AUDIT & ACCOUNTING GUIDE

Not-for-Profit Entities

WITH CONFORMING CHANGES AS OF

MARCH 1, 2011

This edition of the AICPA Audit and Accounting Guide *Not-for-Profit Entities*, which was originally issued in 1996, has been modified by the AICPA staff to include certain changes necessary because of the issuance of authoritative pronouncements since the guide was originally issued and other changes necessary to keep the guide current on industry and regulatory matters. The schedule of changes appendix identifies all changes made in this edition of the guide. The changes do *not* include all those that might be considered necessary if the guide was subjected to a comprehensive review and revision.

1 2 3 4 5 6 7 8 9 0 AAP 1 9 8 7 6 5 4 3 2 1

ISBN 978-0-87051-953-6

Preface

About AICPA Audit and Accounting Guides

This AICPA Audit and Accounting Guide has been prepared by the AICPA Not-for-Profit Organizations Committee to assist management of not-for-profit entities (NFPs) in the preparation of their financial statements in conformity with U.S. generally accepted accounting principles (GAAP) and to assist auditors in auditing and reporting on those financial statements. (The entities to which this guide applies are described in paragraphs 1.01–.04 of this guide.)

The financial accounting and reporting guidance contained in this guide has been approved by the affirmative vote of at least two-thirds of the members of the Financial Reporting Executive Committee (FinREC), which is the senior technical body of the AICPA authorized to speak for the AICPA in the areas of financial accounting and reporting.

This guide does the following:

- Identifies certain requirements set forth in the Financial Accounting Standards Board (FASB) *Accounting Standards Codification*™ (ASC).
- Describes FinREC's understanding of prevalent or sole industry practice concerning certain issues. In addition, this guide may indicate that FinREC expresses a preference for the prevalent or sole industry practice, or it may indicate that FinREC expresses a preference for another practice that is not the prevalent or sole industry practice; alternatively, FinREC may express no view on the matter.
- Identifies certain other, but not necessarily all, industry practices concerning certain accounting issues without expressing FinREC's views on them.
- Provides guidance that has been supported by FinREC on the accounting, reporting, or disclosure treatment of transactions or events that are not set forth in FASB ASC.
- Applies to NFPs that meet the definition of a *not-for-profit entity* included in the FASB ASC glossary.

Accounting guidance for nongovernmental entities included in an AICPA Audit and Accounting Guide is a source of nonauthoritative accounting guidance. As discussed later in this preface, FASB ASC is the authoritative source of U.S. accounting and reporting standards for nongovernmental entities, in addition to guidance issued by the Securities and Exchange Commission (SEC). Accounting guidance for governmental entities included in an AICPA Audit and Accounting Guide is a source of authoritative accounting guidance described in category *b* of the hierarchy of GAAP for state and local governmental entities, and has been cleared by Governmental Accounting Standards Board. AICPA members should be prepared to justify departures from GAAP as discussed in Rule 203, *Accounting Principles* (AICPA, *Professional Standards*, ET sec. 203 par. .01).

Auditing guidance included in an AICPA Audit and Accounting Guide is recognized as an interpretive publication pursuant to AU section 150, *Generally Accepted Auditing Standards* (AICPA, *Professional Standards*). Interpretive publications are recommendations on the application of Statements on Auditing Standards (SASs) in specific circumstances, including engagements for entities in specialized industries. An interpretive publication is issued under the authority of the Auditing Standards Board (ASB) after all ASB members have been provided an opportunity to consider and comment on whether the proposed interpretive publication is consistent with the SASs. The members of the ASB have found this guide to be consistent with existing SASs.

The auditor should be aware of and consider interpretive publications applicable to his or her audit. If an auditor does not apply the auditing guidance included in an applicable interpretive publication, the auditor should be prepared to explain how he or she complied with the SAS provisions addressed by such auditing guidance.

Recognition

Richard Paul
Chair, Financial Reporting Executive Committee

Darrel R. Schubert
Chair, Auditing Standards Board

Not-for-Profit Organizations Committee (1995–1996)

Kenneth D. Williams, *Chair*

Elaine T. Allen

Katherine K. Anderson

Martha L. Benson

Walter D. Bristol

Gregory B. Capin

Gregory A. Coursen

Lawrence A. Dollinger

John H. Fisher

Mary F. Foster

Stephen H. Kattell

Robert C. Kovarik, Jr.

Richard F. Larkin

Louis J. Mezzina

Richard E. Mills

AICPA Staff

Christopher Cole
Technical Manager
Accounting and Auditing Publications

Dan Noll
Director
Accounting Standards

The AICPA gratefully acknowledges Gregg Capin, Cathy Clarke, Frank Jakosz, John Mattie, Tim McCutcheon, Mandy Nelson, Susan Stewart, Nancy E. Shelmon, and Andrea Wright for their assistance in reviewing the conforming changes for the March 2011 edition of this guide.

Special thanks to Susan E. Budak for her invaluable help in updating and maintaining the guidance in the guide.

The Not-for-Profit Organizations Committee gratefully acknowledges the contributions made to the development, content, and writing of this Audit and Accounting Guide by Alan S. Glazer, professor of business administration, Franklin and Marshall College, and Henry R. Jaenicke, C.D. Clarkson Emeritus professor of accounting, Drexel University.

Guidance Considered in This Edition

This edition of the Audit and Accounting Guide *Not-for-Profit Entities* has been modified by the AICPA staff to include certain changes necessary due to the issuance of authoritative pronouncements since the guide was originally issued in 1996. Relevant accounting and auditing guidance contained in official pronouncements issued through March 1, 2011, have been considered in the development of this edition of the guide. This includes relevant guidance issued up to and including the following:

- FASB Accounting Standards Update (ASU) No. 2010-11, *Receivables (Topic 310): Deferral of the Effective Date of Disclosures about Troubled Debt Restructurings in Update No. 2010-20*
- SAS No. 121, *Revised Applicability of Statement on Auditing Standards No. 100*, Interim Financial Information (AICPA, *Professional Standards*, AU sec. 722)
- Interpretation No. 19, "Financial Statements Prepared in Conformity With International Financial Reporting Standards as Issued by the International Accounting Standards Board," of AU section 508, *Reports on Audited Financial Statements* (AICPA, *Professional Standards*, AU sec. 9508 par. .93–.97)
- Revised interpretations issued through March 1, 2011, including Interpretation No. 1, "The Use of Electronic Confirmations," of AU section 330, *The Confirmation Process* (AICPA, *Professional Standards*, AU sec. 9330 par. .01–.08)
- Statement of Position 09-1, *Performing Agreed-Upon Procedures Engagements That Address the Completeness, Accuracy, or Consistency of XBRL-Tagged Data* (AICPA, *Technical Practice Aids*, AUD sec. 14,440)

Users of this guide should consider pronouncements issued subsequent to those listed previously to determine their effect on entities covered by this guide. In determining the applicability of recently issued guidance, its effective date should also be considered.

The changes made to this edition of the guide are identified in the schedule of changes in appendix D. The changes do not include all those that might be considered necessary if the guide were subjected to a comprehensive review and revision.

Auditors who perform audits under *Government Auditing Standards*; the Single Audit Act Amendments of 1996; and Office of Management and Budget Circular A-133, *Audits of States, Local Governments, and Non-Profit Organizations*, should also refer to the AICPA Audit Guide Government Auditing Standards *and Circular A-133 Audits*.

References to Professional Standards

In citing the professional standards, references are made to the AICPA *Professional Standards* publication. Additionally, when referencing professional standards, this guide cites section numbers and not the original statement number, as appropriate. For example, SAS No. 54, *Illegal Acts by Clients*, is referred to as AU section 317, *Illegal Acts by Clients* (AICPA, *Professional Standards*).

FASB *Accounting Standards Codification*™

Overview

Released on July 1, 2009, FASB ASC is a major restructuring of accounting and reporting standards designed to simplify user access to all authoritative U.S. GAAP by topically organizing the authoritative literature. FASB ASC disassembled and reassembled thousands of nongovernmental accounting pronouncements (including those of FASB, the Emerging Issues Task Force, and the AICPA) to organize them under approximately 90 topics.

FASB ASC also includes relevant portions of authoritative content issued by the SEC, as well as selected SEC staff interpretations and administrative guidance issued by the SEC; however, FASB ASC is not the official source of SEC guidance and does not contain the entire population of SEC rules, regulations, interpretive releases, and SEC staff guidance. Moreover, FASB ASC does not include governmental accounting standards.

FASB published a notice to constituents that explains the scope, structure, and usage of consistent terminology of FASB ASC. Constituents are encouraged to read this notice to constituents because it answers many common questions about FASB ASC. FASB ASC, and its related notice to constituents, can be accessed at http://asc.fasb.org/home and are also offered by certain third party licensees, including the AICPA. FASB ASC is offered by FASB at no charge in a basic view and for an annual fee in a professional view.

Issuance of Amendments to the Codification

Amendments to FASB ASC are now issued through ASUs and serve only to update FASB ASC. FASB does not consider the ASUs authoritative in their own right; new standards become authoritative when they are incorporated into FASB ASC.

New standards will be in the form of ASU No. 20YY-XX, in which "YY" is the last two digits of the year and "XX" is the sequential number for each update. For example, ASU No. 2011-01 is the first update in the calendar year 2011. The ASUs will include the amendments to the codification and an appendix of FASB ASC update instructions. ASUs also provide background information about the amendments and explain the basis for the board's decisions.

Pending Content in FASB ASC

Amendments to FASB ASC issued in the form of ASUs (or other authoritative accounting guidance issued prior to the release date of FASB ASC) that are not fully effective, or became effective within the last six months, for all entities or transactions within its scope are reflected as "Pending Content" in FASB ASC. This pending content is shown in text boxes below the paragraphs being amended in FASB ASC and includes links to the transition information. The pending content boxes are meant to provide users with information about how a paragraph will change when new guidance becomes authoritative. When an amended paragraph has been fully effective for six months, the outdated guidance will be removed, and the amended paragraph will remain without the pending content box. FASB will keep any outdated guidance in the applicable archive section of FASB ASC for historical purposes.

Because not all entities have the same fiscal year-ends, and certain guidance may be effective on different dates for public and nonpublic entities, the pending content will apply to different entities at different times. As such, pending content will remain in place within FASB ASC until the "roll off" date. Generally, the roll off date is six months following the latest fiscal year end for which the original guidance being amended or superseded by the pending content could be applied as specified by the transition guidance. For example, assume an ASU has an effective date for fiscal years beginning after November 15, 2010. The latest possible fiscal year end of an entity still eligible to apply the original guidance being amended or superseded by the pending content would begin November 15, 2010, and end November 14, 2011. Accordingly, the roll off date would be April 14, 2012.

Entities cannot disregard the pending content boxes. Instead, all entities must review the transition guidance to determine if and when the pending content is applicable to them. This audit and accounting guide identifies pending content where applicable.

New AICPA.org Website

The AICPA encourages you to visit the new website at www.aicpa.org. It was launched in 2010 and provides significantly enhanced functionality and content critical to the success of AICPA members and other constituents. Certain content on the AICPA's website referenced in this guide may be restricted to AICPA members only.

Select Recent Developments Significant to This Guide

ASB Clarity Project

In an effort to make generally accepted auditing standards (GAAS) easier to read, understand, and apply, the ASB launched the Clarity Project. When completed, clarified auditing standards will be issued as one SAS that will supersede all prior SASs. The effective date of the new audit standards will be for audits of financial statements for periods ending on or after December 15, 2012.

The foundation of the ASB's Clarity Project is the establishment of an objective for each auditing standard. These objectives will better reflect a principles-based approach to standard-setting. In addition to having objectives, the clarified standards will reflect new drafting conventions that include

- adding a definitions section, if relevant, in each standard.
- separating requirements from application and other explanatory material.
- numbering application and other explanatory material paragraphs using an A prefix and presenting them in a separate section (following the requirements section).
- using formatting techniques, such as bulleted lists, to enhance readability.
- adding special considerations relevant to audits of smaller, less complex entities.
- adding special considerations relevant to audits of governmental audits.

The project also has an international convergence component. The ASB expects that, upon completion of the project, nearly all the requirements of International Standards on Auditing will also be requirements of U.S. GAAS. AICPA Audit and Accounting Guides, as well as other AICPA publications, will be conformed to reflect the new standards resulting from the Clarity Project after issuance and as appropriate based on the effective dates.

Private Company Financial Reporting Blue Ribbon Panel

The Blue Ribbon Panel on Private Company Financial Reporting was established in December 2009 and is sponsored by the AICPA, the Financial Accounting Foundation (FAF), and the National Association of State Boards of Accountancy. This panel was formed to consider how U.S. accounting standards can best meet the needs of users of private company financial statements. Members of the panel represent a cross-section of financial reporting constituencies, including lenders, investors, owners, preparers, and auditors.

In late 2010, the Blue Ribbon Panel voted to recommend that the FAF accept a new standard-setting model for private companies and the creation of a separate board to set those standards. Work continues related to changes being considered for private company financial reporting. For more information visit www.accountingfoundation.org/home.

Limitations

This guide does not discuss the application of all GAAP and all GAAS that are relevant to the preparation and audit of financial statements of NFPs. This guide is directed primarily to those aspects of the preparation and audit of financial statements that are unique to NFPs or are considered particularly significant to them.

TABLE OF CONTENTS

Chapter		Paragraph
1	Introduction	.01-.28
	Scope	.01-.04
	U.S. GAAP for NFPs	.05-.14
	Grandfathered GAAP Guidance for NFPs, Including Mergers and Acquisitions	.15-.20
	Audited Financial Statements Prepared in Conformity With GAAP	.21
	Fund Accounting and Net Asset Classes	.22-.27
	Appendix A—Understanding Audits, Reviews, and Compilations	.28
2	General Auditing Considerations	.01-.79
	Overview	.01
	Planning and Other Auditing Considerations	.02-.18
	Audit Planning	.03-.04
	Using the Work of a Specialist	.05
	Scope of Services	.06-.07
	Independence	.08-.10
	Audit Risk	.11-.13
	Planning Materiality	.14-.18
	Qualitative Aspects of Materiality	.19-.33
	Related-Party Transactions	.21-.23
	Errors and Fraud	.24
	Illegal Acts	.25-.28
	Compliance Auditing Under *Government Auditing Standards*	.29
	Single Audits and Related Considerations	.30-.32
	Processing of Transactions by Service Organizations	.33
	Use of Assertions in Obtaining Audit Evidence	.34-.38
	Understanding the Entity, Its Environment, and Its Internal Control	.39-.59
	Risk Assessment Procedures	.41
	Analytical Procedures	.42-.43
	Discussion Among the Audit Team	.44
	Understanding of the Entity and Its Environment	.45-.53
	Understanding of Internal Control	.54-.59
	Risk Assessment and the Design of Further Audit Procedures	.60-.71
	Assessing the Risks of Material Misstatement	.61-.63
	Designing and Performing Further Audit Procedures	.64-.71
	Evaluating Misstatements	.72-.73

Chapter		Paragraph
2	General Auditing Considerations—continued	
	Completing the Audit	.74-.78
	Management Representations	.75-.76
	Going-Concern Considerations	.77-.78
	Appendix A—Consideration of Fraud in a Financial Statement Audit	.79
3	Basic Financial Statements and General Financial Reporting Matters	.01-.107
	Introduction	.01-.04
	Statement of Financial Position	.05-.11
	Statement of Activities	.12-.21
	Reporting Expenses, Including in a Statement of Functional Expenses	.21
	Statement of Cash Flows	.22-.31
	Comparative Financial Information	.30-.31
	Reporting of Related Entities, Including Consolidation	.32-.57
	Relationships With Another NFP	.34-.43
	Relationships With a For-Profit Entity	.44-.54
	Consolidation of a Special-Purpose Leasing Entity	.55-.56
	Combined Financial Statements	.57
	Mergers and Acquisitions	.58-.71
	Merger of Not-for-Profit Entities	.60-.61
	Acquisition by a Not-for-Profit Entity	.62-.71
	Collaborative Arrangements	.72
	The Use of Fair Value Measures	.73-.97
	Definition of *Fair Value*	.76-.81
	Valuation Techniques	.82-.88
	The Fair Value Hierarchy	.89-.93
	Disclosures	.94
	Fair Value Option	.95-.97
	Financial Statement Disclosures Not Considered Elsewhere	.98-.107
	Noncompliance With Donor-Imposed Restrictions	.99-.101
	Risks and Uncertainties	.102
	Subsequent Events	.103-.106
	Appendix A—Flowcharts and Decision Trees	.107
4	Cash and Cash Equivalents	.01-.06
	Introduction	.01-.02
	Financial Statement Presentation	.03-.06
5	Contributions Received and Agency Transactions	.01-.141
	Introduction	.01-.04
	Distinguishing Contributions From Other Transactions	.05-.49

Chapter | Paragraph

5 Contributions Received and Agency Transactions—continued
- Agency Transactions .07-.20
- Variance Power .21-.25
- Financially Interrelated Entities .26-.29
- Similar Transactions That Are Revocable, Repayable or Reciprocal .30-.35
- Exchange Transactions .36-.49

Recognition Principles for Contributions .50-.103
- Recognition if a Donor Imposes a Condition .58-.61
- Recognition if a Donor Imposes a Restriction .62-.77
- Promises to Give .78-.89
- Contributed Services .90-.93
- Gifts in Kind .94-.99
- Contributed Utilities and Use of Long-Lived Assets .100-.101
- Contributed Collection Items .102
- Split-Interest Agreements .103

Measurement Principles for Contributions .104-.128
- Discounting .113-.116
- Subsequent Measurement .117-.128

Financial Statement Presentation .129-.133

Illustrative Disclosures .134

Auditing .135-.141

6 Split-Interest Agreements .01-.64

Introduction .01

Types of Split-Interest Agreements .02-.03

Recognition and Measurement Principles .04-.31
- Recognition of Revocable Agreements .07
- Initial Recognition and Measurement of Unconditional Irrevocable Agreements Other Than Pooled Income Funds or Net Income Unitrusts .08-.17
- Initial Recognition and Measurement of Pooled Income Funds and Net Income Unitrusts .18
- Recognition and Measurement During the Agreement's Term for Unconditional Irrevocable Agreements Other Than Pooled Income Funds or Net Income Unitrusts .19-.29
- Recognition and Measurement During the Agreement's Term for Pooled Income Funds and Net Income Unitrusts .30
- Recognition Upon Termination of Agreement .31

Financial Statement Presentation .32-.36

Examples of Split-Interest Agreements .37-.59
- Charitable Lead Trust .38-.42
- Perpetual Trust Held by a Third Party .43-.46
- Charitable Remainder Trust .47-.51

Chapter		Paragraph
6	Split-Interest Agreements—continued	
	Charitable Gift Annuity	.52-.55
	Pooled (Life) Income Fund	.56-.59
	Auditing	.60-.63
	Appendix A—Journal Entries	.64
7	Other Assets	.01-.28
	Introduction	.01
	Inventory	.02-.05
	Prepaid Expenses, Deferred Charges, and Similar Costs	.06
	Collections	.07-.17
	Financial Statement Presentation	.14-.16
	Illustrative Disclosures	.17
	Goodwill	.18-.20
	Intangible Assets Other Than Goodwill	.21-.22
	Auditing	.23-.28
	Inventory	.24
	Collection Items	.25-.28
8	Investments	.01-.65
	Introduction	.01-.04
	Initial Recognition	.05-.06
	Investment Income	.07-.09
	Valuation Subsequent to Acquisition	.10-.18
	Equity Securities With Readily Determinable Fair Value (Other Than Consolidated Subsidiaries and Equity Securities Reported Under the Equity Method) and All Debt Securities	.10
	Investments That Are Accounted for Under the Equity Method or a Fair Value Election	.11-.13
	Derivative Instruments	.14
	Other Investments	.15
	Fair Value Measurements	.16-.18
	Unrealized and Realized Gains and Losses	.19-.21
	Investment Pools	.22
	Donor-Restricted Endowment Funds	.23-.32
	Financial Statement Presentation	.33-.48
	Accounting for Derivative Instruments and Hedging Activities	.49-.56
	Auditing	.57-.65
	Net Appreciation on Endowment Funds	.59-.64
	Audit Objectives and Procedures	.65
9	Property, Plant, and Equipment	.01-.28
	Introduction	.01-.02
	Recognition and Measurement Principles	.03-.19

Chapter		Paragraph
9	Property, Plant, and Equipment—continued	
	Contributed Property and Equipment	.05-.08
	Depreciation and Amortization	.09-.13
	Impairment or Disposal of Long-Lived Assets	.14-.16
	Asset Retirement Obligations	.17-.18
	Gains and Losses	.19
	Financial Statement Presentation	.20-.25
	Auditing	.26-.28
10	Debt and Other Liabilities	.01-.27
	Introduction	.01-.03
	Tax-Exempt Financing and Long-Term Debt	.04-.06
	Current and Deferred Tax Liabilities	.07-.08
	Deferred Revenue	.09
	Refunds Due to and Advances From Third Parties	.10
	Promises to Give	.11-.15
	Annuity Obligations	.16
	Amounts Held for Others Under Agency Transactions	.17
	Revenue Sharing and Other Agreements	.18
	Exit or Disposal Activities	.19
	Guarantees	.20-.21
	Contingencies	.22
	Pension and Other Defined Benefit Postretirement Plan Obligations	.23-.25
	Auditing	.26-.27
11	Net Assets	.01-.32
	Introduction	.01-.02
	Net Asset Classes	.03-.06
	Permanently Restricted Net Assets	.07-.09
	Temporarily Restricted Net Assets	.10-.12
	Unrestricted Net Assets	.13-.19
	Noncontrolling Interests	.20-.21
	Reclassifications	.22-.23
	Disclosure	.24-.29
	Changing Net Asset Classifications Reported in a Prior Year	.30
	Auditing	.31-.32
12	Revenues and Receivables From Exchange Transactions	.01-.09
	Introduction	.01-.02
	Revenues	.03-.05
	Recognition, Measurement, and Display	.06-.09

Chapter		Paragraph
13	Expenses, Gains, and Losses	.01-.101
	Introduction	.01
	Expenses	.02-.06
	Expense Recognition Issues	.07-.17
	Fundraising Costs	.08
	Financial Aid and Other Reductions in Amounts Charged for Goods and Services	.09
	Advertising Costs	.10-.12
	Start-Up Costs	.13-.15
	Internal Use Computer Software Costs	.16
	Contributions Made	.17
	Gains and Losses	.18-.34
	Reporting Costs Related to Sales of Goods and Services	.25-.27
	Reporting the Cost of Special Events and Other Fundraising Activities	.28-.32
	Investment Revenues, Expenses, Gains, and Losses	.33-.34
	Functional Reporting of Expenses	.35-.94
	Functional Classifications	.37-.44
	Classification of Expenses Related to More Than One Function	.45-.93
	Expenses of Federated Fundraising Entities	.94
	Income Taxes	.95
	Auditing	.96-.97
	Appendix A—Accounting for Joint Activities	.98
	Appendix B—Examples of Applying the Criteria of Purpose, Audience, and Content to Determine Whether a Program or Management and General Activity Has Been Conducted	.99
	Appendix C—Allocation Methods	.100
	Appendix D—Examples of Disclosures	.101
14	Reports of Independent Auditors	.01-.17
	Reports on Financial Statements	.01-.04
	Reports on Comparative Financial Statements	.05-.07
	Unqualified Opinions	.08
	Modified Reports and Departures From Unqualified Opinions	.09
	Going Concern	.10
	Reporting on Supplementary Information	.11-.12
	Bases of Accounting Other Than GAAP	.13-.14
	Reporting on Prescribed Forms	.15-.16
	Reports Required by *Government Auditing Standards*, the Single Audit Act Amendments of 1996, and OMB Circular A-133	.17

Chapter Paragraph

15 Tax Considerations .01-.24
Introduction .01-.03
Basis of Exemption .04-.15
Federal and State Filing Requirements .16
Public Charities and Private Foundations .17
Unrelated Business Income .18-.21
Auditing .22-.24

16 Fund Accounting .01-.22
Introduction .01
Fund Accounting and External Financial Reporting .02-.05
Unrestricted Current (or Unrestricted Operating or General) Funds .06-.07
Restricted Current (or Restricted Operating or Specific-Purpose) Funds .08-.09
Plant (or Land, Building, and Equipment) Funds .10-.12
Loan Funds .13-.14
Endowment Funds .15-.18
Annuity and Life-Income (Split-Interest) Funds .19-.20
Agency (Or Custodian) Funds .21
Summary .22

Appendix

A Financial Accounting Standards Board Accounting Standards Codification 958, Not-For-Profit Entities, Topic Hierarchy

B Information Sources

C References to AICPA Technical Practice Aids

D Schedule of Changes Made to the Text From the Previous Edition

Glossary

Index

Chapter 1

Introduction

Scope

1.01 This Audit and Accounting Guide covers entities that meet the definition of a *not-for-profit entity* (NFP) included in the Financial Accounting Standards Board (FASB) *Accounting Standards Codification* (ASC) glossary. That definition is

> an entity that possesses the following characteristics, in varying degrees, that distinguish it from a business entity:
>
> *a.* Contributions of significant amounts of resources from resource providers who do not expect commensurate or proportionate pecuniary return
>
> *b.* Operating purposes other than to provide goods or services at a profit
>
> *c.* Absence of ownership interests like those of business entities
>
> Entities that clearly fall outside this definition include the following:
>
> *a.* All investor-owned entities
>
> *b.* Entities that provide dividends, lower costs, or other economic benefits directly and proportionately to their owners, members, or participants, such as mutual insurance entities, credit unions, farm and rural electric cooperatives, and employee benefit plans

As noted in the preceding definition, NFPs have characteristics (*a*), (*b*), and (*c*) in varying degrees. An entity could meet the definition of an NFP without possessing characteristic (*a*), (*b*), or (*c*). For example, some NFPs, such as those that receive all their revenue from exchange transactions, receive no contributions.

1.02 This guide applies to the following nongovernmental NFPs:

- Cemetery organizations
- Civic and community organizations
- Colleges and universities
- Elementary and secondary schools
- Federated fund-raising organizations
- Fraternal organizations
- Labor unions
- Libraries
- Museums
- Other cultural organizations
- Performing arts organizations
- Political parties

- Political action committees
- Private and community foundations
- Professional associations
- Public broadcasting stations
- Religious organizations
- Research and scientific organizations
- Social and country clubs
- Trade associations
- Voluntary health and welfare entities
- Zoological and botanical societies

Additionally, the guidance in this guide applies to all entities that meet the definition of an NFP in paragraph 1.01, regardless of whether they are included in this list.

1.03 Paragraph 1.02 provides that this guide applies to certain nongovernmental NFPs. *Nongovernmental entities* are all entities other than governmental organizations. Public corporations[1] and bodies corporate and politic are governmental organizations. Other organizations are governmental organizations if they have one or more of the following characteristics:

a. Popular election of officers or appointment (or approval) of a controlling majority of the members of the organization's governing body by officials of one or more state or local governments

b. The potential for unilateral dissolution by a government with the net assets reverting to a government

c. The power to enact and enforce a tax levy

Furthermore, organizations are presumed to be governmental if they have the ability to issue directly (rather than through a state or municipal authority) debt that pays interest exempt from federal taxation. However, organizations possessing only that ability (to issue tax-exempt debt) and none of the other governmental characteristics may rebut the presumption that they are governmental if their determination is supported by compelling, relevant evidence.

1.04 NFPs that are providers of health care services[2] are not covered by this guide and should refer to the AICPA Audit and Accounting Guide *Health Care Entities*.

---

[1] *Black's Law Dictionary* defines a public corporation as: An artificial person (for example, [a] municipality or a governmental corporation) created for the administration of public affairs. Unlike a private corporation it has no protection against legislative acts altering or even repealing its charter. Instrumentalities created by [the] state, formed and owned by it in [the] public interest, supported in whole or part by public funds, and governed by managers deriving their authority from [the] state. Sharon Realty Co. v. Westlake, Ohio Com. Pl., 188 N.E.2d 318, 323, 25 O.O.2d 322. A public corporation is an instrumentality of the state, founded and owned in the public interest, supported by public funds and governed by those deriving their authority from the state. York County Fair Ass'n v. South Carolina Tax Commission, 249 S.C. 337, 154 S.E.2d 361, 362.

[2] Providers of health care services that meet the definition of a voluntary health and welfare entity in the glossary of Financial Accounting Standards Board (FASB) *Accounting Standards Codification*™ should follow this guide.

U.S. GAAP for NFPs[3]

1.05 FASB ASC is the single authoritative source of U.S. accounting and reporting standards for nongovernmental entities; that is, it is the source of U.S. generally accepted accounting principles (GAAP). The AICPA Council has resolved that FASB ASC constitutes accounting principles as contemplated in Rule 203, *Accounting Principles* (AICPA, *Professional Standards*, ET sec. 203 par. .01), of the AICPA Code of Professional Conduct.

1.06 Per FASB ASC 105-10-05-2, if the guidance for a transaction or event is not specified within a source of authoritative GAAP for that entity, an entity shall first consider accounting principles for similar transactions or events within a source of authoritative GAAP for that entity and then consider nonauthoritative guidance from other sources. An entity shall not follow the accounting treatment specified in accounting guidance for similar transactions or events if that guidance either (*a*) prohibits the application of the accounting treatment to the particular transaction or event or (*b*) indicates that the accounting treatment should not be applied to other transactions or events by analogy.

1.07 Accounting and financial reporting practices not included in FASB ASC are nonauthoritative. Sources of nonauthoritative accounting guidance and literature include, for example, practices that are widely recognized and prevalent either generally or in the industry; FASB Concepts Statements; AICPA Audit and Accounting Guides; AICPA Issues Papers; International Financial Reporting Standards of the International Accounting Standards Board; pronouncements of professional associations or regulatory agencies; Technical Questions and Answers included in AICPA *Technical Practice Aids*; and accounting textbooks, handbooks, and articles. The appropriateness of other sources of accounting guidance depends on its relevance to particular circumstances, the specificity of the guidance, the general recognition of the issuer or author as an authority, and the extent of its use in practice. For example, FASB Concepts Statements would normally be more influential than other sources in this category.

1.08 NFPs should follow the guidance in all effective provisions of FASB ASC unless the specific provision explicitly exempts NFPs or its subject matter

---

[3] The International Accounting Standards Board (IASB) has been designated by the Council of the AICPA as the body to establish international financial reporting standards (IFRSs) for both private and public entities pursuant to Rule 202, *Compliance With Standards* (AICPA, *Professional Standards*, ET sec. 202 par. .01), and Rule 203, *Accounting Principles* (AICPA, *Professional Standards*, ET sec. 203 par. .01), of the AICPA Code of Professional Conduct; and as of May 18, 2008, an auditor may report on general purpose financial statements presented in conformity with IFRSs as issued by the IASB. When the auditor reports on financial statements prepared in conformity with IFRSs, the auditor would refer, in the auditor's report, to IFRSs rather than U.S. generally accepted accounting principles (GAAP). For more information, readers should refer to Interpretation No. 19, "Financial Statements Prepared in Conformity With International Financial Reporting Standards as Issued by the International Accounting Standards Board," of AU section 508, *Reports on Audited Financial Statements* (AICPA, *Professional Standards*, AU sec. 9508 par. .93–.97). AU section 534, *Reporting on Financial Statements Prepared for Use in Other Countries* (AICPA, *Professional Standards*), applies to such financial statements prepared for use outside the United States, and paragraphs .14–.15 of AU section 534 and paragraphs .35–.60 of AU section 508 apply to financial statements prepared for more than limited distribution in the United States. Paragraph 14.03 of this guide discusses reporting when an auditor is engaged to report on the financial statements of a U.S. entity for use outside of the United States in conformity with accounting principles generally accepted in another country or in accordance with the International Standards on Auditing.

precludes such applicability. FASB ASC 958, *Not-for-Profit Entities*, contains only incremental industry-specific guidance. NFPs should follow that industry-specific guidance and all other relevant guidance contained in other FASB ASC topics that does not conflict with the industry guidance.

1.09 Accounting Standards Updates issued by FASB subsequent to this guide's effective date apply to NFPs unless those pronouncements explicitly exempt NFPs or their subject matter precludes such applicability.

1.10 NFPs may follow and are not prohibited from following the guidance in effective provisions of FASB ASC that specifically exempt NFPs from their application, unless FASB ASC 958 provides different guidance. The guidance that specifically exempts NFPs includes guidance on earnings per share, reporting comprehensive income, segment disclosure, and variable interest entities, among others. However, the guidance included in the effective provisions of FASB ASC that specifically exempt NFPs applies to all for-profit entities owned, whether owned all or in part, by NFPs. The discussion in paragraphs 1.11–.14 of this guide should be considered in determining the relevance of such guidance and of guidance issued by the AICPA.

1.11 Certain financial reporting guidance, such as that concerning common stock, convertible debt, stock purchase warrants, share-based payments, and certain financial instruments with characteristics of both liabilities and equity, generally does not apply to the kinds of entities covered by this guide because such entities do not enter into the kinds of transactions covered by that guidance. However, the guidance included in the effective provisions of those pronouncements applies to all for-profit entities owned, whether owned all or in part, by NFPs. Also, NFPs should follow the effective provisions of those pronouncements if they enter into the kinds of transactions covered by that guidance.

1.12 Certain FASB ASC guidance applies primarily to entities operating in certain industries. An example of such guidance is FASB ASC 920, *Entertainment—Broadcasters*. Some NFPs conduct activities[4] in some of those industries and should apply the guidance concerning the recognition and measurement of assets, liabilities, revenues, expenses, and gains and losses to the transactions unique to those industries. However, in applying that guidance, NFPs should follow the financial statement display guidance in FASB ASC 958, even though it may conflict with display that would result from applying the industry guidance.

1.13 Certain FASB ASC guidance, although it does not exempt NFPs and does cover transactions conducted by NFPs, includes some provisions whose application by NFPs may be unclear. Nevertheless, NFPs are required to follow those effective provisions. These provisions and their applicability are discussed in the next paragraph.

1.14 Some provisions of FASB ASC specify the financial statement display of certain financial statement elements or items (such as gains and losses, extraordinary items, translation adjustments, income tax expense, and prepaid or deferred income taxes) without considering the net asset reporting model included in FASB ASC 958 and this guide. Therefore, FASB ASC 958-10-45-1

---

[4] Such activities may be conducted by (*a*) for-profit entities owned and consolidated by not-for-profit entities (NFPs), (*b*) divisions of NFPs, or (*c*) entire NFPs, such as those operating as not-for-profit broadcasters.

states that NFPs should consider the reporting objectives of the guidance when exercising judgment about how to best display elements, such as in which net asset class. Examples of those provisions follow:

- FASB ASC 205-20, about discontinued operations[*]
- FASB ASC 225-20, about extraordinary and unusual items
- FASB ASC 250, *Accounting Changes and Error Corrections*
- FASB ASC 470-50, about modifications and extinguishments of debt
- FASB ASC 740, *Income Taxes*
- FASB ASC 830, *Foreign Currency Matters*

Grandfathered GAAP Guidance for NFPs, Including Mergers and Acquisitions

1.15 As described in FASB ASC 105-10-70-2, certain accounting standards have allowed for the continued application of superseded accounting standards for transactions that have an ongoing effect in an entity's financial statements. That superseded guidance has not been included in FASB ASC, shall be considered grandfathered, and shall continue to remain authoritative for those transactions after the effective date of FASB Statement No. 168, *The* FASB Accounting Standards Codification™ *and the Hierarchy of Generally Accepted Accounting Principles*. FASB ASC 105-10-70-2(h) lists pooling of interests as allowed for NFPs under Accounting Principles Board (APB) Opinion No. 16, *Business Combinations*, even though it has been superseded by FASB Statement No. 141, until FASB Statement No. 164, *Not-for-Profit Entities: Mergers and Acquisitions—Including an amendment of FASB Statement No. 142*, is effective (that is, for accounting periods beginning after December 15, 2009).[†]

1.16 Until the effective date of FASB Statement No. 164, which is codified in FASB ASC 958-805, NFPs should

- continue to follow the guidance in the following three paragraphs.
- follow the guidance in APB Opinion No. 16 as amended by pronouncements prior to the issuance of FASB Statement No. 141. In applying the guidance included in APB Opinion No. 16, NFPs should continue to apply the amendments to that opinion that

[*] On September 25, 2008, FASB issued an exposure draft of a proposed FASB Staff Position (FSP) FAS 144-d, *Amending the Criteria for Reporting a Discontinued Operation*. The proposed FSP would define when a component of an entity should be reported in the discontinued operations section of the statement of activities and enhance the disclosure requirements for all components of an entity that have been disposed of or are classified as held for sale. On December 17, 2009, FASB decided that its proposed guidance should be re-exposed. Readers should be alert to the issuance of a final Accounting Standards Update (ASU).

[†] In April 2009, FASB issued FASB Statement No. 164, *Not-for-Profit Entities: Mergers and Acquisitions—Including an amendment of FASB Statement No. 142*, which improves the relevance, representational faithfulness, and comparability of the information that an NFP reporting entity provides in its financial reports about a combination with one or more other NFPs, businesses, or nonprofit activities. FASB Statement No. 164 also improves the relevance, representational faithfulness, and comparability of the information an NFP provides about goodwill and other intangible assets after an acquisition by making the standards of FASB ASC 350-20 fully applicable to NFPs. FASB Statement No. 164 was codified by ASU No. 2010-07, *Not-for-Profit Entities (Topic 958): Not-for-Profit Entities: Mergers and Acquisitions*, issued in January 2010. These standards, which are effective for accounting periods beginning on or after December 15, 2009, are discussed beginning in paragraph 3.58 of this guide.

were included in FASB Statement No. 121, *Accounting for the Impairment of Long-Lived Assets and for Long-Lived Assets to Be Disposed Of*, even though FASB Statement No. 121 was superseded by FASB Statement No. 144, *Accounting for the Impairment or Disposal of Long-Lived Assets*. (FASB Statement No. 144 did not carry forward the amendments to APB Opinion No. 16 because APB Opinion No. 16 had been superseded.)

- follow the guidance in the other pronouncements superseded by FASB Statement Nos. 141 and 141 (revised 2007).
- apply pronouncements that were amended by FASB Statement Nos. 141 and 141(R) as though FASB Statement Nos. 141 and 141(R) had not amended them.

1.17 Because the conditions for applying the pooling of interests method of accounting described in APB Opinion No. 16 for a business combination generally include an exchange of common stock of the combining entities, NFPs generally would not meet the conditions for applying that method. The AICPA Financial Reporting Executive Committee believes that circumstances exist under which reporting on the combination of two or more NFPs (or that of an NFP with a formerly for-profit entity) by the pooling of interests method better reflects the substance of the transaction than reporting by the purchase method. Therefore, an NFP is, under certain circumstances, permitted to report by the pooling of interests method, even though it generally does not issue common stock. Such circumstances include the combination of two or more entities to form a new entity without the exchange of consideration.

1.18 An example of acceptable practice, in some circumstances, for reporting business combinations by NFPs if there has been no exchange of consideration is to report the (*a*) assets, (*b*) liabilities, and (*c*) net asset balances of the combined entities as of the beginning of the year and disclose the information that would be required to be disclosed for a pooling of interests under APB Opinion No. 16. APB Opinion No. 16 is available in the FASB publication *Original Pronouncements*, and in the "Pre-Codification AICPA Copyrighted Standards" section of the FASB website.

1.19 In addition, FASB ASC 105-10-70-2(i) states that APB Opinion No. 16 and APB Opinion No. 17, *Intangible Assets*, are effective for goodwill and intangible assets arising from a combination between two or more NFPs or acquired in the acquisition of a for-profit business entity by an NFP until FASB Statement No. 164 is effective. Thus, the provisions of FASB ASC 350-20 and FASB ASC 350-30 should not be applied to goodwill and intangible assets arising from a merger or acquisition between two or more NFPs or acquired in the acquisition of a for-profit business entity by an NFP until accounting periods beginning on or after December 15, 2009. FASB ASC 350-30 is effective for intangible assets acquired in transactions other than combinations, for example, the purchase or gift of patent or royalty rights from the holder of the patent or copyright.

1.20 When applying APB Opinion No. 17, an NFP should continue to apply the amendments to that opinion found in other literature even though that other literature may have been superseded by FASB Statement Nos. 141; 141(R); 142, *Goodwill and Other Intangible Assets*; and 144. For example, when applying APB Opinion No. 17, an NFP should continue to apply the amendments to that opinion found in FASB Statement No. 121, even though that

FASB statement was superseded by FASB Statement No. 144. APB Opinion No. 17 is available in the "Pre-Codification AICPA Copyrighted Standards" section of the FASB website and in the FASB publication *Original Pronouncements*.

Audited Financial Statements Prepared in Conformity With GAAP

1.21 The purpose of this guide is to assist preparers of financial statements in preparing financial statements in conformity with GAAP and to assist auditors in auditing and reporting on such financial statements in accordance with generally accepted auditing standards. Other comprehensive bases of accounting are sometimes used to prepare financial statements, and other levels of service are offered by certified public accountants, but those are not the focus of this guide. Appendix A to this chapter discusses the benefits of an audit and provides a general overview of audit, review, and compilation engagements.

Fund Accounting and Net Asset Classes

1.22 Fund accounting is a technique used by some NFPs for purposes of internal recordkeeping and managerial control and to help ensure that the use of resources is in accordance with stipulations imposed by donors and other resource providers and with self-imposed limitations designated by those charged with governance, hereafter referred to as governing board. Under fund accounting, resources are classified into funds associated with specific activities and objectives.

1.23 *Montgomery's Auditing* notes that

> as used in nonprofit accounting, a fund is an accounting entity with a self-balancing set of accounts for recording assets, liabilities, the fund balance, and changes in the fund balance. Separate accounts are maintained for each fund to ensure that the limitations and restrictions on the use of resources are observed. Though the fund concept involves separate accounting records, it does not entail the physical segregation of resources. Fund accounting is basically a mechanism to assist in exercising control over the purpose of particular resources and amounts of those resources available for use.[5]

Fund accounting is discussed further in chapter 16, "Fund Accounting," of this guide.

1.24 FASB ASC 958-205-05-7 states that "The Not-for-Profit Entities Topic does not use the terms *fund balance* or *changes in fund balances* because in current practice those terms are commonly used to refer to individual groups of assets and related liabilities rather than to an entity's net assets or changes in net assets taken as a whole . . ." As discussed in chapter 3, "Basic Financial Statements and General Financial Reporting Matters," of this guide, FASB ASC 958-210-45-1 requires that the amounts for each of three classes of net assets (permanently restricted, temporarily restricted, and unrestricted) be displayed in a statement of financial position. FASB ASC 958-225-45-1 also requires that the amounts of change in each of those classes of net assets be displayed in a statement of activities.

---

[5] Vincent M. O'Reilly, Murray B. Hirsch, Philip L. Defliese, and Henry R. Jaenicke, *Montgomery's Auditing*, 11th ed. (New York: John Wiley & Sons, 1990), 791.

1.25 Therefore, reporting by individual funds or fund groups is not required. However, FASB ASC 958-205-45-3 does not preclude providing disaggregated information by individual funds or fund groups, as long as the required aggregated amounts for each of the three classes of net assets are displayed as indicated previously. How an NFP maintains its internal accounting and recordkeeping systems is a matter outside the purview of standard setting.

1.26 Some NFPs may continue to use fund accounting for purposes other than reporting in conformity with GAAP, and some may provide disaggregated information in the financial statements beyond the minimum requirements of GAAP. A particular fund balance may fall completely into one of the three net asset classes or may be allocated to more than one net asset class, as discussed in chapter 16 of this guide.

1.27 The accounting and auditing issues concerning each particular asset, liability, or class of net assets (financial statement elements) are not a function of the element's internal classification or financial statement subclassification. Accordingly, this guide is organized by financial statement elements and not by type of fund or groups of funds. Chapter 16 of this guide contains a discussion of the relationship of an NFP's fund balances to its net asset classes.

1.28

Appendix A—Understanding Audits, Reviews, and Compilations

A-1 CPAs perform various services for not-for-profit entities (NFPs) and other entities. For example, an NFP may engage a CPA to audit, review, or compile its financial statements. In addition, an NFP may engage a CPA to prepare or review its IRS Form 990 and other tax filings. This appendix discusses the benefits of an audit and provides a general overview of audit, review, and compilations engagements.

Benefits of an Audit

A-2 A financial statement audit provides management (including those charged with governance, which is sometimes referred to in this appendix as the *governing board*) and other financial statement users an independent CPA's opinion about whether the financial statements present fairly the entity's financial position, changes in net assets, and cash flows in conformity with generally accepted accounting principles (GAAP). In order for auditors to express their opinion, they must perform certain procedures in accordance with generally accepted auditing standards (GAAS). Among other requirements, GAAS requires auditors to plan and perform their audit to obtain reasonable assurance (which is a high, but not absolute, level of assurance) that the financial statements are free of material misstatement, whether caused by error or fraud.

A-3 The auditor, therefore, provides a second set of eyes in the event that management has inadvertently (or intentionally) omitted or misstated important financial statement information. Additionally, the audit process tends to strengthen management's discipline towards improving internal control over financial reporting. That in turn helps management prepare more accurate financial information. It is imperative that the auditor be independent of management, the entity, and others related to the entity, both in fact and in appearance, so the auditor has no incentive for the financial statements to be anything other than fairly presented.

A-4 Financial statement audits are performed by CPAs subject to rigorous licensing and other requirements. CPAs must pass the CPA exam and fulfill requisite education, experience and continuing professional education. In addition, members of the AICPA must adhere to the AICPA *Professional Standards*, including the AICPA Code of Conduct and peer review requirements.

A-5 The following questions and answers provide additional information about the benefits of an audit.

Frequently Asked Questions

A-6 *Why is it important that someone other than management be associated with the financial statements?*

A-7 Independent auditors provide an impartial second set of eyes that examine the financial statements with the objective of obtaining a high level of assurance about whether the financial statements as a whole are free of material misstatement. The auditor then expresses an opinion on whether the financial statements are presented fairly, in all material respects. This process not only provides comfort for users of the audited financial statements, but it also helps to bring a discipline to management that helps them refine their internal control and procedures to improve financial reporting in the future. Because CPAs performing audits are skilled in both audit procedures and GAAP, they are in an ideal position to provide such services.

A-8 *What procedures does an auditor perform as part of an audit?*

A-9 The auditor performs extensive procedures in performing an audit. Among other things, the auditor obtains a sufficient understanding of the entity and its environment, including its internal control, to assess the risk of material misstatement of the financial statements whether due to error or fraud, and to design the nature, timing, and extent of further audit procedures. Further audit procedures include observing certain assets, verifying a sample of transactions with third parties, testing revenues, expenses, assets, and liabilities, searching for unreported liabilities, and performing other procedures to search for misstatements. In addition to performing certain required audit procedures, auditors use their judgment in determining additional needed procedures.

A-10 *What procedures does an auditor perform to verify transactions with third parties and other recorded transactions?*

A-11 The auditor confirms bank balances, examines paid invoices, confirms accounts receivable, observes and recounts inventory items, tests recordings to the general ledger, analyzes general ledger accounts, and performs analytical procedures to name a few. Due to inherent cost constraints, the auditor must perform many of these procedures on a test or sample basis, rather than examining 100 percent of transactions and items.

A-12 *What procedures does an auditor perform with respect to fraud?*

A-13 Two types of fraud misstatements are relevant to the auditor's consideration of fraud: (1) intentional misstatements of the financial statements, and (2) misappropriation of assets. To begin every audit, auditors meet in brainstorming sessions in which all engagement personnel discuss the opportunities for fraud to occur. Auditors brainstorm about how and where they believe the entity's financial statements might be susceptible to fraud, how management could perpetrate and conceal fraudulent financial reporting, and how assets of the entity could be misappropriated. Additionally, as part of planning every audit, the auditor must interview or inquire of management and others whether any of them are aware of or suspect fraud. Auditors also perform analytical procedures designed to look for unusual ratios or amounts that are unexpected.

A-14 Based on these planning procedures, auditors then design audit procedures that are responsive to the nature and significance of the fraud risks that they've identified as being present and the entity's programs and controls that address those identified risks. Because many financial frauds are perpetrated in revenue accounts, auditors are now required to ordinarily presume that improper revenue recognition is a risk in all audits. Of course, the first line of defense against fraud is management and that increases the need to have adequate internal controls and a management that sets a high tone at the top.

A-15 *What are some of the byproducts to management of an audit?*

A-16 This depends on each entity and the auditor involved, but it may include some or all of the following:

> *Training and assistance.* Some entities, particularly smaller entities, may benefit from periodic assistance with their accounting processes and the drafting of the financial statements. The auditor may provide

these services while maintaining their independence, assuming certain management conditions are met. In many cases the audit is a time when the entity's financial staff receives a great deal of training and assistance.

Identification of control weaknesses and recommendations for improvements in control and operations. As a result of the procedures performed during the audit, the auditor may become aware of weaknesses in an entity's internal control over financial reporting. Also, though not required, an audit may bring an evaluation of operations and controls that enables the auditor to provide input to the board and management. This helps the board and management understand risks, evaluate their internal control, and establish procedures to safeguard assets and to improve financial reporting in the future. All of which ultimately help the entity govern and operate more effectively and efficiently. (The auditor is required to communicate internal control weaknesses identified as a result of the audit. The auditor typically communicates other identified opportunities for improvements and efficiencies as well.)

Reduced cost of capital. In the for-profit arena, better, transparent, and more reliable financial reporting reduces the cost of capital. We expect that it follows in the NFP arena, that better, transparent, and more reliable financial reporting not only reduces the cost of capital in the traditional sense, such as lower interest rates on borrowings, but likely increases the NFP's ability to raise contributions. For example, many donors will not even consider contributing to an NFP if that NFP does not make available audited financial statements.

A-17 *What are some common misconceptions about an audit?*

A-18 The auditor's report is not a "clean bill of health." Although a clean opinion from the auditor states that the financial statements, including the entity's assets, liabilities, net assets, revenues, expenses, cash flows, and note disclosures, are fairly presented, it is not an opinion about the entity's policy decisions, effective use of assets, programmatic outcomes and outputs.

A-19 *Does a clean opinion guarantee that the NFP will continue to operate?*

A-20 No, but the auditor has a responsibility to evaluate whether there is substantial doubt about the NFP's ability to continue as a going concern for a reasonable period of time, not to exceed one year beyond the date of the financial statements being audited. If the auditor concludes that substantial doubt does exist, the audit report should include an explanatory paragraph to reflect that conclusion.

A-21 *What are the benefits of an audit to an external financial statement user?*

A-22 From the perspective of an external financial statement user, an audit provides reasonable confidence that the financial statements are materially correct. Audited financial statements can lend credibility to an NFP's financial status and demonstrate an entity's willingness to submit its financial affairs to independent scrutiny. In addition, it reduces the risk of fraud, and the risk that the NFP is not complying with donor restrictions.

A-23 *What are the benefits of an audit to an internal financial statement user?*

A-24 From the perspective of an internal user, an audit tends to provide information to help the entity govern and operate effectively and efficiently. Also, it tends to add a self-imposed discipline to the NFP's finances and related activities, from requiring adequate backup for routine cash disbursements and preparing bank reconciliations, to designing and implementing effective accounting systems, to properly reporting the results of capital campaigns, making sure the NFP is complying with donor restrictions, and avoiding inappropriate conflicts of interest, private inurement, and prohibited transactions.

A-25 *When would an entity use a review instead of an audit?*

A-26 An audit requires more extensive procedures than a review. As a result, an auditor obtains a higher level of assurance than does an accountant conducting a review, but because more procedures are performed an audit is more expensive than a review. In determining whether to have an audit or a review, management and those responsible for governance must make a decision as to whether to expend more resources for a higher level of benefits. In situations in which a statement that the accountant is not aware of any material modifications that should be made to the financial statements is sufficient, a review may be an appropriate level of service. During a review, the CPA performs analytical procedures and makes certain inquiries of management and accounting personnel for the purpose of identifying inadvertent or intentional misstatements.

A-27 *Why is it that some believe an audit is unnecessary?*

A-28 If management prepares the financial statements with competence and integrity, an audit may provide only confirmation of that fact. As a result, management or the governing board may not sense much benefit for the cost. This is a decision that management and the governing board should weigh very carefully.

Discussion of an Audit, Review, and Compilation

Audit

A-29 During an audit performed in accordance with GAAS,[1] an auditor obtains a high, but not absolute, level of assurance about whether the financial statements are free of material misstatement. The end product of an audit is the auditor's report. The auditor's report states the scope of the auditor's work (for example, which financial statements have been audited) and provides the auditor's opinion about whether the financial statements are presented fairly in conformity with GAAP.[2]

A-30 The financial statements are prepared by and are the responsibility of the NFP's management. The auditor's responsibility is to express an opinion on those financial statements based on the audit. GAAS require that the auditor plan and perform the audit to obtain reasonable assurance about whether the financial statements are free of material misstatement, whether caused by error or fraud. Though this is a reasonable or high level of assurance, an audit does not provide a guarantee of accuracy.

---

[1] This document discusses audits performed in accordance with generally accepted auditing standards (GAAS). GAAS are the most prevalent auditing standards used. Additionally, *Government Auditing Standards*, promulgated by the GAO and commonly referred to as the Yellow Book, build on GAAS. These generally accepted government auditing standards (GAGAS) generally apply to entities that expend $500,000 or more of federal assistance or to other entities where GAGAS is required by a governmental entity. The federal government has a formal process for developing those standards and monitoring compliance with them.

[2] This document discusses financial statements prepared in conformity with generally accepted accounting principles (GAAP). Entities may prepare their financial statements in accordance with a comprehensive basis of accounting other than GAAP, such as the cash basis or income tax basis.

A-31 An audit includes obtaining knowledge about and an understanding of the industry in which the entity operates. It includes acquiring information on key aspects of the entity, including operating methods, products and services, material transactions with related parties, and internal controls. Auditors make inquiries concerning financial statement related matters, such as accounting principles and practices; recordkeeping practices, accounting policies, actions of the governing board, and changes in business activities. Auditors apply analytical procedures designed to identify unusual items or trends in the financial statements that may need explanation. An audit also includes assessing the accounting principles used and significant estimates made by management, as well as evaluating the overall financial statement presentation. Essentially, many of the preceding procedures are designed to determine whether the financial statements make sense, prior to applying additional audit procedures.

A-32 An audit includes examining, on a test basis, evidence supporting the amounts and disclosures in the financial statements. Typical audit procedures might include confirming balances with banks or creditors, observing inventory counting, and testing selected transactions by examining supporting documents. In addition, the auditor contacts other sources outside of the client to gather information that may be more objective than that obtained from internal sources. For example, the auditor may decide to obtain written confirmation from an NFP's donors about promises to give. While accumulating this type of evidence, the auditor tries to reduce the risk that the financial statements will be materially misstated.

A-33 Because an audit must be performed at a reasonable cost, an auditor tests a portion of the transactions and does not examine 100 percent of all transactions. The auditor must exercise skill and judgment in deciding what evidence to look at, when to look at it, and how much to look at. The auditor must also exercise skill and judgment in evaluating and interpreting the results of the tests performed. Additionally, because management in preparing its financial statements must use estimates and because estimates are inherently imprecise, an audit cannot guarantee exactness.

A-34 The auditor plans and performs the audit with an attitude of professional skepticism; that is, the auditor designs the audit to obtain reasonable assurance that material errors or fraud are detected. An audit, however, does not and cannot provide a guarantee that fraud does not exist. For example, the auditor may not find fraud concealed through forgery or collusion, because the auditor is not trained to catch forgeries, nor will customary audit procedures detect all conspiracies.

A-35 Procedures the auditor performs pertaining to consideration of fraud in a financial statement audit include, but are not limited to, the following:

- Discussion among the engagement personnel regarding the risks of material misstatement due to fraud
- Identifying risks that may result in a material misstatement due to fraud
- Assessing identified risks after taking into account an evaluation of the entity's programs and controls
- Responding to the results of the assessment
- Evaluating audit evidence
- Communicating about fraud to management, the audit committee, and others

Review

A-36 During a review performed in accordance with Statements on Standards for Accounting and Review Services (SSARSs), an accountant obtains limited assurance that material changes to the financial statements are not necessary in order for the financial statements to be in conformity with GAAP. With respect to the auditor's level of assurance that the financial statements are presented fairly, a review falls between a compilation, in which an accountant obtains no assurance (as discussed subsequently), and an audit, in which an auditor obtains a high level of assurance (as discussed previously).

A-37 The end product of a review is the CPA's report on the accompanying financial statements. The CPA's report states the scope of the CPA's work (for example, which financial statements have been reviewed) and provides a statement that the CPA is not aware of any material modifications that should be made to the financial statements in order for them to be in conformity with GAAP.

A-38 As with all levels of service (for example, audit, review or compilation) the financial statements are the responsibility of the NFP's management. The primary difference between a review and an audit is that in an audit, the auditor verifies management's amounts and disclosures with evidence provided by third parties. In a review, the CPA ordinarily does not verify management's amounts and disclosures with outside evidence unless the CPA believes that the amounts and disclosures are materially inaccurate.

A-39 In performing a review, the CPA performs inquiries and analytical procedures designed to identify unusual items or trends that may need further explanation by management. Essentially, the review is designed to determine whether the financial statements make sense without applying audit-like procedures. A review of financial statements does not require that the CPA obtain an understanding of an entity's internal control, assess control risk, test accounting records and responses to inquiries by obtaining corroborating evidential matter, or perform certain other procedures ordinarily performed during an audit. A review does include assessing the accounting principles used and significant estimates made by management, as well as evaluating the overall financial statement presentation.

Compilation

A-40 A compilation performed in accordance with SSARSs, does not provide a basis for obtaining or providing any assurance regarding the financial statements. An accountant does not obtain any assurance that material changes to the financial statements are not necessary in order for the financial statements to be in conformity with GAAP. In a compilation, the CPA simply presents, in the form of financial statements, the client's financial data and does not probe beneath the surface unless he or she becomes aware that the information management provided is in error or is incomplete. As with an audit and a review, the compiled financial statements are the responsibility of the NFP's management.

A-41 The end product of a compilation is the CPA's report on the compiled financial statements. The CPA's report states that the financial statements were compiled, but because they were not audited or reviewed, the CPA expresses no opinion or any other form of assurance on them.

A-42 A compilation includes becoming familiar with the accounting principles and practices common to the client's industry and obtaining a general understanding all of the client's transactions and how they are recorded.

A-43 As part of a compilation, the CPA takes a commonsense look at the entity's accounting system to decide whether the client needs other accounting services, such as adjusting the accounting records. In addition, the CPA is obliged to read the financial statements and to consider whether they are appropriate in form and free from obvious material errors.

Comparison of an Audit, Review, and Compilation

Attribute	*Audit*	*Review*	*Compilation*
Engagement performed for the purpose of providing an opinion or report about whether the financial statements are presented fairly in conformity with generally accepted accounting principles	The auditor obtains a high, but not absolute, level of assurance about whether the financial statements are free of material misstatement	Accountant obtains limited assurance that no material modifications should be made to the financial statements	Accountant does not obtain or provide any assurance that no material modifications should be made to the financial statements
CPA obtains an understanding of internal control over financial statements	Yes	No	No
CPA tests the effectiveness of internal control	Frequently, but not always. The nature and extent of internal control testing depends on the auditor's judgment and conclusions pertaining to risk assessment	No	No
CPA verifies certain balances and transactions with third parties	Yes	No	No
CPA performs procedures to obtain reasonable assurance that financial statements are free of material misstatements whether caused by fraud or error	Yes	No	No

(continued)

Attribute	*Audit*	*Review*	*Compilation*
Financial statements are the responsibility of management	Yes	Yes	Yes
Financial statements are prepared by and are the responsibility of management	Yes, but the CPA may assist in drafting	Yes, but the CPA may assist in drafting	Yes, but the CPA may assist in drafting
CPA guarantees that the financial statements are accurate and free of fraud	No	No	No
CPA evaluates the entity's policy decisions and use of resources	No	No	No
CPA reports material weaknesses in internal control over financial reporting noted during the engagement to management or audit committee	Yes	Not required, though may be done if matters come to the CPA's attention	Not required, though may be done if matters come to the CPA's attention
CPA acts as a whistleblower internally and reports identified fraud to management or audit committee	Yes	Yes, unless clearly inconsequential	Yes, unless clearly inconsequential
CPA acts as a whistleblower externally and reports fraud and other matters to third parties, such as the IRS or state attorneys general	No	No	No
Cost	The cost of an audit, review or compilation will vary depending on many factors, including the quality of the not-for-profit entity's (NFP's) financial records (auditor readiness); size and complexity of the NFP; its geographic market; and the CPA		

Chapter 2

General Auditing Considerations*, 1

Overview

2.01 In accordance with AU section 150, *Generally Accepted Auditing Standards* (AICPA, *Professional Standards*), an independent auditor plans, conducts, and reports the results of an audit in accordance with generally accepted auditing standards (GAAS). Auditing standards provide a measure of audit quality and the objectives to be achieved in an audit. This chapter of the guide provides guidance, primarily on the application of the standards of fieldwork. Specifically, this chapter provides guidance on the risk assessment process and general auditing considerations for not-for-profit entities (NFPs).

Planning and Other Auditing Considerations

2.02 The objective of an audit of an NFP's financial statements is to express an opinion on whether its financial statements present fairly, in all material respects, its financial position, changes in net assets, and its cash flows in conformity with generally accepted accounting principles (GAAP) or other comprehensive bases of accounting. To accomplish that objective, the independent auditor's responsibility is to plan and perform the audit to obtain reasonable assurance (a high, but not absolute, level of assurance) that material misstatements, whether caused by errors or fraud, are detected. This section addresses general planning considerations and other auditing considerations relevant to NFPs.

Audit Planning

2.03 The first standard of field work states, "The auditor must adequately plan the work and must properly supervise any assistants." AU section 311, *Planning and Supervision* (AICPA, *Professional Standards*), establishes standards and provides guidance on the considerations and activities applicable to planning and supervision of an audit conducted in accordance with GAAS, including appointment of the independent auditor, preliminary engagement activities, establishing an understanding with the client, preparing a detailed, written audit plan, determining the extent of involvement of professionals with specialized skills, and communicating with those charged with governance and management. Audit planning also involves developing an overall audit strategy for the expected conduct, organization, and staffing of the audit. The nature, timing, and extent of planning vary with the size and complexity of the entity and with the auditor's experience with the entity, understanding of the entity, and its environment, including its internal control.

---

* Refer to the preface of this Audit and Accounting Guide for important information about the references to the professional standards from Statements on Auditing Standards (SASs) to AU sections and for information about the Auditing Standards Board's (ASB's) Clarity Project to revise all existing auditing standards so they are easier to read and understand.

1 Not-for-profit entities (NFPs) are not issuers subject to oversight by the Public Company Accounting Oversight Board (PCAOB). Thus, auditing standards issued by the PCAOB do not apply to audits of NFPs. The ASB sets auditing and assurance standards for nonissuers.

2.04 Paragraph .03 of AU section 311 states that the auditor must plan the audit so that it is responsive to the assessment of the risks of material misstatement based on the auditor's understanding of the entity and its environment, including its internal control. Planning is not a discrete phase of the audit, but rather an iterative process that begins with engagement acceptance and continues throughout the audit as the auditor performs audit procedures and accumulates sufficient appropriate audit evidence to support the audit opinion.

Using the Work of a Specialist

2.05 Management or the auditor may engage a specialist to provide special skill or knowledge about complex or subjective matters that are potentially material to the financial statements. Auditors of NFPs, for example, may need to use the work of a specialist with respect to the valuation of contributed assets, particularly contributed collection items that the NFP capitalizes. AU section 336, *Using the Work of a Specialist* (AICPA, *Professional Standards*), provides guidance to an auditor who uses the work of a specialist.

Scope of Services

2.06 The scope of services rendered by independent auditors depends on the kinds of reports to be issued as a result of the engagement. AU section 311 states the auditor should establish an understanding with the NFP regarding the services to be performed for each engagement. This understanding should be documented through a written communication with the NFP in the form of an engagement letter. The understanding generally includes the objectives of the engagement, management's responsibilities, the auditor's responsibilities, and limitations of the engagement. AU section 311 also identifies specific matters that would generally be included in the understanding with the client and other contractual matters an auditor might wish to include in the understanding. So that the understanding does not misinterpret the need and expectations of the NFP, the scope of the understanding should, where applicable, address all relevant contractual, legal, and regulatory requirements. For example, the auditor may be engaged to issue reports that meet requirements found in *Government Auditing Standards* as amended (often called the Yellow Book) issued by the Comptroller General of the United States.[2] Also, the auditor may be engaged to perform tests and issue reports required by the Single Audit Act Amendments of 1996 and United States Office of Management and Budget (OMB) Circular A-133, *Audits of States, Local Governments, and Non-Profit Organizations*.[3] The auditor may also be engaged to prepare special reports

---

[2] In practice, the standards included in *Government Auditing Standards* (July 2007 revision) are sometimes referred to as generally accepted government auditing standards (GAGAS). Government auditing standards includes standards for performance audits as well as standards for financial audits. The references to government auditing standards in this guide pertain only to the standards for financial audits. In August 2010, the U.S. Government Accountability Office (GAO; formerly U.S. General Accounting Office) issued an exposure draft of the ninth edition of *Government Auditing Standards*. The proposed changes contained in the exposure draft update GAGAS to reflect major developments in the accountability and audit profession and emphasize specific considerations applicable to the government environment. Readers should be alert for the issuance of final standards.

[3] United States Office of Management and Budget (OMB) Circular A-133 includes requirements that the auditor perform tests and report on compliance with the cost principles and matching or cost-sharing requirements set forth in various other government regulations, such as OMB Circulars A-21, *Cost Principles for Colleges and Universities*; A-110, *Uniform Administrative Requirements for Grants and Agreements with Institutions of Higher Education, Hospitals, and Other Nonprofit Organizations*; and A-122, *Cost Principles for Nonprofit Organizations*. OMB Circular A-133 *Compliance Supplement 2010*, issued in June 2010, assists auditors in performing the audits required under the Single Audit Act Amendments of 1996.

on various financial data prepared by the NFP, such as those related to bond indentures and other debt instruments and annual state information returns required by state attorneys general. AU section 380, *The Auditor's Communication With Those Charged With Governance* (AICPA, *Professional Standards*), states that the auditor should communicate to those charged with governance of the NFP the auditor's responsibilities under GAAS and an overview of the planned scope and timing of the audit.

2.07 An auditor may become aware that the entity is subject to an audit requirement that may not be encompassed in the terms of the engagement. If the auditor becomes aware of information concerning an instance of noncompliance or suspected noncompliance with laws and regulations, the auditor should obtain (*a*) an understanding of the nature of the noncompliance and the circumstances in which it has occurred and (*b*) further information to evaluate the possible effect on the financial statements. Noncompliance with laws and regulations may result in fines, litigation, or other consequences for the entity that may have a material effect on the financial statements. If the auditor suspects noncompliance may exist, the auditor should discuss the matter with management (at a level above those involved with the suspected noncompliance, if possible) and those charged with governance, such as the audit committee. Paragraph .22 of AU section 317, *Illegal Acts by Clients* (AICPA, *Professional Standards*), discusses considerations if management does not take the remedial action that the auditor considers necessary in the circumstances (such as not arranging for an audit that meets the applicable requirements).

Independence

2.08 Paragraph .11 of AU section 311 states at the beginning of an audit engagement, in addition to performing procedures regarding the continuance of the client relationship and the specific audit engagement, auditors should evaluate their compliance with ethical requirements, including independence. Members of the AICPA who are engaged to audit the financial statements of an NFP in accordance with GAAS are required to be independent. In making judgments about whether they are independent, members should be guided by Rule 101, *Independence* (AICPA, *Professional Standards*, ET sec. 101 par. .01), of the AICPA Code of Professional Conduct, its interpretations, and the ethics rulings under it. Although a number of ethics interpretations specifically address matters of independence as it relates to NFPs, members should use ET section 100-1, *Conceptual Framework for AICPA Independence Standards* (AICPA, *Professional Standards*), when making decisions on independence matters that are not explicitly addressed by the AICPA Code of Professional Conduct.

2.09 Interpretation No. 101-3, "Performance of nonattest services," under Rule 101 (AICPA, *Professional Standards*, ET sec. 101 par. .05), states that a member who performs attest services (audits, examinations, reviews, compilations, and agreed-upon procedures services) should not perform management functions or make management decisions for an attest client. (However, the member may provide advice, research materials, and recommendations to assist the client's management in performing its functions and making decisions.) If a member is engaged to perform nonattest services, the client must agree to perform the following functions in connection with the engagement:

- Make all management decisions and perform all management functions.

- Designate a competent employee, preferably within senior management, to oversee the services.
- Evaluate the adequacy and results of the services performed.
- Accept responsibility for the results of the services.

2.10 The member should be satisfied that the client will be able to meet all of these criteria and make an informed judgment on the results of the member's nonattest services. Assessing the competency of the client's designated employee is a matter of professional judgment. A Q&A issued by the Professional Ethics Executive Committee on January 27, 2005, provides guidance in assessing the client's competency. The member should be satisfied that the employee understands the services to be performed sufficiently to oversee them. In cases where the client is unable or unwilling to assume these responsibilities (for example, the client does not have an individual with the necessary competence to oversee the nonattest services provided or is unwilling to perform such functions due to lack of time or desire), the member's provision of nonattest services would impair independence. Before performing nonattest services, the member should establish and document in writing the client's acceptance of its responsibilities, as well as the objectives of the nonattest engagement, services to be performed, member's responsibilities, and any limitations of the engagement. ET section 101, *Independence* (AICPA, *Professional Standards*), provides examples of nonattest services and whether performance of those services would impair independence.

Audit Risk

2.11 AU section 312, *Audit Risk and Materiality in Conducting an Audit* (AICPA, *Professional Standards*), states that *audit risk* is a function of the risk that the financial statements prepared by management are materially misstated and the risk that the auditor will not detect such material misstatement. The auditor should consider audit risk in relation to the relevant assertions related to individual account balances, classes of transactions, and disclosures and at the overall financial statement level.

2.12 At the account balance, class of transactions, relevant assertion, or disclosure level, audit risk consists of (*a*) the risks of material misstatement (consisting of inherent risk and control risk) and (*b*) the detection risk. An auditor is required to assess the combined risks of material misstatement. An auditor cannot ignore the assessment of control risk regardless of his or her assessment of inherent risk. Although auditing standards do not require separate assessments to be performed, they do require an assessment of risks of material misstatement that includes control risk. Paragraph .23 of AU section 312 states that auditors should assess the risks of material misstatement at the relevant assertion level as a basis for further audit procedures (tests of controls or substantive procedures). It is not acceptable to simply deem risk to be "at the maximum." This assessment may be in qualitative terms such as high, medium, and low, or in quantitative terms such as percentages.

2.13 In considering audit risk at the overall financial statement level, the auditor should consider risks of material misstatement that relate pervasively to the financial statements taken as a whole and potentially affect many relevant assertions. Risks of this nature often relate to the entity's control environment and are not necessarily identifiable with specific relevant assertions at the class of transactions, account balance, or disclosure level. Such risks may be especially relevant to the auditor's consideration of the risks of material misstatement arising from fraud, for example, through management override of internal control.

Planning Materiality

2.14 The auditor's consideration of materiality is a matter of professional judgment and is influenced by the auditor's perception of the needs of users of financial statements. Materiality judgments are made in light of surrounding circumstances and necessarily involve both quantitative and qualitative considerations.

2.15 In accordance with paragraph .27 of AU section 312, the auditor should determine a materiality level for the financial statements taken as a whole when establishing the overall audit strategy for the audit. The auditor often may apply a percentage to a chosen benchmark as a step in determining materiality for the financial statements taken as a whole.

2.16 Expenditures of NFPs are often tightly controlled and based on the concept of a balanced budget with relatively small or zero operating margins. Examples of appropriate benchmarks include total net assets, various net asset classes, changes in net assets, changes in each class of net assets, total revenues, revenues of each net asset class, total expenses, total unrestricted contributions, total program expenses, or the effect on important measures, such as the ratio of program expenses to total expenses and the ratio of fund-raising expenses to contributions.

2.17 In an audit of compliance, the auditor should establish and apply materiality levels based on the governmental audit requirement. For example, for purposes of reporting findings of noncompliance, OMB Circular A-133 requires that noncompliance that is material in relation to 1 of the 14 types of compliance requirements identified in the OMB *Compliance Supplement* be reported.

Tolerable Misstatement

2.18 The initial determination of materiality is made for the financial statement taken as a whole. However, the auditor should allow for the possibility that some misstatements of lesser amounts than the materiality levels could, in the aggregate, result in a material misstatement of the financial statements. To do so, the auditor should determine one or more levels of tolerable misstatement. Paragraph .34 of AU section 312 defines *tolerable misstatement* (or *tolerable error*) as the maximum error in a population (for example, the class of transactions or account balance) that the auditor is willing to accept. Such levels of tolerable misstatement are normally lower than the materiality levels.

Qualitative Aspects of Materiality

2.19 As indicated previously, judgments about materiality include both quantitative and qualitative information. As a result of the interaction of quantitative and qualitative considerations in materiality judgments, misstatements of relatively small amounts that come to the auditor's attention could have a material effect on the financial statements. For example, it was revealed that an officer of an NFP had been improperly spending the NFP's money to support a lavish personal lifestyle. Although the amount of the improper spending was only a small fraction of 1 percent of the charity's annual budget, the wide publicity surrounding the officer's behavior led to an estimated 10 percent decrease in public contributions for several years and severely affected the charity's ability to fund its programs. Further, as discussed in paragraphs 3.99–.101 of this guide, noncompliance with donor-imposed restrictions (even of an otherwise immaterial amount) could be material if there is a reasonable possibility that the noncompliance could lead to a material loss of revenue or could cause an entity to be unable to continue as a going concern.†

2.20 Qualitative considerations also influence the auditor in reaching a conclusion about whether misstatements are material. Paragraph .60 of AU section 312 provides qualitative factors that the auditor may consider relevant in determining whether misstatements are material.

Related-Party Transactions

2.21 Obtaining knowledge of the client's organization and operations should include performing the procedures in AU section 334, *Related Parties* (AICPA, *Professional Standards*), to determine the existence of related-party relationships and transactions with such parties and to examine those transactions. The definition of *related parties* in Financial Accounting Standards Board (FASB) *Accounting Standards Codification* (ASC) 850, *Related Party Disclosures*, includes an NFP's management and members of management's immediate family, as well as affiliated entities. Accordingly, transactions with brother-sister entities and certain national and local affiliates as well as entities whose officers or directors are members of the NFP's governing board may have to be disclosed under FASB ASC 850-10-50.

2.22 AU section 334 provides guidance on, among other matters, procedures that the auditor should consider to identify related party relationships and transactions and to obtain satisfaction about the related financial statement reporting and disclosure. Obtaining that information will be enhanced if the NFP has a policy that requires an annual written disclosure by governing board members of the details of their transactions and other business involvements with the NFP, as well as disclosure of their other board memberships. Some states require that these kinds of disclosures be made on the annual reporting form filed by the NFP.

2.23 Some states have exhibited a heightened concern about whether the governing board members of NFPs are meeting their stewardship responsibilities, particularly if there are potential conflicts between the governing board members' financial interests and their duties as governing board members. Responses by an NFP to that concern might include increased sensitivity when it enters into business relationships with governing board members and might include developing appropriate controls for addressing potential conflicts of interests that could arise in related-party transactions and for ensuring that such transactions are disclosed to and approved by the governing board.

---

† On October 10, 2008, the Financial Accounting Standards Board (FASB) issued an exposure draft of a proposed statement, *Going Concern*, which would carry forward into the accounting standards the going concern guidance from AU section 341, *The Auditor's Consideration of an Entity's Ability to Continue as a Going Concern* (AICPA, *Professional Standards*), subject to several modifications to align the guidance with International Financial Reporting Standards. In June 2009, the project (renamed *Disclosures about Risks and Uncertainties and the Liquidation Basis of Accounting*) was broadened to address three additional areas: enhancing the disclosures of short-term and long-term risks, specifically risks for which there is more-than-remote likelihood of occurrence; defining *substantial doubt* in terms of an entity's ability to continue as a going concern; and defining when it is appropriate for an entity to apply the liquidation basis of accounting. Readers should be alert to the issuance of the final Accounting Standards Update (ASU).

Errors and Fraud

2.24 The auditor has a responsibility to plan and perform the audit to obtain reasonable assurance about whether the financial statements are free of material misstatement, whether caused by error or fraud.[4] AU section 312 establishes standards and provides guidance on the auditor's consideration of the risk that the financial statements are materially misstated by error or fraud. AU section 316, *Consideration of Fraud in a Financial Statement Audit* (AICPA, *Professional Standards*), establishes standards and provides guidance to auditors in fulfilling their responsibility, as it relates to fraud, in an audit of financial statements conducted in accordance with GAAS. AU section 316 describes fraud and its characteristics; discusses the importance of exercising professional skepticism; requires the engagement personnel to discuss how and where the NFP's financial statements might be susceptible to material misstatement due to fraud; requires the auditor to gather information necessary to identify risks of material misstatement due to fraud, to use the information gathered to identify risks that may result in a material misstatement due to fraud, and to evaluate the NFP's programs and controls that address the identified risks; provides guidance on how the auditor responds to the results of the assessment; provides guidance on the evaluation of audit evidence as it relates to the risk of material misstatement due to fraud; describes related documentation requirements; and provides guidance regarding the auditor's communication about fraud to management, the audit committee, and others. As described in paragraph .33 of AU section 316, risk factors that relate to misstatements arising from fraudulent financial reporting and misappropriation of assets may be grouped into three categories based on the conditions generally present when fraud exists: incentive or pressure, or both, opportunity, and attitude or rationalization, or both. Additional information about the implementation of AU section 316 is provided in appendix A (paragraph 2.79) to this chapter.

Illegal Acts

2.25 AU section 317 prescribes the nature and extent of the consideration the auditor should give to the possibility of illegal acts by a client. It also provides guidance on the auditor's responsibilities when a possible illegal act is detected, including the responsibility to be assured that the audit committee or its equivalent is adequately informed about illegal acts that come to the auditor's attention.

2.26 AU section 317 notes that illegal acts vary considerably in their relation to the financial statements. Some laws and regulations—such as sections of the tax law that affect tax provisions and accruals because of unrelated business income and government regulations that affect the amount of revenue accrued under government contracts—may have a direct and material effect on the determination of financial statement amounts. The auditor's responsibility to detect misstatements resulting from direct-effect illegal acts is the same as for errors and fraud (see footnote 4). Accordingly, management generally should identify federal, state, and local laws and regulations that may have a direct

---

[4] The auditor's consideration of illegal acts and responsibility for detecting misstatements resulting from illegal acts is defined in AU section 317, *Illegal Acts by Clients* (AICPA, *Professional Standards*). For those illegal acts that are defined in that section as having a direct and material effect on the determination of financial statement amounts, the auditor's responsibility to detect misstatements resulting from such illegal acts is the same as that for errors or fraud.

and material effect on the determination of financial statement amounts. The auditor should make inquiries of management concerning the client's compliance with laws and regulations.

2.27 NFPs frequently receive financial assistance—such as grants, loans, loan guarantees, and interest-rate subsidies—from federal, state, and local governmental entities. By accepting such assistance, NFPs often become subject to laws and regulations that may have a direct and material effect on the determination of amounts in their financial statements. Such laws and regulations may specifically address (*a*) the types of goods or services that NFPs may purchase with the assistance, (*b*) the eligibility of those to whom NFPs may provide benefits, (*c*) amounts NFPs must contribute from their own resources toward projects for which financial assistance is provided, and (*d*) principles and standards for determining the direct and indirect costs that are allowable as charges to governmental financial assistance programs.

2.28 Other laws and regulations relate more to an NFP's operating aspects than to its financial and accounting aspects, and violations of these laws and regulations have only an indirect effect on the financial statements. (The indirect effect is usually limited to the need to disclose a contingent liability under FASB ASC 450, *Contingencies*, because of the allegation or determination of illegality and the possibility of fines, penalties, or damages.)[‡] Such laws and regulations may concern securities trading, occupational safety and health, food and drug administration, environmental protection, equal employment opportunities, or antitrust violations. An example particular to the not-for-profit environment might be the requirement that an NFP inform contributors of the portion of their contributions that is tax deductible; the failure to do so could subject the NFP to financial penalties. Normally, an audit in accordance with GAAS does not include audit procedures specifically designed to detect illegal acts. AU section 317 specifies the auditor's responsibilities when he or she becomes aware of possible illegal acts as defined in that section.

Compliance Auditing Under *Government Auditing Standards*[||]

2.29 NFPs that receive government financial assistance may be required to have audits in accordance with *Government Auditing Standards* (the Yellow Book).[5] Government auditing standards pertain to auditors' professional qualifications, the quality of the work performed, and the characteristics of the reports issued. In performing an audit in accordance with the Yellow Book, the auditor assumes reporting responsibilities beyond those required by GAAS. The auditor must report on compliance with laws and regulations, violations of which may affect financial statement amounts, and on the NFP's internal

---

‡ On July 20, 2010, FASB issued a proposed ASU, *Disclosure of Certain Loss Contingencies*. The proposed ASU would retain the current qualitative disclosures in FASB *Accounting Standards Codification* (ASC) 450-20 for loss contingencies and enhance them by requiring additional disclosures, particularly for litigation contingencies. Readers should be alert to the issuance of a final ASU.

|| In August 2010, the U.S. GAO issued an exposure draft of the ninth edition of *Government Auditing Standards*. The proposed changes contained in the exposure draft update GAGAS to reflect major developments in the accountability and audit profession and emphasize specific considerations applicable to the government environment. Readers should be alert for the issuance of final standards.

5 Though government auditing standards primarily apply to federal financial assistance, some states have adopted government auditing standards.

control over financial reporting.[6] AU section 801, *Compliance Audits* (AICPA, *Professional Standards*), establishes standards and provides guidance when an auditor is engaged, or required by law or regulation, to perform a compliance audit in accordance with all of the following:

- GAAS
- *Government Auditing Standards*
- A governmental audit requirement that requires an auditor to express an opinion on compliance

It requires the auditor to adapt and apply the AU sections of AICPA *Professional Standards* to a compliance audit and provides guidance on how to do so. It identifies the AU sections that are not applicable to a compliance audit, defines terms related to compliance audits, and identifies the elements to be included in an auditor's report on a compliance audit.

Single Audits and Related Considerations

2.30 OMB Circular A-133 also prescribes audit requirements for NFPs receiving federal awards.[7] The audit requirements of Circular A-133 vary with the amount of federal awards an NFP receives.[8]

2.31 For audits performed in accordance with OMB Circular A-133, the auditor has responsibilities specified in the circular that go beyond GAAS. In such audits, the auditor must perform additional procedures to test and report on compliance with specified laws, regulations, and the provisions of contracts or grant agreements that may have a direct and material effect on major federal award programs (as defined in the circular). Other requirements of OMB Circular A-133 include reports on the financial statements, on the supplementary schedule of expenditures of federal awards, and on internal control relevant to major federal award programs.

2.32 AU section 801 and AICPA Audit Guide Government Auditing Standards *and Circular A-133 Audits* provide guidance on testing and reporting on compliance with laws and regulations in engagements performed under GAAS, the Yellow Book, and OMB Circular A-133. They provide auditors of NFPs with a basic understanding of the work they should do and the reports they should issue under the Yellow Book and OMB Circular A-133. AU section 801 is not

---

[6] Auditors reports on compliance are restricted-use reports under the provisions of AU section 532, *Restricting the Use of an Auditor's Report* (AICPA, *Professional Standards*). Paragraph 14.15 provides further information about restricted-use reports.

[7] A single audit is an audit of an entity's financial statements and of compliance with federal regulations relating to federal financial assistance, such as the audits required by Single Audit Act of 1984, as amended by the Single Audit Act Amendments of 1996, and OMB Circular A-133. OMB Circular A-133 *Compliance Supplement 2010*, issued in June 2010, assists auditors in performing the audits required. Program-specific audits may be conducted in accordance with specific government audit guides, such as the U.S. Department of Education's Audit Guide titled *Compliance Audit (Attestation Engagements) of Federal Student Financial Assistance Programs at Participating Institutions*.

[8] OMB Circular A-133 requires NFPs that expend $500,000 or more in federal awards in a year to have an audit in accordance with the circular. (Generally, NFPs that expend $500,000 or more, but under only 1 program, have the option of having a program-specific audit or a single audit in accordance with OMB Circular A-133.) NFPs that expend less than $500,000 must maintain records and make them available for review, if requested, but they are exempt from OMB Circular A-133 audit requirements.

applicable when the governmental audit requirement calls for an examination, in accordance with Statements on Standards for Attestation Engagements, of an entity's compliance with specified requirements or an examination of an entity's internal control over compliance. AT section 601, *Compliance Attestation* (AICPA, *Professional Standards*), is applicable to these engagements. If the NFP is required to undergo a compliance audit and an examination of internal control over compliance, AU section 801 is applicable to performing and reporting on the compliance audit, and AT section 601 is applicable to performing and reporting on the examination of internal control over compliance. An engagement might also be performed under AT section 101, *Attest Engagements* (AICPA, *Professional Standards*), or AT section 201, *Agreed-Upon Procedures Engagements* (AICPA, *Professional Standards*), depending on the requirements of the government. Law or regulation will not always indicate which standards to follow. In such cases, auditor judgment will be needed to determine, based on the circumstances, the appropriate standards to follow.

Processing of Transactions by Service Organizations

2.33 In addition to transactions, such as discretionary investment management services and payroll, for which for-profit entities might use service organizations, NFPs may also use such organizations to process transactions, such as student financial aid payments and receipt of contributions, that are unique to that industry. AU section 324,[9] *Service Organizations* (AICPA, *Professional Standards*), provides requirements and guidance for auditing the financial statements of an entity that uses a service organization to provide services that are part of the entity's information system for accounting or financial reporting.

Use of Assertions in Obtaining Audit Evidence

2.34 Paragraphs .14–.19 of AU section 326, *Audit Evidence* (AICPA, *Professional Standards*), discuss the use of assertions in obtaining audit evidence. In representing that the financial statements are fairly presented in accordance with GAAP, management implicitly or explicitly makes assertions regarding the recognition, measurement, and disclosure of information in the financial statements and related disclosures. Assertions used by the auditor fall into the following categories:

---

[9] The ASB has issued clarified SAS *Audit Considerations Relating to an Entity Using a Service Organization* and Statement on Standards for Attestation Engagements (SSAE) No. 16, *Reporting on Controls at a Service Organization* (AICPA, *Professional Standards*, AT sec. 801). These two standards will replace AU section 324, *Service Organizations* (AICPA, *Professional Standards*). The SAS will supersede the requirements and guidance for user auditors in SAS No. 70, *Service Organizations* (AICPA, *Professional Standards*, AU sec. 324), and address the user auditor's responsibility for obtaining sufficient appropriate audit evidence in an audit of the financial statement of an entity that uses one or more service organizations. This SAS has been released but not yet issued as authoritative. Upon the finalization of all remaining SASs to be issued as part of the Clarity Project (that is, "clarified" SASs), one SAS will be issued containing all finalized but unissued clarified SASs in a codified format. The effective date will be the same as the other clarified standards, which is for periods ending on or after December 15, 2012 (early implementation is not permitted). Until the new SAS is effective, user auditors will still use the guidance currently contained in AU section 324.

SSAE No. 16 addresses examination engagements undertaken by a service auditor to report on controls at organizations that provide services to user entities when those controls are likely to be relevant to user entities' internal control over financial reporting. It is effective for service auditors' reports for periods ending on or after June 15, 2011. Early implementation is permitted.

Categories of Assertions

	Description of Assertions		
	Classes of Transactions and Events During the Period	*Account Balances at the End of the Period*	*Presentation and Disclosure*
Occurrence/ Existence	Transactions and events that have been recorded have occurred and pertain to the entity.	Assets and liabilities exist.	Disclosed events and transactions have occurred.
Rights and Obligations	—	The entity holds or controls the rights to assets, and liabilities are the obligations of the entity.	Disclosed events and transactions pertain to the entity.
Completeness	All transactions and events that should have been recorded have been recorded.	All assets, liabilities, and restricted net assets that should have been recorded have been recorded.	All disclosures that should have been included in the financial statements have been included.
Accuracy/ Valuation and Allocation	Amounts and other data relating to recorded transactions and events have been recorded appropriately.	Assets, liabilities, and restricted net assets are included in the financial statements at appropriate amounts and any resulting valuation or allocation adjustments are recorded appropriately.	Financial and other information is disclosed fairly and at appropriate amounts.
Cut-off	Transactions and events have been recorded in the correct accounting period.	—	—
Classification and Under-standability	Transactions and events have been recorded in the proper accounts.	—	Financial information is appropriately presented and described and information in disclosures is expressed clearly.

2.35 The auditor should use relevant assertions for classes of transactions, account balances, and presentation and disclosures in sufficient detail to form a basis for the assessment of risks of material misstatement and the design and performance of further audit procedures. The auditor should use relevant assertions in assessing risks by considering the different types of potential misstatements that may occur and then designing further audit procedures that are responsive to the assessed risks.

2.36 The purpose of the use of assertions, specific audit objectives, examples of controls, and examples of auditing procedures in the tables titled "Auditing Considerations," which are presented in the auditing sections of several of the following chapters, is to assist the auditor in linking the auditor's risk assessments and further audit procedures. The tables include only those matters that are unique to NFPs. Accordingly, they should not be considered a complete listing of all of the audit objectives, controls, and auditing procedures that the auditor should consider when auditing an NFP. In addition, the absence of examples of selected controls related to a particular assertion is intended to indicate that the assertion does not ordinarily lend itself to specific controls that would provide reasonable assurance that the related audit objective has been achieved.

2.37 There is not necessarily a one-to-one relationship between audit objectives and auditing procedures. Some procedures may relate to more than one objective. On the other hand, a combination of procedures may be necessary to achieve a single objective. The tables are not intended to be all-inclusive or to suggest that specific audit objectives, controls, and auditing procedures should be applied. Some of the audit objectives may not be relevant to a particular NFP because of the nature of its operations or the absence of certain types of transactions. The absence of one or more of the illustrative controls would not necessarily indicate a deficiency in internal control.

2.38 Many of the illustrative controls are premised on the existence of certain essential characteristics of internal control: authorization of transactions, segregation of duties, documentation, supervision and review, and timeliness of controls. To avoid repetition, these characteristics have not been explicitly incorporated in the tables.

Understanding the Entity, Its Environment, and Its Internal Control

2.39 AU section 314, *Understanding the Entity and Its Environment and Assessing the Risks of Material Misstatement* (AICPA, *Professional Standards*), establishes standards and provides guidance about implementing the second standard of field work, as follows: "The auditor must obtain a sufficient understanding of the entity and its environment, including its internal control, to assess the risks of material misstatement of the financial statements whether due to error or fraud, and to design the nature, timing, and extent of further audit procedures."

2.40 Obtaining an understanding of the entity and its environment, including its internal control, is a continuous, dynamic process of gathering, updating, and analyzing information throughout the audit. Throughout this process, the auditor should also consider the guidance in AU section 316. See appendix A of this chapter for additional guidance pertaining to AU section 316.

This section addresses the unique aspects of NFPs that may be helpful in developing the required understanding of the entity, its environment, and its internal control.

Risk Assessment Procedures

2.41 As described in AU section 326, audit procedures performed to obtain an understanding of the entity and its environment, including its internal control, to assess the risks of material misstatement at the financial statement and relevant assertion levels are referred to as *risk assessment procedures*. Paragraph .21 of AU section 326 states that the auditor must perform risk assessment procedures to provide a satisfactory basis for the assessment of risks at the financial statement and relevant assertion levels. Risk assessment procedures by themselves do not provide sufficient appropriate audit evidence on which to base the audit opinion and must be supplemented by further audit procedures in the form of tests of controls, when relevant or necessary, and substantive procedures. In accordance with paragraph .06 of AU section 314, the auditor should perform the following risk assessment procedures to obtain an understanding of the entity and its environment, including its internal control:

a. Inquiries of management and others within the entity

b. Analytical procedures

c. Observation and inspection

See paragraphs .06–.13 of AU section 314 for more guidance on risk assessment procedures.

Analytical Procedures

2.42 AU section 329, *Analytical Procedures* (AICPA, *Professional Standards*), provides guidance on the use of analytical procedures. Paragraphs .04 and .06 of AU section 329 specify that the auditor should apply analytical procedures in planning the audit to assist in understanding the entity and its environment and to identify areas that may represent specific risks relevant to the audit. In performing analytical procedures as risk assessment procedures, the auditor should develop expectations about plausible relationships that are reasonably expected to exist. When comparison of those expectations with recorded amounts or ratios developed from recorded amounts yields unusual or unexpected relationships, the auditor should consider those results in identifying risks of material misstatement. However, when such analytical procedures use data aggregated at a high level (which is often the situation), the results of those analytical procedures provide only a broad initial indication about whether a material misstatement may exist. Accordingly, the auditor should consider the results of such analytical procedures along with other information gathered in identifying the risks of material misstatement.

2.43 Paragraph .05 of AU section 329 provides examples of sources of information that can be used to develop the necessary expectations for applying analytical procedures. The sources of information that may be unique to NFPs are (1) "information regarding the industry in which the client operates" and (2) "relationships of financial information with relevant nonfinancial information." The first of these utilizes industry-wide data for comparisons (such as data on endowment return, contributions, or program, fund-raising, and management and general costs that can be obtained from industry trade and professional associations). The second uses the auditor to formulate relevant relationships that are usually unique to a particular type of NFP, such as the relationship that might be expected to exist at a college or university between the number of students registered at standard tuition rates and tuition revenues, the relationship between the number of members in an NFP and its dues revenue, and the relationship between stagehand costs and the number of theatrical, dance, orchestral, or similar performances.

Discussion Among the Audit Team

2.44 In obtaining an understanding of the entity and its environment, including its internal control, AU section 314 states that there should be discussion among the audit team. In accordance with paragraph .14 of AU section 314, the members of the audit team, including the auditor with final responsibility for the audit, should discuss the susceptibility of the entity's financial statements to material misstatements. This discussion could be held concurrently with the discussion among the audit team that is specified by AU section 316 to discuss the susceptibility of the entity's financial statements to fraud.

Understanding of the Entity and Its Environment

2.45 AU section 314 requires auditors to obtain an understanding of the entity and its environment, including its internal control. In accordance with paragraph .04 of AU section 314, the auditor should use professional judgment to determine the extent of the understanding required of the entity and its environment, including its internal control. The auditor's primary consideration is whether the understanding that has been obtained is sufficient (1) to assess risks of material misstatement of the financial statements and (2) to design and perform further audit procedures (tests of controls and substantive tests).

2.46 The auditor's understanding of the entity and its environment consists of an understanding of the following aspects:

a. Industry, regulatory, and other external factors

b. Nature of the entity

c. Objectives and strategies and the related business risks that may result in a material misstatement of the financial statements

d. Measurement and review of the entity's financial performance

e. Internal control, which includes the selection and application of accounting policies (see subsequent section for further discussion)

Refer to appendix A of AU section 314 for examples of matters that the auditor may consider in obtaining an understanding of the entity and its environment relating to categories (*a*)–(*d*) previously. Industry characteristics that are particularly relevant to NFPs are discussed subsequently.[#]

Industry Characteristics

2.47 The operations of NFPs differ from those of for-profit entities in several significant ways, and those differences affect the auditor's assessment of the risk of material misstatement. NFPs use their resources to accomplish the purpose or mission for which they exist, not to generate net income. These

[#] In addition to industry characteristics, the auditor's understanding of the entity and its environment also consists of regulatory and other external factors; the nature of the entity; objectives and strategies and related business risks; and measurement and review of the entity's financial performance. The Audit Risk Alert *Not-for-Profit Entities Industry Developments* is intended to provide auditors of financial statements of NFPs with an overview of recent economic, industry, technical, regulatory, and professional developments that may affect the audits and other engagements they perform.

resources often come from contributions, grants, or appropriations, some of which may be subject to limitations on how the resources may be used.[10] These limitations, which may be imposed by donor restrictions, by contractual terms, or by the NFP's governing board, may affect the way in which revenues and net assets are recorded and presented in the financial statements.

2.48 NFPs are also required to comply with numerous other provisions of statutes, contractual agreements, terms of grants and trust agreements, and similar limitations. As discussed earlier in this chapter, these compliance requirements may have an effect on the financial statements. Finally, though NFPs are usually eligible for tax-exempt status under section 501 of the Internal Revenue Code, income from activities not related to an NFP's exempt purpose may be subject to tax and that the NFP may own or control for-profit subsidiaries. Taxes on unrelated business income and other tax matters related to the assessment of the risk of material misstatement for an NFP are addressed in chapter 15, "Tax Considerations," of this guide.

2.49 NFPs often have revenue and expenditure transactions that are unique to the industry, and these transactions have attendant implications for assessing the risk of material misstatement. For example, some NFPs solicit contributions from various sources, some receive revenues from grants, and some NFPs collect dues from members. Fund-raising may take place through telemarketing, direct mail solicitations, door-to-door solicitations, telethons, various kinds of special events, and other activities. Some NFPs collect substantial amounts of contributions in the form of currency. Each of these sources of cash flows is associated with different kinds of risk. On the expenditure side, some NFPs must also comply with restrictions imposed by resource providers. The revenue and expenditure transaction cycles of NFPs may also include transactions that are similar to those entered into by for-profit entities—for example, buying and selling merchandise, purchasing investments, property and equipment, and other assets; providing services for fees, and earning income from investments. These cycles may include transactions that do not immediately result in revenues and expenses.

2.50 FASB ASC 958-605-25-8 requires NFPs to recognize agreements for future nonreciprocal transfers of cash, other assets, and services that are unconditional (that is, promises to give). Chapter 5, "Contributions Received and Agency Transactions," of this guide, discusses recognition and measurement principles for the assets and revenues related to such transactions. Applying those principles often involves the use of significant accounting estimates. AU section 342, *Auditing Accounting Estimates* (AICPA, *Professional Standards*), provides guidance on obtaining and evaluating sufficient appropriate audit evidence to support those estimates. AU section 328, *Auditing Fair Value Measurements and Disclosures* (AICPA, *Professional Standards*), addresses audit considerations relating to the measurement and disclosure of assets, liabilities, and specific components of equity presented or disclosed at fair value in financial statements.

2.51 NFPs also have unique reporting requirements under GAAP. For example, they must report their expenses by function, such as major classes

---

[10] As used in this guide, *limitation* refers broadly to any constraints imposed on the use of assets or net assets, restriction refers to donor-imposed limitations, and *designation* refers to governing-board-imposed limitations.

of program services and supporting activities, in conformity with FASB ASC 958-720-45-2. They are also subject to specific disclosure requirements under FASB ASC 958-310-50 and FASB ASC 958-605-50, such as disclosures about promises to give, contributed services, and collections.

2.52 Each of these kinds of transactions and reporting requirements increases the risk of material misstatement. NFPs usually have controls designed to achieve control objectives related to these transactions.

2.53 Many NFPs face financial and operating pressures that are similar to those faced by for-profit entities. NFPs may also face pressures that are unique to entities that seek revenues in the form of contributions and grants, transactions that often depend on the state of the economy. These pressures generate operating, financial, and accounting responses by management, and such responses may increase the risk of material misstatement, which the auditor should assess and, when necessary, respond to by performing appropriate further audit procedures. The following are examples:

- Certain donors may tie contribution allocation formulas to the NFP's actual or budgeted revenues, leading management to attempt to manage revenues to achieve the largest allocation possible.
- A sluggish economy may reduce contributions and the collection of promises to give that were made in prior years. The reduced receipts may lead the NFP to pursue a more aggressive investment strategy involving complex financial instruments. Accounting for these instruments may represent significant risks. As part of performing his or her risk assessment procedures, the auditor should understand the substance of these instruments and determine that they are reported in conformity with GAAP.
- Adverse demographics may lead an NFP that charges fees for its services to pursue a more aggressive marketing strategy in its quest for constituents; this could decrease the collectibility of its receivables.
- Shortfalls in unrestricted contributions may induce an NFP to use restricted contributions for purposes that violate donor restrictions.
- Acceptance by an NFP of federal research and other grants carries with it an obligation to comply with federal regulations when the NFP administers those grants. Such regulations include those governing overhead and other costs charged to these grants. The terms of the grants may induce NFPs to charge unallowable costs to the grants, possibly resulting in liabilities for fines and repayment of any unallowable costs.
- An attempt to appear as efficient as possible may increase the likelihood of misstatement of the allocation of costs between program services and supporting activities. (Because some financial statement users view program expenses more favorably than supporting services, some NFPs have incentive to report costs as program rather than supporting services.)

Understanding of Internal Control

2.54 AU section 314 states that the auditor should obtain an understanding of the five components of internal control sufficient to assess the risks of material misstatement of the financial statements whether due to error or fraud, and to design the nature, timing, and extent of further audit procedures. The auditor is required to obtain an understanding of the control environment, even if the control environment might be less formal at smaller entities than at larger entities. The auditor should obtain a sufficient understanding by performing risk assessment procedures to

a. evaluate the design of controls relevant to an audit of financial statements and

b. determine whether they have been implemented.

2.55 The auditor should use such knowledge to

- identify types of potential misstatements;
- consider factors that affect the risks of material misstatement; and
- design tests of controls, when applicable, and substantive procedures.

2.56 Obtaining an understanding of the internal controls is distinct from testing the operating effectiveness of internal controls. The objective of obtaining an understanding of internal control is to evaluate the design of controls and determine whether they have been implemented for the purpose of assessing the risks of material misstatement. In contrast, the objective of testing the operating effectiveness of internal controls is to determine whether the controls, as designed, prevent or detect a material misstatement.

2.57 Paragraph .41 of AU section 314 defines *internal control* as "a process—effected by those charged with governance, management, and other personnel—designed to provide reasonable assurance about the achievement of the entity's objectives with regard to reliability of financial reporting, effectiveness and efficiency of operations, and compliance with applicable laws and regulations." Internal control consists of five interrelated components:

a. The control environment

b. Risk assessment

c. Information and communication systems

d. Control activities

e. Monitoring

Refer to paragraphs .40–.101 of AU section 314 for a detailed discussion of the internal control components. Those paragraphs recognize the definition and description of internal control contained in *Internal Control—Integrated Framework, published by the Committee of Sponsoring Organizations of the Treadway Commission.*

2.58 Certain characteristics of internal control, particularly in the control environment, may be unique to NFPs. Paragraph .70 of AU section 314 states that auditors should obtain sufficient knowledge of the control environment to understand the attitudes, awareness, and actions of those charged with governance concerning the entity's internal control and its importance in achieving reliable financial reporting. In understanding the control environment, the auditor should concentrate on the implementation of controls because controls may be established but not acted upon. The following are examples of characteristics of an NFP's control environment that the auditor may consider in obtaining an understanding of that environment:

- The role of management and the governing board
- The frequency of governing board meetings
- The qualifications of management and governing board members
- The governing board members' involvement in the NFP's operations
- The organizational structure

2.59 The other four components of internal control of NFPs may also include characteristics that would not ordinarily exist in for-profit entities. The auditor should obtain sufficient knowledge of the other four components to understand how

- restricted contributions are identified, evaluated, and accepted;
- promises to give are valued and recorded;
- contributed goods, services, utilities, facilities, and the use of long-lived assets are valued and recorded;
- compliance with donor restrictions and board designations is monitored;
- reporting requirements imposed by donors, contractors, and regulators are met;
- conformity with accounting presentation and disclosure principles, including those related to functional and natural expense reporting and allocation of joint costs, is achieved; and
- new programs are identified and accounted for.

Risk Assessment and the Design of Further Audit Procedures

2.60 As discussed previously, risk assessment procedures allow the auditor to gather the information necessary to obtain an understanding of the entity and its environment, including its internal control. This knowledge provides a basis for assessing the risks of material misstatement of the financial statements. These risk assessments are then used to design further audit procedures, such as tests of controls, substantive tests, or both. This section provides guidance on assessing the risk of material misstatement and how to design further audit procedures that effectively respond to those risks.

Assessing the Risks of Material Misstatement

2.61 Paragraph .102 of AU section 314 states that the auditor should identify and assess the risks of material misstatement at the financial statement level and at the relevant assertion level related to classes of transactions, account balances, and disclosures. For this purpose, the auditor should

a. identify risks throughout the process of obtaining an understanding of the entity and its environment, including relevant controls that relate to the risks, and considering the classes of transactions, account balances, and disclosures in the financial statements;

b. relate the identified risks to what can go wrong at the relevant assertion level;

c. consider whether the risks are of a magnitude that could result in a material misstatement of the financial statements; and

d. consider the likelihood that the risks could result in a material misstatement of the financial statements.

2.62 The auditor should use information gathered by performing risk assessment procedures, including the audit evidence obtained in evaluating the design of controls and determining whether they have been implemented, as audit evidence to support the risk assessment. The auditor should use the assessment of the risk of material misstatement at the relevant assertion level as the basis to determine the nature, timing, and extent of further audit procedures to be performed.

Identification of Significant Risks

2.63 As part of the assessment of the risks of material misstatement, the auditor should determine which of the risks identified are, in the auditor's judgment, risks that require special audit consideration (such risks are defined as *significant risks*). In considering the nature of the risks, the auditor should consider a number of matters, including whether the risk is related to recent significant economic, accounting, or other developments; whether the risk involves significant transactions with related parties; whether the risk involves significant nonroutine transactions that are outside the normal course of business for the entity, or that otherwise appear to be unusual; the degree of subjectivity in the measurement of financial information; the complexity of the transactions; and whether the risk is a risk of fraud. Examples of risks of material misstatements due to fraud can be found in paragraphs A-6–A-8 in appendix A of this chapter. One or more significant risks normally arise on most audits. In exercising this judgment, the auditor should consider inherent risk to determine whether the nature of the risk, the likely magnitude of the potential misstatement including the possibility that the risk may give rise to multiple misstatements, and the likelihood of the risk occurring are such that they require special audit consideration. Refer to paragraphs .45 and .53 of AU section 318, *Performing Audit Procedures in Response to Assessed Risks and Evaluating the Audit Evidence Obtained* (AICPA, *Professional Standards*), for further audit procedures pertaining to significant risks.

Designing and Performing Further Audit Procedures

2.64 AU section 318 provides guidance about implementing the third standard of field work, as follows: "The auditor must obtain sufficient appropriate audit evidence by performing audit procedures to afford a reasonable basis for an opinion regarding the financial statements under audit."

2.65 To reduce audit risk to an acceptably low level, the auditor (1) should determine overall responses to address the assessed risks of material misstatement at the financial statement level and (2) should design and perform further audit procedures whose nature, timing, and extent are responsive to the assessed risks of material misstatement at the relevant assertion level. The purpose is to provide a clear linkage between the nature, timing, and extent of the auditor's further audit procedures and the assessed risks. The overall responses and the nature, timing, and extent of the further audit procedures to be performed are matters for the professional judgment of the auditor and should be based on the auditor's assessment of the risk of material misstatement.

Overall Responses

2.66 The auditor's overall responses to address the assessed risks of material misstatement at the financial statement level may include emphasizing to the audit team the need to maintain professional skepticism in gathering and evaluating audit evidence, assigning more experienced staff or those with specialized skills or using specialists, providing more supervision, or incorporating additional elements of unpredictability in the selection of further audit procedures to be performed. Additionally, the auditor may make general changes to the nature, timing, or extent of further audit procedures as an overall response, for example, performing substantive procedures at period end instead of at an interim date.

Further Audit Procedures

2.67 Further audit procedures provide important audit evidence to support an audit opinion. These procedures consist of tests of controls and substantive tests. The nature, timing, and extent of the further audit procedures to be performed by the auditor should be based on the auditor's assessment of risk of material misstatement at the relevant assertion level.

2.68 In some cases, an auditor may determine that performing only substantive procedures is appropriate. However, the auditor often will determine that a combined audit approach using both tests of the operating effectiveness of controls and substantive procedures is an effective audit approach.

2.69 The auditor should perform tests of controls when the auditor's risk assessment includes an expectation of the operating effectiveness of controls or when substantive procedures alone do not provide sufficient appropriate audit evidence at the relevant assertion level. The phrase expectation of the operating effectiveness of controls means that the auditor's understanding of the five components of internal control has enabled him or her to initially assess control risk at less than maximum; and the auditor's strategy contemplates a combined approach of designing and performing tests of controls and substantive procedures. After obtaining an understanding of the five components of internal control sufficient to assess the risks of material misstatement and identifying and assessing the risks of material misstatement at the assertion level, the auditor's decision about whether to test the operating effectiveness of controls may be considered within a cost-benefit framework. The auditor may adopt a substantive audit strategy that excludes testing controls (as described in Technical Questions and Answers section 8200.07, "Considering a Substantive Audit Strategy" [AICPA, *Technical Practice Aids*], which is nonauthoritative) if the auditor believes that the benefit of testing control operating effectiveness—both in terms of audit efficiency and effectiveness—is less than the cost of testing controls. If testing the operating effectiveness of controls would not be effective or efficient, it will then be necessary to perform substantive procedures that respond to the assessed risks for specific assertions.[11]

2.70 Regardless of the audit approach selected, the auditor should design and perform substantive procedures for all relevant assertions related to each material class of transactions, account balance, and disclosure.

2.71 The auditor's substantive procedures should include the following audit procedures related to the financial statement reporting process:

- Agreeing the financial statements, including their accompanying notes, to the underlying accounting records.
- Examining material journal entries and other adjustments made during the course of preparing the financial statements. The nature and extent of the auditor's examination of journal entries and other adjustments depend on the nature and complexity of the entity's financial reporting system and the associated risks of material misstatement.

Evaluating Misstatements

2.72 Based on the results of the audit procedures performed, the auditor may identify misstatements in accounts or notes to the financial statements. Paragraph .42 of AU section 312 states that auditors must accumulate all known and likely misstatements identified during the audit, other than those that the auditor believes are trivial, and communicate them to the appropriate level of management. AU section 312 further states that auditors must consider the effects, both individually and in the aggregate, of misstatements (known and likely) that are not corrected by the entity. This consideration includes, among other things, the effect of misstatements related to prior periods.

2.73 For detailed guidance on evaluating audit findings and audit evidence, refer to AU section 312 and AU section 326, respectively.

Completing the Audit

2.74 The procedures involved in completing the audit include the following:

- Performing analytical procedures in the overall review stage
- Evaluating whether the financial statements are free of material misstatements. Procedures include the following:
  - Evaluating uncorrected misstatements and concluding whether the accumulated misstatements cause the financial statements to be materially misstated (AU section 312)
  - Evaluating whether the accumulated results of audit procedures and other observations affect the assessment of the risks of material misstatement due to fraud made earlier in the audit (AU section 316)

---

[11] For nonauthoritative guidance pertaining to internal control and the risk assessment standards (SAS Nos. 104–111), refer to Technical Questions and Answers (TIS) sections 8200.05–.16 in TIS section 8200, *Internal Control* (AICPA, *Technical Practice Aids*).

- — Considering the effect of undetected misstatements
- — Considering the possibility of management's bias

- Obtaining legal letters
- Reviewing for subsequent events[12]
- Obtaining written management representations
- Evaluating whether there is a substantial doubt about the NFP's ability to continue as a going concern for a reasonable period of time[†]
- Preparing the auditor's reports
- Communicating, in writing, to management and those charged with governance, significant deficiencies and material weaknesses identified in the audit (AU section 325, *Communicating Internal Control Related Matters Identified in an Audit* [AICPA, *Professional Standards*])[13]
- Communicating the auditor's views about qualitative aspects of the NFP's significant accounting policies; significant difficulties encountered during the audit; uncorrected misstatements (other than those the auditor believes are trivial); disagreements with management; material, corrected misstatements; representations that the auditor is requesting of management; management's consultations with other accountants; significant issues discussed with management; and other significant findings or issues that the auditor believes are significant and relevant to those charged with governance (AU section 380)

This section of the guide discusses aspects of these procedures that are unique to NFPs.

Management Representations

2.75 AU section 333, *Management Representations* (AICPA, *Professional Standards*), sets forth requirements that the auditor obtain written representations from management as a part of an audit of financial statements performed

---

[12] Nonauthoritative guidance about the auditor's responsibilities for subsequent events and the effects of FASB ASC 855, *Subsequent Events*, on AU section 560, *Subsequent Events* (AICPA, *Professional Standards*), can be found in TIS sections 8700, *Subsequent Events*, and 9070, *Subsequent Events*. The ASB finalized a new clarified SAS, *Subsequent Events and Subsequently Discovered Facts*, which would remove the accounting guidance for subsequent events from AU section 560, and converge with International Standard on Auditing No. 560, *Subsequent Events*. The SAS has been finalized by the ASB but is not yet issued as authoritative. Upon the finalization of the AICPA Clarity Project, one SAS will be issued containing all finalized but unissued clarified SASs in codified format. See the preface of this guide for further information on the ASB's Clarity Project. This SAS is effective for audits of financial statements for periods ending on or after December 15, 2012.

[†] See footnote † in paragraph 2.19.

[13] Interpretation No. 1 of AU section 325, *Communicating Internal Control Related Matters Identified in an Audit* (AICPA, *Professional Standards*, AU sec. 9325 par. .01–.03), clarifies use of the terms *deficiency in internal control, significant deficiencies* and *material weaknesses*, in the context of reporting on internal control over compliance in a single audit. It reflects the March 11, 2010, statement of the OMB, (which appears in the introductory section of Circular A-133), which states that those terms are to be used as defined in generally accepted auditing standards issued by the AICPA and *Government Auditing Standards* issued by the GAO. Interpretation Nos. 2–4 of AU section 325 (AICPA, *Professional Standards*, AU sec. 9325 par. .04–.13) discuss interim communications to management of identified significant deficiencies and material weaknesses before the completion of a compliance audit, including compliance audits conducted under the OMB pilot project for auditees receiving awards under the American Recovery and Reinvestment Act of 2009.

in accordance with GAAS and provides guidance concerning the representations to be obtained. Written representations from management should be obtained for all financial statements and periods covered by the auditor's report. The specific written representations to be obtained depend on the circumstances of the engagement and the nature and basis of the presentation of the financial statements. Paragraph .06 of AU section 333 lists matters ordinarily included in management's representation letter. Paragraph .06*g* of AU section 333 states that the representation letter should include an acknowledgment by management that it has considered the financial statement misstatements aggregated by the auditor during the current engagement and pertaining to the latest period presented, and has concluded that any uncorrected misstatements are immaterial, both individually and in the aggregate to the financial statements taken as a whole. Also, a summary of the uncorrected misstatements should be included in or attached to the representation letter. Additional representations specific to NFPs that may be obtained include the following:

- Compliance with contractual agreements, grants, and donor restrictions
- Maintenance of an appropriate composition of assets in amounts needed to comply with all donor restrictions
- Taxation and tax-exempt status
- Reasonableness of bases for allocation of functional expenses
- Inclusion in the financial statements of all assets and liabilities under the entity's control
- Adequacy of internal control over the receipt and recording of contributions
- Propriety of reclassifications between net asset classes
- The governing board's interpretation concerning whether laws place restrictions on net appreciation of donor-restricted endowments
- Appropriateness of the methods and significant assumptions used by management to determine fair value, their consistency in application, and the completeness and adequacy of fair value information for financial statement measurement and disclosure purposes

2.76 Paragraphs .23–.24 of AU section 801 note that an auditor should request from management written representations that are tailored to the entity and the governmental audit requirements. Paragraph .23 includes a list of 12 items to include in the representation letter.

Going-Concern Considerations†

2.77 AU section 341, *The Auditor's Consideration of an Entity's Ability to Continue as a Going Concern* (AICPA, *Professional Standards*), provides guidance to the auditor in meeting the responsibility to evaluate whether there is substantial doubt about the client's ability to continue as a going concern for a reasonable period of time not to exceed one year beyond the date of the balance sheet. AU section 341 gives examples of conditions and events that might indicate that there could be substantial doubt about the entity's continued existence. Additional examples of such conditions and events that are particularly applicable to NFPs include the following:

† See footnote† in paragraph 2.19.

- Insufficient unrestricted revenues to provide supporting services to activities funded by restricted contributions
- A high ratio of fund-raising expenses to contributions received or a low ratio of program expenses to total expenses
- Insufficient resources to meet donor's restrictions (this may result from the use of restricted net assets for purposes that do not satisfy the donor's restrictions, sometimes referred to as interfund borrowing)
- Activities that could jeopardize the NFP's tax-exempt status and thus endanger current contribution levels
- Concerns expressed by governmental authorities regarding alleged violations of state laws governing an NFP's maintenance or preservation of certain assets, such as collection items
- A loss of key governing board members or volunteers
- External events that could affect donors' motivations to continue to contribute
- Decreases in revenues contributed by repeat donors
- A loss of major funding sources

2.78 Paragraph .18 of AU section 341 states that if, after considering the identified conditions and events in the aggregate, the auditor believes there is substantial doubt about the ability of the entity to continue as a going concern for a reasonable period of time, he or she should follow the guidance in paragraphs .07–.16 of AU section 341. In connection with that guidance, the auditor should document all of the following:

a. The conditions or events that led him or her to believe that there is substantial doubt about the entity's ability to continue as a going concern for a reasonable period of time.

b. The elements of management's plans that the auditor considered to be particularly significant to overcoming the adverse effects of the conditions or events.

c. The auditing procedures performed and evidence obtained to evaluate the significant elements of management's plans.

d. The auditor's conclusion as to whether substantial doubt about the entity's ability to continue as a going concern for a reasonable period of time remains or is alleviated. If substantial doubt remains, the auditor also should document the possible effects of the conditions or events on the financial statements and the adequacy of the related disclosures. If substantial doubt is alleviated, the auditor also should document the conclusion as to the need for disclosure of the principal conditions and events that initially caused him or her to believe there was substantial doubt.

e. The auditor's conclusion as to whether he or she should include an explanatory paragraph in the audit report. If disclosures with respect to an entity's ability to continue as a going concern are inadequate, the auditor also should document the conclusion as to whether to express a qualified or adverse opinion for the resultant departure from GAAP.

2.79

Appendix A—Consideration of Fraud in a Financial Statement Audit

A-1 AU section 316, *Consideration of Fraud in a Financial Statement Audit* (AICPA, *Professional Standards*), is the primary source of authoritative guidance about an auditor's responsibilities concerning the consideration of fraud in a financial statement audit. AU section 316 establishes standards and provides guidance to auditors in fulfilling their responsibility to plan and perform the audit to obtain reasonable assurance about whether the financial statements are free of material misstatement, whether caused by error or fraud as stated in paragraph .02 of AU section 110, *Responsibilities and Functions of the Independent Auditor* (AICPA, *Professional Standards*).

A-2 Two types of misstatements are relevant to the auditor's consideration of fraud in a financial statement audit:

- Misstatements arising from fraudulent financial reporting
- Misstatements arising from misappropriation of assets

A-3 Three conditions generally are present when fraud occurs. First, management or other employees have an *incentive* or are under *pressure,* which provides a reason to commit fraud. Second, circumstances exist—for example, the absence of controls, ineffective controls, or the ability of management to override controls—that provide an *opportunity* for a fraud to be perpetrated. Third, those involved are able to *rationalize* committing a fraudulent act.

The Importance of Exercising Professional Skepticism

A-4 Because of the characteristics of fraud, the auditor's exercise of professional skepticism is important when considering the risk of material misstatement due to fraud. Professional skepticism is an attitude that includes a questioning mind and a critical assessment of audit evidence. The auditor should conduct the engagement with a mindset that recognizes the possibility that a material misstatement due to fraud could be present, regardless of any past experience with the entity and regardless of the auditor's belief about management's honesty and integrity. Furthermore, professional skepticism requires an ongoing questioning of whether the information and evidence obtained suggests that a material misstatement due to fraud has occurred.

Discussion Among Engagement Personnel Regarding the Risks of Material Misstatement Due to Fraud[1]

A-5 Members of the audit team should discuss the potential for material misstatement due to fraud in accordance with the requirements of paragraphs .14–.18 of AU section 316. The discussion among the audit team members about the susceptibility of the entity's financial statements to material misstatement due to fraud should include a consideration of the known external and internal

---

[1] The brainstorming session to discuss the entity's susceptibility to material misstatements due to fraud could be held concurrently with the brainstorming session required under AU section 314, *Understanding the Entity and Its Environment and Assessing the Risks of Material Misstatement* (AICPA, *Professional Standards*), to discuss the potential of the risk of material misstatement.

factors affecting the entity that might (*a*) create incentives or pressures, or both, for management and others to commit fraud, (*b*) provide the opportunity for fraud to be perpetrated, and (*c*) indicate a culture or environment that enables management to rationalize committing fraud. Communication among the audit team members about the risks of material misstatement due to fraud also should continue throughout the audit.

A-6 When brainstorming about the incentives and pressures for management and others to commit fraud, the audit team members may want to discuss whether any of the following exist:

- Incentive to minimize reported fundraising and management and general expenses, and maximize reported program expenses, to make the not-for-profit entity (NFP) appear worthy of contributions, especially if some potential resource providers have stated or implied limits in these areas (for example, the resource provider will not fund NFPs with more than 25 percent overhead), or if the NFP desires to be in compliance with standards of the charitable organization rating agencies
- Incentive to defer fundraising expenses to future periods if the related contributions will not be received until those future periods
- Incentive to make the NFP look poor (but not *too* poor) to induce contributors to contribute
- Incentive to mischaracterize the relationship with related parties (for example, affiliated chapters, fundraising organizations, foundations, guilds, trusts, funds, student clubs, and auxiliaries) to avoid consolidating those entities or reporting the assets held by them for the NFP's benefit if the NFP wants to appear poorer
- Incentive to achieve certain fundraising goals, especially to meet terms of matching gifts
- Incentive to misstate financial information if contributions are conditioned on achieving certain financial performance goals
- Incentive to report that donor gifts (or restricted income from donor endowments) have been used in accordance with donor restrictions when, in fact, that is not the case (this incentive may be particularly strong if there is a deficit change in unrestricted net assets)
- Incentive to "borrow" from restricted funds to cover a current unrestricted deficit
- Incentive to mischaracterize revenue so as not to fail the IRS public support test
- Incentive to recognize intentions to give as contributions made in order to reduce the private foundation excise tax on the net investment income, avoid the excise tax for failure to distribute income, or both
- Incentive to misallocate expenses to avoid exceeding IRS limits on allowable lobbying

- Incentive to inappropriately minimize unrelated business income taxes, such as by over-allocating costs against taxable unrelated business income
- Incentive to mischaracterize overhead expenses as direct program expenses when grantors limit the amount of their grants that may be used for overhead (sometimes such limits are zero)
- Incentive to avoid surplus funds in grants that require that surplus funds be returned to the grantor

A-7 When brainstorming about the opportunities for fraud to be perpetrated, the audit team members may want to discuss whether the following exist:

- Domination of management by a single person (such as an executive director) or small group without compensating controls, for example, a charismatic executive combined with a reluctance of employees or those charged with governance to disagree with him or her
- Limited number of staff involved in the accounting functions, if the result is inadequate internal control over assets that increases the susceptibility of misappropriation of those assets
- The attitude among management of, "We're a charity, no one would steal from us!" with an attendant lack of appreciation for the importance of strong internal controls
- Unjustified trust in employees or volunteers because "we know they are committed to the cause"
- Key management functions and controls are in the hands of volunteers not subject to normal levels of supervision
- Management lacks the necessary background, experience, or commitment to fulfill their duties
- A hands-off governing board or one with insufficient financial expertise to oversee the financial reporting process and internal controls
- Special events or fundraising methods result in large amounts of cash on hand or processed, for example, church plate collections, and door-to-door and other off-premises fundraising
- Revenue (including contributions) received in the form of coins or currency, or both, or in the form of checks personally handed to the NFP's staff and volunteers
- Inadequate investigation of past-due promises to give, especially conditional promises, which are not recognized in the financial statements
- Numerous restricted grants received under the control of a single individual or a small group of individuals, which could lead to allocating expenses to an inappropriate grant account when grant limits are reached on the appropriate one
- Programs are supported by mixed types of grants (fixed price, units of service, cost reimbursement) that could motivate charging inappropriate expenses against certain grants or charging multiple grants for the same expenditure

- Fixed assets not subject to existing general ledger controls because they are not recorded, for example, fixed assets legally owned by a grantor or collection items that the NFP has chosen not to capitalize
- Grant programs for which the recipients are individuals (for example, food, clothing, or other assets are distributed) or scholarships, fellowships, or other financial assistance is paid out
- Research projects where payments to test subjects are made in cash, especially if lists of payments are not prepared so as to preserve the confidentiality of the subjects' identities
- A complex organizational structure (often including several entities under common control), especially if there are numerous inter-entity transactions

A-8 When brainstorming about a culture or environment that enables management to rationalize committing fraud, the audit team members may want to discuss whether any of the following exist:

- An organizational culture that lets concern for provision of program services completely override sound internal controls
- Misguided attempts to preserve the NFP's program services no matter what the cost or risk, for example, by not remitting payroll withholdings
- An employee's attitude that because his or her compensation is lower than what the employee perceives could be earned in the for-profit sector, special perquisites are justified (such as rights to take donated noncash items for personal use)
- An employee who has access to assets subject to misappropriation is dissatisfied, perhaps because of long work hours or inability to get resources assigned to the employee's projects
- Governing board members have personally guaranteed debt of the NFP and the NFP is experiencing a deteriorating financial condition

A-9 The preceding lists highlight incentives or pressures, or both, opportunities, and cultures or environments that are unique to or more common in the not-for-profit industry than in other industries. Additionally, the appendix of AU section 316 provides examples of fraud risk factors that the audit team members might consider.

Obtaining the Information Needed to Identify the Risks of Material Misstatement Due to Fraud

A-10 AU section 314, *Understanding the Entity and Its Environment and Assessing the Risks of Material Misstatement* (AICPA, *Professional Standards*), establishes standards and provides guidance about how the auditor obtains an understanding of the entity and its environment, including its internal control for the purpose of assessing the risks of material misstatement. In performing that work, information may come to the auditor's attention that should be considered in identifying risks of material misstatement due to fraud. As part of this work, the auditor should perform the following procedures to obtain information that is used (as described in paragraphs .35–.42 of AU section 316) to identify the risks of material misstatement due to fraud:

a. Make inquiries of management and others within the entity to obtain their views about the risks of fraud and how they are addressed (see paragraphs .20–.27 of AU section 316)

b. Consider any unusual or unexpected relationships that have been identified in performing analytical procedures in planning the audit (see paragraphs .28–.30 of AU section 316)

c. Consider whether one or more fraud risk factors exist (see paragraphs .31–.33 of AU section 316, the appendix to AU section 316, and paragraphs A-5–A-9 of this appendix)

d. Consider other information that may be helpful in the identification of risks of material misstatement due to fraud (see paragraph .34 of AU section 316)

A-11 In planning the audit, the auditor also should perform analytical procedures relating to revenue with the objective of identifying unusual or unexpected relationships involving revenue accounts that may indicate a material misstatement due to fraudulent financial reporting. For example, in the not-for-profit industry, the following unusual or unexpected relationships may indicate a material misstatement due to fraud:

- Changes in contribution revenue as compared to a prior period are not as expected, considering changes in the surrounding circumstances (state of the economy, changed fundraising efforts, known major gifts or grants, or both)
- Revenue does not change in the direction or magnitude, or both, that is expected based on observed changes in related expenses (for example, revenue and expenses of a clinic)
- Earned revenue is inconsistent with known levels of services provided
- A significant amount of expenditures on cost-reimbursement grants are recognized at the tail end of the grant period
- Investment return overall, or for an individual fund, is not reasonable

A-12 *Considering Fraud Risk Factors.* As indicated in item (*c*) previously, the auditor may identify events or conditions that indicate incentives or pressures, or both, to perpetrate fraud, opportunities to carry out the fraud, or attitudes or rationalizations, or both, to justify a fraudulent action. Such events or conditions are referred to as *fraud risk factors*. Fraud risk factors do not necessarily indicate the existence of fraud; however, they often are present in circumstances where fraud exists.

A-13 AU section 316 provides fraud risk factor examples that have been written to apply to most enterprises. The section about brainstorming sessions that are conducted by the audit team members (paragraphs A-5–A-9 of this appendix) contains a list of fraud risk factors specific to the not-for-profit industry. Remember that fraud risk factors are only one of several sources of information an auditor considers when identifying and assessing risk of material misstatement due to fraud.

Identifying Risks That May Result in a Material Misstatement Due to Fraud[2]

A-14 In identifying risks of material misstatement due to fraud, it is helpful for the auditor to consider the information that has been gathered in accordance with the requirements of paragraphs .19–.34 of AU section 316. The auditor's identification of fraud risks may be influenced by characteristics such as the size, complexity, and ownership attributes of the entity. In addition, the auditor should evaluate whether identified risks of material misstatement due to fraud can be related to specific financial-statement account balances or classes of transactions and related assertions, or whether they relate more pervasively to the financial statements as a whole. Certain accounts, classes of transactions, and assertions that have high inherent risk because they involve a high degree of management judgment and subjectivity also may present risks of material misstatement due to fraud because they are susceptible to manipulation by management.

A-15 Recognition of the following items might involve a high degree of management judgment and subjectivity:

Contributions Receivable and Revenue

- Measurement of noncash contributions in the absence of publicly available market quotations
- Whether the allowance for uncollectible pledges is appropriate (This involves a higher degree of subjectivity than normal trade or loans receivable, due to the voluntary nature of the underlying transaction.)
- Whether a donor communication is an expression of an intention to give or a promise to give
- Whether promises to give are conditional or unconditional
- Whether donor stipulations are conditions or restrictions
- Whether a donor-imposed condition on a promise to give has been substantially met
- Whether donated services require specialized skills
- Whether the NFP would typically have had to purchase services if they were not provided by donation
- Whether assets received that must be passed on to another entity meet the criteria for recognition as contribution revenue by the reporting (recipient) entity (That is, is there variance power; are the NFPs financially interrelated; is a transfer revocable; and so forth?)

Revenues Other Than Contributions

- Whether revenue transactions (for example, membership dues, grants, contracts) are contributions or exchange transactions (or whether they have a contribution element)

---

[2] Paragraph .102 of AU section 314 states that the auditor should to identify and assess the risk of material misstatement at the financial statement level and at the relevant assertion level related to classes of transactions, account balances and disclosures. This requirement provides a link between the auditor's consideration of fraud and the auditor's assessment of risk, and the auditor's procedures in response to those assessed risks.

- Whether a revenue source results from an activity that is subject to tax as an unrelated business

Contributions Payable and Expense

- Whether a communication with another NFP is an expression of an intention to give or a promise to give
- Whether promises to give are conditional or unconditional
- Whether stipulations are conditions or restrictions
- Whether a condition on a promise to give to another NFP has been met, especially if the donor NFP's monitoring system is inadequate

Expenses, in General

- Allocation of costs of joint activities, both as to whether the criteria for allocation are met and whether the allocation bases and methods chosen are appropriate
- Allocation of expenses among functional categories, especially if that allocation is made at year end based on percentages
- Whether an expenditure satisfies a restriction on net assets

Other Items

- Whether an NFP maintains its collection in a manner that qualifies for nonrecognition, especially if they have occasionally sold collection items in the past without purchasing new items for the collection
- Recoverability of assets with possibly limited future use (for example, sets and costumes owned by a theater)
- Whether a related entity meets the criteria for consolidation or for financially interrelated entities accounted for under the equity method, especially if one NFP has significant influence over the other but not a majority voting interest in the governing board of the other

A Presumption That Improper Revenue Recognition Is a Fraud Risk

A-16 Material misstatements due to fraudulent financial reporting often result from an overstatement of revenues (for example, through premature revenue recognition or recording fictitious revenues) or an understatement of revenues (for example, through improperly shifting revenues to a later period). Therefore, the auditor should ordinarily presume that there is a risk of material misstatement due to fraud relating to revenue recognition (see paragraph .41 of AU section 316).

A-17 Revenue may be improperly recognized due to fraudulent financial reporting if

- revenue is improperly classified among the three net asset classes, restrictions are released before they are met, or restrictions are not released even though they are met;
- conditional promises to give are recognized as unconditional, or vice versa;

- intentions to give are recognized as promises to give, or promises to give are not recognized because it is asserted that they are intentions to give;
- unconditional grants that are in substance contributions are recognized as exchange transactions, or vice versa;
- membership dues that are in substance contributions are recognized as exchange transactions, or vice versa;
- improper periods for amortization of income from membership dues, tuition, and season ticket sales are used;
- agency transactions are recognized as contribution revenue and program expense, particularly if the reported fair value of noncash items changes without cause between receipt and disbursement;
- works of art, historical treasures, and similar items are not recognized but should be because the collection does not meet the criteria for nonrecognition;
- in-kind contributions are selectively recognized to maximize the reported ratio of program expenses to total expenses (that is, the NFP makes every attempt to recognize and maximize the fair value of contributions of items for program purposes, but ignores or minimizes the estimated fair value of items used for management and general or fundraising purposes);
- discount rates used in measuring promises to give or split-interest gifts are inappropriate;
- revenue is recognized for services that were not delivered; and
- sliding scales used to charge service recipients are not appropriately applied.

A Consideration of the Risk of Management Override of Controls

A-18 Even if specific risks of material misstatement due to fraud are not identified by the auditor, there is a possibility that management override of controls could occur, and accordingly, the auditor should address that risk (see paragraph .57 of AU section 316) apart from any conclusions regarding the existence of more specifically identifiable risks. Specifically, the procedures described in paragraphs .58–.67 of AU section 316 should be performed to further address the risk of management override of controls. These procedures include (1) examining journal entries and other adjustments for evidence of possible material misstatement due to fraud, (2) reviewing accounting estimates for biases that could result in material misstatement due to fraud, and (3) evaluating the business rationale for significant unusual transactions.

Key Estimates

A-19 Fraudulent financial reporting is often accomplished through the intentional misstatement of accounting estimates. Estimates by management are common in the following areas:

- Measurement of noncash contributions other than marketable securities and especially of unusual noncash assets
- Allowance for uncollectible promises to give
- Present value calculations for unconditional promises to give and split-interest agreements

- Methods and factors used in allocating the costs of joint activities
- Allocation of expenses to functional categories
- Future cash flows related to assets that are possibly impaired

A-20 Review and evaluation of the financial results reported by the NFP or its individual operating units also may detect fraudulent financial reporting. Unusual fluctuations in results of a particular reporting unit, or the lack of expected fluctuations, may indicate potential manipulation by management. Examples of key ratios or trends to evaluate include the following:

- Percentage of revenue by major source, particularly if compared over a series of years or between similar individual operating units
- Percentage of expenses in each of the major programs and in management and general and fundraising categories, particularly if compared over a series of years or between similar individual operating units
- Fundraising expenses as a percentage of contribution revenue
- Investment income as a percentage of investment assets
- Comparisons of budget to actual for revenues and expenses
- Per capita calculations such as payroll expense per employee, average fee per service recipient, average gift shop sales per person admitted, and average contribution per person solicited, particularly if the denominator (head count) can be determined independent of the accounting function
- Comparison of the amount of gifts received in the accounting records and the development records

Assessing the Identified Risks After Taking Into Account an Evaluation of the Entity's Programs and Controls That Address the Risks

A-21 Paragraphs .43–.45 of AU section 316 provide requirements and guidance for the evaluation of entity programs and controls and assessing identified risks of material misstatement due to fraud.

A-22 The exhibit to AU section 316 discusses examples of programs and controls an entity may implement to prevent, deter, and detect fraud. It includes sections on creating a culture of honesty and high ethics, evaluating antifraud processes and controls, and developing an appropriate oversight process. Some example recommendations from the exhibit to AU section 316 are included in the following two paragraphs.

A-23 The NFP should attract individuals to serve on the governing board who are financially literate and who have an understanding of generally accepted accounting principles and audits of financial statements prepared under those principles. It is also helpful if some members of the governing board have experience in the preparation or the auditing, or both, of financial statements of an NFP of similar size, scope and complexity, an appreciation of what is necessary to maintain a good internal control environment and experience in internal governance and procedures of audit committees. (Additional desirable characteristics of board members are discussed in the exhibit to AU section 316.) Members of the governing board should set the "tone at the top" for ethical behavior within the NFP, including making sure that transactions do not result in private inurement or violate the IRS Intermediate Sanctions. (Intermediate sanctions are designed to protect donors and charities from insider dealing and excessive compensation for executives.)

A-24 Management also participates in setting the tone for ethical behavior. It also should create a positive workplace environment, hire and promote appropriate employees, provide training upon hiring and periodically thereafter, hold all employees accountable to act within the entity's code of conduct, investigate all suspected incidents of fraud, and discipline for actual violations.

A-25 In addition, management has primary responsibility for establishing and monitoring all aspects of the entity's fraud risk-assessment and prevention activities. Among the processes that management should design and monitor are those that

- satisfy management that substantially all contributions intended for the NFP have been received, recorded, and deposited;
- satisfy management that services are provided only to authorized persons and properly billed (members have paid dues, patients have paid proper fees, beneficiaries meet eligibility criteria, only ticketholders are admitted to events);
- satisfy management that expenses are being properly allocated to functions and to individual funds or grants;
- monitor and explain budget variances, including by fund or grant; and
- ensure that related party transactions and relationships have a valid business purpose and are conducted in a manner that does not result in private inurement.

A-26 The auditor should consider whether such programs and controls mitigate the identified risks of material misstatement due to fraud or whether specific control deficiencies exacerbate the risks. After the auditor has evaluated whether the entity's programs and controls have been suitably designed and placed in operation, the auditor should assess these risks taking into account that evaluation. This assessment should be considered when developing the auditor's response to the identified risks of material misstatement due to fraud.

Responding to the Results of the Assessment[3]

A-27 Paragraphs .46–.67 of AU section 316 provide requirements and guidance about an auditor's response to the results of the assessment of the risks of material misstatement due to fraud. The auditor responds to risks of material misstatement due to fraud in the following three ways:

a. A response that has an overall effect on how the audit is conducted—that is, a response involving more general considerations apart from the specific procedures otherwise planned (see paragraph .50 of AU section 316).

---

[3] Paragraph .03 of AU section 318, *Performing Audit Procedures in Response to Assessed Risks and Evaluating the Audit Evidence Obtained* (AICPA, *Professional Standards*), states that, to reduce audit risk to an acceptably low level, the auditor should determine overall responses to address the assessed risks of material misstatement at the financial statement level and should design and perform further audit procedures whose nature, timing, and extent are responsive to the assessed risks of material misstatement at the relevant assertion level. See paragraphs .04–.07 of AU section 318. This requirement provides a link between the auditor's consideration of fraud and the auditor's assessment of risk and the auditor's procedures in response to those assessed risks.

b. A response to identified risks involving the nature, timing, and extent of the auditing procedures to be performed (see paragraphs .51–.56 of AU section 316). Audit tests that are unique to NFPs are included at the ends of chapters 5–11, 13, and 15 of this guide.

c. A response involving the performance of certain procedures to further address the risk of material misstatement due to fraud involving management override of controls, given the unpredictable ways in which such override could occur (see paragraphs .57–.67 of AU section 316 and paragraph A-18–A-20 of this appendix).

Evaluating Audit Evidence

A-28 Paragraphs .68–.78 of AU section 316 provide requirements and guidance for evaluating audit evidence. The auditor should evaluate whether analytical procedures that were performed as substantive tests or in the overall review stage of the audit indicate a previously unrecognized risk of material misstatement due to fraud. The auditor also should consider whether responses to inquiries throughout the audit about analytical relationships have been vague or implausible or have produced evidence that is inconsistent with other audit evidence accumulated during the audit.

A-29 At or near the completion of fieldwork, the auditor should evaluate whether the accumulated results of auditing procedures and other observations affect the assessment of the risks of material misstatement due to fraud made earlier in the audit. As part of this evaluation, the auditor with final responsibility for the audit should ascertain that there has been appropriate communication with the other audit team members throughout the audit regarding information or conditions indicative of risks of material misstatement due to fraud.

Responding to Misstatements That May Be the Result of Fraud

A-30 When audit test results identify misstatements in the financial statements, the auditor should consider whether such misstatements may be indicative of fraud. See paragraphs .75–.78 of AU section 316 for requirements and guidance about an auditor's response to misstatements that may be the result of fraud. If the auditor believes that misstatements are or may be the result of fraud, but the effect of the misstatements is not material to the financial statements, the auditor nevertheless should evaluate the implications, especially those dealing with the organizational position of the person(s) involved.

A-31 If the auditor believes that the misstatement is or may be the result of fraud, and either has determined that the effect could be material to the financial statements or has been unable to evaluate whether the effect is material, the auditor should

a. attempt to obtain additional audit evidence to determine whether material fraud has occurred or is likely to have occurred, and, if so, its effect on the financial statements and the auditor's report thereon;[4]

b. consider the implications for other aspects of the audit (see paragraph .76 of AU section 316);

---

[4] See AU section 508, *Reports on Audited Financial Statements* (AICPA, *Professional Standards*), for guidance on auditors' reports issued in connection with audits of financial statements.

c. discuss the matter and the approach for further investigation with an appropriate level of management that is at least one level above those involved, and with senior management and the audit committee; and[5]

d. if appropriate, suggest that the client consult with legal counsel.

A-32 The auditor's consideration of the risks of material misstatement and the results of audit tests may indicate such a significant risk of material misstatement due to fraud that the auditor should consider withdrawing from the engagement and communicating the reasons for withdrawal to the audit committee or others with equivalent authority and responsibility. The auditor may wish to consult with legal counsel when considering withdrawal from an engagement.

Communicating About Possible Fraud to Management, the Audit Committee, and Others

A-33 Whenever the auditor has determined that there is evidence that fraud may exist, that matter should be brought to the attention of an appropriate level of management. See paragraphs .79–.82 of AU section 316 for further requirements and guidance about communications with management, the audit committee, and others.

Documenting the Auditor's Consideration of Fraud

A-34 Paragraph .83 of AU section 316 requires certain items and events to be documented by the auditor. Auditors should comply with those requirements.

Practical Guidance

A-35 The AICPA practice aid *Fraud Detection in a GAAS Audit* provides a wealth of information and help on complying with the provisions of AU section 316. This practice aid is an other auditing publication as defined in AU section 150, *Generally Accepted Auditing Standards* (AICPA, *Professional Standards*). Other auditing publications have no authoritative status; however, they may help the auditor understand and apply Statements on Auditing Standards.

---

[5] If the auditor believes senior management may be involved, discussion of the matter directly with the audit committee may be appropriate.

Chapter 3

Basic Financial Statements and General Financial Reporting Matters

Introduction

3.01 Financial Accounting Standards Board (FASB) *Accounting Standards Codification*™ (ASC) includes the unique standards relating to the general-purpose external financial statements for a not-for-profit entity (NFP) in four subtopics, as follows:

a. FASB ASC 958-205, about presentation of financial statements

b. FASB ASC 958-210, about the statement of financial position

c. FASB ASC 958-225, about the statement of activities

d. FASB ASC 958-230, about the statement of cash flows

An NFP should follow that industry-specific guidance and all effective provisions of FASB ASC unless the specific provision explicitly exempts NFPs or its subject matter precludes such applicability. For example, FASB ASC contains presentation topics (FASB ASC 205 to FASB ASC 280), many of which provide guidance for general presentation and display items applicable to NFPs. The guidance in this chapter summarizes many of those unique standards but is not intended as a substitute for reading those topics and subtopics.

3.02 FASB ASC 958-205-45-4 specifies that a complete set of financial statements should include a statement of financial position as of the end of the reporting period, a statement of activities and a statement of cash flows for the reporting period, and accompanying notes to financial statements. In addition, a voluntary health and welfare entity should provide a statement of functional expenses.[1]

3.03 FASB ASC 958-205-45-5 requires that a set of financial statements include, either in the body of the financial statements or in the accompanying notes, information required by generally accepted accounting principles (GAAP) that do not specifically exempt NFPs and required by applicable specialized accounting and reporting principles and practices. Per FASB ASC 958-205-45-1, the requirements generally are no more stringent than the requirements for business entities. The degree of aggregation and order of presentation of items of assets and liabilities in statements of financial position or of items of revenues and expenses in statements of activities of NFPs, although not

---

[1] Financial Accounting Standards Board (FASB) *Accounting Standards Codification*™ (ASC) and this guide use certain statement titles and the terms *permanently restricted*, *temporarily restricted*, and *unrestricted net assets*. Other titles and other labels may also be used, pursuant to FASB ASC 958-205-55-2 and FASB ASC 958-210-55-3. The terms *statement of financial position* and *statement of activities* indicate the content and purpose of the respective statements and serve as possible titles for those statements. Other appropriately descriptive titles may also be used. Similarly, a statement of functional expenses might have another appropriately descriptive title. For example, a statement reporting financial position could be called a *balance sheet* as well as a *statement of financial position*. Current practice and the statement's purpose suggest, however, that a statement of cash flows only be titled "Statement of Cash Flows." FASB ASC 958-210-55-3 states that other labels exist for net assets and its classes. For example, *equity* may be used for net assets, and *other* or *not donor-restricted* may be used with care to distinguish unrestricted net assets from the temporarily and permanently restricted classes of net assets.

specified, generally should be similar to those required or permitted for business entities. Particular formats for a statement of financial position, a statement of activities, or a statement of cash flows are neither prescribed nor prohibited in part because similar prescriptions and proscriptions do not exist for business entities.

3.04 FASB ASC 958-205-55 includes illustrations of the required financial statements that illustrate some of the ways in which the requirements can be met.

Statement of Financial Position

3.05 FASB ASC 958-210 describes the unique standards relating to a statement of financial position of an NFP. An NFP should follow industry-specific guidance and all effective provisions of FASB ASC unless the specific provision explicitly exempts NFPs or its subject matter precludes such applicability. For example, NFPs should apply the guidance contained in FASB ASC 210, *Balance Sheet*, that does not conflict with the industry guidance.

3.06 FASB ASC 958-210-45-1 requires that a statement of financial position focus on the NFP as a whole and report all of the following amounts:

- Total assets
- Total liabilities
- Total net assets
- Permanently restricted net assets
- Temporarily restricted net assets
- Unrestricted net assets

FASB ASC 958-210-45-5 describes how classifying assets and liabilities into reasonably homogeneous groups increases the usefulness of information. FASB ASC 958-210-45-6 states that assets need not be disaggregated on the basis of the presence of donor-imposed restrictions on their use; for example, cash available for unrestricted current use need not be reported separately from cash received with donor-imposed restrictions that is also available for current use.[2] However, cash or other assets received with a donor-imposed restriction that limits their use to long term purposes should not be classified with cash or other assets that are unrestricted and available for current use. FASB ASC 958-210-45-6 also states that the kind of asset whose use is limited should be described in the notes to the financial statements if its nature is not clear from the description on the face of the statement of financial position.

3.07 FASB ASC 958-210-45-8 requires that information about the NFP's liquidity be provided by any of the following:

a. Sequencing assets according to their nearness of conversion to cash and sequencing liabilities according to the nearness of their maturity and resulting use of cash

b. Classifying assets and liabilities as current and noncurrent, as defined by FASB ASC 210-10

---

[2] FASB ASC 958-205-45-6 notes that assets may be restricted by donors. For example, land could be restricted to use as a public park. Generally, however, restrictions apply to net assets, not to specific assets.

c. Disclosing in notes to financial statements relevant information about the liquidity or maturity of assets and liabilities, including restrictions on the use of particular assets

Per FASB ASC 958-210-50-1, information about the liquidity or maturity of assets and liabilities, including restrictions on the use of particular items, should be disclosed in notes to financial statements unless that information is provided on the face of the statement of financial position. FASB ASC 958-205-55-7 explains that when a statement of financial position that sequences assets and liabilities based on their relative liquidity is presented, cash and cash equivalents of permanent endowment funds held temporarily until suitable long term investment opportunities are identified and are included in the classification long term investments. Similarly, cash and contributions receivable restricted by donors to investment in land, buildings, and equipment are not included with the line items cash and cash equivalents or contributions receivable. Rather, those items are reported as assets restricted to investment in land, buildings, and equipment and are sequenced closer to land, buildings, and equipment. Similarly, FASB ASC 210-10-45-4 states that the concept of the nature of current assets contemplates the exclusion from that classification of such resources as cash that is designated for expenditure in the acquisition or construction of noncurrent assets or is segregated for the liquidation of long term debts. Even though not actually set aside in special accounts, funds that are clearly to be used in the near future for the liquidation of long term debts, payments to sinking funds, or for similar purposes should also, under this concept, be excluded from current assets.

3.08 Thus, cash that has been received with donor-imposed restrictions limiting its use to the acquisition of long-lived assets should be reported under a separate caption, such as "cash restricted to investment in property and equipment," and displayed near the section of the statement where property and equipment is displayed. Cash or other assets designated for long term purposes generally is not aggregated on a statement of financial position with cash or other assets that are available for current use.

3.09 Classification of net assets is discussed in paragraphs 9–11 of FASB ASC 958-210-45. The amounts for each of the three net asset classes are based on the existence or absence of donor-imposed restrictions. (As discussed in paragraph 3.11, board-designated limitations on the use of unrestricted net assets are permitted to be disclosed.)

3.10 The FASB ASC glossary defines *permanently restricted net assets* as the part of net assets of an NFP resulting from the following: (*a*) contributions and other inflows of assets whose use by the NFP is limited by donor-imposed stipulations that neither expire by passage of time nor can be fulfilled or otherwise removed by the actions of the NFP, (*b*) other asset enhancements and diminishments subject to the same kinds of stipulations and (*c*) reclassifications from or to other classes of net assets as a consequence of donor-imposed stipulations. The FASB ASC glossary defines *temporarily restricted net assets* as the part of the net assets of an NFP that result from the following: (*a*) contributions and other inflows of assets whose use by the NFP is limited by donor-imposed stipulations that either expire by passage of time or can be fulfilled and removed by actions of the NFP pursuant to those stipulations, (*b*) other asset enhancements and diminishments subject to the same kinds of stipulations, and (*c*) reclassifications from or to other classes of net assets as a consequence of donor-imposed stipulations, their expiration by passage of time, or their fulfillment and removal by actions of the NFP pursuant to those stipulations. Paragraphs 9–10 of FASB ASC 958-210-45 describe various purposes for which net assets might be restricted, such as use in future periods or use for specified purposes.

3.11 The FASB ASC glossary defines *unrestricted net assets* as the part of net assets of an NFP that is neither permanently restricted nor temporarily restricted by donor-imposed stipulations. FASB ASC 958-210-45-11 permits information about self-imposed limits, including voluntary resolutions by the governing board to designate a portion of unrestricted net assets (such as board-designated endowments) to be provided in the notes to or on the face of financial statements, provided that the requirement of FASB ASC 958-210-45-1 to display total unrestricted net assets is also met. FASB ASC 958-210-45-7 requires that, if not disclosed in the notes to financial statements, contractual limitations on the use of particular assets (such as cash held on deposit as a compensating balance) should be displayed on the face of the statement of financial position.

Statement of Activities

3.12 FASB ASC 958-225 describes the unique standards relating to a statement of activities of an NFP. An NFP should follow industry-specific guidance and all effective provisions of FASB ASC unless the specific provision explicitly exempts NFPs or its subject matter precludes such applicability. For example, NFPs should apply the guidance contained in FASB ASC 225, *Income Statement*, that does not conflict with the industry guidance.

3.13 Paragraphs 1–2 of FASB ASC 958-225-45 require that a statement of activities focus on the NFP as a whole and report the following amounts for the period: the change in net assets, using a descriptive term such as *change in net assets* or *change in equity*; the change in permanently restricted net assets; the change in temporarily restricted net assets; and the change in unrestricted net assets.

3.14 Paragraphs 4–8 of FASB ASC 958-225-45 discuss the classification by net asset class of revenues, expenses, and gains and losses. The determination of the net asset class in which revenues and gains and losses are reported is based on the existence or absence of donor-imposed restrictions and the type of restriction. A statement of activities should report revenues as increases in unrestricted net assets unless the use of the assets received is limited by donor imposed restrictions. All expenses should be reported as decreases in unrestricted net assets. Gains should be reported as increases and losses as decreases in unrestricted net assets unless their use is temporarily or permanently restricted by explicit donor stipulations or by law.

3.15 Pursuant to FASB ASC 958-225-45-3, *reclassifications*, which are defined in the FASB ASC glossary as the simultaneous increase of one net asset class and decrease of another, should be reported as separate items. FASB ASC 958-225-45-13 describes the events that require reclassifications of net assets, including donor-imposed restrictions that are fulfilled by the NFP or that expire with the passage of time or the death of a split-interest agreement's beneficiary.

3.16 FASB ASC 958-225-55-7 illustrates the requirement for the display of an appropriately labeled subtotal within a statement of activities for the change in a class of net assets before the effects of an extraordinary item. NFPs should also apply the appropriate disclosure and display requirements of, among other things, FASB ASC 250, *Accounting Changes and Error Corrections*, FASB 205-20-45 for discontinued operations,* and FASB ASC 225-20-45-16 for unusual or infrequently occurring items.

3.17 As noted in FASB ASC 958-205-45-1, particular formats for the statement of activities are neither prescribed nor prohibited, in part because similar prescriptions and proscriptions do not exist for business entities. FASB ASC 958-205-55-11 suggests three ways that items could be sequenced: (*a*) revenues and gains first, then expenses, then losses, reclassifications, which must be shown separately, are reported with revenues and gains; (*b*) revenues, expenses, gains and losses, and reclassifications shown last; and (*c*) certain revenues, less directly related expenses, followed by a subtotal, then other revenues, other expenses, gains and losses, and reclassifications. Those items could be arranged in other ways, and other subtotals may be included.

3.18 Pursuant to FASB ASC 958-225-45-9, classifying revenues, expenses, gains, and losses within classes of net assets does not preclude incorporating additional classifications within a statement of activities. For example, within a class or classes of net assets, an NFP may classify items as follows: operating and nonoperating, expendable and nonexpendable, earned and unearned, recurring and nonrecurring, or in other ways.

3.19 Paragraphs 9–12 of FASB ASC 958-225-45 discuss reporting a measure of operations. If an intermediate measure of operations, such as an excess or deficit of operating revenues over expenses, is reported in a statement of activities, (*a*) a note to financial statements should describe the nature of the reported measure of operations or the items excluded from operations if the NFP's use of the term *operations* is not apparent from the details provided on the face of the statement and (*b*) it must be in a financial statement that, at a minimum, reports the change in unrestricted net assets for the period. Some limitations on an NFP's use of an intermediate measure of operations are imposed by other standards. For example, if a subtotal such as income from operations is presented, it must include (*a*) an impairment loss recognized for a long-lived asset (or asset group) to be held and used pursuant to FASB ASC 360-10-45-4, (*b*) any gain or loss recognized on the sale of a long-lived asset (or disposal group) if that asset (or group) is not a component of the NFP pursuant to FASB ASC 360-10-45-5, and (*c*) costs associated with an exit or disposal activity that does not involve a discontinued operation pursuant to FASB ASC 420-10-45-3.

3.20 Classification of revenues, expenses, gains and losses, and reclassifications is discussed in greater detail in subsequent chapters of this guide. Paragraphs 8.35–.38 describe reporting investment return in a statement of activities that includes an intermediate measure of operations. Chapter 13, "Expenses, Gains, and Losses," of this guide discusses alternative ways of reporting costs related to sales of goods and services and the direct costs of special events.

---

* On September 25, 2008, FASB issued an exposure draft of proposed FASB Staff Position (FSP) FAS 144-d, *Amending the Criteria for Reporting a Discontinued Operation*. The proposed FSP would define when a component of an entity should be reported in the discontinued operations section of the statement of activities and enhance the disclosure requirements for all components of an entity that have been disposed of or are classified as held for sale. In December 2009, FASB decided that the proposed guidance would be re-exposed. Readers should be alert to the issuance of a final Accounting Standards Update (ASU).

Reporting Expenses, Including in a Statement of Functional Expenses[3]

3.21 FASB ASC 958-720-05-4 states that to help donors, creditors, and others assess an NFP's service efforts, including the costs of its services and how it uses resources, a statement of activities or notes to financial statements should provide information about expenses reported by their functional classification, such as major classes of program services and supporting activities. FASB ASC 958-205-45-6 provides guidance for presenting a statement of functional expenses, which is useful in associating expenses with service efforts and accomplishments. Voluntary health and welfare entities should report information about expenses by their functional classes, such as major classes of program services and supporting activities, as well as information about expenses by their natural classification in a matrix format in a separate financial statement—the statement of functional expenses. A natural classification of expenses would include expense categories such as salaries, rent, electricity, interest expense, depreciation, awards and grants to others, and professional fees. To the extent that expenses are reported by other than their natural classification (such as salaries included in cost of goods sold or facility rental costs of special events reported as direct benefits to donors), they should be reported by their natural classification if a statement of functional expenses is presented. For example, salaries, wages, and fringe benefits that are included as part of the cost of goods sold on the statement of activities should be included with other salaries, wages, and fringe benefits in the statement of functional expenses. In addition, as discussed in FASB ASC 958-205-45-6, expenses that are netted against investment revenues should be reported by their functional classification on the statement of functional expenses (if the NFP presents that statement). Pursuant to FASB ASC 958-720-45-16, other NFPs are encouraged, but not required, to provide information about expenses by their natural expense classification.

Statement of Cash Flows

3.22 FASB ASC 958-230 describes the unique standards relating to a statement of cash flows of an NFP. An NFP should follow industry-specific guidance and all effective provisions of FASB ASC unless the specific provision explicitly exempts NFPs or its subject matter precludes such applicability. For example, NFPs should apply the guidance contained in FASB ASC 230, *Statement of Cash Flows*, that does not conflict with the industry guidance.

3.23 FASB ASC 230-10-10-1 explains that the primary purpose of a statement of cash flows is to provide relevant information about the cash receipts and cash payments of an entity during a period. FASB ASC 230-10-45-10 requires that the statement of cash flows classify cash receipts and cash payments as resulting from investing, financing, or operating activities. FASB ASC 958-230-55-5 requires separate disclosure of noncash investing and financing activities (for example, receiving contributions of buildings, securities, or recognized collection items).

---

[3] The FASB ASC glossary definition of *voluntary health and welfare entity* includes a provision that those not-for-profit entities (NFPs) derive their revenue primarily from voluntary contributions from the general public. It specifies that for purposes of that definition, the *general public* excludes governmental entities when determining whether an NFP is a voluntary health and welfare entity.

3.24 The FASB ASC glossary defines *operating activities* as including all transactions and other events that are not defined as investing or financing activities. Operating activities generally involve producing and delivering goods and providing services. Per FASB ASC 958-230-55-4, operating activities also include cash received and paid in agency transactions.

3.25 Some NFPs receive resources in agency transactions, as discussed in chapter 5, "Contributions Received and Agency Transactions," of this guide. For some of those NFPs, receiving resources as agents may be a primary component of their mission. Because cash flows from operating activities include cash flows from agency transactions, an NFP that acts as an agent as a primary component of its mission might consider presenting the statement of cash flows as the first financial statement in its set of financial statements to emphasize the importance of the information presented in that statement.

3.26 FASB ASC 230-10-45-25 encourages entities to report major classes of gross cash receipts and gross cash payments and their arithmetic sum—the net cash flow from operating activities (the direct method). Paragraphs 28–31 of FASB ASC 230-10-45 describe how to determine and report the amount of net cash flow from operating activities indirectly by adjusting the change in (total) net assets to reconcile it to net cash flow from operating activities (the indirect or reconciliation method). That reconciliation of the change in (total) net assets to the net cash flow from operating activities should be provided in a separate schedule if the direct method of reporting net cash flow from operating activities is used.

3.27 As discussed in FASB ASC 958-210-45-6, cash received with a donor-imposed restriction that limits its use to long term purposes should not be classified on a statement of financial position with cash that is unrestricted and available for current use.[4] FASB ASC 958-230-55-3 explains that when an NFP reports cash received with a donor-imposed restriction that limits its use to long-term purposes in conformity with FASB ASC 958-210-45-6, an adjustment is necessary for the statement of cash flows to reconcile beginning and ending cash and cash equivalents. To report in conformity with FASB ASC 230, the receipt of a cash contribution that is restricted for the purchase of equipment should be reported as a cash flow from financing activities (using a caption such as contributions restricted for purchasing equipment), and it should be simultaneously reported as a cash outflow from investing activities (using a caption such as purchase of assets restricted to investment in property and equipment or, if the equipment was purchased in the same period, purchase of equipment). An adjustment to reconcile the change in net assets to net cash used or provided by operating activities would also be needed if the contributed asset is not classified as cash or cash equivalents on the statement of financial position. When the equipment is purchased in a subsequent period, both the proceeds from the sale of assets restricted to investment in the equipment and the purchase of the equipment should be reported as cash flows from investing activities.

3.28 FASB ASC 958-230-55-2 notes that not all assets of NFPs that meet the definition of *cash equivalents* in the FASB ASC glossary are cash equivalents for purposes of preparing statements of financial position and cash flows. Restrictions can prevent them from being included as cash equivalents even if they

---

[4] Paragraphs 3.06 and 3.28 of this guide discuss the classification on a statement of financial position of cash received with donor-imposed restrictions limiting its use to long term purposes.

otherwise qualify. For example, short-term highly liquid investments are not cash equivalents if they are purchased with resources that have donor-imposed restrictions that limit their use to long-term investment. Further, FASB ASC 230-10-45-6 states that an entity should establish a policy concerning which short-term, highly liquid investments that satisfy the definition of cash equivalents are treated as cash equivalents. FASB ASC 230-10-50-1 requires entities to disclose their policy for determining which items are treated as cash equivalents.

3.29 For example, an NFP may hold a portion of its endowment portfolio in cash or other instruments with maturities of less than three months and exclude the cash and other instruments from cash and cash equivalents. Similarly, cash and investments of endowment funds held temporarily until suitable long-term investments are identified may be excluded from cash equivalents.

Comparative Financial Information

3.30 FASB ASC 958-205-45-8 provides guidance if NFPs present comparative information for a prior year or years only in total rather than by net asset class. Such summarized information may not include sufficient detail to constitute a presentation in conformity with GAAP. If the prior year's financial information is summarized and does not include the minimum information required by FASB ASC 958, *Not-for-Profit Entities* (for example, if the statement of activities does not present revenues, expenses, gains, and losses by net asset class), the nature of the prior year information should be described by the use of appropriate titles on the face of the financial statements and in a note to the financial statements. The use of appropriate titles includes a phrase such as with summarized financial information for the year ended June 30, 20PY, following the title of the statement or column headings that indicate the summarized nature of the information. Labeling the prior year summarized financial information for comparative purposes only without further disclosure in the notes to financial statements would not constitute the use of an appropriate title.

3.31 An example of a note to the financial statements[5,6] that describes the nature of the prior period(s) information would be as follows:

> The financial statements include certain prior year summarized comparative information in total but not by net asset class. Such information does not include sufficient detail to constitute a presentation in conformity with GAAP. Accordingly, such information should be read in conjunction with the organization's financial statements for the year ended June 30, 20PY, from which the summarized information was derived.

Reporting of Related Entities, Including Consolidation

3.32 FASB ASC 810-10-10-1 states that the purpose of consolidated financial statements is to present, primarily for the benefit of the shareholders

---

[5] Chapter 14, "Reports of Independent Auditors," of this guide discusses auditors' reports on comparative financial information.

[6] Because the note discusses information that does not pertain to the current-period financial statements, the note is not considered to be part of the current-period financial statements.

and creditors of the parent entity, the results of operations and the financial position of a parent entity and its subsidiaries essentially as if the group were a single entity with one or more branches or divisions. There is a presumption that consolidated financial statements are more meaningful than separate statements and that they are usually necessary for a fair presentation when one of the entities in the group directly or indirectly has a controlling financial interest in the other entities.

3.33 The guidance for reporting of related entities in this chapter is organized as follows:

- Relationships with another NFP
- Relationships with a for-profit entity
- Consolidation of a special-purpose leasing entity

Pursuant to FASB ASC 810-10-15-17, NFPs do not apply the guidance for variable interest entities in FASB ASC 810, *Consolidation*,[7] to their relationships with other entities.

Relationships With Another NFP

3.34 FASB ASC 958-810-05-3 explains that ownership of NFPs may be evidenced in various ways because NFPs may exist in various legal forms, such as corporations issuing stock, corporations issuing ownership certificates, membership corporations issuing membership certificates, joint ventures, and partnerships, among other forms. FASB ASC 958-810-25-1 states that a relationship with another NFP can take any one of the following forms, which determines the appropriate reporting:

---

[7] In December 2007, FASB issued FASB Statement No. 160, *Noncontrolling Interests in Consolidated Financial Statements—an amendment of ARB No. 51*, which establishes accounting and reporting standards for a noncontrolling interest in a subsidiary (sometimes called *minority interests*) and for the deconsolidation of a subsidiary. As noted in FASB ASC 810-10-65-1, NFPs should apply the standards prospectively in the first set of initial or annual financial statements for a reporting period beginning on or after December 15, 2009. Until then, neither FASB Statement No. 160 nor its amendments to the following pronouncements apply to NFPs:

- Accounting Research Bulletin (ARB) No. 51, *Consolidated Financial Statements*
- Accounting Principles Board (APB) Opinion No. 18, *The Equity Method of Accounting for Investments in Common Stock*
- APB Opinion No. 29, *Accounting for Nonmonetary Transactions*
- FASB Statement No. 60, *Accounting and Reporting by Insurance Enterprises*
- FASB Statement No. 89, *Financial Reporting and Changing Prices*
- FASB Statement No. 128, *Earnings per Share*
- FASB Statement No. 130, *Reporting Comprehensive Income*
- FASB Statement No. 142, *Goodwill and Other Intangible Assets*
- FASB Interpretation No. 37, *Accounting for Translation Adjustments upon Sale of Part of an Investment in a Foreign Entity—an interpretation of FASB Statement No. 52*
- FIN 46(R), *Consolidation of Variable Interest Entities (revised December 2003)—an interpretation of ARB No. 51*
- AICPA Interpretation No. 1, "Intercompany Profit Eliminations under Equity Methods," of APB Opinion No. 18
- AICPA Statement of Position (SOP) 04-2, *Accounting for Real Estate Time-Sharing Transactions* (AICPA, *Technical Practice Aids*, ACC sec. 10,910)
- Several Emerging Issues Task Force issues

NFPs should continue to apply the guidance in ARB No. 51 before the amendments made by FASB Statement No. 160; SOP 94-3, *Reporting of Related Entities by Not-for-Profit Organizations* (AICPA, *Technical Practice Aids*, ACC sec. 10,610); and other applicable standards until the effective date of FASB Statement No. 160.

a. A controlling financial interest through direct or indirect ownership of a majority voting interest or sole corporate membership in the other NFP (see FASB ASC 958-810-25-2)

b. [Subparagraph not used.]

c. Control of a related but separate NFP through a majority voting interest in the board of that NFP by means other than ownership or sole corporate membership and an economic interest in other such organizations (see paragraph 958-810-25-3)

d. An economic interest in the other NFP combined with control through means other than those listed in (*a*)–(*c*) (see FASB ASC 958-810-25-4)

e. Either an economic interest in the other NFP or control of the other NFP, but not both (see FASB ASC 958-810-25-5)

3.35 FASB ASC 958-810-25-2 states that an NFP with a controlling financial interest in another NFP through direct or indirect ownership of a majority voting interest or sole corporate membership in that other NFP should consolidate that other NFP, unless control does not rest with the majority owner or sole corporate member (for instance, if the other NFP is in legal reorganization or in bankruptcy or if other legal or contractual limitations are so severe that control does not rest with the sole corporate member), in which case consolidation is prohibited, as discussed in FASB ASC 810-10-15-8. See FASB ASC 958-810-25-2A for an example in which control may not rest with the holder of the majority voting interest. (This example is included in paragraph 3.40 of this guide.) Sole corporate membership in an NFP, like ownership of a majority voting interest in a for-profit entity, should be considered a controlling financial interest, unless control does not rest with the sole corporate member (for instance, if the other [membership] entity is in bankruptcy or if other legal or contractual limitations are so severe that control does not rest with the sole corporate member).

3.36 FASB ASC 958-810-25-3 states that in the case of control of a related but separate NFP through a majority voting interest in the board of the other NFP by means other than ownership or sole corporate membership and an economic interest in other such organizations, consolidation is required, unless control does not rest with the holder of the majority voting interest, in which case consolidation is prohibited. An NFP has a majority voting interest in the board of another NFP if it has the direct or indirect ability to appoint individuals that together constitute a majority of the votes of the fully constituted board (that is, including any vacant board positions). See FASB ASC 958-810-55-5 for an example of a majority voting interest in the board of another NFP.

3.37 FASB ASC 958-810-25-4 states that control of a related but separate NFP in which the reporting entity has an economic interest may take forms other than majority ownership interest, sole corporate membership, or majority voting interest in the board of the other NFP; for example, control may be through contract or affiliation agreement. In circumstances such as these, consolidation is permitted but not required, and the reporting entity should disclose the following information required by FASB ASC 958-810-50-2 if it does not present consolidated financial statements:

a. Identification of the other NFP and the nature of its relationship with the reporting entity that results in control *b.* Summarized financial data of the other NFP, which shall include the following information:

   i. Total assets, liabilities, net assets, revenue, and expenses

   ii. Resources that are held for the benefit of the reporting entity or that are under its control

c. The disclosures required by paragraphs 1–6 of FASB ASC 850-10-50

3.38 FASB ASC 958-810-25-5 states that the existence of control or an economic interest, but not both, precludes consolidation. Pursuant to FASB ASC 958-810-50-3, the reporting entity should disclose the information about related parties required by paragraphs 1–6 of FASB ASC 850-10-50 for these relationships.

3.39 For purposes of applying the guidance stated in the preceding paragraphs, the FASB ASC glossary defines *control* as the direct or indirect ability to determine the direction of management and policies through ownership, contract, or otherwise. The FASB ASC glossary defines *economic interest* as an NFP's interest in another entity that exists if any of the following criteria are met: (*a*) the other entity holds or utilizes significant resources that must be used for the unrestricted or restricted purposes of the NFP, either directly or indirectly by producing income or providing services, or (*b*) the NFP is responsible for the liabilities of the other entity. FASB ASC 958-810-55-6 provides the following examples of economic interests:

a. Other entities solicit funds in the name of and with the expressed or implied approval of the NFP, and substantially all of the funds solicited are intended by the contributor or are otherwise required to be transferred to the NFP or used at its discretion or direction.

b. An NFP transfers significant resources to another entity whose resources are held for the benefit of the NFP.

c. An NFP assigns certain significant functions to another entity.

d. An NFP provides or is committed to provide funds for another entity or guarantees significant debt of another entity.

e. An NFP has a right to or a responsibility for the operating results of another entity. Or upon dissolution, the reporting entity is entitled to the net assets or is responsible for any deficit of another entity.

3.40 FASB ASC 958-810-55-5 provides the following example of a majority voting interest in the board of another entity. Entity B has a five-member board, and a simple voting majority is required to approve board actions. Entity A will have a majority voting interest in the board of Entity B if Entity A has the ability to appoint three or more of Entity B's board members. If three of Entity A's board members, employees, or officers serve on the board of Entity B but Entity A does not have the ability to require that those members serve on the Entity B board, Entity A does not have a majority voting interest in the board of Entity B. FASB ASC 958-810-25-2A provides the following example of a situation in which control might not rest with the holder of the majority voting interest. In some situations, certain actions require approval by a supermajority vote of the board. Such voting requirements might overcome the presumption of control by the owner or holder of a majority voting interest. FASB ASC 958-810-55-4A provides the following implementation advice for that paragraph. An NFP shall exercise judgment in evaluating such situations. If supermajority voting requirements exist—for example, a specified supermajority of the board is needed to approve fundamental actions such as amending the articles of incorporation or dissolving the entity—an NFP should consider whether those voting requirements have little or no effect on the ability to control the other entity's operations or assets or, alternatively, whether those voting requirements are so restrictive as to call into question whether control rests with the holder of the majority voting interest. Paragraphs 2–14 of FASB ASC 810-10-25 may be helpful in considering whether the inability of the majority voting interest to unilaterally approve certain actions due to supermajority voting requirements is substantial enough to overcome the presumption of control.

3.41 FASB ASC 958-810-25-6 discusses an interest by an NFP in another NFP that is less than a complete interest. For example, an NFP may appoint 80 percent of the board of the other NFP. For NFPs other than health care entities (that is, within the scope of FASB ASC 954, *Health Care Entities*), if the conditions for consolidation in paragraphs 2–4 of FASB ASC 958-810-25 are met, the basis of that consolidation would not reflect a noncontrolling interest for the portion of the board that the reporting entity does not control because there is no ownership interest other than the interest of the reporting entity.

3.42 FASB ASC 958-810-50-1 requires that if consolidated financial statements are presented, the reporting entity (parent) should disclose any restrictions made by entities outside of the reporting entity on distributions from the controlled NFP (subsidiary) to the parent and any resulting unavailability of the net assets of the subsidiary for use by the parent.

3.43 NFPs that otherwise would be prohibited from presenting consolidated financial statements under paragraph 3.38 of this guide, but that presented consolidated financial statements prior to December 1994 in conformity with the guidance in AICPA Statement of Position 78-10, *Accounting Principles and Reporting Practices for Certain Nonprofit Organizations*, may continue to do so.

Relationships With a For-Profit Entity

3.44 FASB ASC 958-810-15-4 lists the locations of guidance for reporting relationships between NFPs and for-profit entities. Paragraphs 3.45–.53 provide a brief summary of that guidance but are not intended as a substitute for reading the referenced subtopics.

3.45 FASB ASC 958-810-15-4(a) states that an NFP with a controlling financial interest in a for-profit entity through direct or indirect ownership of a majority voting interest in that entity should apply the guidance in the "General" subsections of FASB ASC 810-10. (Per FASB ASC 810-10-15-8, the usual condition for a controlling financial interest is ownership of a majority voting interest, and, therefore, as a general rule ownership by one reporting entity, directly or indirectly, of more than 50 percent of the outstanding voting shares of another entity is a condition pointing toward consolidation. The power to control may also exist with a lesser percentage of ownership, for example, by contract, lease, agreement with other stockholders, or by court decree. Noncontrolling rights may prevent the owner of over 50 percent of the voting shares from having a controlling financial interest.) However, pursuant to FASB ASC 810-10-15-17, NFPs are not subject to the guidance for variable interest entities in FASB ASC 810.

3.46 FASB ASC 958-810-15-4(b) states that an NFP that is a general partner of a for-profit limited partnership or a similar entity (such as a limited liability company that has governing provisions that are the functional equivalent of a limited partnership) should apply the guidance in FASB ASC 810-20 unless that partnership interest is reported at fair value in conformity with the guidance described in FASB ASC 958-810-15-4(e).

3.47 FASB ASC 810-20-25-3 states that the general partners in a limited partnership are presumed to control a limited partnership regardless of the extent of the general partners' ownership interest in the limited partnership. Paragraphs 4–20 of FASB ASC 810-20-25 provide guidance for purposes of assessing whether the limited partners' rights might preclude a general partner from controlling a limited partnership. Paragraphs 10–11 of FASB ASC 810-20-25 state that if the presumption of control by the general partners is overcome, each of the general partners would account for its investment in the limited partnership using the equity method of accounting. In accordance with FASB ASC 958-810-15-4(e), an NFP that is a general partner of a for-profit limited partnership or similar entity may be permitted to report the partnership interest at fair value in conformity with FASB ASC 958-325-35 (see paragraph 8.15 of this guide) or make an election pursuant to FASB ASC 825-10-25-1 (the fair value option).

3.48 FASB ASC 958-810-15-4(c) states that an NFP that owns 50 percent or less of the voting stock in a for-profit business entity should apply the guidance in FASB ASC 323-10 unless that investment is reported at fair value in conformity with the guidance described in FASB ASC 958-810-15-4(e).

3.49 FASB ASC 323-10 requires that the equity method of accounting be used if investments in common stock or in-substance common stock (or both common stock and in-substance common stock), including investments in common stock of joint ventures, give the investor the ability to exercise significant influence over operating and financial policies of an investee even though the investor holds 50 percent or less of the common stock or in-substance common stock (or both common stock and in-substance common stock). *Significant influence* is defined by paragraphs 6–11 of FASB ASC 323-10-15. In accordance with FASB ASC 958-810-15-4(e), an NFP that would otherwise be required to use the equity method may be permitted to report at fair value in conformity with FASB ASC 958-325-35 (see paragraph 8.15 of this guide) or make an election pursuant to FASB ASC 825-10-25-1 (the fair value option).

3.50 FASB ASC 958-810-15-4(e) also states that an NFP (other than health care entities) may be required to report an investment in voting stock in a for-profit business entity at fair value in conformity with FASB ASC 958-320-35-1. FASB ASC 958-320 applies to equity securities with a readily determinable fair value other than consolidated subsidiaries and investments reported under the equity method.

3.51 FASB ASC 958-810-15-4(d) states that an NFP with a more than minor interest in a for-profit real estate partnership, (a for-profit real estate) limited liability company, or similar (for-profit real estate) entity shall report its noncontrolling interest in such an entity using the equity method in accordance with the guidance in FASB ASC 970-323 unless that interest is reported at fair value in conformity with the guidance described in FASB ASC 958-810-15-4(e). An NFP should apply the guidance in FASB ASC 970-323-25-2 to help determine whether its interest in a for-profit (real estate) partnership, (for-profit real estate) limited liability company, or similar (for-profit real estate) entity is a controlling interest or a noncontrolling interest. An NFP should apply the guidance in FASB ASC 323-30-35-3 to determine whether a limited liability company should be viewed as similar to a partnership, as opposed to a corporation, for purposes of determining whether noncontrolling interests in a for-profit real estate limited liability company or a similar entity should be accounted for in accordance with FASB ASC 970-323 or FASB ASC 323-10. However, pursuant to FASB ASC 810-10-15-17, when applying the guidance in FASB ASC 970-323, NFPs apply the guidance without considering whether the for-profit real estate entity is possibly a variable interest entity (VIE).

3.52 FASB ASC 970-323-25-2 states that a noncontrolling investor in a real estate general partnership should account for its investment by the equity method and should be guided by the provisions of FASB ASC 323, *Investments—Equity Method and Joint Ventures*. FASB ASC 970-810-25-3 requires that the general partners of a real estate limited partnership apply the equity method of accounting to their interests in either of the following circumstances: (1) if the presumption of control by the general partners is overcome by the rights of the limited partners, (2) or if the presumption of control by the general partners is not overcome by the rights of the limited partners and no single general partner controls the limited partnership. In accordance with FASB ASC 958-810-15-4(e), an NFP that would otherwise be required to use the equity method may be permitted to report at fair value in conformity with FASB ASC 958-325-35 (see paragraph 8.15 of this guide) or make an election pursuant to FASB ASC 825-10-25-1 (the fair value option).

3.53 Additional guidance for determining whether a controlling financial interest exists is located as follows:

a. Per FASB ASC 810-30-15, if the reporting entity has a research and development arrangement in which all of the funds for the research and development activities are provided by the sponsor, the reporting entity should follow the guidance in FASB ASC 810-30 to determine whether and how the sponsor should consolidate that arrangement. Per FASB ASC 810-10-15-17, NFPs do not apply tests to determine whether the research and development entity is determined to be a VIE.

b. Per FASB ASC 810-10-15-3(c), if the reporting entity has a contractual management relationship with another entity, the reporting entity should use the guidance in the "Consolidation of Entities Controlled by Contract" subsections of FASB ASC 810-10 to determine whether the arrangement constitutes a controlling financial interest. Per FASB ASC 810-10-15-17, NFPs do not apply tests to determine whether the other entity is a VIE.

3.54 Chapter 8, "Investments," provides guidance about reporting ownership of for-profit entities in circumstances in which those entities are not consolidated.

Consolidation of a Special-Purpose Leasing Entity

3.55 FASB ASC 958-810-25-8 states that an NFP lessee shall consolidate a special-purpose-entity lessor (SPE) if all of the following conditions are met:

a. Substantially all of the activities of the SPE involve assets that are to be leased to a single lessee.

b. The expected substantive residual risks and substantially all the residual rewards of the leased asset(s) and the obligation imposed by the underlying debt of the SPE reside directly or indirectly with the lessee through means such as any of the following:

i. The lease agreement.

ii. A residual value guarantee through, for example, the assumption of first-dollar-of-loss provisions.

iii. A guarantee of the SPE's debt.

iv. An option granting the lessee a right to either (*a*) purchase the leased asset at a fixed price or at a defined price other than fair value determined at the date of exercise or (*b*) receive any of the lessor's sales proceeds in excess of a stipulated amount.

c. The owner (or owners) of record of the SPE has not made an initial substantive residual equity capital investment that is at risk during the entire lease term. This criterion shall be considered met if the majority owner (or owners) of the lessor is not an independent third party, regardless of the level of capital investment.

3.56 Additional information about the application of the preceding criteria and guidance for consolidation of the SPE is located in FASB ASC 958-840.

Combined Financial Statements

3.57 FASB ASC 810-10-55-1B provides guidance for circumstances in which combined financial statements of commonly controlled entities would be useful. It states that there are circumstances in which combined financial statements (as distinguished from consolidated financial statements) of commonly controlled entities are likely to be more meaningful than their separate financial statements. For example, combined financial statements would be useful if one individual owns a controlling financial interest in several entities that are related in their operations. Combined financial statements might also be used to present the financial position and the results of operations of entities under common management. FASB ASC 810-10-45-10 states that if combined statements are prepared for a group of related entities, such as a group of commonly controlled entities, intra-entity transactions and profits or losses should be eliminated, and noncontrolling interests, foreign operations, different fiscal periods, or income taxes, shall be treated in the same manner as in consolidated statements.

Mergers and Acquisitions[†]

3.58 FASB ASC 958-805 provides guidance on a transaction or other event in which an NFP that is the reporting entity combines with one or more other

[†] The guidance from FASB ASC 958-805 is labeled as "Pending Content" due to the transition and open effective date information discussed in FASB ASC 958-805-65-1 and FASB ASC 805-10-65-1. It reflects guidance included in FASB Statement No. 164, *Not-for-Profit Entities: Mergers and Acquisitions—Including an amendment of FASB Statement No. 142*, which was codified by ASU No. 2010-07, *Not-for-Profit Entities (Topic 958): Not-for-Profit Entities: Mergers and Acquisitions*, issued in January 2010. This guidance improves the relevance, representational faithfulness, and comparability of the information that a not-for-profit reporting entity provides in its financial reports about a combination with one or more other NFPs, businesses, or nonprofit activities. It also improves the relevance, representational faithfulness, and comparability of the information an NFP provides about

(continued)

NFPs, businesses, or nonprofit activities. Paragraphs 3.59–.71 of this guide summarize the guidance in FASB ASC 958-805, but are not intended as a substitute for reading that subtopic.

3.59 FASB ASC 958-805-25-1 requires that an NFP determine whether that transaction or other event is a merger of NFPs or an acquisition by an NFP by applying the definitions. FASB ASC 958-805-55-1 states that ceding control to a new NFP is the sole definitive criterion for identifying a merger, and one entity obtaining control over the other is the sole definitive criterion for an acquisition. Paragraphs 1–31 of FASB ASC 958-805-55 provide guidance on distinguishing between a merger and an acquisition.

Merger of Not-for-Profit Entities

3.60 The FASB ASC glossary defines *merger of not-for-profit entities* as a transaction or other event in which the governing bodies of two or more NFPs cede control of those entities to create a new NFP. FASB ASC 958-805-25 requires that the NFP resulting from a merger (the new entity) account for the merger by applying the carryover method described in the "Merger of Not-for-Profit Entities" subsections of FASB ASC 958-805.

3.61 Applying the carryover method requires combining the assets and liabilities recognized in the separate financial statements of the merging entities as of the merger date (or that would be recognized if the entities issued financial statements as of that date), with certain adjustments. The new NFP does not recognize additional assets or liabilities, such as internally developed intangible assets, that GAAP did not require or permit the merging entities to recognize. However, if a merging entity's separate financial statements are not prepared in accordance with GAAP, those statements should be adjusted to GAAP before the new entity recognizes the assets and liabilities. The new NFP should carry forward at the merger date the merging entities' classifications and designations of their assets and liabilities unless one of the exceptions in FASB ASC 958-805-25-9 applies. Those exceptions are for certain modifications in contracts as a result of the merger and for conforming accounting policies to reflect a consistent method of accounting.

Acquisition by a Not-for-Profit Entity

3.62 The FASB ASC glossary defines *acquisition by a not-for-profit entity* as a transaction or other event in which an NFP acquirer obtains control of one or more nonprofit activities or businesses and initially recognizes their assets and liabilities in the acquirer's financial statements. An NFP should account for each acquisition of a business or nonprofit activity by applying the acquisition method described in the "Acquisition by a Not-for-Profit Entity" subsections of FASB ASC 958-805. That acquisition method is the same as the acquisition method described in FASB ASC 805, *Business Combinations*; however, FASB ASC 958-805 includes guidance on aspects of the items that are unique or especially significant to an NFP.

(footnote continued)

goodwill and other intangible assets after an acquisition by making the standards of FASB ASC 350-20 fully applicable to NFPs. These standards are effective for accounting periods beginning on or after December 15, 2009. Paragraphs 1.15–.20 provide guidance for mergers and acquisitions occurring before the effective date of FASB Statement No. 164.

3.63 Pursuant to FASB ASC 805-10-05-4 as modified by FASB ASC 958-805-25, the steps for applying the acquisition method are:

a. Identifying the acquirer

b. Identifying the acquisition date

c. Recognizing the identifiable assets acquired, the liabilities assumed, and any noncontrolling interest in the acquiree

d. Recognizing goodwill acquired or a contribution received, including consideration transferred

3.64 FASB ASC 805-10-25-4 requires that one of the combining entities be identified as the acquirer. The guidance on control and consolidation of NFPs should be used to identify the acquirer: For an NFP acquirer other than a health care entity the guidance to be used is the guidance in FASB ASC 958-810, including the guidance referenced in paragraph 958-810-15-4. (Consolidation of NFPs is discussed beginning at paragraph 3.32 of this guide.) If that guidance does not clearly indicate which of the combining entities is the acquirer, the factors in paragraphs 42–46 of FASB ASC 958-805-55 should be considered in making that determination.

3.65 Paragraphs 6–7 of FASB ASC 805-10-25 require that the acquirer identify the acquisition date, which is the date on which it obtains control of the acquiree. The date on which the acquirer obtains control of the acquiree generally is the date on which the acquirer legally transfers the consideration (if any), acquires the assets, and assumes the liabilities of the acquiree—the closing date. In addition, FASB ASC 958-805-25-17 states that the date on which an NFP acquirer obtains control of an NFP with sole corporate membership generally also is the date on which the acquirer becomes the sole corporate member of that entity.

3.66 FASB ASC 805-20 requires that as of the acquisition date, the acquirer recognize, separately from goodwill, the identifiable assets acquired, the liabilities assumed, and any noncontrolling interest in the acquiree.[8]

3.67 In conformity with FASB ASC 958-805-30-6(b), an NFP acquirer determines the net of the acquisition-date amounts of the identifiable assets acquired and the liabilities assumed measured in accordance with FASB ASC 805-20 and FASB ASC 958-805. Most assets and liabilities are measured at fair value. However, FASB ASC 805-20-25-16 notes that there are limited exceptions to the recognition and measurement principles applicable to business combinations, including acquisitions by an NFP. The limited exceptions are specified in paragraphs 16–28 of FASB ASC 805-20-25, paragraphs 12–23 of FASB ASC 805-20-30, and paragraphs 11–26 of FASB ASC 958-805-25. Examples of items that are either not recognized or are measured at an amount other than their acquisition-date fair values include income taxes, employee benefits, assets held for sale, collections, conditional promises to give, donor relationships, and certain assets and liabilities arising from contingencies.

3.68 Next, in conformity with FASB ASC 958-805-30-6(a), an NFP acquirer determines the aggregate of the following:

a. The consideration transferred measured at its acquisition-date fair value (see paragraphs 10–13 of FASB ASC 958-805-30)

---

[8] Reporting noncontrolling interests in financial statements is discussed in chapter 11, "Net Assets," of this guide.

b. The fair value of any noncontrolling interest in the acquiree

c. In an acquisition by a NFP achieved in stages, the acquisition-date fair value of the acquirer's previously held equity interest in the acquiree

3.69 If the amount in FASB ASC 958-805-30-6(a) is greater than the amount in FASB 958-805-30-6(b), an NFP acquirer should determine whether the operations of the acquiree as part of the combined entity are expected to be predominantly supported by contributions and returns on investments. If the operations of the acquiree are not expected to be predominantly supported by contributions and returns on investments, in conformity with FASB ASC 958-805-25-28, an NFP acquirer should recognize goodwill as of the acquisition date, measured as of the acquisition date as the excess of FASB ASC 958-805-30-6(a) over FASB 958-805-30-6(b). (Accounting for goodwill after acquisition is discussed in chapter 7, "Other Assets," of this guide.) If instead the operations of the acquiree as part of the combined entity are expected to be predominantly supported by contributions and returns on investments, FASB ASC 958-805-25-29 states that an NFP acquirer should recognize a separate charge in its statement of activities as of the acquisition date, measured as the excess of FASB ASC 958-805-30-6(a) over FASB 958-805-30-6(b), rather than goodwill. *Predominantly supported* by means that contributions and returns on investments are expected to be significantly more than the total of all other sources of revenues.

3.70 If the amount in FASB ASC 958-805-30-6(b) is greater than the amount in FASB 958-805-30-6(a), FASB ASC 958-805-25-31 requires an NFP acquirer to recognize an inherent contribution received, measured as the excess of the amount in paragraph 958-805-30-6b over the amount in FASB ASC 958-805-30-6(a). The inherent contribution is reported as a separate credit in the statement of activities as of the acquisition date and, in accordance with FASB ASC 958-805-45-6, is classified on the basis of the type of restrictions imposed on the related net assets. FASB ASC 958-805-45-6 states that those restrictions include restrictions imposed on the net assets of the acquiree by a donor before the acquisition and those imposed by the donor of the business or nonprofit activity acquired, if any. Donor-restricted contributions are reported as restricted support even if the restrictions are met in the same reporting period in which the acquisition occurs. That is, the acquirer should not apply the reporting exception in FASB ASC 958-605-45-4 (see paragraph 5.68 of this guide) to restricted net assets acquired in an acquisition.

Disclosures

3.71 FASB ASC 958-805-50 requires an NFP to disclose information that enables users of its financial statements to evaluate the nature and financial effect of a merger of NFPs or an acquisition by an NFP. If acquisitions are individually immaterial but are material collectively, the NFP should disclose the required information in the aggregate. Disclosures are also required if an acquisition date is after the reporting date but before the financial statements are issued or available for issue. If the initial accounting for an acquisition by an NFP is incomplete, the NFP should disclose information that enables users of its financial statements to evaluate the financial effects of adjustments recognized in the current reporting period that relate to acquisitions that occurred in the current or previous reporting periods.

Collaborative Arrangements

3.72 FASB ASC 808, *Collaborative Arrangements*, provides display and disclosure guidance for a collaborative arrangement. The FASB ASC glossary defines a *collaborative arrangement* as a contractual arrangement that involves a joint operating activity (see FASB ASC 808-10-15-7) that involves two (or more) parties who are both (*a*) active participants in the activity (see paragraphs 8–9 of FASB ASC 808-10-15) and (*b*) exposed to significant risks and rewards dependent on the commercial success of the activity (see paragraphs 10–13 of FASB ASC 808-10-15). A collaborative arrangement within the scope of FASB ASC 808 is not primarily conducted through a separate legal entity created for that activity. FASB ASC 808-10-45-1 states that an entity should not apply the equity method of accounting to the activities of a collaborative arrangement. Per FASB ASC 808-10-15-3, the guidance in FASB ASC 808 does not apply to arrangements for which the accounting is specifically addressed within the scope of other authoritative accounting literature.

The Use of Fair Value Measures ‡

3.73 The use of fair value measures is pervasive in the preparation of financial statements. Among other uses, fair value is used in the following items:

- Measurement of noncash contributions received (discussed in chapter 5 of this guide)
- Measurement of financial assets held as an agent (discussed in chapter 5 of this guide)
- Measurement of a beneficial interest in a trust (discussed in chapters 5 and 6 of this guide)
- Measurement of the contribution portion of a split-interest agreement (discussed in chapter 6, "Split-Interest Agreements," of this guide)
- Measurement of certain investments (discussed in chapter 8 of this guide)
- Measurement of derivative instruments (discussed in chapter 8 of this guide)
- Disclosures about the fair value of financial instruments (discussed in chapter 8 of this guide)
- Measurement of impairment losses for long-lived assets (discussed in chapter 9, "Property, Plant, and Equipment," of this guide)

‡ On June 29, 2010, FASB issued a proposed ASU, *Amendments for Common Fair Value Measurement and Disclosure Requirements in U.S. GAAP and IFRSs*, intended to develop common requirements for measuring fair value and for disclosing information about fair value measurements in U.S. generally accepted accounting principles (GAAP) and International Financial Reporting Standards (IFRSs). For many of the proposed requirements, FASB does not expect the amendments to result in changes in the application of FASB ASC 820, *Fair Value Measures and Disclosures*. Other amendments would change a particular principle or requirement. The most notable of these changes are: highest and best use and valuation premise, measuring the fair value of an instrument classified in shareholders' equity, measuring the fair value of instruments that are managed within a portfolio, and application of blockage factors and other premiums and discounts in a fair value measurement. The proposed standards also include additional disclosure requirements. Readers should be alert to the issuance of a final ASU.

- Measurement of asset retirement obligations (discussed in chapter 9 of this guide)
- Measurement of a guarantee obligation (discussed in chapter 10, "Debt and Other Liabilities," of this guide)
- Measurement of exit and disposal costs (discussed in chapter 10 of this guide)
- Measurement of an underfunded or overfunded pension or other postretirement benefit plan (discussed in chapter 10 of this guide)
- Measurement of nonmonetary transactions in conformity with FASB ASC 845, *Nonmonetary Transactions*
- Measurement of transfers of financial assets in conformity with FASB ASC 860, *Transfers and Servicing*
- Measurement of a financial asset or financial liability for which an election is made pursuant to FASB ASC 815-15-25 or the "Fair Value Option" subsections of FASB ASC 825-10 (discussed in paragraphs 3.95–.97)

3.74 FASB ASC 820, *Fair Value Measurements and Disclosures*, defines fair value, establishes a framework for measuring fair value, and expands disclosures about fair value measurements.[||] The following paragraphs summarize FASB ASC 820 but are not intended as a substitute for the reading FASB ASC 820 itself.

3.75 Technical Questions and Answers section 1800.05, "Applicability of Fair Value Disclosure Requirements and Measurement Principles in Financial Accounting Standards Board (FASB) *Accounting Standards Codification* (ASC) 820, *Fair Value Measurements and Disclosures*, to Certain Financial Instruments" (AICPA, *Technical Practice Aids*), clarifies that the measurement principles of FASB ASC 820 apply both when determining fair value of items recognized at fair value in the statement of financial position and when determining fair value for disclosure purposes.

Definition of *Fair Value*

3.76 The FASB ASC glossary defines *fair value* as "the price that would be received to sell an asset or paid to transfer a liability in an orderly transaction between market participants at the measurement date." That definition retains the exchange price notion in earlier definitions of fair value, but clarifies that the exchange price is the price in a hypothetical transaction at the measurement date in the market in which the reporting entity would transact for the asset or liability. A fair value measurement assumes that the transaction to sell the asset or transfer the liability occurs in the principal market for the asset or liability or, in the absence of a principal market, the most advantageous market for the asset or liability. FASB ASC 820-10-35-5 defines the *principal market* as the market in which the reporting entity would sell the asset or transfer the liability with the greatest volume and level of activity for the asset or liability.

[||] Some of the guidance in FASB ASC 820 is labeled as "Pending Content" due to the transition and open effective date information discussed in FASB ASC 820-10-65. For example, ASU No. 2010-06, *Improving Disclosures about Fair Value Measurements* is effective for interim and annual reporting periods beginning after December 15, 2009, except for the separate disclosures about purchases, sales, issuances, and settlements relating to level 3 measurements (see FASB ASC 820-10-50-2(c)(2)), which shall be effective for fiscal years beginning after December 15, 2010, and for interim periods within those fiscal years. Early adoption is permitted.

3.77 FASB ASC 820-10-35-10 provides that a fair value measurement of an asset assumes the highest and best use of the asset by market participants, considering the use of the asset that is physically possible, legally permissible, and financially feasible at the measurement date. Highest and best use is determined based on the use of the asset by market participants that would maximize the value of the asset or the group of assets within which the asset would be used, even if the intended use of the asset by the reporting entity is different.

3.78 FASB ASC 820-10-35-10 provides that the highest and best use for an asset is established by one of two valuation premises: value in-use or value in-exchange. The highest and best use of the asset is in-use if the asset would provide maximum value to market participants principally through its use in combination with other assets as a group (as installed or otherwise configured for use). For example, value in-use might be appropriate for certain nonfinancial assets. An asset's value in-use should be based on the price that would be received in a current transaction to sell the asset assuming that the asset would be used with other assets as a group and that those other assets would be available to market participants. The highest and best use of the asset is in-exchange if the asset would provide maximum value to market participants principally on a standalone basis. For example, value in-exchange might be appropriate for a financial asset. An asset's value in-exchange is determined based on the price that would be received in a current transaction to sell the asset standalone.

3.79 Paragraphs 17–18 of FASB ASC 820-10-35 provide that a fair value measurement for a liability reflects its nonperformance risk (the risk that the obligation will not be fulfilled). Because nonperformance risk includes the reporting entity's credit risk, the reporting entity should consider the effect of its credit risk (credit standing) on the fair value of the liability in all periods in which the liability is measured at fair value.

3.80 FASB ASC 820-10-35-3 provides that the hypothetical transaction to sell the asset or transfer the liability is considered from the perspective of a market participant that holds the asset or owes the liability. Therefore, the definition of fair value focuses on the price that would be received to sell the asset or paid to transfer the liability (an exit price), not the price that would be paid to acquire the asset or received to assume the liability (an entry price). Conceptually, entry prices and exit prices are different. However, FASB ASC 820-10-30-3 explains that, in many cases, a transaction price (entry price) will equal the exit price and, therefore, will represent the fair value of the asset or liability at initial recognition.

3.81 Paragraphs 7–8 of FASB ASC 820-10-35 provide that the price should not be adjusted for transaction costs. If location is an attribute of the asset or liability (as might be the case for a commodity), the price in the principal (or most advantageous) market used to measure the fair value of the asset or liability should be adjusted for the costs, if any, that would be incurred to transport the asset or liability to (or from) its principal (or most advantageous) market.

Valuation Techniques

3.82 Paragraphs 24–35 of FASB ASC 820-10-35 describe the valuation techniques that should be used to measure fair value. Valuation techniques consistent with the market approach, income approach, or cost approach, or any combination thereof, should be used to measure fair value, as follows:

- The market approach uses prices and other relevant information generated by market transactions involving identical or comparable assets or liabilities. Valuation techniques consistent with the market approach include matrix pricing and often use market multiples derived from a set of comparables.
- The income approach uses valuation techniques to convert future amounts (for example, cash flows or earnings) to a single present amount (discounted). The measurement is based on the value indicated by current market expectations about those future amounts. Valuation techniques consistent with the income approach include present value techniques, option-pricing models, and the multiperiod excess earnings method.
- The cost approach is based on the amount that currently would be required to replace the service capacity of an asset (often referred to as current replacement cost). Fair value is determined based on the cost to a market participant (buyer) to acquire or construct a substitute asset of comparable utility, adjusted for obsolescence.

3.83 Valuation techniques that are appropriate in the circumstances and for which sufficient data are available should be used to measure fair value. In some cases, a single valuation technique will be appropriate (for example, when valuing an asset or liability using quoted prices in an active market for identical assets or liabilities). In other cases, multiple valuation techniques will be appropriate and the respective indications of fair value should be evaluated and weighted, as appropriate, considering the reasonableness of the range indicated by those results. Example 3 (paragraphs 35–38) of FASB ASC 820-10-55 illustrates the use of multiple valuation techniques. A fair value measurement is the point within that range that is most representative of fair value in the circumstances.

3.84 Valuation techniques used to measure fair value should be consistently applied. However, a change in a valuation technique or its application is appropriate if the change results in a measurement that is equally or more representative of fair value in the circumstances. Such a change would be accounted for as a change in accounting estimate in accordance with the provisions of FASB ASC 250.

Present Value Techniques

3.85 Paragraphs 4–20 of FASB ASC 820-10-55 provide guidance on present value techniques. Those paragraphs neither prescribe the use of one specific present value technique nor limit the use of present value techniques to the three techniques discussed therein. They say that a fair value measurement of an asset or liability using present value techniques should capture the following elements from the perspective of market participants as of the measurement date: an estimate of future cash flows, expectations about possible variations in the amount or timing (or both) of the cash flows, the time value of money, the price for bearing the uncertainty inherent in the cash flows (risk premium), other case-specific factors that would be considered by market participants, and in the case of a liability, the nonperformance risk relating to that liability, including the reporting entity's (obligor's) own credit risk.

3.86 FASB ASC 820-10-55-6 provides the general principles that govern any present value technique, as follows:

- Cash flows and discount rates should reflect assumptions that market participants would use in pricing the asset or liability.
- Cash flows and discount rates should consider only factors attributed to the asset (or liability) being measured.
- To avoid double counting or omitting the effects of risk factors, discount rates should reflect assumptions that are consistent with those inherent in the cash flows. For example, a discount rate that reflects expectations about future defaults is appropriate if using the contractual cash flows of a loan, but is not appropriate if the cash flows themselves are adjusted to reflect possible defaults.
- Assumptions about cash flows and discount rates should be internally consistent. For example, nominal cash flows (that include the effects of inflation) should be discounted at a rate that includes the effects of inflation.
- Discount rates should be consistent with the underlying economic factors of the currency in which the cash flows are denominated.

3.87 Present value techniques differ in how they adjust for risk and in the type of cash flows they use. For example, the discount rate adjustment technique (also called the traditional present value technique) uses a risk-adjusted discount rate and contractual, promised, or most likely cash flows. In contrast, expected present value techniques use the probability-weighted average of all possible cash flows (referred to as expected cash flows). The traditional present value technique and two methods of expected present value techniques are discussed more fully in paragraphs 4–20 of FASB ASC 820-10-55.

3.88 This guide includes guidance about measuring assets (promises to give and beneficial interests in trusts) and liabilities (split-interest obligations) using traditional present value techniques. That guidance is not intended to suggest that the income approach is the only one of the three approaches that is appropriate in the circumstances, nor is it intended to suggest that the traditional present value technique described in the guide is preferred over other present value techniques. Rather, the inclusion of that guidance in the guide merely reflects that prior to the issuance of the framework for fair value measurement, present value techniques were specifically mentioned in the standards, as appropriate for measuring promises to give cash and beneficial interests in trusts, and the guide had been drafted reflecting those standards. In conforming this guide to the framework for fair value measurement, guidance that previously specified the use of the traditional present value technique was modified to indicate that the technique was a possible technique to consider for fair value measurement.

The Fair Value Hierarchy

3.89 FASB ASC 820 emphasizes that fair value is a market-based measurement, not an entity-specific measurement. Therefore, a fair value measurement should be determined based on the assumptions that market participants would use in pricing the asset or liability (referred to in the statement as inputs). Paragraphs 37–57 of FASB ASC 820-10-35 establish a fair value hierarchy that distinguishes between (1) market participant assumptions developed based on market data obtained from sources independent of the reporting entity (observable inputs) and (2) the reporting entity's own assumptions about market participant assumptions developed based on the best information available in the circumstances (unobservable inputs). Valuation techniques used to measure fair value should maximize the use of observable inputs and minimize the use of unobservable inputs.

3.90 The fair value hierarchy in FASB ASC 820 prioritizes the inputs to valuation techniques used to measure fair value into three broad levels, which are described in paragraphs 39–57 of FASB ASC 820-10-35. The three levels are described in the following list:

- Level 1 inputs are quoted prices (unadjusted) in active markets for identical assets or liabilities that the reporting entity has the ability to access at the measurement date. An active market is a market in which transactions for the asset or liability occur with sufficient frequency and volume to provide pricing information on an ongoing basis. A quoted price in an active market provides the most reliable evidence of fair value and should be used to measure fair value whenever available, except as discussed in paragraphs 16D and 42–43 of FASB ASC 820-10-35. Further, FASB ASC 820-10-35-44 states that the quoted price shall not be adjusted because of the size of the position relative to trading volume (blockage factor). The fair value of the position should be measured within level 1 as the product of the quoted price for the individual instrument and the quantity held. The use of a blockage factor is prohibited, even if a market's normal daily trading volume is not sufficient to absorb the quantity held and placing orders to sell the position in a single transaction might affect the quoted price. As discussed in paragraphs 16–18A of FASB ASC 820-10-35, liabilities are rarely transferred in the marketplace because of contractual or other legal restrictions preventing the transfer of liabilities. If a quoted price in an active market for the identical liability is available, it represents a level 1 measurement. FASB ASC 820-10-35-41A states that in addition, the quoted price for the identical liability when traded as an asset in an active market also is a level 1 fair value measurement for that liability when no adjustments to the quoted price of the asset are required. (Paragraph 3.92 of this guide describes circumstances in which adjustments are necessary.)

- Level 2 inputs are inputs other than quoted prices included within level 1 that are observable for the asset or liability, either directly or indirectly. Adjustments to level 2 inputs will vary depending on factors specific to the asset or liability. An adjustment that is significant to the fair value measurement in its entirety might render the measurement a level 3 measurement, depending on the level in the fair value hierarchy within which the inputs used to determine the adjustment fall. Level 2 inputs include the following:

  — Quoted prices for similar assets or liabilities in active markets

  — Quoted prices for identical or similar assets or liabilities in markets that are not active

   - Inputs other than quoted prices that are observable for the asset or liability (for example, interest rates and yield curves observable at commonly quoted intervals, volatilities, prepayment speeds, loss severities, credit risks, and default rates)
   - Inputs that are derived principally from or corroborated by observable market data by correlation or other means (market-corroborated inputs)

- Level 3 inputs are unobservable inputs for the asset or liability. Unobservable inputs should be used to measure fair value to the extent that observable inputs are not available, thereby allowing for situations in which there is little, if any, market activity for the asset or liability at the measurement date. In developing unobservable inputs, the reporting entity need not undertake all possible efforts to obtain information about market participant assumptions. Unobservable inputs should reflect the reporting entity's own assumptions about the assumptions that market participants would use in pricing the asset or liability (including assumptions about risk). The reporting entity should not ignore information about market participant assumptions that is reasonably available without undue cost and effort.

In some cases, the inputs used to measure fair value might fall in different levels of the fair value hierarchy. The level in the fair value hierarchy within which the fair value measurement in its entirety falls should be determined based on the lowest level input that is significant to the fair value measurement in its entirety.

3.91 As discussed in FASB ASC 820-10-35-38, the availability of inputs relevant to the asset or liability and the relative reliability of the inputs might affect the selection of appropriate valuation techniques. However, the fair value hierarchy prioritizes the inputs to valuation techniques, not the valuation techniques. For example, a fair value measurement using a present value technique might fall within level 2 or level 3, depending on the inputs that are significant to the measurement in its entirety and the level in the fair value hierarchy within which those inputs fall.

3.92 FASB ASC 820-10-35 provides additional guidance for certain fair value measurements. Paragraphs 51A–51H of FASB ASC 820-10-35 clarify how to determine fair value when the volume and level of activity for the asset or liability have significantly decreased or when transactions are not orderly. If the reporting entity concludes there has been a significant decrease in the volume and level of activity for the asset or liability in relation to normal market activity for the asset or liability (or similar assets or liabilities), transactions or quoted prices may not be determinative of fair value (for example, there may be increased instances of transactions that are not orderly). Further analysis of the transactions or quoted prices is needed, and a significant adjustment to the transactions or quoted prices may be necessary to estimate fair value. Paragraphs 16–18A of FASB ASC 820-10-35 clarify the measurement of the fair value of a liability. If a quoted price for the identical liability when traded as an asset in an active market is used to measure the fair value of a liability, a reporting entity needs to determine whether the quoted price should be adjusted for factors specific to the liability and the asset, as described in FASB ASC

820-10-35-16D. The quoted price of the liability when traded as an asset should be adjusted for factors specific to the asset that are not applicable to the fair value measurement of the liability, such as the effect of a third-party credit enhancement (as discussed in paragraph 10.03 of this guide). However, the reporting entity should not adjust the quoted price of the asset for the effect of a restriction preventing its sale. Any adjustment to the quoted price of the asset renders the fair value measurement of the liability a lower level measurement.

3.93 FASB ASC 820-10-35-15 states that market participant assumptions should include assumptions about the effect of a restriction on the sale or use of an asset if market participants would consider the effect of the restriction in pricing the asset. Example 6 (paragraphs 51–55) of FASB ASC 820-10-55 illustrates that restrictions that are an attribute of an asset, and, therefore, would transfer to a market participant, are the only restrictions reflected in fair value. Donor restrictions that are specific to the donee are reflected in the classification of net assets, not in the measurement of fair value.

Disclosures

3.94 Paragraphs 1–9 of FASB ASC 820-10-50 expand the disclosures required for assets and liabilities measured at fair value. For assets and liabilities that are measured at fair value on a recurring basis in periods subsequent to initial recognition or that are measured on a nonrecurring basis in periods subsequent to initial recognition, FASB ASC 820-10-50 requires the reporting entity to disclose certain information that enables users of its financial statements to assess the inputs used to develop those measurements. For recurring fair value measurements using significant unobservable inputs (level 3), the reporting entity is required to disclose certain information to help users assess the effect of the measurements on earnings (or changes in net assets) for the period.

Fair Value Option[#]

3.95 The "Fair Value Option" subsections of FASB ASC 825-10 permit an entity to irrevocably elect fair value as the initial and subsequent measure for many financial instruments and certain other items, with changes in fair value recognized in the statement of activities as those changes occur. Paragraphs 4–6 of FASB ASC 815-15-25 similarly permits an elective fair value remeasurement for any hybrid financial instrument that contains an embedded derivative, if that embedded derivative would otherwise have to be separated from its debt host contract in conformity with FASB ASC 815-15. An election is made on an instrument-by-instrument basis (with certain exceptions), generally when an instrument is initially recognized in the financial statements.

[#] On May 26, 2010, FASB issued a proposed ASU, *Accounting for Financial Instruments and Revisions to the Accounting for Derivative Instruments and Hedging Activities*, intended to improve accounting for financial instruments. Among other changes, the proposed ASU reconsiders the recognition and measurement of financial instruments, addresses issues related to impairment of financial instruments, simplifies hedge accounting, and, increases convergence in accounting for financial instruments with IFRSs. It would incorporate both amortized cost and fair value information about financial instruments held for collection or payment of cash flows. On January 31, 2011, FASB and the International Accounting Standards Board jointly issued a supplementary document, *Accounting for Financial Instruments and Revisions to the Accounting for Derivative Instruments and Hedging Activities: Impairment*, to address a number of questions that arose from the comments received on the proposed ASU. Readers should be alert for the issuance of a final ASU.

3.96 The "Fair Value Option" subsection of FASB ASC 825-10-15 describes the financial assets and liabilities for which the option is available. Most financial assets and financial liabilities are eligible to be recognized using the fair value option, as are firm commitments for financial instruments and certain nonfinancial contracts. Specifically excluded from eligibility are investments in other entities that are required to be consolidated, employer's and plan's obligations under postemployment, postretirement plans, and deferred compensation arrangements (or assets representing overfunded positions in those plans), financial assets and liabilities recognized under leases, deposit liabilities of depository institutions, and financial instruments that are, in whole or in part, classified by the issuer as a component of shareholder's equity. Additionally, the election cannot be made for most nonfinancial assets and liabilities or for current or deferred income taxes.

3.97 FASB ASC 825-10-45 and FASB ASC 825-10-50 establish presentation and disclosure requirements designed to facilitate comparisons between entities that choose different measurement attributes for similar types of assets and liabilities. Entities should report assets and liabilities that are measured using the fair value option in a manner that separates those reported fair values from the carrying amounts of similar assets and liabilities measured using another measurement attribute. To accomplish that, an entity should either (*a*) report the aggregate carrying amount for both fair value and nonfair value items on a single line, with the fair value amount parenthetically disclosed or (*b*) present separate lines for the fair value carrying amounts and the nonfair value carrying amounts.

Financial Statement Disclosures Not Considered Elsewhere

3.98 Financial statement disclosures are generally discussed in this guide in connection with the specific financial statement items to which they pertain. This section discusses disclosures that are unique to NFPs and that are not discussed elsewhere in this guide.

Noncompliance With Donor-Imposed Restrictions[9]

3.99 An NFP may not be in compliance with donor-imposed restrictions, including requirements that it maintain an appropriate composition of assets (usually cash and marketable securities in amounts needed to comply with all donor restrictions). Such noncompliance could result in a material contingent liability, result in a material loss of future revenue, or cause the NFP to be unable to continue as a going concern.[**]

---

[9] As discussed in chapter 11 of this guide, and throughout other sections of this guide, NFPs report amounts for each of three classes of net assets. Noncompliance with donor-imposed restrictions may result in net assets being reported other than in accordance with donor-imposed restrictions. For example, net assets would be reported other than in accordance with donor-imposed restrictions if restricted net assets were reported as unrestricted net assets. If net assets are reported other than in accordance with donor-imposed restrictions, the financial statements are not presented in conformity with GAAP.

[**] On October 10, 2008, FASB issued an exposure draft of a proposed statement, *Going Concern*, which would carry forward into the accounting standards the going concern guidance from AU section 341, *The Auditor's Consideration of an Entity's Ability to Continue as a Going Concern* (AICPA, *Professional Standards*), subject to several modifications to align the guidance with International Financial Reporting Standards. In June 2009, the project was broadened to address three additional

(continued)

3.100 FASB ASC 450, *Contingencies*, provides guidance for accruing and disclosing contingent liabilities.[††] AU section 317, *Illegal Acts by Clients* (AICPA, *Professional Standards*), addresses disclosure of illegal acts that could lead to a material loss of revenue. AU section 341, *The Auditor's Consideration of an Entity's Ability to Continue as a Going Concern* (AICPA, *Professional Standards*), contains broad guidance on disclosures when there is a substantial doubt about an entity's ability to continue as a going concern.

3.101 FASB ASC 958-450-50-2 requires noncompliance with donor-imposed restrictions to be disclosed if either of the following is true: (*a*) there is a reasonable possibility that a material contingent liability has been incurred at the date of the financial statements or (*b*) there is at least a reasonable possibility that the noncompliance could lead to a material loss of revenue or could cause an entity to be unable to continue as a going concern.[10] That paragraph requires that if the noncompliance results from an NFP's failure to maintain an appropriate composition of assets in amounts needed to comply with all donor restrictions, the amounts and circumstances be disclosed.

Risks and Uncertainties

3.102 FASB ASC 275, *Risks and Uncertainties*, requires entities to include in their financial statements information about the following:

- The nature of their operations
- Use of estimates in the preparation of financial statements

In addition, if specified disclosure criteria are met, it requires entities to include in their financial statements disclosures about the following:

- Certain significant estimates
- Current vulnerability due to certain concentrations

FASB ASC 958-605-55-70 includes an example of a vulnerability of concentration of risk because of reliance on major donors. FASB ASC 275-10-55 includes other examples of disclosures that may be pertinent for NFPs.

Subsequent Events

3.103 FASB ASC 855, *Subsequent Events*, establishes standards for accounting for and disclosure of events that occur after the balance sheet date but before financial statements are issued or are available to be issued. In accordance with FASB ASC 855-10-25, an NFP should recognize in the financial statements the effects of all subsequent events that provide additional evidence about conditions that existed at the date of the balance sheet, including the estimates inherent in the process of preparing financial statements. An NFP

(footnote continued)

areas: enhancing the disclosures of short-term and long-term risks, specifically risks for which there is more-than-remote likelihood of occurrence; defining *substantial doubt* in terms of an entity's ability to continue as a going concern; and defining when it is appropriate for an entity to apply the liquidation basis of accounting. Readers should be alert to the issuance of the final ASU.

[††] On July 20, 2010, FASB issued a proposed ASU, *Disclosure of Certain Loss Contingencies*. The proposed ASU would retain the current qualitative disclosures in FASB ASC 450-20 for loss contingencies and enhance them by requiring additional disclosures, particularly for litigation contingencies. Readers should be alert to the issuance of a final ASU.

[10] As discussed in paragraph 10.14, noncompliance with donor-imposed restrictions may require accrual of a liability in conformity with FASB ASC 450-20.

should not recognize subsequent events that provide evidence about conditions that did not exist at the date of the balance sheet but arose after the balance sheet date but before financial statements are issued or are available to be issued. Instead, nonrecognized subsequent events are disclosed if they are of such a nature that they must be disclosed to keep the financial statements from being misleading.

3.104 FASB ASC 855-10-50-1 requires the disclosure of the date through which an NFP has evaluated subsequent events and whether that date is the date the financial statements were issued or the date the financial statements were available to be issued. The FASB ASC glossary states that "Financial statements are considered issued when they are widely distributed to shareholders and other financial statement users for general use and reliance in a form and format that complies with GAAP." The FASB ASC glossary also states that "Financial statements are considered available to be issued when they are complete in a form and format that complies with GAAP and all approvals necessary for issuance have been obtained, for example, from management, the board of directors, and/or significant shareholders. The process involved in creating and distributing the financial statements will vary depending on an entity's management and corporate governance structure as well as statutory and regulatory requirements."

3.105 FASB ASC 855-10-25-1A requires that a conduit bond obligor for conduit debt securities that are traded in a public market (a domestic or foreign stock exchange or an over-the-counter market, including local or regional markets) should evaluate subsequent events through the date the financial statements are issued. All other entities should evaluate subsequent events through the date that the financial statements are available to be issued.

3.106 Because of their use of conduit debt that trades in public markets, some NFPs fall into the class of entities that are required to evaluate subsequent events through the issuance date of their financial statements. If an NFP does not have conduit debt that trades in a public market, it is required to evaluate subsequent events up through the date the financial statements are available to be issued.

3.107

Appendix A—Flowcharts and Decision Trees[1]

Ownership of a For-Profit Entity

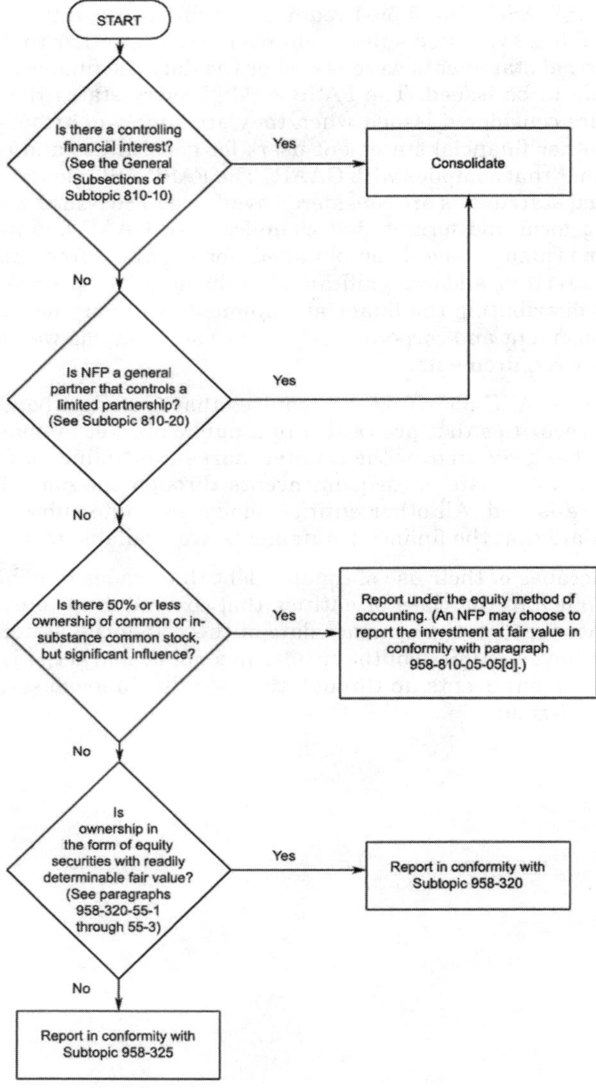

---

[1] The flowcharts and decision trees summarize certain guidance in the Financial Accounting Standards Board (FASB) *Accounting Standards Codification* (ASC) 958-810 for interests in entities that are neither special-purpose leasing entities (FASB ASC 958-810-25-8) nor for-profit real estate entities (FASB ASC 958-810-15-4(d)). They are not intended as substitutes for the guidance in that subtopic.

Relationship With Another Not-for-Profit Organization

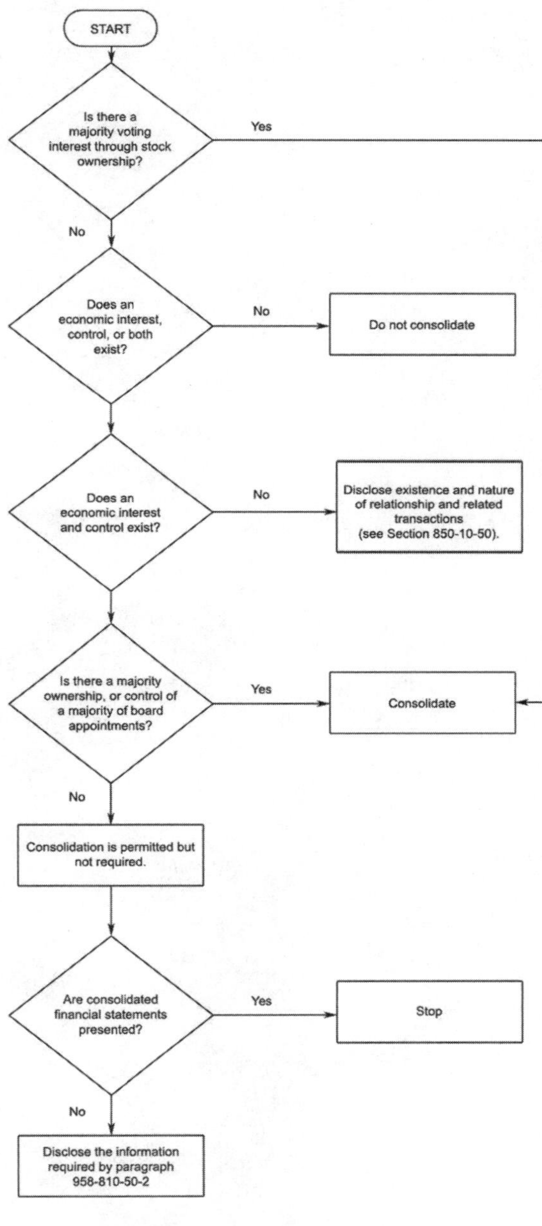

Chapter 4

Cash and Cash Equivalents

Introduction

4.01 Like for-profit enterprises, not-for-profit entities (NFPs) hold cash balances to meet payments arising in the ordinary course of operations and payments for unanticipated contingencies. These balances may be held as cash or cash equivalents. Cash includes currency on hand and deposits held by financial institutions that can be added to or withdrawn without limitation, such as demand deposits. NFPs may invest excess cash in cash equivalents (such as treasury bills, commercial paper, and money-market mutual funds) to earn greater returns.

4.02 The Financial Accounting Standards Board (FASB) *Accounting Standards Codification* (ASC) glossary defines *cash equivalents* as

> short-term, highly liquid investments that have both of the following characteristics: (*a*) readily convertible to known amounts of cash [and] (*b*) so near their maturity that they present insignificant risk of changes in value because of changes in interest rates. Generally, only investments with original maturities of three months or less qualify under that definition. Original maturity means original maturity to the entity holding the investment. For example, both a three-month U.S. Treasury bill and a three-year Treasury note purchased three months from maturity qualify as cash equivalents. However, a Treasury note purchased three years ago does not become a cash equivalent when its remaining maturity is three months. Examples of items commonly considered to be cash equivalents are Treasury bills, commercial paper, money market funds, and federal funds sold (for an entity with banking operations).

Financial Statement Presentation

4.03 A statement of financial position should include a separate line item for "Cash" or "Cash and Cash Equivalents." As noted in paragraphs 3.06–.07, cash and cash equivalents received with donor-imposed stipulations restricting the use of the cash contributed to long-term purposes and cash set aside for long-term purposes should not be classified on a statement of financial position with assets that are available for current use. As noted in paragraph 3.08, NFPs are required to provide information about liquidity or maturity of assets and liabilities, including restriction on the use of particular items.

4.04 Some limitations may exist on an NFP's ability to withdraw or use cash and cash equivalents. These limitations may be imposed by (*a*) creditors and other outside parties (such as limitations on cash held by financial institutions to meet compensating balance requirements, cash and cash equivalents held as collateral on debt obligations, cash received as collateral on loaned securities, and cash held for students, clients, and others under agency agreements); (*b*) donors, who place permanent or temporary restrictions on their cash contributions (such as restricting the contributions to investments in buildings or requiring that the principal be maintained permanently or for a specified time period); or (*c*) governing boards, which may designate cash for investment purposes (traditionally known as "funds functioning as endowment" or "quasi endowment"). NFPs are permitted, but not required, to disaggregate assets into unrestricted and donor-restricted classes when there are donor restrictions on the use of specific donated assets.

4.05 FASB ASC 958-210-45-7 requires that relevant information about the nature and amount of limitations on the use of cash and cash equivalents (such as cash held on deposit as a compensating balance) be included on the face of the financial statements or in the notes. Information about the nature and amount of donor-imposed restrictions should also be disclosed in the net asset section of the statement of financial position or in the notes to the financial statements. (Chapter 11, "Net Assets," of this guide discusses accounting for net assets.) FASB ASC 958-210-50-2 requires disclosure in the notes to the financial statements if unusual circumstances (such as special borrowing arrangements, requirements imposed by resource providers that cash be held in separate accounts, and known significant liquidity problems) are present, or if the NFP has not maintained appropriate amounts of cash and cash equivalents to comply with donor-imposed restrictions. (Paragraphs 3.99–.101 of this guide discuss reporting requirements if an NFP is not in compliance with donor-imposed restrictions.)

4.06 Technical Questions and Answers sections 2130.38–.40 (AICPA, *Technical Practice Aids*) discuss the balance sheet classification of certificates of deposit and whether certificates of deposit are debt securities that must be recognized at fair value. Certificates of deposit with original maturities of 90 days or less are commonly considered "cash and cash equivalents" under FASB ASC 305, *Cash and Cash Equivalents*. A certificate of deposit with an original maturity greater than 90 days would not be included in cash and cash equivalents. Certificates of deposit generally are not debt securities as defined in FASB ASC 958-320. However, some negotiable certificates of deposit may meet the definition of a security. Certificates of deposit that are not debt securities are "other investments," as discussed in paragraph 8.15 of this guide.

Chapter 5

Contributions Received and Agency Transactions

Introduction

5.01 Some not-for-profit entities (NFPs) receive contributions of cash, other assets, and services from individuals, for-profit entities, other NFPs, and governments. Other assets include securities, land, buildings, use of facilities or utilities, material and supplies, intangible assets, and unconditional promises to give in the future.

5.02 The Financial Accounting Standards Board (FASB) *Accounting Standards Codification* (ASC) glossary, defines a *contribution* as

> an unconditional transfer of cash or other assets to an entity or a settlement or cancellation of its liabilities in a voluntary nonreciprocal transfer by another entity acting other than as an owner. Those characteristics distinguish contributions from exchange transactions, which are reciprocal transfers in which each party receives and sacrifices approximately equal value; from investments by owners and distributions to owners, which are nonreciprocal transfers between an entity and its owners; and from other nonreciprocal transfers, such as impositions of taxes or legal judgments, fines, and thefts, which are not voluntary transfers. In a contribution transaction, the value, if any, returned to the resource provider is incidental to potential public benefits. In an exchange transaction, the potential public benefits are secondary to the potential proprietary benefits to the resource provider. The term contribution revenue is used to apply to transactions that are part of the entity's ongoing major or central activities (revenues), or are peripheral or incidental to the entity (gains).

5.03 The "Contributions Received" subsections of FASB ASC 958-605 provide guidance for contributions of cash and other assets received, including promises to give. FASB ASC 958-605-15-6 states that the guidance in those subsections do not apply to the following transactions and activities:

- Transfers of assets that are in substance purchases of goods or services—exchange transactions, in which each party receives and sacrifices commensurate value. However, if an entity voluntarily transfers assets to another or performs services for another in exchange for assets of substantially lower value and no unstated rights or privileges are involved, the contribution received that is inherent in that transaction is within the scope of the "Contributions Received" subsections.
- Transfers of assets in which the reporting entity is acting as an agent, trustee, or intermediary rather than as a donor or donee. (Those transactions are within the scope of the "Transfers of Assets to a Not-for Profit Entity or Charitable Trust that Raises or Holds Contributions for Others" subsections of FASB ASC 958-605.)
- Tax exemptions, tax incentives, and tax abatements.

5.04 This chapter provides guidance for distinguishing contributions from other kinds of transactions. It also discusses recognition, measurement, and disclosure principles for contribution revenues[1] and related receivables.[2] Chapter 12, "Revenue and Receivables from Exchange Transactions," of this guide discusses accounting principles for revenues, gains, and receivables from providing services and from other exchange transactions. Chapter 13, "Expenses, Gains, and Losses," of this guide, discusses reporting contributions made by NFPs.

Distinguishing Contributions From Other Transactions[3]

5.05 A contribution by definition must be a voluntary transfer. Some resource providers may be required to transfer assets or provide services to NFPs involuntarily; for example, to settle legal disputes or to pay fines. Those transactions are not contributions. Accounting for contributions is different from accounting for other kinds of voluntary transfers, such as conditional transfers, agency transactions, and exchange transactions. Accounting for transfers with donor-imposed conditions is discussed in paragraphs 5.50–.61 of this guide.

5.06 To determine the accounting for transactions in which an entity voluntarily transfers assets to an NFP, it is first necessary to assess the extent of discretion the NFP has over the use of the assets that are received. If it has little or no discretion, the transaction is an agency transaction. If it has discretion over the assets' use, the transaction is a contribution, an exchange, or a combination of the two.

Agency Transactions

5.07 The FASB ASC glossary defines an *agency transaction* as "a type of exchange transaction in which the reporting organization acts as an agent, trustee, or intermediary for another party that may be a donor or donee."

5.08 When NFPs act as agents, trustees, or intermediaries helping donors to make a contribution to another entity or individual, they do not receive a contribution when they receive the assets, nor do they make a contribution when they disburse the assets to the other entity or individual. Instead, they act as go-betweens, passing the assets from the donor through their organization to the specified entity or individual. Federated fundraising organizations, community foundations, and institutionally related entities are examples of NFPs that commonly serve as agents, trustees, or intermediaries, but any NFP can function in those capacities.

---

[1] For purposes of this chapter, the term *contribution revenue* is used to apply transactions that are part of the not-for-profit entity's (NFP's) ongoing major or central activities (revenues), or are peripheral or incidental to the NFP (gains). Chapter 12, "Revenues and Receivables From Exchange Transactions," of this Audit and Accounting Guide, discusses the distinction between ongoing major activities and peripheral or incidental transactions and events.

[2] Unconditional promises to give cash or other financial instruments, such as an ownership interest in an entity, are financial instruments as defined in the Financial Accounting Standards Board (FASB) *Accounting Standards Codification* (ASC) glossary, and thus requirements for recognition and disclosure of financial instruments apply.

[3] Federal rules specify the classification of certain transactions for purposes other than reporting in conformity with generally accepted accounting principles (GAAP), such as contractual reporting requirements. For example, certain transactions should be classified as federal awards received and expended by NFPs. The guidance in this guide pertains to financial reporting in conformity with GAAP. Classifications in conformity with GAAP may differ from classifications in accordance with federal rules.

5.09 The "Transfers of Assets to a Not-for-Profit Entity or Charitable Trust That Raises or Holds Contributions for Others" subsections of FASB ASC 958-605 establish standards for transactions in which an entity—the donor—makes a contribution by transferring assets to an NFP or charitable trust—a recipient entity—that accepts the assets from the donor and agrees to use those assets on behalf of or transfers those assets, the return on investment of those assets, or both to an unaffiliated entity—the beneficiary—that is specified by the donor. Paragraphs 5.30–.35 discuss the standards for transactions that take place in a similar manner, but are not contributions because the transfers are revocable, repayable, or reciprocal. FASB ASC 958-605 does not set standards for recipient entities that are trustees.[4]

5.10 FASB ASC 958-605-55-76 states that a recipient entity has discretion sufficient to recognize a contribution received if it can choose the beneficiaries of the assets. Paragraphs 76–79 of FASB ASC 958-605 provide guidance to help determine whether a recipient entity has discretion to choose the beneficiary. FASB ASC 958-605-25-24 states that except as described in FASB ASC 958-605-25-25 [variance power] and FASB ASC 958-605-25-27 [financially interrelated entities], a recipient entity that accepts assets from a donor and agrees to use those assets on behalf of [a specified beneficiary] or transfer those assets, the return on investment of those assets, or both to a specified beneficiary is [an agent and] not a donee. (The exceptions for variance power are discussed in paragraphs 5.21–.25 and for financially interrelated entities in paragraphs 5.26–.29.) FASB ASC 958-605-55-78 states that a donor may specify the beneficiary (*a*) by name, (*b*) by stating that all entities that meet a set of donor-defined criteria are beneficiaries, or (*c*) by actions surrounding the transfer that made clear the identity of the beneficiary. (Paragraphs 80–115 of FASB ASC 958-605-55 provide examples of donor stipulations and discuss whether those stipulations specify a beneficiary.)

5.11 The following are three examples of circumstances in which donors specify a beneficiary and the recipient entity should not recognize a contribution. (The exceptions for variance power are discussed in paragraphs 5.21–.25 and for financially interrelated entities in paragraphs 5.26–.29.) If a donor selects a beneficiary from among a list of potential beneficiaries that have been prequalified or otherwise identified by the recipient entity, the assets received are not contributions to that recipient entity. Similarly, if a grantor specifies eligibility criteria and states that the grant proceeds must be transferred to all who meet those criteria, the recipient entity has not received a contribution even though it may be responsible for determining whether individuals or entities meet those grantor-specified eligibility criteria. Likewise, if a donor responds to a campaign request from an NFP that indicates that the proceeds of the campaign will be distributed to a named beneficiary, that recipient entity has not received a contribution.

5.12 In contrast, if neither the language used by the donor, the representations of the recipient entity, nor the actions surrounding the transfers cause the donor to believe that he or she is directing the gift to a specified beneficiary, then the NFP is a donee and should recognize a contribution received. For example, an NFP is a donee and should recognize a contribution if it asks the

---

[4] Chapter 6, "Split-Interest Agreements," of this guide discusses split-interest and similar agreements in which NFPs act as trustee for a resource provider and have a beneficial interest in the assets transferred.

donor to select one or more fields of interest from among a list of community needs prepared by the NFP. Similarly, if a donor uses broad generalizations to describe the beneficiaries, such as homeless individuals, the NFP has received a contribution because the choice of the beneficiary is within its control. Likewise, if an NFP asks its donors to indicate an NFP for consideration by its allocation committee, the NFP is the donee if that request is conveyed in a manner that leads the donor to conclude that its role is merely to propose possible allocations.

5.13 The representations made to the donor during the solicitation of a gift are important in determining whether a transaction is an agency transaction. If an NFP creates a donor's reasonable expectation that a contribution will be transferred to a beneficiary specified by the donor, the NFP is an agent or intermediary. Unless the NFP has variance power or is financially interrelated to the specified beneficiary, it should not recognize a contribution received.

5.14 FASB ASC 958-605-55-75 states that discretion to determine the timing of the distribution to the specified beneficiary, by itself, does not give the recipient entity discretion sufficient to recognize a contribution. That limited discretion is not sufficient. The ability to choose a payment date does not relieve an entity from its obligation to pay.

5.15 Pursuant to FASB ASC 958-605-25-24, an agent should recognize its liability to the specified beneficiary concurrent with its recognition of cash or other financial assets received from the donor. As discussed in FASB ASC 958-605-30-13, both the asset and the liability should be measured at the fair value of the assets received from the donor. FASB ASC 958-605-25-24 states that except as described in [the paragraphs about variance power and financially interrelated entities], a recipient entity that receives nonfinancial assets is permitted, but not required, to recognize its liability and those assets provided that the recipient entity reports consistently from period to period and discloses its accounting policy. An NFP should consider the need for disclosure of its accounting policy in the notes to the financial statements pursuant to FASB ASC 235-10-50-1.

5.16 Thus, if the assets received from the donor are donated materials, supplies, or other nonfinancial assets, the recipient entity may choose either to (*a*) report the receipt of the assets as a liability to the beneficiary concurrent with recognition of the assets received or (*b*) not report the transaction at all. Distributions of cash or other assets to the specified third-party beneficiaries should be reported as decreases in the assets and liabilities.

5.17 FASB ASC 958-230-55-4 states that cash received and paid in agency transactions should be reported as cash flows from operating activities in a statement of cash flows. If the statement of cash flows is presented using the indirect method, cash received and paid in such transactions is permitted to be reported either gross or net. FASB ASC 958-605-50-5 states that additional information about transactions in which an NFP acts as an agent, trustee, or intermediary may be required to be disclosed under FASB ASC 850, *Related Party Disclosures*.

5.18 Paragraphs 28–30 of FASB ASC 958-605-25 provide guidance for recognition of an agency transaction by the specified beneficiary. A specified beneficiary should recognize its rights to the assets (financial or nonfinancial) held by a recipient entity as an asset unless the recipient entity is explicitly granted variance power. Those rights are any one of the following: (*a*) an interest in the net assets of the recipient entity (which is discussed in paragraphs 5.26–.29), (*b*) a beneficial interest (which is discussed in this paragraph), or (*c*) a receivable (which is discussed in the following paragraph). If the beneficiary has an unconditional right to receive all or a portion of the specified cash flows from a charitable trust or other identifiable pool of assets, the beneficiary should recognize that beneficial interest. Pursuant to FASB ASC 958-605-30-14 and FASB ASC 958-605-35-3, the beneficiary should measure and subsequently remeasure its beneficial interest at fair value. The fair value of a perpetual trust held by a third party generally can be measured using the fair value of the assets contributed to the trust, unless facts and circumstances indicate that the fair value of the beneficial interest differs from the fair value of the assets contributed to the trust. (Although FASB ASC 958-605 does not establish standards for the trustee, it does establish standards for the beneficiaries' rights to trust assets.)

5.19 FASB ASC 958-605-25-30 states that if the beneficiary's rights are neither an interest in the net assets of the recipient entity nor a beneficial interest, a beneficiary should recognize its rights to the assets held by a recipient entity as a receivable and contribution revenue in accordance with paragraphs 8–10 of FASB ASC 958-605-25 and FASB ASC 958-605-45-5 for unconditional promises to give. (Paragraphs 5.78–.89 and 5.109–.116 discuss recognition of promises to give.)

5.20 Present value techniques are one valuation technique for measuring the fair value of the contribution and the beneficial interest or receivable; other valuation techniques also are available, as described in FASB ASC 820, *Fair Value Measurements and Disclosures*.[5,*] If present value techniques are used, the contribution revenue and the beneficial interest or receivable should be measured as the present value of the future cash inflows over the expected term of the agreement. The choice of accounting policies regarding recognition of nonfinancial assets, as discussed in paragraph 5.15, applies only to the agent or intermediary; beneficiaries should recognize their rights to nonfinancial assets held by the recipient entity.

---

[5] Paragraphs 3.73–.94 of this guide discuss FASB ASC 820, *Fair Value Measurements and Disclosures*, which defines fair value, establishes a framework for measuring fair value, and expands disclosures about fair value measurements. Paragraphs 4–20 of FASB ASC 820-10-55 provide standards for using present value techniques when the measurement objective is fair value. Some of the guidance in FASB ASC 820 is labeled as "Pending Content" due to the transition and open effective date information discussed in FASB ASC 820-10-65. For example, Accounting Standards Update (ASU) No. 2010-06, *Fair Value Measurements and Disclosures (Topic 820): Improving Disclosures about Fair Value Measurements*, is effective for interim and annual reporting periods beginning after December 15, 2009, except for the separate disclosures about purchases, sales, issuances, and settlements relating to level 3 measurements (see FASB ASC 820-10-50-2(c)(2)), which shall be effective for fiscal years beginning after December 15, 2010, and for interim periods within those fiscal years. Early adoption is permitted.

[*] On June 29, 2010, FASB issued a proposed ASU, *Amendments for Common Fair Value Measurement and Disclosure Requirements in U.S. GAAP and IFRSs*, intended to develop common requirements for measuring fair value and for disclosing information about fair value measurements in U.S. GAAP and International Financial Reporting Standards (IFRSs). For many of the proposed requirements, FASB does not expect the amendments to result in changes in the application of FASB ASC 820. Other amendments would change a particular principle or requirement. The most notable of these changes are: highest and best use and valuation premise, measuring the fair value of an instrument classified in shareholders' equity, measuring the fair value of instruments that are managed within a portfolio, and application of blockage factors and other premiums and discounts in a fair value measurement. The proposed standards also include additional disclosure requirements. Readers should be alert to the issuance of a final ASU.

Variance Power

5.21 The FASB ASC glossary defines *variance power* as

> [t]he unilateral power to redirect the use of the transferred assets to another beneficiary. A donor explicitly grants variance power if the recipient entity's unilateral power to redirect the use of the assets is explicitly referred to in the instrument transferring the assets. Unilateral power means that the recipient entity can override the donor's instructions without approval from the donor, specified beneficiary, or any other interested party.

5.22 Paragraphs 25–26 of FASB ASC 958-605-25 discuss the effects of variance power on recognition of the transferred assets by the recipient entity. A recipient entity that is directed by a donor to distribute the transferred assets, the return on investment of those assets, or both to a specified unaffiliated beneficiary acts as a donee, rather than an agent, trustee, or intermediary, if the donor explicitly grants the recipient entity variance power. A recipient entity that is explicitly granted variance power has the ability to use assets it receives to further its own purpose from the date it accepts the assets. In that situation, the recipient entity should account for receipt of funds by recognizing an asset and corresponding contribution revenue unless the transfer is revocable, repayable, or reciprocal as described in FASB ASC 958-605-25-33 (paragraph 5.31 of this guide).

5.23 Variance power provides the recipient entity with discretion sufficient to recognize a contribution received despite the specification of a beneficiary by the donor, subject to the exception in the following paragraph. If a donor explicitly grants a recipient entity variance power and names an unaffiliated beneficiary, the recipient entity is a donee and recognizes contribution revenue. Unaffiliated means that the beneficiary is other than the donor or the donor's affiliate as defined in the FASB ASC glossary.

5.24 A recipient entity that receives variance power should not report a contribution if the resource provider specifies itself or its affiliate(s) as the beneficiary of the transferred assets. Because of their reciprocal nature, those transfers are not contributions received by the recipient entity—even if the resource provider granted the recipient entity variance power at the time of the transfer. Paragraphs 5.30–.35 discuss transactions in which a resource provider names itself or its affiliate as beneficiary of a transfer of assets to a recipient entity.

5.25 As discussed in FASB ASC 958-605-25-31, if the donor explicitly grants a recipient entity variance power, the specified unaffiliated beneficiary should not recognize its potential for future distributions from the assets held by the recipient entity. Those future distributions, if they occur, should be recognized as contributions by the specified beneficiary when received or unconditionally promised.

Financially Interrelated Entities

5.26 The FASB ASC glossary defines financially interrelated entities stating that a recipient entity and a specified beneficiary are financially interrelated if the relationship between them has both of the following characteristics: (*a*) one of the entities has the ability to influence the operating and financial decisions of the other and (*b*) one of the entities has an ongoing economic interest in the net assets of the other.

5.27 FASB ASC 958-20-15-2 states that the ability to exercise that influence (of the operating and financial decisions of the other) may be demonstrated in several ways, including the following:

a. The entities are affiliates as defined in the FASB ASC glossary.

b. One entity has considerable representation on the governing board of the other entity.

c. The charter or bylaws of one entity limit its activities to those that are beneficial to the other entity.

d. An agreement between the entities allows one entity to actively participate in the policy making processes of the other, such as setting organizational priorities, budgets, and management compensation.

The FASB ASC glossary defines an *ongoing economic interest in the net assets of another* as a residual right to another NFP's net assets that results from an ongoing relationship. The value of those rights increases or decreases as a result of the investment, fundraising, operating, and other activities of the other entity.

5.28 FASB ASC 958-605-25-27 states that if a recipient entity and a specified beneficiary are financially interrelated entities and the recipient entity is not a trustee, the recipient entity should recognize a contribution received when it receives assets (financial or nonfinancial) from the donor that are specified for the beneficiary. FASB ASC 958-20-25 provides the following example. A foundation that exists to raise, hold, and invest assets for the specified beneficiary or for a group of affiliates of which the specified beneficiary is a member generally is financially interrelated with the NFP or NFPs it supports. The foundation should recognize contribution revenue when it receives assets from the donor. Pursuant to FASB ASC 958-20-25-2, the beneficiary should recognize its interest in the net assets of the recipient entity and adjust that interest for its share of the change in net assets of the recipient entity using a method similar to the equity method of accounting for investments in common stock.[6] Examples 1–3 (paragraphs 3–17) of FASB ASC 958-20-55 provide examples of this guidance.

5.29 FASB ASC 958-20-55-2A states that although most of the relationships described in the definition of *economic interest* used in FASB ASC 958-810 (see FASB ASC 958-810-55-6) are potentially ongoing economic interests in the net assets of the other, some do not meet the criterion in paragraph 958-20-15-2(b). (The examples of economic interest in FASB ASC 958-810-55-6 are included at paragraph 3.39 of this guide.) Only economic interests that are both ongoing and residual interests in the net assets are ongoing economic interests in the net assets of another.

Similar Transactions That Are Revocable, Repayable or Reciprocal

5.30 In addition to establishing standards for contributions transferred to beneficiaries via agents, trustees, and intermediaries, the "Transfers of Assets to a Not-for-Profit Entity or Charitable Trust that Raises or Holds Contributions

---

[6] FASB ASC 958-20-55-11 states that an interest in the net assets of an affiliate would be eliminated if that affiliate were included in consolidated financial statements of the interest holder.

for Others" subsections of FASB ASC 958-605 also set standards for transactions that take place in a similar manner (that is, there is a resource provider, a recipient entity, and a specified beneficiary), but that are not contributions because the terms of the transfer or the relationships between the parties make the transfer revocable, repayable, or reciprocal.

5.31 FASB ASC 958-605-25-33 describes four types of transfers that are not contributions to either the recipient entity or the specified beneficiary. The first three types are the following:

a. The transfer is subject to the resource provider's unilateral right to redirect the use of the transferred assets to another beneficiary.

b. The transfer is accompanied by the resource provider's conditional promise to give or is otherwise revocable or repayable.

c. The resource provider controls the recipient entity and specifies an unaffiliated beneficiary. Several definitions of control exist. The definition of control in FASB ASC 958-810 and FASB ASC 850 should be considered when determining whether one entity controls another.[7]

Those transfers should be reported as an asset of the resource provider and as a liability of the recipient entity.

5.32 Sometimes a resource provider specifies itself or its affiliate as beneficiary of a transfer of assets to a recipient entity. Those transfers are reciprocal and thus are not contributions. Examples of those types of transfers are (*a*) an NFP transfers assets to a community foundation to establish an endowment for the benefit of the NFP and (*b*) an NFP transfers assets to a foundation it creates to hold those assets.

5.33 Paragraphs 4–7 of FASB ASC 958-20-25 describe two types of reciprocal transactions, which are as follows:

a. An equity transaction—A transfer of assets to a recipient entity that meets all of the following conditions: (i) the resource provider specifies itself or its affiliate as the beneficiary, (ii) the resource provider and the recipient entity are financially interrelated entities (paragraphs 5.26–.29 of this guide discusses financially interrelated organizations), and (iii) neither the resource provider nor its affiliate expects payment of the transferred assets, although payment of investment return on the transferred assets may be expected.

b. The resource provider specifies itself or its affiliate as the beneficiary and any of the conditions (ii) and (iii) in paragraph (*a*) are not met (that is, the transfer is not an equity transaction).

5.34 Per FASB ASC 958-605-25-33, if the transfer in which the resource provider specifies itself or its affiliate as the beneficiary is not an equity transaction, the resource provider should report an asset and the recipient entity should report a liability. If the transaction is an equity transaction, the reporting depends upon whether the resource provider or its affiliate is the specified

---

[7] FASB ASC 850, *Related Party Disclosures*, defines *control* as "the possession, direct or indirect, of the power to direct or cause the direction of the management and policies of an enterprise through ownership, by contract, or otherwise." FASB ASC 958-810 defines *control* as "the direct or indirect ability to determine the direction of management and policies through ownership, contract, or otherwise."

beneficiary. Per FASB ASC 958-605-25-5 and FASB ASC 958-20-45-1, if the resource provider specifies itself as the beneficiary, the resource provider should report an equity transaction as an interest in the net assets of the recipient entity (or an increase in a previously recognized interest), and the recipient entity should report an equity transaction as a separate line in its statement of activities. Per FASB ASC 958-605-25-6 and FASB ASC 958-20-45-1, if the resource provider specifies an affiliate as the beneficiary, the resource provider and the recipient entity should report an equity transaction as separate lines in their statements of activities, and the affiliate named as beneficiary should report an interest in the net assets of the recipient entity.

5.35 In accordance with FASB ASC 958-20-45-3, if the beneficiary (resource provider or its affiliate) and the recipient entity are included in consolidated financial statements, the beneficiary's interest in the net assets of the recipient entity (recognized in the previous paragraph) should be eliminated.

Exchange Transactions[8]

5.36 The FASB ASC glossary defines *exchange transaction* as a reciprocal transfer between two entities that results in one of the entities acquiring assets or services or satisfying liabilities by surrendering other assets or services or incurring other obligations. The FASB ASC glossary definition of *contribution* states that contributions differ from exchange transactions, which are reciprocal transfers in which each party receives and sacrifices something of approximately equal value.

5.37 In some situations, exchange transactions can be easily distinguished from contributions. For example, purchases of assets or payments of employees' salaries clearly are exchange transactions: each party gives up and receives equivalent economic value. In contrast, an example of a contribution is a donation to an NFP's mass fund-raising appeal: donors are providing resources in support of the NFP's mission and expect to receive nothing of direct value in exchange.

5.38 Paragraphs 18–19 of FASB ASC 958-720-45 discuss the cost of premiums and whether premiums are given in exchange for resources provided. The guidance is included in this paragraph and the following paragraph. The cost of premiums (such as postcards or calendars) given to potential donors as part of mass fund-raising appeals is a fundraising expense, and the classification of the donations received from the appeal as contributions is unaffected by the fact that premiums were given to potential donors. The premiums are not provided to potential donors in exchange for the assets contributed; they can be kept by all those from whom funds are solicited, regardless of whether a contribution is made.

5.39 The cost of premiums (such as coffee mugs) that are given to resource providers to acknowledge receipt of a contribution also should be reported as fundraising expenses if those costs are nominal in value compared with the value of the goods or services donated by the resource provider. For example, an NFP may provide a coffee mug to people making a contribution of $50 or more; the mug costs the NFP $1. The NFP should recognize contributions for the total amount contributed and fund-raising expense of $1 for each mug provided to donors. The cost of premiums that are greater than nominal in value

---

[8] Certain reciprocal transactions that involve transfers to recipient entities are discussed in paragraphs 5.24 and 5.30–.35.

should be reported as cost of sales. If premiums are greater than nominal in value, transactions shall be reported as part exchange transaction and part contribution.

5.40 Chapter 12 of this guide provides guidance concerning reporting exchange transactions.

5.41 Classifying asset transfers as exchange transactions or as contributions may require the exercise of judgment concerning whether a reciprocal transaction has occurred, that is, whether a recipient NFP has given up assets, rights, or privileges approximately equal to the value of the assets, rights, or privileges received. Value should be assessed from both the recipient NFP's and the resource provider's points of view and can be affected by a wide variety of factors; for example, resource providers can retain the right to share in the use of or income from an asset provided to the NFP.

5.42 Table 5-1 contains the list of indicators from FASB ASC 958-605-55-8 that may be helpful in determining whether individual asset transfers are contributions, exchange transactions, or a combination of both. Depending on the facts and circumstances, some indicators may be more significant than others; however, no single indicator is determinative of the classification of a particular transaction. Indicators of a contribution tend to describe transactions in which the value, if any, returned to the resource provider is incidental to potential public benefits. Indicators of an exchange tend to describe transactions in which the potential public benefits are secondary to the potential proprietary benefits to the resource provider.

5.43 Several kinds of voluntary asset transfers that may be difficult to classify are discussed in the following four paragraphs.

5.44 Paragraphs 9–12 of FASB ASC 958-605-55 discuss NFPs that receive dues from their members. This paragraph and the following paragraph and table reproduce that guidance. The term "members" is used broadly by some NFPs to refer to their donors and by other NFPs to refer to individuals or other entities that pay dues in exchange for a defined set of benefits. These transfers often have elements of both a contribution and an exchange transaction because members receive tangible or intangible benefits from their membership in the NFP. Usually, the determination of whether membership dues are contributions rests on whether the value received by the member is commensurate with the dues paid. For example, if an NFP has annual dues of $100 and the only benefit members receive is a monthly newsletter with a fair value of $25, $25 of the dues are received in an exchange transaction and should be recognized as revenue as the earnings process is completed and $75 of the dues are a contribution.

5.45 Member benefits generally have value regardless of how often (or whether) the benefits are used. For example, most would agree that a health club membership is an exchange transaction, even if the member stops using the facilities before the completion of the membership period. It may be difficult, however, to measure the benefits members receive and to determine whether the value of those benefits is approximately equal to the dues paid by the members. Table 5-2 contains the list of indicators from FASB ASC 958-605-55-12 that may be helpful in determining whether membership dues are contributions, exchange transactions, or a combination of both. Depending on the facts and circumstances, some indicators may be more significant than others; however, no single indicator is determinative of the classification of a particular transaction.

Table 5-1

Indicators Useful in Distinguishing Contributions From Exchange Transactions

Indicator	*Contribution*	*Exchange Transaction*
Recipient not-for-profit entity's (NFP's) intent in soliciting the asset*	Recipient NFP asserts that it is soliciting the asset as a contribution.	Recipient NFP asserts that it is seeking resources in exchange for specified benefits.
Resource provider's expressed intent about the purpose of the asset to be provided by recipient NFP	Resource provider asserts that it is making a donation to support the NFP's programs.	Resource provider asserts that it is transferring resources in exchange for specified benefits.
Method of delivery	The time or place of delivery of the asset to be provided by the recipient NFP to third-party recipients is at the discretion of the NFP.	The method of delivery of the asset to be provided by the recipient NFP to third-party recipients is specified by the resource provider.
Method of determining amount of payment	The resource provider determines the amount of the payment.	Payment by the resource provider equals the value of the assets to be provided by the recipient NFP, or the assets' cost plus markup; the total payment is based on the quantity of assets to be provided.
Penalties assessed if NFP fails to make timely delivery of assets	Penalties are limited to the delivery of assets already produced and the return of the unspent amount. (The NFP is not penalized for nonperformance.)	Provisions for economic penalties exist beyond the amount of payment. (The NFP is penalized for nonperformance.)
Delivery of assets to be provided by the recipient NFP	Assets are to be delivered to individuals or organizations other than the resource provider.	Assets are to be delivered to the resource provider or to individuals or organizations closely connected to the resource provider.

* This table refers to assets. Assets may include services. The terms *assets* and *services* are used interchangeably in this table.

Table 5-2

Indicators Useful for Determining the Contribution and Exchange Portions of Membership Dues

Indicator	*Contribution*	*Exchange Transaction*
Recipient not-for-profit entity's (NFP's) expressed intent concerning purpose of dues payment	The request describes the dues as being used to provide benefits to the general public or to the NFP's service beneficiaries.	The request describes the dues as providing economic benefits to members or to other entities or individuals designated by or related to the members.
Extent of benefits to members	The benefits to members are negligible.	The substantive benefits to members (for example, publications, admissions, educational programs, and special events) may be available to nonmembers for a fee.
NFP's service efforts	The NFP provides service to members and nonmembers.	The NFP benefits are provided only to members.
Duration of benefits	The duration is not specified.	The benefits are provided for a defined period; additional payment of dues is required to extend benefits.
Expressed agreement concerning refundability of the payment	The payment is not refundable to the resource provider.	The payment is fully or partially refundable if the resource provider withdraws from membership.
Qualifications for membership	Membership is available to the general public.	Membership is available only to individuals who meet certain criteria (for example, requirements to pursue a specific career or to live in a certain area).

5.46 FASB ASC 958-605-25-1 states that revenue derived from membership dues in exchange transactions should be recognized over the period to which the dues relate. Nonrefundable initiation and life membership fees received in exchange transactions should be recognized as revenues in the period in which the fees become receivable if future fees are expected to cover the costs of future services to be provided to members. If nonrefundable initiation and life membership fees, rather than future fees, are expected to cover those costs, nonrefundable initiation and life member fees received in exchange transactions should be recognized as revenue over the average duration of membership, the life expectancy of members, or other appropriate time periods.

5.47 Paragraphs 2–5 of FASB ASC 958-605-55 discuss transactions in which foundations, business organizations, and other types of entities provide resources to NFPs under programs referred to as *grants*, *awards*, or *sponsorships*. A grant or sponsorship may be entirely a contribution, entirely an exchange transaction, or a combination of the two. In addition, those transactions may also have characteristics of agency transactions.[9] Those asset transfers are contributions if the resource providers receive no value in exchange for the assets transferred or if the value received by the resource providers is incidental to the potential public benefit from using the assets transferred. A grant made by a resource provider to an NFP would likely be a contribution if the activity specified by the grant is to be planned and carried out by the NFP and the NFP has the right to the benefits of carrying out the activity. If, however, the grant is made by a resource provider that provides materials to be tested in the activity and that retains the right to any patents or other results of the activity, the grant would likely be an exchange transaction.

5.48 Some transfers of assets between NFPs and governments (such as the sale of goods and services) are exchange transactions. Other transfers of assets between NFPs and governments (such as unrestricted support given by state and local governments) are contributions. Other kinds of government transfers (sometimes referred to as *grants*, *awards*, or *appropriations*) have unique characteristics that may make it difficult to determine whether they are contributions or exchange transactions. The indicators described in table 5-1 provide guidance on how to classify such transfers. Depending on the facts and circumstances, some indicators may be more significant than others; however, no single indicator is determinative of the classification of a particular transaction.

5.49 FASB ASC 958-605-45-1 states that resources received in exchange transactions should be classified as unrestricted revenues and net assets, even in circumstances in which resource providers place limitations on the use of the resources. For example, resources received from governments in exchange transactions in which those governments have placed limitations on the use of the resources should be reported as unrestricted revenues and net assets, because those limitations are not donor-imposed restrictions on contributions. (Classification of net assets is discussed further in paragraphs 5.62–.77 and in chapters 3, "Basic Financial Statements and General Financial Reporting Matters," and 11, "Net Assets," of this guide.)

Recognition Principles for Contributions

5.50 The recognition principles for contributions are discussed in the "Contributions Received" subsections of FASB ASC 958-605. Accounting for contributions depends on whether the transfer of assets, including promises to give, is received by the NFP with donor-imposed conditions, donor-imposed restrictions, or both. Donor-imposed conditions create a barrier that must be overcome before a contribution can be recognized; by definition, a contribution is unconditional. Donor-imposed restrictions do not affect recognition; instead, they affect the classification of the contribution revenue.

5.51 The FASB ASC glossary defines a *donor-imposed condition* as a donor-imposed stipulation that specifies a future and uncertain event whose occurrence or failure to occur gives the donor the right of return of the assets or releases the donor from the obligation to transfer assets in the future.

---

[9] Paragraphs 5.07–.35 discuss agency transactions.

5.52 Some promises to give are in part conditional and in part unconditional. For example, an NFP may guarantee the debt of an unaffiliated entity without receiving commensurate consideration in return. That guarantee is in part conditional—the promise to make payments in future periods upon default—and in part unconditional—the gift of the guarantor's credit support, which enables the entity to obtain a lower interest rate on its borrowing. (Paragraphs 10.20–.21 provide additional information about guarantees.)

5.53 The FASB ASC glossary defines a *donor-imposed restriction* as

> [a] stipulation that specifies a use for a contributed asset that is more specific than the broad limits resulting from the following: (*a*) the nature of the NFP, (*b*) the environment in which it operates, and (*c*) the purposes specified in its articles of incorporation or bylaws or comparable documents for an unincorporated association. A donor-imposed restriction on an NFP's use of the asset contributed may be temporary or permanent. Some donor-imposed restrictions impose limits that are permanent, for example, stipulating that resources be invested in perpetuity (not used up). Others are temporary, for example, stipulating that resources may be used only after a specified date, for particular programs or services, or to acquire buildings and equipment.

5.54 Paragraphs 15–17 of FASB ASC 958-605-55 provide guidance for distinguishing between a condition stipulated by a donor and a restriction on the use of a contribution imposed by a donor. Those paragraphs are summarized in this paragraph and the next. Making that determination may require the exercise of judgment. Conditional transfers are not contributions yet; they may become contributions upon the occurrence of one or more future and uncertain events. Because of the uncertainty about whether they will be met, conditions imposed by resource providers may cast doubt on whether the resource provider's intent was to make a contribution, to make a conditional contribution, or to make no contribution. As a result of this uncertainty, donor-imposed conditions should be substantially met by the entity before the receipt of assets (including contributions receivable) is recognized as a contribution. In contrast to donor-imposed conditions, donor-imposed restrictions limit the use of the contribution, but they do not change the transaction's fundamental nature from that of a contribution.

5.55 If donor stipulations do not state clearly whether the right to receive payment or take delivery depends on meeting those stipulations, or if those stipulations are ambiguous, distinguishing a conditional promise to give from an unconditional promise to give may be difficult. First, review the facts and circumstances surrounding the gift and communicate with the donor. If the ambiguity cannot be resolved as a result of those efforts, presume a promise containing stipulations that are not clearly unconditional is a conditional promise to give. However, if the possibility that the condition will not be met is remote,[10] a conditional promise to give is considered unconditional. For example, a stipulation that an annual report must be provided by the donee to receive subsequent annual payments on a multiyear promise is not a condition if the possibility of not meeting that administrative requirement is remote. A challenge (or matching) grant is a common form of conditional promise to give.

---

[10] The FASB ASC glossary defines *remote* as "the chance of the future event or events occurring is slight."

5.56 FASB ASC 958-605-25-2 states that except as provided (for contributed services and collections), contributions received shall be recognized as revenues or gains in the period received and as assets, decreases of liabilities, or expenses depending on the form of the benefits received.[11] The classification of contributions received as revenues or gains depends on whether the transactions are part of the NFP's ongoing major or central activities (revenues), or are peripheral or incidental to the NFP (gains).

5.57 Depending on the kind of benefit received, in addition to recognizing contribution revenue, the NFP should also recognize (*a*) an increase in assets (for example, cash, securities, contributions receivable, collections [if capitalized, see chapter 7, "Other Assets," of this guide], and property and equipment); (*b*) a decrease in liabilities (for example, accounts payable or notes payable); or (*c*) an expense (for example, donated legal services).

Recognition if a Donor Imposes a Condition

5.58 Per FASB ASC 958-605-25-13, a transfer of assets with a conditional promise to contribute them should be accounted for as a refundable advance until the conditions have been substantially met or explicitly waived by the donor. A change in the original conditions of the agreement between the promisor and the promisee should not be implied without an explicit waiver.

5.59 Transfers of assets, including promises to give, on which resource providers have imposed conditions should be recognized as contributions if the likelihood of not meeting the conditions is remote (because the transfer is considered unconditional as discussed in paragraph 5.54–.55).

5.60 FASB ASC 958-605-55-21 discusses promises that become unconditional in stages because they are dependent on several or a series of conditions—milestones—rather than on a single future and uncertain event. Those promises are recognized in increments as each of the conditions is met. Similarly, other promises are conditioned on promisees' incurring certain qualifying expenses (or costs). Those promises become unconditional and are recognized to the extent that the expenses are incurred. A portion of those contributions should be recognized as revenue as each of those stages is met.

5.61 FASB ASC 958-605-55-17 provides the following example. A resource provider promises to contribute $1 for each $1 of contributions received by an NFP, up to $100,000, over the next 6 months. As contributions are received from other resource providers, the conditions would be met and the promise would become unconditional. For example, if $10,000 is received in the first month from donors, $10,000 of the conditional promise would become unconditional and should be recognized as contribution revenue.

Recognition if a Donor Imposes a Restriction

5.62 Contributions may be received with donor-imposed restrictions. Some restrictions permanently limit the NFP's use of contributed assets. Other restrictions are temporary in nature, limiting the NFP's use of contributed assets to (*a*) later periods or after specific dates (time restrictions), (*b*) specific purposes (purpose restrictions), or (*c*) both.

---

[11] Unconditional contributions of services and collection items are subject to different recognition criteria. Paragraphs 5.90–.93 and chapter 7, "Other Assets," of this guide discuss those transactions.

5.63 FASB ASC 958-605-45-3 notes that a restriction on an NFP's use of the assets contributed results either from a donor's explicit stipulation or from circumstances surrounding the receipt of the contribution that make clear the donor's implicit restriction on use.

5.64 For example, restrictions may (*a*) be stipulated explicitly by the donor in a written or oral communication accompanying the contribution or (*b*) result implicitly from the circumstances surrounding receipt of the contributed asset—for example, making a gift to a capital campaign whose stated objective is to raise funds for a new building.

5.65 FASB ASC 958-225-45-13(d) notes that a donor can impose restrictions on otherwise unrestricted net assets. For example, a donor may make a restricted contribution that is conditioned on the NFP restricting a stated amount of its unrestricted net assets. Such restrictions that are not reversible without donors' consent result in a reclassification of unrestricted net assets to restricted net assets.

5.66 Paragraphs 3–7 of FASB ASC 958-605-45 provide guidance on classification of contributions received. Contributions without donor-imposed restrictions should be reported as unrestricted support that increases unrestricted net assets. Contributions with donor-imposed restrictions should be reported as restricted support, which increases permanently restricted or temporarily restricted net assets, depending on the nature of the restriction.

5.67 The permanently restricted classification should be used if the limits imposed on the use of the contributed assets are permanent (for example, contributions of cash or securities that must be invested in perpetuity to provide a permanent source of income for the NFP or contributions of permanently restricted collection items or of cash that must be used to purchase permanently restricted collection items). The temporarily restricted classification should be used for contributions if the limitations are temporary (for example, a restriction that contributed assets may be used only after some future date, or for some specific program, or to acquire a specific asset).

5.68 In some situations, an NFP may meet donor-imposed restrictions on all or a portion of the amount contributed in the same reporting period in which the contribution is received. In those cases, pursuant to FASB ASC 958-605-45-4, the contribution (to the extent that the restrictions have been met) may be reported as unrestricted support provided that the NFP has a similar policy for reporting investment gains and income (see FASB ASC 958-320-45-3),[12] reports consistently from period to period, and discloses its accounting policy in notes to financial statements.

5.69 In other cases, a subsequent event may arise that raises the possibility that the NFP may not satisfy a donor-imposed restriction. FASB ASC 855, *Subsequent Events*, provides guidance on the recognition and disclosure of subsequent events. Paragraphs 3.103–.106 of this guide provides additional information about subsequent events.

5.70 Paragraphs 9–12 of FASB ASC 958-205-45 and FASB ASC 958-225-45-13 provide guidance for reporting reclassifications for the expiration

---

[12] FASB ASC 958-320-45-3 (paragraph 8.32) discusses the accounting policy for reporting investment gains and income if the NFP meets donor-imposed restrictions on all or a portion of such gains and income in the same reporting period as the gains and income are recognized.

of donor-imposed restrictions. A restriction expires when the stipulated time has elapsed, when the stipulated purpose for which the resource was restricted has been fulfilled, or both. If two or more temporary restrictions are imposed on a contribution, the effect of the expiration of those restrictions should be recognized in the period in which the last remaining restriction has expired.

5.71 The expiration of donor-imposed restrictions on contributions should be reported in the period or periods in which (*a*) a donor-stipulated time has elapsed (for example, the restriction on a term endowment in which contributed cash is to be invested for 10 years expires at the end of the tenth year) or (*b*) a donor-stipulated purpose for which the contribution was restricted has been fulfilled by the NFP (for example, the restriction on a contribution to acquire operating supplies expires when those supplies are acquired by the NFP). Expirations of donor-imposed restrictions should be reported in a statement of activities as reclassifications, decreasing temporarily restricted net assets and increasing unrestricted net assets.

5.72 Expenses may be incurred for purposes for which both unrestricted and temporarily restricted net assets are available. FASB ASC 958-205-45-11 states that if an expense is incurred for a purpose for which both unrestricted and temporarily restricted net assets are available, a donor-imposed restriction is fulfilled to the extent of the expense incurred unless the expense is for a purpose that is directly attributable to another specific external source of revenue.

5.73 For example, an employee's salary may meet donor-imposed restrictions to support the program on which the employee is working. In that situation, the restriction is met to the extent of the salary expense incurred unless incurring the salary will lead to inflows of revenues from a specific external source, such as revenues from a cost reimbursement contract or a conditional promise to give that becomes unconditional when the NFP incurs the salary expense.

5.74 NFPs may receive contributions of long-lived assets (such as property and equipment) or of cash and other assets restricted to the purchase of long-lived assets, for which donors have not expressly stipulated how or how long the long-lived asset must be used by the NFP or how to use any proceeds resulting from the asset's disposal. FASB ASC 958-605-45-6 states that gifts of long-lived assets received without stipulations about how long the donated asset must be used should be reported as restricted support if it is an NFP's policy to imply a time restriction that expires over the useful life of the donated assets. NFPs that adopt a policy of implying time restrictions also shall imply a time restriction on long-lived assets acquired with gifts of cash or other assets restricted for those acquisitions.

5.75 If an NFP adopts such a policy, the contributions of long-lived assets or of cash and other assets restricted to the purchase of long-lived assets it receives should be reported as restricted support that increases temporarily restricted net assets. Depreciation should be recorded over the asset's useful life, and net assets should be reclassified periodically from temporarily restricted to unrestricted as depreciation is recognized. Paragraph 9.12 of this guide includes additional guidance about the reclassification of net assets upon the expiration of donor restrictions related to property, plant, and equipment.

5.76 FASB ASC 958-360-40-1 discusses long-lived assets that are subject to an accounting policy implying time restrictions on the use of contributed long-lived assets if those assets are disposed of before the end of their useful lives. In those situations, the gain or loss on the disposal of that asset should be reported as a change in unrestricted net assets and a reclassification should be reported for any remaining temporarily restricted net assets.

5.77 Alternatively, an NFP may adopt a policy of not implying time restrictions on contributions of long-lived assets (or of other assets restricted to the purchase of long-lived assets) received without donor stipulations about how long the contributed assets must be used. If an NFP adopts such a policy, contributions of long-lived assets with no donor-imposed time restrictions should be reported as unrestricted support. Contributions of cash and other assets restricted to the acquisition of long-lived assets should be reported as restricted support that increases temporarily restricted net assets; those restrictions expire when the long-lived assets are placed in service by the NFP.

Promises to Give

5.78 The FASB ASC glossary defines *promise to give* as

> A written or oral agreement to contribute cash or other assets to another entity. A promise carries rights and obligations—the recipient of a promise to give has a right to expect that the promised assets will be transferred in the future, and the maker has a social and moral obligation, and generally a legal obligation, to make the promised transfer. A promise to give may be either conditional or unconditional.

An unconditional promise to give is a promise to give that depends only on passage of time or demand by the promisee for performance. A conditional promise to give is a promise to give that depends on the occurrence of a specified future and uncertain event to bind the promisor.

5.79 NFPs may enter into written or oral agreements with donors involving future nonreciprocal transfers of cash, other assets, and services.[13] These items are sometimes referred to as pledges, a term that FASB ASC 958, *Not-for-Profit Entities*, and this guide avoid because it may be misinterpreted. Such agreements between NFPs and potential donors should be reported as contribution revenue and receivables if such agreements are, in substance, unconditional promises to give, even if the promises are not legally enforceable.

5.80 Paragraphs 8–10 of FASB ASC 958-605-25 provide recognition guidance for unconditional promises to give. An unconditional promise to give shall be recognized when it is received. However, to be recognized there must be sufficient evidence in the form of verifiable documentation that a promise was made and received. A communication that does not indicate clearly whether it is a promise is considered an unconditional promise to give if it indicates an unconditional intention to give that is legally enforceable. Legal enforceability refers to the availability of legal remedies, not the intent to use them.

5.81 Paragraphs 11–13 of FASB ASC 958-605-25 provide recognition guidance for conditional promises to give. Conditional promises to give cash or other assets (such as securities or property and equipment) should be recognized as

---

[13] FASB ASC 958-605-55-20 notes that "promises to give services generally involve personal services that, if not explicitly conditional, are often implicitly conditioned upon the future and uncertain availability of specific individuals whose services have been promised." It is assumed in the remainder of this chapter that promises to give services are conditional and, hence, not recognized until the services are performed.

contribution revenue and receivables when the conditions on which they depend are substantially met or explicitly waived by the donor, that is, when the conditional promise becomes unconditional.

5.82 Per FASB 958-605-45-5, contributions of unconditional promises to give with payments due in future periods should be reported as restricted support unless explicit donor stipulations or circumstances surrounding the receipt of a promise make clear that the donor intended it to be used to support activities of the current period. It is reasonable to assume that by specifying future payment dates donors indicate that their gift is to support activities in each period in which a payment is scheduled. For example, receipts of unconditional promises to give cash in future years generally increase temporarily restricted net assets.

5.83 Depending on the existence and nature of donor-imposed restrictions, unconditional promises to give should be reported either as unrestricted support that increases unrestricted net assets, or as restricted support that increases permanently restricted or temporarily restricted net assets. Use of the *permanently restricted* classification is appropriate if donor-imposed restrictions stipulate that the resources must be maintained permanently (for example, donors' promises to give cash or securities that must be invested in perpetuity). Use of the temporarily restricted classification is appropriate if donor-imposed restrictions (*a*) expire by passage of time or (*b*) can be fulfilled or removed by actions of the NFP pursuant to donor stipulations.

5.84 Unconditional promises to give that are due in future periods and are not permanently restricted generally increase temporarily restricted net assets, rather than unrestricted net assets. If, however, the donor explicitly stipulates that the promise to give is to support current-period activities or if other circumstances surrounding the promise make it clear that the donor's intention is to support current-period activities, unconditional promises to give should be reported as unrestricted support that increases unrestricted net assets.

5.85 Per FASB ASC 958-605-55-19, the requirement (that there be sufficient evidence that a promise was received and made) does not preclude recognition of verifiable oral promises, such as those documented by tape recordings, written registers, or other means that permit subsequent verification.

5.86 Other forms of sufficient verifiable evidence documenting that a promise was made by the donor and received by the NFP include (*a*) written agreements, (*b*) pledge cards, (*c*) oral promises documented by contemporaneous written logs, and (*d*) oral promises documented by follow-up written confirmations.

5.87 Promises to give that do not discuss the specific time or place for the contribution but that are otherwise clearly unconditional in nature should be considered unconditional promises to give.

5.88 NFPs may receive communications that are intentions to give, rather than promises to give. For example, communications from individuals indicating that the NFP has been included in the individual's will as a beneficiary are intentions to give. Such communications are not unconditional promises to give, because individuals retain the ability to modify their wills during their lifetimes. (When the probate court declares the will valid, the NFP should recognize contribution revenue and a receivable at the fair value of its interest in the estate, unless the promise is conditioned upon future or uncertain events, in which case a contribution should not be recognized until the conditions are substantially met.) Paragraphs 49–51 of FASB ASC 958-605-55 provide an example of an individual naming an NFP as a beneficiary in her will. NFPs should disclose information about conditional promises in valid wills in conformity with FASB ASC 958-310-50-4.

5.89 Per FASB ASC 958-605-25-10, solicitations for donations that clearly include wording such as "information to be used for budget purposes only" or that clearly and explicitly allow resource providers to rescind their indications that they will give are intentions to give rather than promises to give and should not be reported as contributions.

Contributed Services

5.90 FASB ASC 958-605-25-16 requires that contributions of services be recognized if the services received meet any of the following criteria:

a. They create or enhance a nonfinancial asset. The FASB ASC glossary defines a *nonfinancial asset* as an asset that is not a financial asset. Nonfinancial assets include land, buildings, use of facilities or utilities, materials and supplies, intangible assets, or services.

b. They require specialized skills, are provided by individuals possessing those skills and would typically need to be purchased by the organization if they had not been provided by contribution. Services requiring specialized skills are provided by accountants, architects, carpenters, doctors, electricians, lawyers, nurses, plumbers, teachers, and other professionals and craftspeople.

5.91 Recognized contributed services should be reported as contribution revenue and as assets or expenses. Skills such as accounting, financial, construction, educational, electrical, legal, medical, investment advisory and other services should be recognized if they meet criterion (*a*) or (*b*) in the preceding paragraph or if they meet both criteria. Whether such contributions should be reported is unaffected by whether the NFP could afford to purchase the services at their fair value.

5.92 FASB ASC 958-605-25-16 states that contributed services and promises to give services that do not meet the criteria (in paragraph 5.90) should not be recognized. Examples 7–10 (paragraphs 52–68 of FASB ASC 958-605-55) illustrate the recognition of contributed services. Per FASB ASC 958-605-30-2, if such contributions are recognized, they should be measured at fair value.

5.93 Per FASB ASC 958-605-25-17, contributed services (and the related assets and expenses) should be recognized if employees of separately governed affiliated entities regularly perform services (in other than an advisory capacity) for and under the direction of the donee and the recognition criteria for contributed services are met.

Gifts in Kind

5.94 Some NFPs receive noncash assets—such as property, equipment, and inventory—from resource providers. Reporting these transfers, sometimes referred to as *gifts in kind*, as agency transactions or as contributions depends on the extent of discretion that the NFP recipient has over the use or subsequent disposition of the assets. (Determining whether an NFP recipient receives assets as an agent is discussed in paragraphs 5.07–.14. Paragraphs 5.15–.16

describe the accounting and disclosures of an agent that receives nonfinancial assets.) Information about gifts-in-kind transactions may be required to be disclosed under FASB ASC 850.

5.95 An NFP that is the specified beneficiary of an agency transaction should recognize its rights to gifts in kind held by the agent unless the agent is granted variance power. (Paragraphs 5.18–.19 describe more fully the specified beneficiary's accounting.) If gifts-in-kind transfers are not agency transactions, the noncash assets received by the NFP should be recognized as contributions when received from or unconditionally promised by the donor. If the gifts have no value, as might be the case for certain clothing and furniture that cannot be (*a*) used internally by the NFP or for program purposes or (*b*) sold by the NFP, the item received should not be recognized.

5.96 Per FASB ASC 958-605-30-11, gifts in kind that can be used or sold should be measured at fair value. In determining fair value, entities should consider the quality and quantity of the gifts, as well as any applicable discounts that would have been received by the entity, including discounts based on that quantity if the assets had been acquired in exchange transactions. Fair value would generally not increase when a gift in kind is passed from one entity to another. However, fair value could increase if an entity adds value to the gift, such as by cleaning and packaging the gift. Any increases should be evaluated to determine whether the entity did, in fact, add to the fair value of the assets.

5.97 In some cases, entities other than an NFP use for the NFP's benefit (or provide at no charge to the NFP) certain nonfinancial assets that encourage the public to contribute to the NFP or help the NFP communicate its message or mission. Examples of these include fundraising material, informational material, or advertising, including media time or space for public service announcements or other purposes. Technical Questions and Answers section 6140.24, "Contributions of Certain Nonfinancial Assets, Such as Fundraising Material, Informational Material, or Advertising, Including Media Time or Space for Public Service Announcements or Other Purposes" (AICPA, *Technical Practice Aids*), states that when such nonfinancial assets are used for the NFP's benefit (or provided to the NFP at no charge) and they encourage the public to contribute to an NFP or help the NFP communicate its message or mission, NFPs should consider whether they have received a contribution. If they have received a contribution, it should be measured at fair value, pursuant to FASB ASC 958-605-30-2, and the related expense, at the time the expense is recognized, should be reported by function, based on the nature of the contributed item.

5.98 As discussed in FASB ASC 958-605-25-20, NFPs may also receive items, such as tickets, gift certificates, works of art, and merchandise, that are to be used for fund-raising purposes by transferring them to other resource providers (the ultimate resource provider or recipient) during fundraising events. Those gifts in kind can be linked to asset transfers from the original resource providers to the ultimate resource providers (recipients) because they are, in substance, part of the same transaction; those gifts in kind should be reported as contributions and measured at fair value when originally received by an NFP. The difference between the amount received for those items from the ultimate resource providers (recipients) and the fair value of the gifts in kind when originally contributed to the NFP should be recognized as adjustments to the original contributions when the items are transferred to the ultimate resource providers (recipients).

5.99 For example, a public radio station receives from the local community theater (the original resource provider) a ticket with a fair value of $75, to be auctioned to the highest bidder; a listener (the ultimate resource provider or recipient) subsequently acquires the ticket at auction for $100. The initial transfer of the ticket to the NFP should be reported as a $75 contribution and the ticket should be reported as an asset; an additional $25 contribution should be reported when the ticket is transferred to the listener at auction, and no cost for the ticket should be reported on the statement of activities. In that example, the ultimate resource provider or recipient acquires the ticket in a transaction that is part exchange transaction and part contribution.[14] If instead a listener acquires the ticket for $45, rather than $100, a reduction of $30 in contributions should be reported when the ticket is transferred to the listener at auction, because the transfer at auction is part of the transaction that was initiated when the NFP received the ticket. Holding the ticket from the time of initial receipt to the time of ultimate transfer at auction does not create a transaction separate from the initial contribution.

Contributed Utilities and Use of Long-Lived Assets

5.100 NFPs may receive unconditional contributions of the use of electric, telephone, and other utilities and of long-lived assets (such as a building or the use of facilities) in which the donor retains legal title to the long-lived asset. Pursuant to FASB ASC 958-605-55-23 and FASB ASC 958-605-25-2, an NFP should recognize the fair value of the use of property or utilities as contribution revenue in the period in which the contribution[15] is received and expenses in the period the utilities or long-lived assets are used.[16] If the transaction is an unconditional promise to give (as described in paragraphs 5.78–.89) for a specified number of periods, the promise should be reported as contributions receivable and as restricted support that increases temporarily restricted net assets.[17]

5.101 FASB ASC 958-605-55-24 discusses unconditional promises to give the use of long-lived assets (such as a building or other facilities) for a specified number of periods in which the donor retains legal title to the long-lived asset. Those promises may be received in connection with leases or may be similar to leases but have no lease payments. For example, an NFP may use facilities under lease agreements that call for lease payments at amounts below the fair rental value of the property. In circumstances in which an NFP receives an unconditional promise to give for a specified number of periods, the promise should be reported as revenue and as a contribution receivable for the difference between the fair rental value of the property and the stated amount of the lease payments.[18] Amounts reported as contributions should not exceed the fair value of the long-lived asset at the time the NFP receives the unconditional promise to give. The contribution receivable may be described in the financial statements

---

[14] Paragraphs 13.26–.31 of this guide discuss reporting special events associated with an NFP's fund-raising efforts.

[15] As discussed in FASB ASC 958-605-55-26, contributions are received in several different forms, which include both the use of facilities and utilities, as well as unconditional promises to give those items in the future.

[16] FASB ASC 958-605-55-23 states that whether those contributions should be reported is unaffected by whether the NFP could afford to purchase the utilities or facilities at their fair value.

[17] Paragraphs 5.104–.106 discuss measurement principles for initial recognition of contributions received.

[18] See footnote 17.

based on the item whose use is being contributed, such as a building, rather than as contributions receivable.†

Contributed Collection Items

5.102 NFPs may receive contributions of works of art, historical treasures, and similar items that meet the definition of collections in the FASB ASC glossary. The recognition and measurement principles for contributions of collection items depend on the collections-capitalization policy adopted by the NFP. Accounting for collections is discussed in chapter 7 of this guide.

Split-Interest Agreements

5.103 A *split-interest agreement* is a form of contribution in which an NFP receives benefits that are shared with other beneficiaries designated by the donor. Common kinds of such agreements include charitable lead and remainder trusts, charitable gift annuities, and pooled (life) income funds. Because of the specialized nature of these arrangements, they are discussed separately in chapter 6, "Split-Interest Agreements," of this guide.

Measurement Principles for Contributions

5.104 The "Contributions Received" subsections of FASB ASC 958-605-30 discuss the initial measurement of contributions received at fair value. FASB ASC 820 establishes a framework for measuring fair value.* Per FASB ASC 958-605-30-6, unconditional promises to give that are expected to be collected in less than one year may be measured at net realizable value because that amount results in a reasonable estimate of fair value. FASB ASC 820-10-35-9 states that a fair value measurement should be determined based on the assumptions that market participants would use in pricing the asset. FASB ASC 820-10-35-19 states that market participant assumptions should consider assumptions about the effect of a restriction on the sale or use of an asset if market participants would consider the effect of the restriction in pricing the asset. Example 6 (paragraphs 51–55 of FASB ASC 820-10-55) illustrates that restrictions that are an attribute of an asset, and therefore would transfer to a market participant, are the only restrictions reflected in fair value. Donor restrictions that are specific to the donee are reflected in the classification of net assets, not in the measurement of fair value.

5.105 Contribution revenue should be measured at the fair value of the assets or services received or promised or the fair value of the liabilities satisfied. The use of the word expected in the phrase expected to be received or the phrase expected to be collected, when used to describe the receipt of cash or other assets from an unconditional promise to give, is not intended to limit the NFP's choice of present value techniques to an expected present value technique as described in paragraphs 13–20 of FASB ASC 820-10-55.

5.106 Per FASB ASC 958-605-30-10, the fair value of contributed services that create or enhance nonfinancial assets may be measured by referring to

---

† On August 17, 2010, FASB issued a proposed ASU, *Leases (Topic 840)*, which would make significant changes to the accounting requirements for both lessees and lessors. FASB initiated a joint project with the International Accounting Standards Board (IASB) to develop a new approach to lease accounting that would ensure that assets and liabilities arising under leases are recognized in the statement of financial position. Readers should be alert to the issuance of final ASU.

* See footnote * in paragraph 5.20.

either the fair value of the services received or the fair value of the asset or of the asset enhancement resulting from the services. Fair value should be used for the measure regardless of whether the NFP could afford to purchase the services at their fair value.

5.107 Generally, an NFP would use the fair value measure that is more readily determinable to measure contributed services.

5.108 Per FASB ASC 958-605-25-4, a major uncertainty about the existence of value may indicate that an item received should not be recognized. If an item is accepted solely to be saved for its potential future use in scientific or educational research , it may have uncertain value, or perhaps no value, and should not be recognized. For example, contributions of flora, fauna, photographs, and objects identified with historic persons, places, or events often have no value or have highly restricted alternative uses. Chapter 7 of this guide discusses gifts of clothing or furniture. FASB ASC 958-605-25-5 provides additional information about contributed tangible property.

5.109 Pursuant to FASB ASC 958-605-30-7, if a promise to give has not previously been recognized as contribution revenue because it was conditional, fair value should be measured when the conditions are met.

5.110 FASB ASC 958-605-55-22 states that the present value of the future cash flows is one valuation technique for measuring the fair value of contributions arising from unconditional promises to give cash; other valuation techniques also are available, as described in FASB ASC 820.[19] That paragraph provides the table shown in exhibit 5-1, which illustrates the use of present value techniques for initial recognition and measurement of unconditional promises to give cash that are expected to be collected one year or more after the financial statement date.

---

[19] See footnote 5.

Exhibit 5-1

Initial Recognition of Unconditional Promises to Give Cash

Facts

Assume that a not-for-profit entity receives a promise (or promises from a group of homogeneous donors) to give $100 in 5 years, that the anticipated future cash flows from the promise(s) are $70, and that the present value of the future cash flows is $50.

Solution

dr.		Contributions Receivable	$70	
	cr.	Contribution Revenue—Temporarily Restricted		$50
	cr.	Discount on Contributions Receivable		$20

(To report contributions receivable and revenue using a present value technique to measure fair value.)

[*Note*: Some entities may use a subsidiary ledger to retain information concerning the $100 face amount of contributions promised in order to monitor collections of contributions promised.]

5.111 FASB ASC 958-605-30-4 discusses initial measurement of unconditional promises to give. If present value techniques are used to measure the fair value of unconditional promises to give, an NFP should determine the amount and timing of the future cash flows of unconditional promises to give cash (or, for promises to give noncash assets, the quantity and nature of assets expected to be received). In making that determination, the NFP should consider all the elements in FASB ASC 820-10-55-5, including the following: when the receivable is expected to be collected, the creditworthiness of the other parties, the NFP's past collection experience, the NFP's policies concerning the enforcement of promises to give, expectations about possible variations in the amount or timing of the cash flows (that is, the uncertainty inherent in the cash flows), and other factors concerning the receivable's collectibility.

5.112 FASB ASC 958-605-30-8 discusses initial measurement of unconditional promises to give noncash assets. It states that a present value technique is one valuation technique for measuring the fair value of an unconditional promise to give noncash assets; other valuation techniques also are available, as described in FASB ASC 820.[20] If present value techniques are used, the fair value of contributions arising from unconditional promises to give noncash assets might be determined based on the present value of the projected fair value of the underlying noncash assets at the date that those assets are expected to be received (that projected fair value is referred to in this section as the *future fair value*) and in the quantities that those assets are expected to be received, if the date is one year or more after the financial statement date. Both the likelihood of the promise being fulfilled and the future fair value of those underlying assets, such as the future fair value per share of a promised equity security, should be considered in determining the future amount to be discounted. The quantity, nature, and timing of assets expected to be received, such as the number of shares of a promised equity security, the entity in which those shares represent an equity interest, and when those shares will be received should

[20] See footnote 5.

be considered in determining the likelihood of the promise being fulfilled. In cases in which the future fair value of the underlying asset is difficult to determine, the fair value of an unconditional promise to give noncash assets may be based on the fair value of the underlying asset at the date of initial recognition. No discount for the time value of money should be reported if an asset's fair value at the date of initial recognition is used to measure the fair value of the contribution.

Discounting

5.113 FASB ASC 958-605-30-5 discusses the determination of the discount rate if present value techniques are used to measure fair value. The present value of unconditional promises to give should be measured using a discount rate that is consistent with the general principles for present value measurement discussed in paragraphs 5–9 of FASB ASC 820-10-55-5. In conformity with FASB ASC 835-30-25-11, the discount rate should be determined at the time the unconditional promise to give is initially recognized and should not be revised subsequently unless the NFP has elected to measure the promise to give at fair value in conformity with the "Fair Value Option" subsections of FASB ASC 825-10, as discussed further in paragraphs 5.117–.119.

5.114 FASB ASC 958-310-35-1 states that if an NFP elects to measure a receivable at fair value and uses a present value technique to measure fair value, the discount rate assumptions, and all other elements discussed in FASB ASC 820-10-55-5, should be revised at each measurement date to reflect current market conditions.

5.115 Discounts on contributions receivable that are measured at present value should be amortized between the date the promise to give is initially recognized and the date the cash or other contributed assets are received. In conformity with FASB ASC 835-30-35, the interest method should be used to amortize the discount. Other methods of amortization may be used if the results are not materially different. FASB ASC 958-310-35-6 and FASB ASC 958-310-45-2 require that the subsequent accruals of the interest element be accounted for by donees as contribution revenue that increases either temporarily or permanently restricted net assets if the underlying promise to give is donor restricted.

5.116 Per FASB ASC 958-310-45-1, contributions receivable should be reported net of the discount that arises if measuring a promise to give at present value. The discount should be separately disclosed by reporting it as a deduction from contributions receivable either on the face of a statement of financial position or in the notes to the financial statements.

Subsequent Measurement

5.117 FASB ASC 958-310-35 discusses the subsequent measurement of receivables. It states that after recognition, the value of a contribution arising from an unconditional promise to give cash or noncash assets (contribution receivable) may change because of any of the following reasons: (*a*) accrual of the interest element for a promise to give measured using present value techniques, (*b*) changes in the quantity or nature of assets expected to be received (such as changes in the amounts of future cash flows), (*c*) changes in the projected fair value of the underlying noncash assets at the date that those assets are expected to be received (referred to as the *future fair value* of underlying noncash assets), (*d*) changes in the timing of assets expected to be received, and (*e*) changes in the time value of money.

5.118 Neither FASB ASC 958-310 nor this guide address accounting for changes in the timing of assets expected to be received. FASB Concepts Statement No. 7, *Using Cash Flow Information and Present Value in Accounting Measurements*, provides useful discussion of techniques to address changes in estimated cash flows. Statements of Financial Accounting Concepts are not sources of established accounting principles and, thus, do not amend, modify, or justify a change from generally accepted accounting principles currently in effect.

5.119 Unconditional promises to give cash should be subsequently measured using one of the following:

- Fair value, if an election is made in conformity with the "Fair Value Option" subsections of FASB ASC 825-10
- The guidance in paragraphs 5.120–.121 if the fair value election in conformity with the "Fair Value Option" subsections of FASB ASC 825-10 is not made

Unconditional promises to give financial instruments, including debt or equity securities, should be subsequently measured using one of the following:

- Fair value, if an election is made in conformity with the "Fair Value Option" subsections of FASB ASC 825-10
- The guidance in paragraphs 5.120–.123 for unconditional promises to give equity securities with readily determinable fair values or debt securities (if the fair value election in conformity with the "Fair Value Option" subsections of FASB ASC 825-10 is not made)
- The guidance in paragraphs 5.120–.121 and 5.124–.127 for promises to give financial instruments other than equity securities with readily determinable fair values or debt securities (if the fair value election in conformity with the "Fair Value Option" subsections of FASB ASC 825-10 is not made)

Unconditional promises to give assets other than cash or financial instruments should be subsequently measured using the guidance in paragraphs 5.120–.121 and 5.124–.127.

Changes in the Quantity or Nature of Assets Expected to Be Received

5.120 This paragraph and the next discuss the guidance in paragraphs 7–10 of FASB ASC 958-310-35 for subsequent measurement of unconditional promises to give if there are changes in the quantity or nature of the promised assets. If the fair value of a contribution receivable decreases because of changes in the quantity or nature of assets expected to be received, the decrease should be recognized in the period(s) in which the expectation changes. As discussed in FASB ASC 958-310-45-3, that decrease should be reported as an expense or loss (bad debt) in the net asset class in which the net assets are represented. Because all expenses are reported as decreases in the unrestricted net asset class, those decreases should be reported as losses if they are decreases in temporarily restricted net assets or permanently restricted net assets.

5.121 No increase in net assets should be recognized if the fair value of a contribution receivable increases because of a change in the quantity or nature of assets expected to be received between the date the unconditional promise to give is recognized and the date it is collected, except as provided in (the next sentence). If the fair value of a contribution receivable increases because of changes in the quantity or nature of assets expected to be received, and previous decreases in the value of that unconditional promise to give resulted in expenses or losses from bad debts, the increase should be reported as a recovery of those expenses or losses to the extent that those expenses or losses were previously recognized. The recovery should be reported in the net asset classes in which the net assets are represented. Amounts collected, other than a recovery of bad debt expenses or losses, in excess of the carrying amount of contributions receivable should be reported as contribution revenue in the appropriate net asset class.

Changes in the Fair Value of Underlying Noncash Assets—Gifts of Certain Securities

5.122 As discussed in FASB ASC 958-310-35-11, the fair value of a contribution receivable arising from an unconditional promise to give equity securities with readily determinable fair values or debt securities may change between the date the unconditional promise to give is recognized and the date the asset promised is received because of changes in the future fair value of the underlying securities. For purposes of subsequent measurement, the method of determining the future fair value of the underlying securities shall be the same as the method used for determining that amount for purposes of initial measurement. Thus, if a promise to give securities is measured based on the fair value of the underlying securities at the date of gift, as described in FASB ASC 958-605-30-8 (paragraph 5.112 of this guide), an observed change in the current fair value of the underlying securities shall be recognized. The change should be reported as an increase or decrease in contribution revenue in the period(s) in which the change occurs. The change should be recognized in the net asset class in which the contribution was originally reported or in the net asset class in which the net assets are represented.

5.123 Assumed relationships, such as the relationship between the market price of the security at the time the initial measurement is made and its projected market price at the date the asset is expected to be received, should be presumed to continue in determining whether the future fair value of the underlying noncash asset has changed.

Changes in the Fair Value of Underlying Noncash Assets—Gifts of Other Assets

5.124 As discussed in paragraphs 5.117–.119 and FASB ASC 958-310-35-12, the fair value of a contribution receivable arising from an unconditional promise to give noncash assets other than equity securities with readily determinable fair values or debt securities may change between the date the unconditional promise to give is recognized and the date the asset promised is received because of changes in the future fair value of the underlying noncash assets. If, in a period subsequent to initial measurement, an observed change in the current fair value of the asset to be contributed occurs, that change in fair value may or may not result in changes in the future fair value of the underlying noncash asset, depending on the method and assumptions used for determining the future fair value of the underlying noncash asset.

5.125 As discussed in FASB ASC 958-310-35-12, for purposes of subsequent measurement, the method for determining the future fair value of the underlying noncash asset should be the same as the method used for determining that amount for purposes of initial measurement. (Paragraph 5.112 discusses the measurement principles for initial recognition of unconditional promises to give noncash assets, including consideration of the future fair value of the underlying asset.) Accordingly, assumed relationships, such as the relationship between the market price of the noncash asset at the time the initial measurement is made and its projected market price at the date the asset is expected to be received, should be presumed to continue in determining whether the future fair value of the underlying noncash asset has changed.

5.126 As discussed in paragraph 5.112, the fair value of an unconditional promise to give noncash assets may be based on the fair value of the underlying noncash asset at the date of initial recognition. If that method is used at initial measurement, for subsequent measurement, observed changes in the current fair value of the asset to be contributed should be treated as if they were changes in the fair value of contributions arising from unconditional promises to give noncash assets because of changes in the future fair value of the underlying asset. If that method is not used at initial measurement, for subsequent measurement, observed changes in the current fair value of the asset to be contributed may or may not result in changes in the future fair value of the underlying asset, and, therefore, may or may not result in changes in the fair value of contributions arising from unconditional promises to give noncash assets because of changes in the future fair value of the underlying asset.

5.127 As discussed in FASB ASC 958-310-35-13, if the future fair value of the underlying noncash asset (that is, other than equity securities with readily determinable fair values or debt securities) decreases, that decrease should be reported as a decrease in contribution revenue in the period(s) in which the decrease occurs. The decrease should be reported in the net asset class in which the contribution was originally reported or in the net asset class in which the net assets are represented. Thus, if a promise to give noncash assets is measured based on the fair value of those underlying noncash assets at the date of gift, as described in FASB ASC 958-605-30-8 (paragraph 5.112 of this guide), an observed decrease in the current fair value of the underlying noncash asset shall be recognized. If the future fair value of the underlying noncash asset increases between the date the unconditional promise to give is recognized and the date the asset promised is received, no additional revenue should be recognized.

Illustration

5.128 Table 5-3 reproduces the table in FASB ASC 958-310-55-1, which illustrates the accounting for changes in the fair value of unconditional promises to give subsequent to initial recognition, but before collection if those promises to give are not measured subsequently at fair value.

Table 5-3

Accounting for Unconditional Promises to Give That Are Not Measured Subsequently at Fair Value (Subsequent to Initial Recognition But Before Collection)

	Reason for the Change in Value			
Underlying Asset	*Change in Collectibility of the Receivable*		*Change in the Fair Value of the Underlying Asset*	
	Increase in Fair Value	*Decrease in Fair Value*	*Increase in Future Fair Value*	*Decrease in Future Fair Value*
Cash	No adjustment[a]	Recognize expense or loss (bad debt)	Not applicable	Not applicable
Securities[b]	No adjustment[a]	Recognize expense or loss (bad debt)	Recognize additional contribution revenue	Recognize a decrease in contribution revenue
Other assets	No adjustment[a]	Recognize expense or loss (bad debt)	No adjustment	Recognize a decrease in contribution revenue

[a] Recoveries of previously recognized decreases in fair value resulting from changes in estimates of collectibility (up to the amount of decreases previously recognized), however, should be recognized as reductions of bad debt expense or loss.

[b] For purposes of this table, *securities* are defined as equity securities with readily determinable fair values and all debt securities, consistent with the use of the terms in Financial Accounting Standards Board *Accounting Standards Codification* 958-320.

Financial Statement Presentation

5.129 Contribution revenue may be reported as a separate line item on a statement of activities. However, this does not preclude reporting separate line items for government contracts, membership dues,[21] special events, or similar revenue sources in other revenue categories or in the notes to the financial statements.

5.130 The majority of the disclosures for contributions received and agency transactions are located in the "Disclosure" sections (sections 50) of FASB ASC 958-310 and FASB ASC 958-605. The following paragraphs discuss the more common of those disclosures, but are not intended as a substitute for the "Disclosure" sections of the FASB ASC.

[21] Accounting for the portion of membership dues that is an exchange transaction is different than accounting for the portion that is a contribution. Paragraphs 5.44–.46 discuss revenue recognition principles for membership dues.

5.131 The notes to financial statements should include the following:

- The accounting policies adopted by the NFP concerning the following:
  - — Whether the NFP implies time restrictions on the use of contributed long-lived assets (and contributions of cash and other assets restricted to purchasing them) received without donor stipulations about how long the contributed assets must be used. (Paragraphs 5.74–.77 provide guidance concerning the application of this policy.)
  - — Whether the NFP classifies donor-restricted contributions as unrestricted or restricted support if restrictions are satisfied in the same reporting period in which the contributions are received. (Paragraphs 5.68–.69 provides guidance concerning the application of this policy.)
  - — Whether the NFP recognizes contributions of collection items. (Chapter 7 of this guide provides guidance concerning the application of this policy.)
- Disclosures relating to the liquidity of the NFP's contributions receivable, including the following:
  - — Contributions receivable pledged as collateral or otherwise limited regarding to use.
  - — A schedule of unconditional promises to give (showing the total amount separated into amounts receivable in less than 1 year, in 1-5 years, and in more than 5 years) and the related allowance for uncollectible promises receivable arising from subsequent decreases due to changes in the quantity or nature of assets expected to be received (see paragraph 5.120–.121), and the unamortized discount. As illustrated in FASB ASC 958-605-55-22, the allowance for uncollectible promises to give does not include amounts determined to be uncollectible when the contributions receivable were initially measured. For example, assume that, on the last day of its fiscal year, an NFP receives promises to give $100 in 5 years, that the estimated future cash flows from the promises are $70, and that the present value of the estimated future cash flows is $50. The notes to the financial statements should disclose unconditional promises to give of $70 and unamortized discount of $20.
  - — The amount of conditional promises to give—in total and, with descriptions, the amount of each group of similar promises (for example, those conditioned upon the development of new programs, upon the purchase or construction of new property and equipment, and upon the raising of matching funds within a specified time period).
- Disclosures required by paragraphs 10–19 of FASB ASC 825-10-50, including disclosures of fair value and carrying amounts for all financial instruments for which it is practicable to estimate fair value, the method(s) and significant assumptions used to estimate the fair value of financial instruments, and the changes

in the those methods and significant assumptions, if any, during the period, unless those disclosures are optional because the three criteria of FASB ASC 825-10-50-3 are met.[‡]

- Disclosures required by paragraphs 1–2 of FASB ASC 820-10-50 in the format described in FASB ASC 820-10-50-8, if unconditional promises to give are subsequently measured at fair value.
- Disclosures required by paragraphs 28–31 of FASB ASC 825-10-50, if unconditional promises to give are subsequently measured at fair value.
- Disclosures required by FASB ASC 825-10-50-32, if an election to report unconditional promises to give at fair value is made after initial recognition pursuant to FASB ASC 825-10-25-4(e).
- Disclosures required by FASB ASC 835-30 for imputation of interest.
- Disclosure of how the NFP computes its fund-raising ratio if it includes that ratio in its financial statements, as described in FASB ASC 958-205-50-3.

5.132 The notes to financial statements should include the following disclosures concerning contributions of services received during the period:

- The nature and extent of contributed services received by the NFP
- A description of the programs or activities for which the services were used
- The amount of contributed services recognized during the period

NFPs are encouraged to report in the notes to the financial statements, if practical, the fair value of contributed services received but not recognized.

5.133 If an NFP transfers assets to a recipient entity and specifies itself or its affiliate as beneficiary, the NFP should disclose the following information for each period for which a statement of financial position is presented:

a. The identity of the recipient entity to which the transfer was made

b. Whether variance power was granted to the recipient entity and, if so, a description of the terms of the variance power

c. The terms under which amounts will be distributed to the resource provider or its affiliate

d. The aggregate amount recognized in the statement of financial position for those transfers and whether that amount is recorded as an interest in the net assets of the recipient entity or as another asset (for example, as a beneficial interest in assets held by others or a refundable advance)

[‡] On May 26, 2010, FASB issued a proposed ASU, *Accounting for Financial Instruments and Revisions to the Accounting for Derivative Instruments and Hedging Activities*, intended to improve accounting for financial instruments. Among other changes, the proposed ASU reconsiders the recognition and measurement of financial instruments, addresses issues related to impairment of financial instruments, simplifies hedge accounting, and increases convergence in accounting for financial instruments with IFRSs. It would incorporate both amortized cost and fair value information about financial instruments held for collection or payment of cash flows. On January 31, 2011, FASB and the IASB jointly issued a supplementary document, *Accounting for Financial Instruments and Revisions to the Accounting for Derivative Instruments and Hedging Activities: Impairment*, to address a number of questions that arose from the comments received on the proposed ASU. Readers should be alert for the issuance of a final ASU.

Illustrative Disclosures

5.134 The following section provides examples of notes to financial statements that illustrate some of the disclosures discussed in this chapter.

Example 1—Donor-Imposed Restrictions

Note X: Summary of Significant Accounting Policies

All contributions are considered to be available for unrestricted use unless specifically restricted by the donor. Amounts received that are designated for future periods or restricted by the donor for specific purposes are reported as temporarily restricted or permanently restricted support that increases those net asset classes. However, if a restriction is fulfilled in the same time period in which the contribution is received, the organization reports the support as unrestricted.

Example 2—Promises to Give

Note X: Summary of Significant Accounting Policies

Unconditional promises to give that are expected to be collected within one year are recorded at net realizable value. Unconditional promises to give that are expected to be collected in future years are recorded at fair value, which is measured as the present value of their future cash flows. The discounts on those amounts are computed using risk-adjusted interest rates applicable to the years in which the promises are received. Amortization of the discounts is included in contribution revenue. Conditional promises to give are not included as support until the conditions are substantially met.

Note Y: Promises to Give

Included in "Contributions Receivable" are the following unconditional promises to give:

	20X1	*20X0*
Capital campaign	$1,220	
Restricted to future periods	795	$530
Unconditional promises to give before unamortized discount and allowance for uncollectibles	2,015	530
Less: Unamortized discount	(180)	(24)
Subtotal	1,835	506
Less: Allowance for uncollectibles	(150)	(30)
Net unconditional promises to give	$1,685	$476
Amounts due in:		
Less than one year	$1,220	
One to five years	725	
More than five years	70	
Total	$2,015	

Discount rates ranged from 4 percent to 4.5 percent and from 3.5 percent to 4 percent for 20X1 and 20X0, respectively.

In 20X0, the organization received $650 for a capital campaign which must be returned if the organization does not receive $1,300 in donations to the capital campaign. The $650 received was recorded on the 20X0 statement of financial position as a refundable advance. In 20X1, the organization received $500 in cash donations and $865 in unconditional promises to give to this campaign.

As a result, the $650 was recognized as temporarily restricted contributions in 20X1.

In addition, the organization received the following conditional promises to give that are not recognized as assets in the statements of financial position:

	20X1	*20X0*
Conditional promise to give upon the establishment of a library program	$100	$100
Conditional promise to give upon obtaining $2,500 in unconditional promises to give to the capital campaign	5,000	

[*The following disclosure is encouraged but not required.*]

The organization received an indication of an intention to give from an individual long-time donor. The anticipated gift is an extensive collection of pre-Columbian textiles with great historical and artistic significance. The value of this intended gift has not been established, nor has the gift been recognized as an asset or contribution revenue.

Example 3—Accounting Policy for Contributed Property and Equipment

Note X: Summary of Significant Accounting Policies

Contributed property and equipment is recorded at fair value at the date of donation. In the absence of donor stipulations regarding how long the contributed assets must be used, the organization has adopted a policy of implying a time restriction on contributions of such assets that expires over the assets' useful lives. As a result, all contributions of property and equipment, and of assets contributed to acquire property and equipment, are recorded as restricted support.

OR

Contributed property and equipment is recorded at fair value at the date of donation. If donors stipulate how long the assets must be used, the contributions are recorded as restricted support. In the absence of such stipulations, contributions of property and equipment are recorded as unrestricted support.

Example 4—Contributed Services

The organization recognizes contribution revenue for certain services received at the fair value of those services. Those services include the following items:

	20X1	*20X0*
Home outreach program:		
Salaries:		
Social work interns—261 and 315 hours at $12.00 per hour	$3,132	$3,780
Registered nurse—200 and 220 hours at $15.00 per hour	3,000	3,300
Total salaries	6,132	7,080
Management and general:		
Accounting services	10,000	19,000
Total contributed services	$16,132	$26,080

In addition, approximately 80,000 hours, for which no value has been assigned, were volunteered by tutors in the home outreach program.

Example 5—Beneficial Interest in Assets Held by Others

In 19XX, the organization transferred $1,000,000 from its investment portfolio to the Any Town Community Foundation to establish an endowment fund. Under the terms of the agreement, in the first quarter of each year, the organization receives a distribution equal to the investment return generated by the transferred assets during the prior year. The organization can withdraw all or a portion of the original amount transferred, any appreciation on those transferred assets, or both, provided that a majority of the governing boards of the organization and the Foundation approve of the withdrawal. At the time of the transfer, the organization granted variance power to the Foundation. That power gives the Foundation the right to distribute the investment income to another not-for-profit organization of its choice if the organization ceases to exist or if the governing board of Any Town Community Foundation votes that support of the organization (*a*) is no longer necessary or (*b*) is inconsistent with the needs of the Any Town community. At June 30, 20X1, the endowment fund has a value of $1,234,567, which is reported in the statement of financial position as beneficial interest in assets held by others.

Auditing

5.135 Because for-profit entities do not usually receive contributions or enter into agency transactions, the specific audit objectives, selected controls, and auditing procedures related to contributions, contributions receivable, and agency transactions are unique to NFPs and are presented in the following paragraphs.

5.136 An NFP that receives a significant amount of contributions may have an increased risk of material misstatement if it does not have proper internal controls in place. Paragraph .54 of AU section 314, *Understanding the Entity and Its Environment and Assessing the Risks of Material Misstatement* (AICPA, *Professional Standards*), states that obtaining an understanding of internal control involves evaluating the design of a control and determining whether it has been implemented. Evaluating the design of a control involves considering whether the control, individually or in combination with other controls, is capable of effectively preventing or detecting and correcting material misstatements. Implementation of a control means that the control exists and that the entity is using it. An improperly designed control may represent a significant deficiency or a material weakness in the entity's internal control and the auditor should consider whether to communicate this to those charged with governance and management.

5.137 In order to have an effective system of internal control, an NFP that receives significant amounts of contributions should have an internal control system that provides effective controls to ensure that all contributions received are recorded and that suitable collection efforts are pursued for unconditional promises to give. The internal control system also should provide effective controls to ensure that revenues arising from conditional promises to give are recognized when the conditions have been substantially met and that restrictions on contributions are recognized in the appropriate net asset class.

5.138 Contributions received are measured at fair value. AU section 328, *Auditing Fair Value Measurements and Disclosures* (AICPA, *Professional*

Standards), addresses audit considerations relating to the measurement and disclosure of assets, liabilities and specific components of equity presented or disclosed at fair value in financial statements. Interpretation No. 1, "Auditing Interests in Trusts Held by a Third-Party Trustee and Reported at Fair Value," of AU section 328 (AICPA, *Professional Standards*, AU sec. 9328 par. .01–.04), provides guidance for auditing interests in trusts held by a third-party trustee. That interpretation is discussed further in paragraph 6.62.

5.139 Paragraph .34 of AU section 330, *The Confirmation Process* (AICPA, *Professional Standards*), states that "confirmation of accounts receivable is a generally accepted auditing procedure," and that there is a presumption that the auditor will request the confirmation of accounts receivable except under certain specified circumstances. That paragraph defines *accounts receivable* as "(*a*) the entity's claims against customers that have arisen from the sale of goods or services in the normal course of business, and (*b*) a financial institution's loans." Though under that definition contributions receivable are not accounts receivable to which that presumption would apply, the auditor may nevertheless decide to request confirmation of contributions receivable.

5.140 Receivables are usually confirmed principally to provide evidence about the existence assertion. FASB ASC 958-605-25-8 specifies that for a promise to give to be recognized in financial statements, there must be sufficient evidence in the form of verifiable documentation that a promise was made and received. If the documentation is not present, an asset should not be recognized. The verifiable documentation for recognition of promises to give may not be sufficient evidence concerning the existence assertion. Confirming recorded promises to give (contributions receivable) may provide additional evidence about the existence of promises to give, the existence or absence of restrictions, the existence or absence of conditions, and the periods over which the promises to give become due. If the auditor confirms promises to give, AU section 330 provides requirements and guidance concerning the confirmation process.

5.141 The following table illustrates the use of assertions in developing audit objectives and designing substantive tests. The examples are not intended to be all-inclusive nor is it expected that all the procedures would necessarily be applied in an audit. The auditor should design and perform substantive procedures for all relevant assertions related to each material class of transactions, account balance, and disclosure to obtain sufficient appropriate audit evidence. The use of assertions in assessing risks and designing appropriate audit procedures to obtain audit evidence is described in paragraphs .14–.26 of AU section 326, *Audit Evidence* (AICPA, *Professional Standards*). Various audit procedures and the purposes for which they may be performed are described in paragraphs .27–.41 of AU section 326.

Auditing Considerations

Financial Statement Assertions	*Specific Audit Objectives*	*Examples of Selected Controls*	*Examples of Auditing Procedures*
Transactions			
Contributions			
Occurrence	Amounts recognized as contribution revenues represent valid unconditional contributions.	Controls ensure that only unconditional contributions are recognized in the financial statements.	Examine documentation supporting recognition of contribution revenues noting information such as absence of conditions.
Completeness	All unconditional contributions are recognized.	Controls ensure that all unconditional contributions are recognized in the financial statements. Controls ensure that revenue is recognized when the conditions on conditional promises to give have been substantially met.	Select from data accumulated and maintained by the fund-raising function, determine whether a contribution should have been recognized and, if so, vouch it to a recognized contribution, investigating reconciling items.
Valuation and Allocation	Contribution revenues are appropriately valued.	Controls ensure the appropriate valuation of contribution revenue at the time of initial recognition.	Review and test the methods and assumptions used to measure contribution revenue at the time of initial recognition.
Cut-off	Contributions are reported in the period in which they were given.	Controls ensure that contributions occurring near fiscal period end are recorded in the proper period.	Examine contributions reported before and after fiscal period end to determine if they are reported in the appropriate period.

(continued)

Auditing Considerations—continued

Financial Statement Assertions	*Specific Audit Objectives*	*Examples of Selected Controls*	*Examples of Auditing Procedures*
Transactions—continued			
Contributed Services, Utilities, Facilities, and Use of Long-Lived Assets			
Occurrence completeness; valuation and allocation	Assets, expenses, and revenues from contributed services, utilities, facilities, and use of long-lived assets meet the appropriate recognition criteria; all such contributions that meet the recognition criteria are recognized and appropriately measured.	Controls ensure that only contributed services, utilities, facilities, and use of long-lived assets that meet the appropriate recognition criteria are recognized; controls ensure that all such contributions that meet the recognition criteria are recognized and appropriately measured.	Review the documentation underlying recognition of contributed services, utilities, facilities, and use of long-lived assets for completeness and propriety of amounts recognized.
Account Balances			
Contributions Receivable			
Occurrence	Amounts recognized as contributions receivable represent valid unconditional promises to give.	Controls ensure that only unconditional promises to give are recognized in the financial statements.	Examine documentation supporting recognition of promises to give, noting information such as absence of conditions and the periods over which the promises to give become due.
Completeness	All unconditional promises to give are recognized.	Controls ensure that all unconditional promises to give are recognized in the financial statements. Controls ensure that conditional promises to give are recognized when the conditions have been substantially met.	Compare detail of contributions receivable with data accumulated and maintained by the fund-raising function and investigate reconciling items.

Auditing Considerations—continued

Financial Statement Assertions	*Specific Audit Objectives*	*Examples of Selected Controls*	*Examples of Auditing Procedures*
Account Balances—continued			
Valuation and Allocation	Contributions receivable are appropriately valued.	Controls ensure the appropriate valuation of promises to give at the time of initial recognition.	Review and test the methods and assumptions used to measure promises to give at the time of initial recognition.
		The valuation of promises to give is periodically reviewed by management.	Review promises to give for collectibility, and, if appropriate, changes in fair value of the underlying asset.
		Writeoffs of uncollectible promises to give are identified and approved in accordance with the entity's established policy.	
Agency Transactions			
Occurrence and Completeness	Assets and liabilities from agency transactions meet the criteria for classification and recognition as agency transactions.	Controls ensure that (1) only resources received and paid in agency transactions are recognized as agency transactions and (2) all such transactions are recognized.	Review the documentation underlying the receipt of assets from resource providers for propriety of classification and recognition as resources that are to be transferred to others.
	All agency transactions are recognized.		Review the documentation underlying the distribution of assets to others for propriety of classification and recognition.
			Review the historical patterns of the distribution

(continued)

Auditing Considerations—continued

Financial Statement Assertions	*Specific Audit Objectives*	*Examples of Selected Controls*	*Examples of Auditing Procedures*
Account Balances—continued			
			of gifts in kind and other assets to determine the extent of the not-for-profit entity's discretion over those distributions.
Presentation and Disclosures			
Contribution Revenues and Contributions Receivable			
Classification and under-standability	Restricted contributions are reported in the proper net asset class.	Contributions are reviewed for restrictions and other limitations.	Review the documentation underlying contributions and promises to give (including donor correspondence and governing board minutes) for propriety of classification.
	Disclosures related to contributions are clear and understandable.	Controls ensure that contributions are appropriately presented and disclosed.	Determine the appropriateness of disclosures for conditional and unconditional promises to give.
Agency Transactions			
Rights and obligations	Agency transactions are not included in reported amounts of contributions.	Controls ensure that agency transactions are identified and are not included in contribution totals.	Determine whether agency transactions are excluded from the statement of activities. If they are not, determine that agency transactions are reported as described in the "Transfers of Assets to a Not-for-Profit Entity or Charitable Trust that Raises or Holds Contributions for Others" subsections of Financial Accounting Standards Board *Accounting Standards Codification* 958-605.

Chapter 6

Split-Interest Agreements

Introduction

6.01 Some donors enter into trust or other arrangements under which not-for-profit entities (NFPs) receive benefits that are shared with other beneficiaries. Recognition and measurement principles for these arrangements, commonly known as *split-interest agreements*, are discussed in Financial Accounting Standards Board (FASB) *Accounting Standards Codification* (ASC) 958-30 and this chapter. The application of these principles to five widely used types of such agreements—charitable lead trusts, perpetual trusts held by third parties,[1] charitable remainder trusts, charitable gift annuities, and pooled (life) income funds—is also illustrated.

Types of Split-Interest Agreements

6.02 Under a *split-interest agreement*, a donor makes an initial gift to a trust, a fiscal agent, or directly to the NFP in which the NFP has a beneficial interest but is not the sole beneficiary. The terms of some agreements do not allow donors to revoke their gifts; other agreements may be revocable by donors in certain situations. Still others may be irrevocable by the donor, but the NFP's rights to distributions are revocable because the agreement allows the donor to change the beneficiaries. The time period covered by the agreement is expressed either as a specific number of years (or in perpetuity) or as the remaining life of an individual or individuals designated by the donor. The assets are invested and administered by the NFP, a trustee, or a fiscal agent, and distributions are made to a beneficiary or beneficiaries during the term of the agreement. At the end of the agreement's term, the remaining assets covered by the agreement are distributed to or retained by either the NFP or another beneficiary or beneficiaries.

6.03 Under some kinds of agreements, referred to in this guide as *lead interests*, the NFP receives the distributions during the agreement's term. In other kinds of agreements, referred to as *remainder interests*, the donor (or other individuals or entities designated by the donor) receives those distributions and the NFP receives all or a portion of the assets remaining at the end of the agreement's term. Under either kind of agreement, donors may impose restrictions on the NFP's use of all or a portion of any assets received.

Recognition and Measurement Principles

6.04 In accordance with FASB ASC 958-30-45-7, the contribution portion of a split-interest agreement (that is, the part that represents the unconditional transfer of assets in a voluntary nonreciprocal transaction) should be recognized as revenue or gain. (As discussed in the FASB ASC glossary definition of

[1] Though perpetual trusts held by third parties may not meet the definition of a split-interest agreement because the not-for-profit entity (NFP) may be the sole beneficiary, they are included in this chapter because they present some of the same accounting issues as do split-interest agreements.

contribution, the term *contribution revenue* in the FASB ASC is used to apply to transactions that are part of the entity's ongoing major or central activities [revenues], or are peripheral or incidental to the entity [gains]. This guide also uses that convention.) In accordance with FASB ASC 958-605-30-2, a contribution should be measured at its fair value.

6.05 Recognition of split-interest agreements also requires assets and liabilities to be initially measured at fair value, and in certain cases requires them to be remeasured at fair value subsequently. FASB ASC 820, *Fair Value Measurements and Disclosures*, establishes a framework for measuring fair value.[*] This guide uses present value techniques as one possible technique to measure the contribution revenue and obligation to other beneficiaries of a split-interest agreement. See paragraphs 4–20 of FASB ASC 820-10-55 for implementation guidance for using present value techniques if the measurement objective is fair value. Other valuation techniques are also available, as described in FASB ASC 820-10-35.

6.06 Reference to IRS guidelines and actuarial tables used in calculating the donor's charitable deduction for income tax purposes may be helpful in assessing the reasonableness of the method used for measuring fair value. Some split-interest agreements include promises to give noncash assets, such as homes. Paragraph 5.112 of this guide includes guidance concerning determining the fair value of unconditional promises to give noncash assets.

Recognition of Revocable Agreements

6.07 FASB ASC 958-30-25-2, FASB ASC 958-30-30-3, and paragraphs 11–12 of FASB ASC 958-30-35 discuss recognition and measurement of revocable split interest agreements. Revocable split-interest agreements should be accounted for as intentions to give. Assets received by an NFP acting as a trustee under a revocable split-interest agreement should be recognized at fair value when received as assets and as a refundable advance. If those assets are investments, they should be recognized in conformity with FASB ASC 958-320 or 958-325 as appropriate. Contribution revenue for the assets received should be recognized when the agreements become irrevocable or when the assets are distributed to the NFP for its unconditional use, whichever occurs first. Income earned on assets held under revocable agreements that is not available for the NFP's unconditional use, and any subsequent adjustments to the carrying value of those assets, should be recognized as adjustments to the assets and as refundable advances.

---

[*] On June 29, 2010, the Financial Accounting Standards Board (FASB) issued a proposed Accounting Standards Update (ASU), *Amendments for Common Fair Value Measurement and Disclosure Requirements in U.S. GAAP and IFRSs*, intended to develop common requirements for measuring fair value and for disclosing information about fair value measurements in U.S. generally accepted accounting principles and International Financial Reporting Standards. For many of the proposed requirements, FASB does not expect the amendments to result in changes in the application of FASB *Accounting Standards Codification* (ASC) 820, *Fair Value Measures and Disclosures*. Other amendments would change a particular principle or requirement. The most notable of these changes are: highest and best use and valuation premise, measuring the fair value of an instrument classified in shareholders' equity, measuring the fair value of instruments that are managed within a portfolio, and application of blockage factors and other premiums and discounts in a fair value measurement. The proposed standards also include additional disclosure requirements. Readers should be alert to the issuance of a final ASU.

Initial Recognition and Measurement of Unconditional Irrevocable Agreements Other Than Pooled Income Funds or Net Income Unitrusts

NFP Is the Trustee or Fiscal Agent

6.08 Paragraphs 4–14 of FASB ASC 958-30-25 discuss recognition of unconditional irrevocable agreements for which the NFP serves as trustee or if the assets contributed by the donor are otherwise under the control of the NFP. Per FASB ASC 958-30-25-4, in the absence of donor-imposed conditions, an NFP should recognize contribution revenue and related assets and liabilities when an irrevocable split-interest agreement naming it trustee or fiscal agent is executed. Assets received under those agreements should be recorded when received. If those assets are investments, they should be recognized in conformity with the guidance in FASB ASC 958-320 or FASB ASC 958-325, as appropriate. The contribution portion of an agreement (that is, the part that represents the unconditional transfer of assets in a voluntary nonreciprocal transaction) should be recognized as revenue or gain.

6.09 Per paragraphs 4–6 of FASB ASC 958-30-30, at the date of initial recognition of a split-interest agreement, contributions should be measured at fair value. The cash and other assets received under split-interest agreements should be recognized at fair value at the date of initial recognition. If the transferred assets, or a portion of those assets, are being held for the benefit of others, such as the donor or third parties designated by the donor, a liability, measured at fair value, should also be recognized at the date of initial recognition. If present value techniques are used to measure fair value, the liability generally is measured at the present value of the future payments to be made to the other beneficiaries. Present value techniques are one valuation technique for measuring fair value; other valuation techniques are also available, as described in FASB ASC 820-10-35.[2, *] Any present value technique for measuring the fair value of the contribution or payments to be made to other beneficiaries must consider the elements described in FASB ASC 820-10-55-5, including (*a*) the estimated return on the invested assets during the expected term of the agreement, (*b*) the contractual payment obligations under the agreement, and (*c*) a discount rate commensurate with the risks involved.

6.10 Per FASB ASC 958-30-30-7, under a lead interest agreement, the fair value of the contribution can be estimated directly based on the present value of the future distributions to be received by the NFP as a beneficiary. Under lead interest agreements, the future payments to be made to other beneficiaries will be made by the NFP only after the NFP receives its benefits. In those situations, the present value of the future payments to be made to other beneficiaries may

---

[2] Chapter 3, "Basic Financial Statements and General Financial Reporting Matters," of this guide discuss FASB ASC 820, which defines *fair value*, establishes a framework for measuring fair value and expands disclosures about fair value measurements. Some of the guidance in FASB ASC 820 is labeled as "Pending Content" due to the transition and open effective date information discussed in FASB ASC 820-10-65. For example, ASU No. 2010-06, *Fair Value Measurements and Disclosures (Topic 820): Improving Disclosures about Fair Value Measurements*, is effective for interim and annual reporting periods beginning after December 15, 2009, except for the separate disclosures about purchases, sales, issuances, and settlements relating to level 3 measurements (see FASB ASC 820-10-50-2(c)(2)), which shall be effective for fiscal years beginning after December 15, 2010, and for interim periods within those fiscal years. Early adoption is permitted.

[*] See footnote * in paragraph 6.05.

be estimated by the fair value of the assets contributed by the donor under the agreement less the fair value of the benefits to be received by the NFP. If present value techniques are used, the fair value of the benefits to be received by the NFP should be measured at the present value of the benefits to be received over the expected term of the agreement.

6.11 Per FASB ASC 958-30-30-8, under remainder interest agreements, the present value of the future payments to be made to other beneficiaries can be estimated directly based on the terms of the agreement. Future distributions will be received by the NFP only after obligations to other beneficiaries are satisfied. In those cases, the fair value of the contribution may be estimated based on the fair value of the assets contributed by the donor less the fair value of the payments to be made to other beneficiaries.

6.12 Per FASB ASC 958-30-45-1, contribution revenues recognized under split-interest agreements should be classified as increases in temporarily restricted net assets unless either of the following conditions exist:

a. The donor has permanently restricted the NFP's use of its interest (lead or remainder) in the assets. If the donor has permanently restricted the NFP's use of its interest, the contribution should be classified as an increase in permanently restricted net assets.

b. The donor gives the NFP the immediate right to use without restrictions the assets it receives. If the NFP has the immediate right to use its interest without restrictions, the contribution should be classified as increases in unrestricted net assets.

6.13 As discussed in FASB ASC 958-30-45-2, under many charitable gift annuity agreements, the assets received from the donor are held by the NFP as part of its general assets and are available for its unrestricted use. The contribution portion of a charitable gift annuity agreement should be recognized as unrestricted support if both (*a*) the donor does not restrict the use of the assets contributed to the NFP and (*b*) neither the agreement nor state law requires the assets received by the NFP to be invested until the income beneficiary's death. If either of those criteria are met, the contribution should be classified as restricted and should be reclassified when temporary restrictions or legal requirements are satisfied.

Unrelated Third Party Is the Trustee or Fiscal Agent

6.14 Paragraphs 16–19 of FASB ASC 958-30-25 and FASB ASC 958-30-30-11 discuss recognition and initial measurement of irrevocable split interest agreements for which a third party maintains control of the donor's contributed assets. In a split-interest agreement in which cash or other assets contributed by a donor are held by an independent trustee (such as a charitable trust for which a bank, trust company, foundation, or private individual is the trustee) or by another fiscal agent of the donor or the cash or other assets are otherwise not controlled by the NFP, the NFP should recognize its beneficial interest in those assets. The contribution should be recognized when the NFP is notified of the agreement's existence. Contribution revenues recognized should be classified in accordance with FASB ASC 958-30-45-1, which is reproduced in paragraph 6.12. If, however, the trustee or fiscal agent has variance power to redirect the benefits to another entity or if the NFP's rights to the benefits are conditional, the NFP should not recognize its potential for future distributions from the split-interest agreement until the NFP has an unconditional right to receive benefits under the agreement. (See FASB ASC 958-605-25-31.)

6.15 Pursuant to FASB ASC 958-605-30-14, if an NFP is the beneficiary of a split-interest agreement held by a trustee or fiscal agent and has an unconditional right to receive all or a portion of the specified cash flows from the assets held pursuant to that agreement, the NFP should measure its beneficial interest at fair value.

6.16 Present value techniques are one valuation technique for measuring the fair value of the contribution and the beneficial interest; other valuation techniques are also available, as described in FASB ASC 820-10-35.[3] If present value techniques are used, the contribution revenue and the beneficial interest in the trust should be measured at the present value of the future distributions expected to be received over the term of the agreement.

6.17 As noted in paragraph 5.09, FASB ASC 958-605-25 establishes standards for a beneficiary's reporting of assets held in trust, but does not establish standards for a trustee's reporting of those assets. Paragraphs 5.30–.35 of this guide discuss the requirements for transactions in which a perpetual trust held by a third party (trustee or other recipient entity) is established by an NFP for its own benefit or for the benefit of its affiliate. Paragraphs 6.43–.46 provide an example of a perpetual trust held by a third party.

Initial Recognition and Measurement of Pooled Income Funds and Net Income Unitrusts

6.18 Per FASB ASC 958-30-25-15 and FASB ASC 958-30-30-10, the assets received from the donor under a pooled income fund agreement or a net income unitrust should be recognized when received and measured at fair value. An NFP should recognize its remainder interest in the assets received as contribution revenue in the period in which the assets are received from the donor. The contribution should be measured at fair value. Present value techniques are one valuation technique for measuring the fair value of the contribution; other valuation techniques are also available, as described in FASB ASC 820-10-35. If present value techniques are used, the contribution may be measured at the fair value of the assets to be received, discounted for the estimated time period until the donor's death. The contributed assets should be recognized at fair value. The difference between the fair value of the assets when received and the revenue recognized should be recorded as deferred revenue, representing the amount of the discount for future interest. Contribution revenues recognized under a pooled income fund agreement or a net income unitrust should be classified in accordance with FASB ASC 958-30-45-1, which is reproduced in paragraph 6.12.

Recognition and Measurement During the Agreement's Term for Unconditional Irrevocable Agreements Other Than Pooled Income Funds or Net Income Unitrusts

6.19 Per FASB ASC 958-30-35-6 and 958-30-45-3, during the term of the agreement, certain transactions and events should be recognized as changes in the value of split-interest agreements in a statement of activities and should be classified as temporarily restricted, permanently restricted, or unrestricted net assets, depending on the classification used when the contribution revenue was recognized initially.

---

[3] See footnote 2.

6.20 Pursuant to FASB ASC 958-30-45-4, amounts should be reclassified from temporarily restricted net assets to unrestricted net assets as distributions are received by NFPs under the terms of split-interest agreements, unless those assets are otherwise temporarily restricted by the donor. In that case, they should be reclassified to unrestricted net assets when the restrictions expire.

Unrelated Third Party Is the Trustee or Fiscal Agent

6.21 Pursuant to FASB ASC 958-30-35-2, in circumstances in which cash or other assets contributed by donors under split-interest agreements are held by independent trustees, such as a charitable trust for which a bank is a trustee, or by other fiscal agents of the donors or otherwise not controlled by the NFP, the measurement objective for the beneficial interest for periods subsequent to the period of initial recognition is fair value. Per FASB ASC 958-30-35-10, the change in the value of split-interest agreements should be the change in the fair value of the NFP's beneficial interest, which should be determined using the same valuation technique that was used to measure the asset initially. In accordance with FASB ASC 958-30-35-3, in circumstances in which the fair value is measured at the present value of the future cash flows, all elements discussed in FASB ASC 820-10-55-5, including discount rate assumptions, should be revised at each measurement date to reflect current market conditions. Distributions from the trust should be reflected as a reduction in the beneficial interest. As discussed in FASB ASC 958-30-45-4, as distributions are received by the NFP under the terms of the split-interest agreement, amounts should be reclassified from temporarily restricted net assets to unrestricted net assets unless those assets are otherwise temporarily restricted by the donor. In that case, they shall be reclassified to unrestricted net assets when the restrictions expire.

NFP Is the Trustee or Fiscal Agent

6.22 FASB ASC 958-30-35-4 states that assets held by the NFP under irrevocable split-interest agreements as investments should be subsequently measured in conformity with FASB ASC 958-320-35 or FASB ASC 958-325-35.

6.23 Paragraphs 5–8 of FASB ASC 958-30-35 discuss the recognition of transactions and events during the term of a split-interest agreement in circumstances in which assets and related liabilities are recognized under lead and remainder interest agreements for which an NFP serves as a trustee or fiscal agent. Pursuant to FASB ASC 958-30-35-6, if the NFP does not elect to measure the liability at the fair value as described in the next paragraph, the following adjustments to the liability should be recognized as changes in the value of split-interest agreements in a statement of activities: (*a*) amortization of the discount associated with the contribution and (*b*) revaluations of future payments to beneficiaries, based on changes in life expectancy, and other actuarial assumptions. In conformity with FASB ASC 310-10-30-6 and FASB ASC 958-30-35-6, the discount rate should not be revised after initial recognition, unless the measurement objective for periods subsequent to the period of initial recognition is fair value.

6.24 As discussed in FASB ASC 958-30-35-2, the measurement objective is fair value for the following split interest obligations: (*a*) embedded derivatives subject to the measurement provisions of FASB ASC 815-15, as discussed in paragraph 6.26 of this guide, (*b*) obligations for which the NFP elects the fair value option pursuant to the "Fair Value Option" subsections of FASB ASC

825-10, as discussed in paragraphs 6.27–.28 of this guide, and (*c*) obligations containing embedded derivatives that the NFP has irrevocably elected to measure in their entirety at fair value in conformity with FASB ASC 815-15-25 as discussed in paragraphs 6.27–.28 of this guide.

6.25 As discussed in paragraphs 7–14 of FASB ASC 958-30-25, the obligation for certain split-interest agreements contains embedded derivatives. Example 2 (paragraphs 6–29) of FASB ASC 958-30-55 provides illustrations for determining whether a split-interest agreement has an embedded derivative. The following paragraph summarizes the subsequent measurement guidance for embedded derivatives, but is not intended as a substitute for the reading of paragraphs 7–8 of FASB ASC 958-30-35 or FASB ASC 815-15.

6.26 If an NFP does not elect to report a split-interest obligation at fair value, a split-interest obligation with an embedded derivative (for example, the liability for remainder unitrusts with either period-certain payments or period-certain-plus-life-contingent payments and certain lead interest trusts) is bifurcated into a debt host contract and an embedded derivative that is measured at fair value. (Paragraph 6.24 of this guide discusses alternative treatments for reporting split-interest agreements that contain embedded derivatives.) The debt host contract is the liability for the payment to the beneficiary that would be required if the fair value of the trust assets does not change over the specified period. The embedded derivative represents the liability (or contra-liability) for the increase (or decrease) in the payments to the beneficiary due to changes in the fair value of the trust assets over the specified period. Thus, in circumstances in which the liability is measured using present value techniques, the discount rate assumptions on the debt host contract should not be revised subsequent to initial recognition, consistent with paragraphs 5.113 and 6.23 of this guide. In accordance with FASB ASC 815-10-35-1, the embedded derivative is subsequently measured at fair value. If the fair value of the embedded derivative is measured using present value techniques, all elements discussed in FASB ASC 820-10-55-5, including the discount rate assumptions on the embedded derivative should be revised at each measurement date to reflect current market conditions. In conformity with FASB ASC 815-15-25-53, if an NFP cannot reliably identify and measure the embedded derivative, the entire split-interest liability should be measured at fair value (that is, all elements discussed in FASB ASC 820-10-55-5, including discount rate assumptions, should be revised to reflect current market conditions).

6.27 If the NFP elects the fair value option pursuant to FASB ASC 958-30-35-6 in circumstances in which assets and related liabilities are recognized under lead and remainder interest agreements for which an NFP serves as a trustee or fiscal agent, the liability for future payments to be made to other beneficiaries is measured at fair value. The following paragraph summarizes the guidance for making the election and subsequently measuring at fair value, but is not intended as a substitute for the reading of FASB ASC 815-15 or the "Fair Value Option" subsections of FASB ASC 825-10.

6.28 The election may be made on an instrument-by-instrument basis, and should be supported by concurrent documentation or a preexisting documented policy for automatic election. If an NFP elects to measure the obligation for future payments to be made to other beneficiaries at fair value, the entire liability should be remeasured at fair value (that is, if the fair value is measured using a present value technique, all the elements discussed in FASB ASC 820-10-55-5, including the discount rate assumptions for the entire obligation should be revised at each measurement date to reflect current market conditions).[4]

6.29 Per FASB ASC 958-30-35-5, when assets and related liabilities are recognized under charitable gift annuity, charitable lead trust, or charitable remainder trust agreements for which an NFP serves as a trustee or fiscal agent, income earned on those assets, gains and losses, and distributions made to other beneficiaries under the agreements should be reported in the NFP's statements of financial position, activities, and cash flows.

Recognition and Measurement During the Agreement's Term for Pooled Income Funds and Net Income Unitrusts

6.30 FASB ASC 958-30-35-4 states that assets held by the NFP under irrevocable split-interest agreements as investments should be subsequently measured in conformity with FASB ASC 958-320-35 or FASB ASC 958-325-35. Per FASB ASC 958-30-35-9, periodic income on a pooled income fund or net income unitrust and payments to the donor should be reflected as increases and decreases in a liability to the donor. Amortization of the discount should be recognized as a reduction in the deferred revenue account and as a change in the value of split-interest agreements. Pursuant to FASB ASC 958-30-45-3, changes in the value of split-interest agreements should be classified as temporarily restricted, permanently restricted, or unrestricted net assets, depending on the classification used when the contribution revenue was recognized initially.

Recognition Upon Termination of Agreement

6.31 Pursuant to FASB ASC 958-30-40-1, upon termination of a split-interest agreement, asset and liability accounts related to the agreement should be closed. Any remaining amounts in the asset or liability accounts should be recognized as changes in the value of split-interest agreements. The changes should be classified as changes in permanently restricted, temporarily restricted, or unrestricted net assets, pursuant to FASB ASC 958-30-45-3, as appropriate. Per FASB ASC 958-30-45-5, if assets previously distributed to the NFP become available for its unrestricted use upon termination of the agreement, appropriate amounts should be reclassified from temporarily restricted to unrestricted net assets.

Financial Statement Presentation

6.32 As discussed in footnote 1 to chapter 5, "Contributions Received and Agency Transactions," of this guide, contributions may be reported as revenues or gains, depending on whether they are part of the NFP's ongoing major activities or are peripheral or incidental transactions. For purposes of this chapter, the term contribution revenue is used to apply to either situation.

6.33 The majority of the unique disclosures for split interest agreements are located in FASB ASC 958-30-50. The following three paragraphs discuss the more common of those disclosures, but are not intended as a substitute for the "Disclosure" sections of the FASB ASC.

6.34 The notes to the financial statements should include all of the following disclosures related to split-interest agreements:

---

[4] Chapter 3 of this guide provides additional information about FASB ASC 815-15 or the "Fair Value Option" subsections of FASB ASC 825-10.

- A description of the general terms of existing split-interest agreements
- Assets and liabilities recognized under split-interest agreements, if not reported separately from other assets and liabilities in a statement of financial position
- The basis used (for example, cost, lower of cost or market, fair market value) for recognized assets
- The discount rates and actuarial assumptions used, if present values techniques are used in reporting the assets and liabilities related to split-interest agreements
- Contribution revenue recognized under such agreements, if not reported as a separate line item in a statement of activities
- Changes in the value of split-interest agreements recognized, if not reported as a separate line item in a statement of activities
- The disclosures required by the "Fair Value Option" subsections of FASB ASC 825-10, if an NFP elects the fair value option pursuant to FASB ASC 958-30-35-2(b) or 958-30-35-2(c)
- The disclosures required by paragraphs 1–2 of FASB ASC 820-10-50 in the format described in FASB ASC 820-10-50-8, if the assets and liabilities of split-interest agreements are measured at fair value on a recurring basis in periods subsequent to initial recognition

6.35 Additional annuity reserves may be required by the laws of the state where the NFP is located or by the state where the donor resides. Legally mandated reserves should be disclosed in the notes to financial statements. If state law imposes other limitations on the NFP, such as limitations on the manner in which some net assets are invested, those limitations also should be disclosed in the notes to financial statements.

6.36 In addition, some NFPs voluntarily set aside additional reserves as a cushion against unexpected actuarial losses. Voluntary reserves should be included as part of unrestricted net assets, but may be disclosed as a separate component, such as board-designated unrestricted net assets (see FASB ASC 958-210-55-3).

Examples of Split-Interest Agreements

6.37 Many kinds of split-interest agreements have been developed. The examples in this section demonstrate how the recognition and measurement principles discussed in this chapter apply to some common kinds of agreements. Appendix A (paragraph 6.64) to this chapter provides journal entries related to these examples.

Charitable Lead Trust

6.38 A charitable lead trust is an arrangement in which a donor establishes and funds a trust with specific distributions to be made to a designated NFP over a specified period. The NFP's use of the assets distributed may be restricted by the donor. The distributions may be for a fixed dollar amount, an arrangement called a charitable lead annuity trust, or for a fixed percentage of the trust's fair market value as determined annually, a charitable lead unitrust. Upon termination of the trust, the remainder of the trust assets is paid to the donor or to the beneficiaries designated by the donor.

6.39 For example, NFP A receives cash from a donor under an irrevocable charitable lead annuity trust agreement designating NFP A as trustee and lead beneficiary. Under the terms of the trust, NFP A will invest the assets and receive a specified dollar amount each year for its unrestricted use until the death of the donor. At that time, the remaining assets in the trust revert to the donor's estate.

6.40 Contribution revenue, assets held in trust, and a liability for amounts held for others should be recognized by NFP A in the period in which the trust is established. Revenue should be reported as temporarily restricted support and measured at fair value. The present value of the specified dollar amount to be received annually over the expected life of the donor is one possible technique to measure the fair value of the contribution; other valuation techniques are also available (as described in FASB ASC 820-10-35).[5] The assets held in trust by NFP A should be recorded at fair value at the date of initial recognition. The difference between the fair value of the assets received and the contribution revenue represents the present value of the liability to pay the donor's estate upon the termination of the trust.

6.41 In subsequent periods, both the income earned on the trust assets and recognized gains and losses should be reflected in the trust asset and liability accounts. Adjustments of the liability to reflect amortization of the discount and revaluations of the future cash flows based on revisions in the donor's life expectancy should be recognized as changes in the value of split-interest agreements and classified as changes in temporarily restricted net assets in a statement of activities. Amounts should be reclassified from temporarily restricted to unrestricted net assets as the annual distributions to NFP A are made and recognized during the term of the trust. Upon the death of the donor, the assets are distributed to the donor's estate, the asset and liability accounts are closed, and any difference between the balances in those accounts should be recognized as a change in the value of split-interest agreements in the temporarily restricted net asset class. (In this example, the timing of the distribution of the remainder interest to the beneficiary was dependent on the donor's death. If instead the distribution were required to be paid at the end of a specified period, the liability to the beneficiary would have contained an embedded derivative as described in paragraph 6.25. Paragraphs 6.24–.28 discuss measuring an obligation that contains an embedded derivative.)

6.42 If NFP A is not the trustee and does not exercise control over the trust's assets, it should recognize its beneficial interest in those assets as temporarily restricted contribution revenue and as a beneficial interest, measured at fair value as discussed in paragraphs 6.14–.17. Distributions from the trust should be reflected as a reduction in the beneficial interest and as reclassifications from temporarily restricted net assets to unrestricted net assets. Changes in the fair value of the beneficial interest should be recognized as adjustments to the beneficial interest in the statement of financial position and as changes in the value of split-interest agreements in the statement of activities in the temporarily restricted net asset class. If present value techniques are used to estimate fair value, those changes would reflect the revision of all elements discussed in FASB ASC 825-10-55-5, including the passage of time, revaluations

---

[5] See footnote 2.

of expected future cash flows based on revisions in the donor's life expectancy, and discount rate assumptions to reflect current market conditions. Any balance in the beneficial interest account remaining upon termination of the trust should be recognized as a change in the value of split-interest agreements in the statement of activities in the temporarily restricted net asset class.

Perpetual Trust Held by a Third Party

6.43 According to the FASB ASC glossary, a *perpetual trust held by a third party* is an arrangement in which a donor establishes and funds a perpetual trust administered by an individual or entity other than the NFP that is the beneficiary.[6] Under the terms of the trust, the NFP has the irrevocable right to receive the income earned on the trust assets in perpetuity, but never receives the assets held in trust. Distributions received by the NFP may be restricted by the donor.

6.44 For example, a donor establishes a trust with the donor's bank serving as trustee. Funds contributed to the trust are to be invested in perpetuity. Under the terms of the trust, NFP B is to be the sole beneficiary and is to receive annually the income on the trust's assets as earned in perpetuity. NFP B can use the distributions from the trust in any way that is consistent with its mission.

6.45 The arrangement should be recognized by NFP B as contribution revenue and as an asset, measured at fair value, when the NFP B is notified of the trust's existence, as discussed in paragraph 6.15–.18.[7] The contribution should be classified as permanently restricted support, because the trust is similar to donor restricted permanent endowment that the NFP B does not control, rather than a multiyear promise to give. Pursuant to FASB ASC 958-605-35-3, annual distributions from the trust are reported as investment income. In this example, the investment income increases unrestricted net assets.

6.46 Periodically in conjunction with preparing its financial statements, NFP B should remeasure its beneficial interest at fair value, using the same valuation technique that was used to measure the asset initially, as described in paragraph 6.22. In this example, the adjustment should be recognized as permanently restricted gains or losses.

Charitable Remainder Trust

6.47 A charitable remainder trust is an arrangement in which a donor establishes and funds a trust with specified distributions to be made to a designated beneficiary or beneficiaries over the trust's term. Upon termination of the trust, an NFP receives the assets remaining in the trust. The NFP may ultimately have unrestricted use of those assets, or the donor may place permanent or temporary restrictions on their use. The distributions to the beneficiaries may be for a specified dollar amount, an arrangement called a charitable remainder annuity trust, or for a specified percentage of the trust's fair market

---

[6] Chapter 5, "Contributions Received and Agency Transactions," of this guide provides guidance for transactions in which a perpetual trust held by a third party (trustee or other recipient organization) is established by an NFP for its own benefit or for the benefit of its affiliate.

[7] FASB ASC 958-605-30-14 states that the fair value of a perpetual trust held by a third party generally can be measured using the fair value of the assets contributed to the trust, unless facts and circumstances indicate that the fair value of the beneficial interest differs from the fair value of the assets contributed to the trust.

value as determined annually, a charitable remainder unitrust. Some charitable remainder unitrusts limit the annual payout to the lesser of the stated percentage or the actual income earned. Obligations to the beneficiaries are limited to the trust's assets.

6.48 For example, a donor establishes a charitable remainder unitrust, with NFP C serving as trustee. Under the trust's terms, the donor's spouse is to receive an annual distribution equal in value to a specified percentage of the fair market value of the trust's assets each year until the spouse dies. The income earned on the trust's assets must remain in the trust until the spouse dies. At that time, the remaining assets of the trust are to be distributed to NFP C for use as a permanent endowment.

6.49 NFP C should recognize the contribution in the period in which the trust is established. The assets held in trust by NFP C and the liability to the donor's spouse should be recorded at fair value when received, as discussed in paragraphs 6.14–.17. If the liability is measured using present value techniques, the liability to the donor's spouse should be recorded at the present value of the future payments to be distributed over the spouse's expected life. The amount of the contribution is the difference between these amounts and should be classified as permanently restricted support.

6.50 In subsequent periods, income earned on trust assets, recognized gains and losses, and distributions paid to the spouse should be reflected in the NFP C's statement of financial position. Adjustments to the liability to reflect amortization of the discount, revaluations of the present value of the estimated future payments to the spouse, and changes in actuarial assumptions should be recognized in a statement of activities as a change in the value of split-interest agreements in the permanently restricted net asset class. Upon the death of the spouse, the liability should be closed and any balance should be recognized as a change in the value of split-interest agreements in the statement of activities in the permanently restricted net asset class. (In this example, the period for which distributions were made to the beneficiary was dependent solely on the donor's death and the payment amounts varied based on the fair value of the unitrust assets. If instead the variable-amount distributions were required to be paid for a specified number of years—or for the greater of the donor's life or a specified number of years, the liability to the beneficiary would have contained an embedded derivative, as discussed in paragraph 6.25. Paragraphs 6.24–.28 discuss measuring an obligation that contains an embedded derivative.)

6.51 If NFP C is not the trustee and does not exercise control over the assets contributed to the trust, the agreement should be recognized as a beneficial interest in a trust. NFP C should recognize, as permanently restricted contribution revenue and as a beneficial interest, the fair value of the beneficial interest, as discussed in paragraphs 6.15–.18. Adjustments to the beneficial interest to reflect changes in the fair value should be measured using the same valuation technique as was used to measure the asset initially and recognized as changes in the value of split-interest agreements. For example, if present value techniques were used to estimate fair value, the adjustment would reflect the revision of all elements discussed in FASB ASC 825-10-55-5, including the passage of time, revaluation of the present value of the future payments to the spouse, changes in actuarial assumptions during the term of the trust, and discount rates based on current market conditions. Upon the death of the spouse, the beneficial interest is closed, the assets received from the trust are recognized at fair value, and any difference is reported as a change in the value of split-interest agreements in permanently restricted net assets.

Charitable Gift Annuity

6.52 A charitable gift annuity is an arrangement between a donor and an NFP in which the donor contributes assets to the NFP in exchange for a promise by the NFP to pay a fixed amount for a specified period of time to the donor or to individuals or entities designated by the donor. The agreements are similar to charitable remainder annuity trusts except that no trust exists, the assets received are held as general assets of the NFP, and the annuity liability is a general obligation of the NFP.

6.53 For example, NFP D and a donor enter into an arrangement whereby assets are transferred from the donor to NFP D. NFP D agrees to pay a stated dollar amount annually to the donor's spouse until the spouse dies.

6.54 NFP D should recognize the agreement in the period in which the contract is executed. The assets received should be recognized at fair value when received, and an annuity payment liability should be recognized at fair value as discussed in paragraphs 6.08–.09. In this example, unrestricted[8] contribution revenue should be recognized as the difference between these two amounts.

6.55 In subsequent periods, payments to the donor's spouse reduce the annuity liability. Adjustments to the annuity liability to reflect amortization of the discount and changes in the life expectancy of the donor's spouse should be recognized in a statement of activities as changes in the value of split-interest agreements in unrestricted net assets. Upon the death of the donor's spouse, the annuity liability should be closed and a change in the value of split-interest agreements should be recognized in the statement of activities.

Pooled (Life) Income Fund

6.56 Some NFPs form, invest, and manage pooled (or life) income funds.[9] These funds are divided into units, and contributions of many donors' life-income gifts are pooled and invested as a group. The FASB ASC glossary defines a *pooled income fund* as a trust in which donors are assigned a specific number of units based on the proportion of the fair value of their contributions to the total fair value of the pooled income fund on the date of the donor's entry to the pooled fund. Until a donor's death, the donor (or the donor's designated beneficiary or beneficiaries) is paid the actual income (as defined under the arrangement) earned on the donor's assigned units. Upon the donor's death, the value of these assigned units reverts to the NFP.

6.57 For example, a donor contributes assets to NFP E's pooled (life) income fund and is assigned a specific number of units in the pool. The donor is to receive a life interest in any income earned on those units. Upon the donor's death, the value of the units is available to NFP E for its unrestricted use.

---

[8] Paragraph 6.08 discusses the classification of the contribution portion of a charitable gift annuity agreement. Paragraphs 6.35–.36 discuss classification and disclosure of reserve requirements or other limitations imposed by state law on NFPs that hold charitable gift annuities.

[9] Net income unitrusts are similar to pooled life-income funds, because the corpus is maintained. Accordingly, financial reporting for net income unitrusts is similar to reporting for pooled life-income funds.

6.58 NFP E should recognize its remainder interest in the assets received as temporarily restricted contribution revenue in the period in which the assets are received from the donor. The contribution should be measured at fair value. Present value techniques are one valuation technique for measuring the fair value of the contribution; other valuation techniques are also available, as described in FASB ASC 820-10-35.[10] If present value techniques are used, the contribution may be measured at the fair value of the assets to be received, discounted for the estimated time period until the donor's death. The contributed assets should be recognized at fair value when received. The difference between the fair value of the assets when received and the revenue recognized should be recorded as deferred revenue, representing the amount of the discount for future interest.

6.59 Periodic income on the fund and payments to the donor should be reflected as increases and decreases in a liability to the donor. Amortization of the discount should be recognized as a reduction in the deferred revenue account and as a change in the value of split-interest agreements and reported as a change in temporarily restricted net assets. Upon the donor's death, any remaining balance in the deferred revenue account should be closed and a change in the value of split-interest agreements should be recognized. A reclassification to unrestricted net assets is also necessary to record the satisfaction of the time restriction on temporarily restricted net assets.

Auditing

6.60 Because for-profit entities do not usually enter into split-interest agreements, the specific audit objectives, selected controls, and auditing procedures related to such agreements are unique to NFPs and are presented in the following paragraphs. (See also the discussion concerning confirming receivables in paragraphs 5.139–.140 of this guide.)

6.61 Reporting split-interest agreements requires the NFP to measure fair value of assets and liabilities. AU section 328, *Auditing Fair Value Measurements and Disclosures* (AICPA, *Professional Standards*), addresses audit considerations relating to the measurement and disclosure of assets, liabilities, and specific components of equity presented or disclosed at fair value in financial statements.

6.62 Interpretation No. 1, "Auditing Interests in Trusts Held by a Third-Party Trustee and Reported at Fair Value," of AU section 328 (AICPA, *Professional Standards*, AU sec. 9328 par. .01–.04), provides additional guidance for auditing interests in trusts held by a third-party trustee. It states that in circumstances in which the auditor determines that the nature and extent of auditing procedures should include verifying the existence and testing the measurement of investments held by a trust, simply receiving a confirmation from the trustee, either in aggregate or on an investment-by-investment basis, does not in and of itself constitute adequate audit evidence with respect to the requirements for auditing the fair value of the interest in the trust under AU section 328. In addition, receiving confirmation from the trustee for investments in aggregate does not constitute adequate audit evidence with respect to the existence assertion. Receiving confirmation from the trustee on

[10] See footnote 2.

an investment-by-investment basis, however, typically would constitute adequate audit evidence with respect to the existence assertion. In circumstances in which the auditor is unable to audit the existence or measurement of interests in trusts at the financial statement date, the auditor should consider whether that scope limitation requires the auditor to either qualify his or her opinion or to disclaim an opinion, as discussed in paragraphs .22–.26 of AU section 508, *Reports on Audited Financial Statements* (AICPA, *Professional Standards*).

6.63 The following table illustrates the use of assertions in developing audit objectives and designing substantive tests. The examples are not intended to be all-inclusive nor is it expected that all the procedures would necessarily be applied in an audit. The auditor should design and perform substantive procedures for all relevant assertions related to each material class of transactions, account balance, and disclosure to obtain sufficient appropriate audit evidence. The use of assertions in assessing risks and designing appropriate audit procedures to obtain audit evidence is described in paragraphs .14–.26 of AU section 326, *Audit Evidence* (AICPA, *Professional Standards*). Various audit procedures and the purposes for which they may be performed are described in paragraphs .27–.41 of AU section 326.

Auditing Considerations

Financial Statement Assertions	*Specific Audit Objectives*	*Examples of Selected Controls*	*Examples of Auditing Procedures*
Transactions			
Occurrence	Amounts recognized as contribution revenues, resulting from split-interest agreements represent valid revenues.	Management authorizes split-interest agreements.	Review split-interest agreements and correspondence with donors or trustees.
Completeness	All unconditional split-interest agreements are recognized.	Controls ensure that split-interest agreements are known and recorded.	Review minutes of governing board and governing board committee meetings for evidence of split-interest agreements.
	All income received under split-interest agreements is recorded.	Management reviews income distribution terms of split-interest agreements and determines that periodic reports and remittances from trustees conform to those terms. Donor relations and fund-raising staff notify appropriate management upon death of beneficiaries.	Compare income distribution terms of split-interest agreements to periodic reports and remittances from trustees; trace periodic reports and remittances from trustees to cash receipts records.

(continued)

Auditing Considerations—continued

Financial Statement Assertions	*Specific Audit Objectives*	*Examples of Selected Controls*	*Examples of Auditing Procedures*
Transactions—continued			
Valuation and Allocation	Assets, liabilities, and revenues recognized at the inception of split-interest agreements are measured at fair value when received. Fair value is measured using appropriate measurement methods.	Documentation supports the determination of assets, liabilities, revenues, and changes in the value of split-interest agreements at the inception of the agreements. If not-for-profit entity (NFP) elects fair value measurements as described in FASB ASC 815-15-25 or the "Fair Value Option" subsections of FASB ASC 825-10, documentation supports the election.	Review documentation, including reports of actuaries, supporting the determination of fair value of assets, liabilities, and revenues. If present value techniques were used, review the techniques to determine if they meet the provisions of paragraphs 4–20 of FASB ASC 820-10-55. Review documentation supporting the present value of future payments to be made to other beneficiaries at the inception of split-interest agreements and over their term (if that valuation technique is used); consider the need to apply provisions of AU section 336, *Using the Work of a Specialist* (AICPA, *Professional Standards*), in conjunction with auditing any actuarial calculations.
Rights and Obligations	Restrictions on contributions arising from split-interest agreements have been met.	Split-interest agreements are reviewed for restrictions.	Review split-interest agreements and donor correspondence.
Account Balances			
Occurrence	Amounts recognized as (1) cash, investments, contributions receivable, and other assets held under split-interest agreements, (2) beneficial interests in trusts held by others, and (3) liabilities for	Management authorizes split-interest agreements. Donor relations and fund-raising staff notify appropriate management upon death of beneficiaries.	Review split-interest agreements and correspondence with donors or trustees. Determine whether beneficiaries are still living if term of agreement is based on a beneficiary's life.

Auditing Considerations—continued

Financial Statement Assertions	*Specific Audit Objectives*	*Examples of Selected Controls*	*Examples of Auditing Procedures*
Account Balances—continued			
	amounts held for others resulting from split-interest agreements represent valid revenues, assets, and liabilities.		
Completeness	All unconditional split-interest agreements are recognized.	Controls ensure that donor relations and fundraising staff notify management upon receipt of a split-interest arrangement. Controls ensure that split-interest agreements are known and recorded.	Review minutes of governing board and governing board committee meetings for evidence of split-interest agreements.
	All income received under split-interest agreements is recorded.	Management reviews income distribution terms of split-interest agreements and determines that periodic reports and remittances from trustees conform to those terms.	Compare income distribution terms of split-interest agreements to periodic reports and remittances from trustees; trace periodic reports and remittances from trustees to cash receipts records.
Valuation and Allocation	Assets and liabilities are measured using appropriate measurement methods. If present value techniques are used to measure the liability to other beneficiaries, amortization of the discount associated with the contribution and revaluations (based on changes in actuarial assumptions) of the liabilities to beneficiaries are recognized during the term of split-interest agreements. (*a*) Beneficial interests in trusts	Documentation supports the determination of assets, liabilities, revenues, and changes in the value of split-interest agreements over the term of the agreements. If the NFP elects fair value measurements as described in FASB ASC 815-15-25 or the "Fair Value Option" subsections of FASB ASC 825-10, documentation supports the election.	Review documentation, including reports of actuaries, supporting the determination of fair value of assets, and the calculation of liabilities, If present value techniques were used, review the techniques to determine if they meet the provisions of paragraphs 4–20 of FASB ASC 820-10-55. Review documentation supporting the future present value of payments to be made to other beneficiaries at the inception of split-interest agreements and over

(continued)

Auditing Considerations—continued

Financial Statement Assertions	*Specific Audit Objectives*	*Examples of Selected Controls*	*Examples of Auditing Procedures*
Account Balances—continued			
	held by others, (*b*) embedded derivatives subject to the measurement provisions of FASB ASC 815-15, and (*c*) assets and liabilities for which an election pursuant to FASB ASC 815-15-25 or the "Fair Value Option" subsections of FASB ASC 825-10, was made are remeasured at fair value and changes recognized during the term of split-interest agreements.		their term (if that valuation technique is used); consider the need to apply provisions of AU section 336 in conjunction with auditing any actuarial calculations.
	Restrictions on contributions arising from split-interest agreements have been met.	Split-interest agreements are reviewed for restrictions.	Review split-interest agreements and donor correspondence.
Presentation and Disclosure			
Rights and Obligations	Restrictions on contributions arising from split-interest agreements have been met.	Split-interest agreements are reviewed for restrictions.	Review split-interest agreements and donor correspondence.
	Contribution revenues recognized under split-interest agreements are reported in the proper net asset class.		Determine that appropriate reclassifications are made on the statement of activities as assets are distributed to the NFP, upon death of beneficiaries, or as restrictions otherwise expire.
	Contribution revenues and changes in the value of split-interest agreements that are recognized during the term of split-interest agreements are reported in the proper net asset class.		
	Temporarily restricted net assets are reclassified as unrestricted net assets as restrictions expire.		

6.64

Appendix A—Journal Entries

1. This appendix provides journal entries related to the examples in paragraphs 6.37–.59.

2. ***Charitable Lead Trust (not-for-profit entity [NFP] is trustee)*** (paragraphs 6.38–.41)

NFP A enters into an irrevocable charitable lead annuity trust arrangement with a donor whereby

- the donor establishes a trust with NFP A serving as trustee.
- the terms of the trust are that NFP A is to receive an annuity of $X per year until the donor's death.
- distributions received from the trust by NFP A are unrestricted.
- upon the death of the donor, the remaining balance in the trust passes to the donor's estate.

Solution:

Creation of the trust:

dr. Assets Held in Charitable Lead Trust

cr. Liability for Amounts Held for Others

cr. Contribution Revenue—Temporarily Restricted

(Assets and revenue measured at fair value when received, as discussed in paragraphs 6.08–.09)

Over the term of the trust:

dr. Assets Held in Charitable Lead Trust

cr. Liability for Amounts Held for Others

(Trust income and changes in fair value of assets held in trust, to the extent recognized)

dr. Cash

cr. Assets Held in Charitable Lead Trust

(Distribution of income to NFP)

dr. Temporarily Restricted Net Assets—Reclassifications Out

cr. Unrestricted Net Assets—Reclassifications In

(Reclassification of amounts received by NFP)

dr. Liability for Amounts Held for Others

cr. Change in Value of Split-Interest Agreements—Temporarily Restricted

(Amortization of discount and revaluation based on changes in actuarial assumptions—debit and credit could be reversed)

Termination of the trust:

dr. Liability for Amounts Held for Others

dr. Change in Value of Split-Interest Agreements—Temporarily Restricted (or cr.)

cr. Assets Held in Charitable Lead Trust

(Return of assets to donor's estate)

3. *Charitable Lead Trust (NFP is not trustee)* (paragraph 6.42)

The fact situation is the same as in the previous example except that the NFP is not the trustee.

Solution:

Creation of the trust:

dr. Beneficial Interest in Lead Trust

cr. Contribution Revenue—Temporarily Restricted

(Beneficial interest in trust assets measured at fair value, as discussed in paragraphs 6.14–.15)

Over the term of the trust:

dr. Cash

cr. Beneficial Interest in Lead Trust

(Distribution of income to NFP)

dr. Temporarily Restricted Net Assets—Reclassifications Out

cr. Unrestricted Net Assets—Reclassifications In

(Reclassification of amount received by NFP)

dr. Beneficial Interest in Lead Trust

cr. Change in Value of Split-Interest Agreements—Temporarily Restricted

(Change in fair value—debit and credit could be reversed)

Termination of the trust:

dr. Change in Value of Split-Interest Agreements—Temporarily Restricted

cr. Beneficial Interest in Lead Trust

(Closeout interest)

4. *Perpetual Trust Held by a Third Party* (paragraphs 6.43–.46)

Donor enters into an irrevocable perpetual trust agreement with a third-party trustee with NFP B as the income beneficiary whereby

- the donor establishes a trust with its bank serving as trustee, with a payment to the trust to be invested in perpetuity by the trustee.

- the terms of the trust are that NFP B is to be the sole beneficiary and receive the income on the trust assets as earned in perpetuity with no restrictions on its use.

Solution:

Creation of the trust:

dr. Beneficial Interest in Perpetual Trust

cr. Contribution Revenue—Permanently Restricted

(Assets and revenue measured at fair value, as discussed in paragraph 6.15–.18 and in footnote 7 to paragraph 6.45)

Each period:

dr. Cash

cr. Investment Income (Unrestricted)

(Income received from trust [net asset class based on stipulations of the trust])

dr. Beneficial Interest in Perpetual Trust

cr. Gain or Loss—Permanently Restricted

(To adjust asset for changes in fair value—debit and credit could be reversed)

5. ***Charitable Remainder Trust (NFP is trustee)*** (paragraphs 6.47–.50)

NFP C enters into a charitable remainder unitrust agreement with a donor whereby

- a trust is established by the donor to be administered by NFP C.
- the donor's spouse is to receive an annual distribution of X percent of the fair market value of the trust's assets each year until the spouse dies.
- at the time of death of the donor's spouse, the remaining assets of the trust are to be distributed to NFP C as permanent endowment.

Solution:

Creation of the trust:

dr. Assets Held in Charitable Remainder Trust

cr. Liability Under Unitrust Agreement

cr. Contribution Revenue—Permanently Restricted

(Assets and liability, as discussed in paragraphs 6.08–.09)

Over the term of the trust:

dr. Assets Held in Charitable Remainder Trust

cr. Liability Under Unitrust Agreement

(Trust income and change in fair value of assets held in trust, to the extent recognized)

dr. Liability Under Unitrust Agreement

cr. Assets Held in Charitable Remainder Trust

(Payment to beneficiary)

dr. Liability Under Unitrust Agreement

cr. Change in Value of Split-Interest Agreements—Permanently Restricted

(Amortization of discount and adjustment of liability to reflect change in actuarial assumptions—debit and credit could be reversed)

Termination of the trust:

dr. Liability Under Unitrust Agreement

cr. Change in Value of Split-Interest Agreements—Permanently Restricted

(To close liability)

dr. Endowment Assets

cr. Assets Held in Charitable Remainder Trust

(To close trust and recognize assets as endowment)

6. *Charitable Remainder Trust (NFP is not trustee)* (paragraph 6.51)

The fact situation is the same as in the previous example, except that the NFP does not serve as trustee.

<u>Solution:</u>

Creation of the trust:

dr. Beneficial Interest in Remainder Trust

cr. Contribution Revenue—Permanently Restricted

(Beneficial interest measured at fair value, as discussed in paragraphs 6.14–.17)

Over the term of the trust:

dr. Beneficial Interest in Remainder Trust

cr. Change in Value of Split-Interest Agreements—Permanently Restricted

(Change in fair value—debit and credit could be reversed)

Termination of the trust:

dr. Endowment Assets

cr. Beneficial Interest in Remainder Trust

cr. Change in Value of Split-Interest Agreements—Permanently Restricted

(NFP receives distribution of trust assets from trustee, measured at fair value; the receivable account is closed and the change in value of split-interest agreements reflects the difference)

7. *Charitable Gift Annuity* (paragraphs 6.52–.55)

NFP D enters into a charitable gift annuity contract with a donor whereby

- assets are transferred to NFP D and are available for unrestricted use by NFP D.
- NFP D agrees to pay a stated dollar amount annually to the donor's spouse until the spouse dies, at which time the remaining assets are available for the unrestricted use of NFP D.

Solution:

Creation of the annuity:

dr. Assets

cr. Annuity Payment Liability

cr. Contribution Revenue—Unrestricted

(Assets and liabilities are measured at fair value when received, as discussed in paragraphs 6.08–.09)

Over the term of the annuity:

dr. Annuity Payment Liability

cr. Cash

(Payment to annuity beneficiary)

dr. Change in Value of Split-Interest Agreements—Unrestricted

cr. Annuity Payment Liability

(Amortization of discount on liability and recording of any change in the life expectancy of the beneficiary—debit and credit could be reversed)

Termination of the annuity:

dr. Annuity Payment Liability

cr. Change in Value of Split-Interest Agreements—Unrestricted

(To close the annuity payment liability)

8. *Pooled (Life) Income Fund* (paragraphs 6.56–.59)

NFP E forms, invests, and manages a pooled income (or life-income) fund. The fund is divided into units, and contributions from many donors are pooled. Donors are assigned a specific number of units based on the proportion of the fair market value of the contribution to the total fair market value of the fund. A donor makes a contribution to the fund, is assigned a specific number of units, and will receive the actual income earned on those units until his or her death. The assets contributed must be invested in the fund until the donor's death. At that time, the value of the units assigned to the donor will revert to NFP E, and those assets will be available to NFP E without restriction.

Solution:

Contribution of assets:

dr. Assets of Pooled Income Fund

cr. Contribution Revenue—Temporarily Restricted

cr. Discount for Future Interest (Deferred Revenue)

(Assets and contribution revenue recorded at fair value on date of receipt, as discussed in paragraph 6.18)

Over the term of the agreement:

dr. Assets of Pooled Income Fund

cr. Liability to Life Beneficiary

(Income earned on units assigned to donor)

dr. Liability to Life Beneficiary

cr. Assets of Pooled Income Fund

(Payment to life beneficiary)

dr. Discount for Future Interest (Deferred Revenue)

cr. Change in Value of Split-Interest Agreements—Temporarily Restricted

(Amortization of discount and changes in the life expectancy of the beneficiary)

Termination of the agreement:

dr. Discount for Future Interest (Deferred Revenue)

cr. Change in Value of Split-Interest Agreement—Unrestricted

(To close discount upon the death of the life beneficiary)

dr. Cash or Investment Assets

cr. Assets of Pooled Income Fund

(To recognize assets available for use upon the death of the life beneficiary)

dr. Temporarily Restricted Net Assets—Reclassification Out

cr. Unrestricted Net Assets—Reclassification In

(Reclassification based on the expiration of the time restriction)

Chapter 7

Other Assets

Introduction

7.01 Some assets held by not-for-profit entities (NFPs) are similar to those held by for-profit entities. This chapter considers assets that are not discussed elsewhere in this Audit and Accounting Guide and that present accounting issues unique to NFPs.

Inventory

7.02 NFPs may acquire merchandise inventory for resale; for example, items held for sale by a bookstore, dining service, kitchen, or thrift shop. Merchandise inventory may be acquired by NFPs in exchange transactions or from contributions. (Paragraphs 5.36–.49 and chapter 12, "Revenues and Receivables From Exchange Transactions," of this guide discuss exchange transactions.) Financial Accounting Standards Board (FASB) *Accounting Standards Codification* (ASC) 330, *Inventory*, discusses the general principles applicable to inventory.

7.03 Pursuant to FASB ASC 958-605-25-2 and FASB ASC 958-605-30-2, contributions of inventory should be reported in the period received and should be measured at fair value. The FASB ASC glossary defines *fair value* as "the price that would be received to sell an asset or paid to transfer a liability in an orderly transaction between market participants at the measurement date." (Paragraphs 3.73–.94 of this guide discuss FASB ASC 820, *Fair Value Measurements and Disclosures*, which defines fair value, establishes a framework for measuring fair value, and expands disclosures about fair value measurements.)[*,†] Consistent with the FASB ASC glossary definition of fair value, the fair value of contributed inventory is its estimated selling price.

7.04 Pursuant to FASB ASC 958-605-25-4, a major uncertainty about the existence of value may indicate that an item received or given should not be recognized. For example, a gift of clothing or furniture has no value unless it

---

[*] Some of the guidance in Financial Accounting Standards Board (FASB) *Accounting Standards Codification* (ASC) 820, *Fair Value Measurements and Disclosures*, is labeled as "Pending Content" due to the transition and open effective date information discussed in FASB ASC 820-10-65. For example, Accounting Standards Update (ASU) No. 2010-06, *Fair Value Measurements and Disclosures (Topic 820): Improving Disclosures about Fair Value Measurements*, is effective for interim and annual reporting periods beginning after December 15, 2009, except for the separate disclosures about purchases, sales, issuances, and settlements relating to level 3 measurements (see FASB ASC 820-10-50-2(c)(2)), which shall be effective for fiscal years beginning after December 15, 2010, and for interim periods within those fiscal years. Early adoption is permitted.

[†] On June 29, 2010, FASB issued a proposed ASU, *Amendments for Common Fair Value Measurement and Disclosure Requirements in U.S. GAAP and IFRSs*, intended to develop common requirements for measuring fair value and for disclosing information about fair value measurements in U.S. generally accepted accounting principles and International Financial Reporting Standards. For many of the proposed requirements, FASB does not expect the amendments to result in changes in the application of FASB ASC 820. Other amendments would change a particular principle or requirement. The most notable of these changes are as follows, highest and best use and valuation premise, measuring the fair value of an instrument classified in shareholders' equity, measuring the fair value of instruments that are managed within a portfolio, and application of blockage factors and other premiums and discounts in a fair value measurement. The proposed standards also include additional disclosure requirements. Readers should be alert to the issuance of a final ASU.

can be utilized in either of the following ways: (*a*) used internally by the NFP or for program purposes or (*b*) sold by the NFP. (Paragraphs 5.94–.99 of this guide discuss gifts in kind.)

7.05 Pursuant to FASB ASC 958-605-30-9, inputs for measuring fair value may be obtained from published catalogs, vendors, independent appraisals, and other sources. If methods such as estimates, averages, or computational approximations, such as average value per pound or subsequent sales, can reduce the cost of measuring the fair value of inventory, use of those methods is appropriate, provided the methods are applied consistently, and the results of applying those methods are reasonably expected not to be materially different from the results of a detailed measurement of the fair value of contributed inventory.

Prepaid Expenses, Deferred Charges, and Similar Costs

7.06 NFPs may incur costs that relate to future rather than to current-period activities. Except as discussed elsewhere in this chapter, the recognition and measurement principles for those costs are similar to those used by business entities. Accordingly, amounts expended for prepaid expenses and deposits should be reported as assets. (In conformity with FASB ASC 340-20 and FASB 720-35, advertising costs should not be capitalized unless they are costs of direct-response advertising that is expected to result in future benefits, such as gift shop sales.)

Collections

7.07 The FASB ASC glossary defines *collections* as follows:

> Works of art, historical treasures, or similar assets that meet all of the following criteria: (*a*) They are held for public exhibition, education, or research in furtherance of public service rather than financial gain, (*b*) They are protected, kept unencumbered, cared for, and preserved, and (*c*) They are subject to an organizational policy that requires the proceeds of items that are sold to be used to acquire other items for collections.

7.08 FASB ASC 958-360-25-3 states that an NFP that holds works of art, historical treasures, and similar items that meet the definition of a collection has the following three alternative policies for reporting that collection: (*a*) capitalization of all collection items, (*b*) capitalization of all collection items on a prospective basis (that is, all items acquired after a stated date), or (*c*) no capitalization. Capitalization of selected collections or items is precluded.

7.09 Accounting for collections depends on whether an NFP adopts a policy of recognizing collections as assets. If an NFP adopts a policy of capitalizing collections, items acquired in exchange transactions should be recognized as assets in the period in which they are acquired and should be measured at cost. Per FASB ASC 958-605-25-19 and FASB ASC 958-605-30-2, contributed collection items should be recognized as assets and as revenues or gains if collections are capitalized[1] and should be measured at fair value. (Paragraphs 3.73–.94

---

[1] As discussed in paragraphs 3–6 of FASB ASC 958-605-45, contributions should be classified as increases in unrestricted, temporarily restricted, or permanently restricted net assets, depending on the existence and type of restrictions imposed by donors. Chapter 5, "Contributions Received and Agency Transactions," of this guide provides guidance concerning accounting for contributions with donor-imposed restrictions.

of this guide discuss FASB ASC 820, which defines *fair value*, establishes a framework for measuring fair value, and expands disclosures about fair value measurements.)[*, †] As discussed in FASB ASC 820-10-35-9, a fair value measurement should be determined based on the assumptions that market participants would use in pricing the asset. Market participant assumptions should include assumptions about the effect of a restriction on the sale or use of an asset if market participants would consider the effect of the restriction in pricing the asset. Example 6 (paragraphs 51–55) of FASB ASC 820-10-55 explains that restrictions that are an attribute of an asset, and therefore would transfer to a market participant, are the only restrictions reflected in fair value. Donor restrictions that are specific to the donee are reflected in the classification of net assets, not in the measurement of fair value. As discussed in FASB ASC 958-605-25-4, if an item is accepted solely to be saved for its potential future use in scientific or educational research and has no alternative use, it may have uncertain value, or perhaps no value, and should not be recognized.

7.10 FASB ASC 958-605-25-19 states that contributed collection items should not be recognized as revenues or gains if collections are not capitalized.

7.11 FASB ASC 958-230-55-5A states that cash flows from purchases, sales, and insurance recoveries of unrecognized, noncapitalized collection items should be reported as investing activities in a statement of cash flows. Additional disclosures described in paragraphs 7.15–.16 should be made if an NFP elects not to capitalize collections.

7.12 Per paragraphs 2–3 of FASB ASC 958-360-40, a contribution made by an NFP of a previously recognized collection item should be reported as an expense and a decrease in assets in the period in which the contribution is made, and should be measured at fair value. A gain or loss should be recognized on that contribution made if the collection item's fair value differs from its carrying amount. A contribution made by an NFP of a previously unrecognized collection item should not be recognized on the face of the financial statements. FASB ASC 958-360-50-6 requires disclosure of those contributions in notes to the financial statements.

7.13 FASB ASC 958-605-25-18 requires that contributions of works of art, historical treasures, and similar assets that are not part of a collection should be recognized as assets and as revenue or gains.[2] Per FASB ASC 958-605-30-2, those contributions should be measured at fair value. Items acquired in exchange transactions should be measured at cost.

Financial Statement Presentation

7.14 In accordance with FASB ASC 958-360-45-3, if an NFP adopts a policy of capitalizing collections (as defined in the FASB ASC glossary) a statement of financial position should include the total amount capitalized on a separate line item, *Collections* or *Collection Items*. Per FASB ASC 958-360-45-4, the amount capitalized for works of art, historical treasures, and similar assets that do not meet the definition of a collection should be disclosed separately on the face of the statement of financial position or in the notes.

---

* See footnote * in paragraph 7.03.

† See footnote † in paragraph 7.03.

[2] See footnote 1.

7.15 FASB ASC 958-360-45-5 states that an NFP that does not recognize and capitalize its collections should report the following on the face of its statement of activities, separately from revenues, expenses, gains, and losses:

- Costs of collection items purchased as a decrease in the appropriate class of net assets
- Proceeds from sale of collection items as an increase in the appropriate class of net assets
- Proceeds from insurance recoveries of lost or destroyed collection items as an increase in the appropriate class of net assets

Similarly, an entity that capitalizes its collections prospectively should report proceeds from sales and insurance recoveries of items not previously capitalized separately from revenues, expenses, gains, and losses. Example 1 (paragraph 2) of FASB ASC 958-360-55 illustrates a statement of activities that satisfies these requirements.

7.16 FASB ASC 958-360-50-6 states that an NFP that does not recognize and capitalize its collections or that capitalizes collections prospectively should describe its collections, including their relative significance, and its stewardship policies for collections. If collection items not capitalized are deaccessed during that period, it also should describe the items given away, damaged, destroyed, lost, or otherwise deaccessed during the period or disclose their fair value. In addition, FASB ASC 958-360-45-3 requires that a line item should be shown on the face of the statement of financial position that refers to the disclosures required by this paragraph. That line item should be dated if collections are capitalized prospectively, for example, "Collections acquired since January 1, 19X1 (Note X)." FASB ASC 958-360-50-1 requires that an NFP disclose [its chosen] capitalization policy for collections (capitalization, prospective capitalization, or no capitalization).

Illustrative Disclosures

7.17 This section provides examples of notes to the financial statements that illustrate some of the financial statement disclosures concerning collection items.

Example 1—NFPs That Capitalize Collections

Note X: Summary of Significant Accounting Policies

The organization has capitalized its collections since its inception. If purchased, items accessioned into the collection are capitalized at cost, and if donated, they are capitalized at their fair value on the accession date (the date on which the item is accepted by the Acquisitions Committee of the Board of Trustees). Gains or losses on the deaccession of collection items are classified on the statement of activities as unrestricted or temporarily restricted support depending on donor restrictions, if any, placed on the item at the time of accession.

Example 2—NFPs That Capitalize Collections Retroactively

Note X: Summary of Significant Accounting Policies

In 19X1, the organization capitalized its collections retroactively. To the extent that reliable records were available, the organization capitalized collection items acquired prior to 19X1 at their cost at the date of purchase or, if the items were contributed, at their fair value at the accession date (the date on which the item was accepted by the Acquisitions Committee of the Board of Trustees).

Other collection items, particularly those acquired prior to 19X1 when detailed curatorial records began to be maintained, have been capitalized at their appraised or estimated current market value. In some cases, collection items held solely for their potential educational value or historical significance were determined to have no alternative use and were not assigned values for the purpose of capitalization. The collection items capitalized retroactively were determined to have a total value of $11,138,100.

Example 3—NFPs That Capitalize Their Collections Prospectively

Note X: Summary of Significant Accounting Policies

Collection items acquired on or after July 1, 19X0: Accessions of these collection items are capitalized at cost, if the items were purchased, or at their fair value on the accession date (the date on which the item is accepted by the Acquisitions Committee of the Board of Trustees), if the items were contributed. Gains or losses from deaccessions of these items are reflected on the statement of activities as changes in the appropriate net asset classes, depending on the existence and type of donor-imposed restrictions.

Collection items acquired prior to July 1, 19X0: Collection items accessioned prior to July 1, 19X0 were recorded as decreases in unrestricted net assets, if the items were purchased. No financial statement recognition was made for contributed collection items. Proceeds from insurance recoveries or deaccessions of these items are reflected on the statements of activities as changes in the appropriate net asset classes, depending on the existence and type of donor-imposed restrictions.

Note Z: Collections

The organization's collections are made up of artifacts of historical significance, scientific specimens, and art objects. Each of the items is cataloged for educational, research, scientific, and curatorial purposes, and activities verifying their existence and assessing their condition are performed continuously.

During 20X1, a significant number of American pioneer artifacts from the 1800s were destroyed while in transit to an exhibition in which they were to be displayed. Because those items were purchased prior to July 1, 19X0, the insurance proceeds of $22,000, which reimbursed the organization in full for the artifacts' fair value, are reflected as an increase in unrestricted net assets on the statement of activities. No other collection items were deaccessioned in 20X1 or 20X0.

Example 4—NFPs That Do Not Capitalize Collections

Note X: Summary of Significant Accounting Policies

The collections, which were acquired through purchases and contributions since the organization's inception, are not recognized as assets on the statement of financial position. Purchases of collection items are recorded as decreases in unrestricted net assets in the year in which the items are acquired, or as temporarily or permanently restricted net assets if the assets used to purchase the items are restricted by donors. Contributed collection items are not reflected on the financial statements. Proceeds from deaccessions or insurance recoveries are reflected as increases in the appropriate net asset classes.

Note Z: Collections

The organization's collections are made up of artifacts of historical significance, scientific specimens, and art objects that are held for educational, research, scientific, and curatorial purposes. Each of the items is cataloged, preserved, and cared for, and activities verifying their existence and assessing their condition are performed continuously. The collections are subject to a policy that requires proceeds from their sales to be used to acquire other items for collections.

During 20X1, a significant number of American pioneer artifacts from the 1800s were destroyed while in transit to an exhibition in which they were to be displayed. These artifacts were contributed in 20XX, with a restriction that limited any future proceeds from deaccessions to acquisitions of artifacts from a similar period. As a result, the insurance proceeds of $22,000, which reimbursed the organization in full for the artifacts' fair value, are reflected as an increase in temporarily restricted net assets on the statement of activities. No other collection items were deaccessioned in 20X1 or 20X0.

Goodwill ‡

7.18 As discussed in paragraph 3.69 of this guide, goodwill is written off as of the acquisition date if the operations of the acquiree as part of the combined entity are expected to be predominantly supported by contributions and returns on investments. If, instead, the operations of the acquiree are not expected to be predominantly supported by contributions and returns on investments, in conformity with FASB ASC 958-805-25-28, an NFP acquirer should recognize goodwill as an asset. FASB ASC 350-20 provides guidance for measuring goodwill subsequent to its acquisition.

7.19 Goodwill that is not written off on the acquisition date should not be amortized. Instead, it should be tested for impairment at a level of reporting referred to as a reporting unit. (Paragraphs 33–46 of FASB ASC 350-20-35 provide guidance on determining reporting units.) Impairment is the condition that exists when the carrying amount of goodwill exceeds its implied fair value. The fair value of goodwill can be measured only as a residual and cannot be measured directly. Therefore, FASB ASC 350-20 includes a methodology to determine an amount that achieves a reasonable estimate of the value of goodwill for purposes of measuring an impairment loss. That estimate is referred to as the implied fair value of goodwill. The two-step impairment test discussed in paragraphs 4–19 of FASB ASC 350-20-35 should be used to identify potential goodwill impairment and measure the amount of a goodwill impairment loss to be recognized (if any).

7.20 FASB ASC 350-10-65-1 provides transition guidance for goodwill that arose from acquisitions whose dates preceded the application of FASB Statement No. 164, *Not-for-Profit Entities: Mergers and Acquisitions—Including an amendment of FASB Statement No. 142*, which is codified in FASB ASC 958-805. (Acquisitions prior to the effective date of FASB Statement No. 164 are discussed beginning at paragraph 1.15 of this guide.) If an NFP is predominantly supported by contributions and returns on investments, it should write

‡ The guidance from FASB ASC 350-20 is labeled as "Pending Content" due to the transition and open effective date information discussed in FASB ASC 350-10-65-1. It reflects guidance included in FASB Statement No. 164, *Not-for-Profit Entities: Mergers and Acquisitions—Including an amendment of FASB Statement No. 142*, which was codified by ASU No. 2010-07, *Not-for-Profit Entities (Topic 958): Not-for-Profit Entities: Mergers and Acquisitions*, issued in January 2010. In addition to providing guidance for mergers and acquisitions, FASB Statement No. 164 improves the relevance, representational faithfulness, and comparability of the information a not-for-profit entity (NFP) provides about goodwill and other intangible assets after an acquisition by making the standards of FASB ASC 350-20 fully applicable to NFPs. These standards are effective for reporting periods beginning on or after December 15, 2009.

off goodwill that arose from acquisitions whose dates preceded the application of FASB ASC 958-805 by a separate charge in the statement of activities for the effect of the accounting change. If an NFP is not predominantly supported by contributions and returns on investments, it should establish its reporting units and subject previously recognized goodwill in each reporting unit to the transitional impairment evaluation required by performing the steps in FASB ASC 350-10-65-1(b)(2).

Intangible Assets Other Than Goodwill

7.21 The cost of an intangible asset acquired other than in an acquisition by an NFP is capitalized in accordance with FASB ASC 350, *Intangibles—Goodwill and Other*. Under the requirements of FASB ASC 350-30, accounting for a recognized intangible asset is based on its useful life to the reporting entity. An intangible asset with a finite useful life should be amortized; an intangible asset with an indefinite useful life should not be amortized. FASB ASC 350-30-55 provides examples of intangible assets other than goodwill. If an intangible asset has a finite useful life, but the precise length of that life is not known, that intangible asset should be amortized over the best estimate of its useful life. The method of amortization should reflect the pattern in which the economic benefits of the intangible asset are consumed or otherwise used up. If that pattern cannot be reliably determined, a straight-line amortization method should be used. An intangible asset that is subject to amortization should be reviewed for impairment in accordance with the "Impairment or Disposal of Long-Lived Assets" subsections of FASB ASC 360-10 by applying the recognition and measurement provisions in paragraphs 17–35 of FASB ASC 360-10-35.

7.22 If an intangible asset is determined to have an indefinite useful life, it should not be amortized until its useful life is determined to be no longer indefinite. Instead, an intangible asset that is not subject to amortization should be tested for impairment annually (or more frequently if events or changes in circumstances indicate that the asset might be impaired), as described in paragraphs 15–20 of FASB ASC 350-30-35. FASB ASC 360-10-35-21 includes examples of impairment indicators. The impairment test should consist of a comparison of the fair value of an intangible asset with its carrying amount. If the carrying amount of an intangible asset exceeds its fair value, an impairment loss should be recognized in an amount equal to that excess.

Auditing

7.23 Many audit objectives, controls, and auditing procedures for other assets of NFPs are similar to those of other entities. In addition, the auditor may need to consider the specific audit objectives, selected controls, and auditing procedures that are unique to NFPs and that are presented at the end of this chapter.

Inventory

7.24 As discussed in paragraph 7.05, in certain circumstances, the fair value of contributed inventory may be measured using methods such as estimates, averages, or computational approximations. Such methods may be used in connection with the financial statement assertion of valuation. However, such methods are unrelated to the assertions of existence and occurrence. AU section 328, *Auditing Fair Value Measurements and Disclosures* (AICPA, *Professional*

Standards), sets forth requirements and guidance when auditing the measurement and disclosure of assets, liabilities, and specific components of equity presented or disclosed at fair value in financial statements, and AU section 331, *Inventories* (AICPA, *Professional Standards*), which provides requirements and guidance concerning inventory observation.

Collection Items

7.25 Examples of auditing procedures that might be applied for collection items are presented in the table at the end of this chapter. If collection items are not capitalized, the auditor should perform procedures to understand the NFP's controls over recording accessions (including contributions) and deaccessions of collection items, controlling the collections, and periodically physically inspecting them. Those auditing procedures are performed, in part, to provide evidence supporting the disclosures required by FASB ASC 958-360-50-6. They are also part of the auditor's work in obtaining an understanding of the NFP's controls over collection items and contributions of such items. The objective of performing those procedures when the collection is not recognized is not to obtain evidence to corroborate a recorded amount, because no amount has been recorded. Instead, the objective is to help the auditor understand the NFP's control environment, which is a component of its internal control.

7.26 As noted in chapter 2, "General Auditing Considerations," of this guide, AU section 314, *Understanding the Entity and Its Environment and Assessing the Risks of Material Misstatement* (AICPA, *Professional Standards*), requires the auditor to understand the NFP's control environment, an important part of which is management's philosophy and operating style and its integrity and ethics. Management's philosophy and operating style include management's approach to taking and monitoring business risks and its attitudes and actions toward financial reporting. Management's integrity and ethics include the emphasis management places on meeting budget, profit, and other financial and operating goals. In addition, AU section 314 requires auditors to understand the effect of information technology on internal control and assessment of risk.

7.27 The required understanding of the control environment should be sufficient to enable the auditor to evaluate the design of the controls and determine whether they have been implemented. To obtain this understanding, the auditor should perform risk assessment procedures such as inquiries, observation, inspection and analytic procedures. What is sometimes referred to as a *transaction review* or *walk-through* of relevant custodial controls might be adequate for the auditor to gain the requisite level of knowledge about controls over the collection as part of understanding the control environment.

7.28 The following table illustrates the use of assertions in developing audit objectives and designing substantive tests. The examples are not intended to be all-inclusive nor is it expected that all the procedures would necessarily be applied in an audit. The auditor should design and perform substantive procedures for all relevant assertions related to each material class of transactions, account balance, and disclosure to obtain sufficient appropriate audit evidence. The use of assertions in assessing risks and designing appropriate audit procedures to obtain audit evidence is described in paragraphs .14–.26 of AU section 326, *Audit Evidence* (AICPA, *Professional Standards*). Various audit procedures and the purposes for which they may be performed are described in paragraphs .27–.41 of AU section 326.

Auditing Considerations

Financial Statement Assertions	*Specific Audit Objectives*	*Examples of Selected Controls*	*Examples of Auditing Procedures*
Transactions			
All Collection Items			
Occurrence	Collection items acquired in the current period by purchase and contribution were authorized.	Controls ensure that purchased collection items are authorized, contributed collection items are appropriately accessioned, and deaccessions are authorized.	Review documentation supporting accessions and deaccessions of collection items.
	Deaccessions from collections occurred and were authorized.		Review minutes of governing board and governing board committee meetings for authorization of major accessions and deaccessions.
			Make inquiries of curatorial personnel about deaccessioned collection items.
Capitalized Collection Items (Excluding Matters Related to Retroactive Capitalization)			
Completeness; valuation and allocation	All collection items acquired in exchange transactions are recognized as assets at cost.	Controls exist to ensure that all purchases and contributions of collection items are recognized as assets (at cost and fair value, respectively) and that contribution revenues are recognized for contributed collection items.	Review minutes of governing board and governing board committee meetings for evidence of current period purchases and contributions.
	All contributed collection items are recognized as assets and as contributions at fair value.		Review documentation and procedures supporting the determination of cost or fair value.

(continued)

Auditing Considerations—continued

Financial Statement Assertions	*Specific Audit Objectives*	*Examples of Selected Controls*	*Examples of Auditing Procedures*
Account Balances			
All Collection Items			
Occurrence	Collection items exist.	Procedures for controlling collections and periodically physically inspecting them.	Review the NFP's procedures for controlling collections and physically inspecting them.
			Consider whether to observe the physical inspection.
			Review actions taken by management to investigate discrepancies disclosed by the physical inspection and to adjust the records.
Rights and obligations	Restrictions on contributed collection items have been met.	Contributions of collection items are reviewed for restrictions and management monitors compliance with restrictions.	Review donor correspondence to determine the presence or absence of restrictions.
			Review minutes of governing board and governing board committee meetings for evidence of restrictions.
			If specific collection items are restricted, review collection item transactions for propriety of use and disposition.

Auditing Considerations—continued

Financial Statement Assertions	*Specific Audit Objectives*	*Examples of Selected Controls*	*Examples of Auditing Procedures*
Account Balances—continued			
Retroactive Capitalization of Collection Items			
Occurrence; completeness; valuation and allocation; rights and obligations; presentation and disclosure	Retroactively capitalized collection items exist, are the property of the NFP, are properly valued, and are reported in the appropriate net asset class; all collection items owned by the NFP are capitalized.	Procedures for controlling collections and determining their cost or fair value at date of acquisition or their current cost or current market value at date of initial recognition.	Review documents and procedures supporting the determination of cost or fair value at date of acquisition or current cost or current market value at date of initial recognition.
			Review donor correspondence to determine the presence or absence of restrictions.
			Review minutes of governing board and governing board committee meetings for evidence of restrictions.
			Review documentation underlying contributed collection items for propriety of classification.
			Consider the need to apply provisions of AU section 336, *Using the Work of a Specialist* (AICPA, *Professional Standards*), in conjunction with determining the reliability of carrying values.

(continued)

Auditing Considerations—continued

Financial Statement Assertions	*Specific Audit Objectives*	*Examples of Selected Controls*	*Examples of Auditing Procedures*
Presentation and Disclosure			
Noncapitalized Collection Items			
Valuation	Noncapitalized works of art, historical treasures, and similar assets meet the definition of *collections* in the FASB ASC glossary.	Policies and procedures for determining that noncapitalized assets are *collections*.	Review policies and procedures determining the appropriateness of classifying assets as noncapitalized collections. Determine whether proceeds of sales of collection items are used to acquire other items for the collection.
Completeness	Appropriate disclosures referenced in a line item on the face of the statement of financial position.		Ensure that required line item is present.
Classification	Purchases, sales, involuntary conversions, and other deaccessions of noncapitalized collection items are appropriately displayed in the statement of activities and the statement of cash flows.		Determine the appropriateness of display and disclosures related to noncapitalized collections.
Capitalized Collection Items (Excluding Matters Related to Retroactive Capitalizations)			
Classification	Contributed and deaccessioned collection items are reported in the appropriate net asset class.		Review documentation underlying collection items for propriety of classification.

Chapter 8

Investments [1,*]

Introduction

8.01 Not-for-profit entities (NFPs) acquire various kinds of investments by contribution or purchase. This chapter discusses the accounting, recognition, measurement, and disclosure requirements for investments. For purposes of this discussion, investments are divided into the following four broad categories:

- Investments in equity securities with readily determinable fair values (other than consolidated subsidiaries and equity securities reported under the equity method) and all investments in debt securities, which are investments that are subject to the requirements of Financial Accounting Standards Board (FASB) *Accounting Standards Codification* (ASC) 958-320.
- Investments that are accounted for under the equity method, which are investments that are subject to the requirements of FASB ASC 323-10, FASB ASC 323-30, and FASB ASC 970-323.
- Investments in derivative instruments that are subject to the requirements of FASB ASC 815, *Derivatives and Hedging*. If an investment would otherwise be in the scope of FASB ASC 958-320 and it has within it an embedded derivative that is subject to FASB ASC 815, the host contract (as described in FASB ASC 815-15-05-1) remains within the scope of FASB ASC 958-320.
- Other investments, which are those included in the scope of FASB ASC 958-325. Those investments include, among others, certain investments in real estate, mortgage notes that are not debt securities, venture capital funds, certain partnership interests, oil and gas interests, and certain equity securities that do not have a readily determinable fair value. Other investments do not include

[1] The Financial Accounting Standards Board (FASB) *Accounting Standards Codification* (ASC) 958-210-45-6 states that cash or other assets received with a donor-imposed restriction that limits their use to long-term purposes should not be classified with cash or other assets that are unrestricted and available for current use. Therefore, as stated in FASB ASC 958-320-45-10 and illustrated in FASB ASC 958-205-55-7, cash and cash equivalents of permanent endowment funds held temporarily until suitable long-term investment opportunities are identified are included in the classification long-term investments on a statement of financial position rather than as cash. Likewise, cash held temporarily by a custodian for investment purposes may be included as part of investments in a statement of financial position rather than as cash.

[*] On May 26, 2010, FASB issued a proposed Accounting Standards Update (ASU), *Accounting for Financial Instruments and Revisions to the Accounting for Derivative Instruments and Hedging Activities*, intended to improve accounting for financial instruments. Among other changes, the proposed ASU reconsiders the recognition and measurement of financial instruments, addresses issues related to impairment of financial instruments, simplifies hedge accounting, and increases convergence in accounting for financial instruments with International Financial Reporting Standards (IFRSs). It would incorporate both amortized cost and fair value information about financial instruments held for collection or payment of cash flows. On January 31, 2011, FASB and the International Accounting Standards Board jointly issued a supplementary document, *Accounting for Financial Instruments and Revisions to the Accounting for Derivative Instruments and Hedging Activities: Impairment*, to address a number of questions that arose from the comments received on the proposed ASU. Readers should be alert for the issuance of a final ASU.

investments described in the preceding 3 bullets or investments in consolidated subsidiaries.

8.02 This chapter does not discuss the standards for investments in consolidated subsidiaries. Those standards are discussed in chapter 3, "Basic Financial Statements and General Financial Reporting Matters," of this guide. It also does not discuss investments held by a financially interrelated entity, which are subject to the requirements of FASB ASC 958-20 rather than the requirements of FASB ASC 958-320 or FASB ASC 958-325. Discussion of financially interrelated entities begins at paragraph 5.26 of this guide. Split-interest gifts, including investments held by others, are discussed in chapter 6, "Split-Interest Agreements," of this guide. Chapter 13, "Expenses, Gains, and Losses," of this guide discusses investment expenses.

8.03 The guidance in this chapter also does not apply to investments held by an NFP as an agent. Pursuant to FASB ASC 958-320-25-3, FASB ASC 958-320-35-3, FASB ASC 958-325-25-2, and FASB ASC 958-325-35-16, if an NFP is holding an investment as an agent and has little or no discretion in determining how the investment income, unrealized gains and losses, and realized gains and losses resulting from those investments will be used, those investment activities should be reported as agency transactions and, therefore, as changes in assets and liabilities rather than as changes in net assets. Chapter 5, "Contributions Received and Agency Transactions," of this guide includes guidance concerning distinguishing contributions from agency transactions, including transactions in which a donor grants variance power and those in which the donor transfers the assets to a financially interrelated entity.

8.04 This chapter provides accounting and auditing guidance concerning the initial recognition and measurement, investment income, the measurement attributes used for subsequent valuation, unrealized and realized gains and losses, and financial statement display and disclosure. Unless specifically stated, that guidance does not apply to investments in equity securities that are accounted for under the equity method and investments in consolidated subsidiaries. Many of the requirements under generally accepted accounting principles in these areas are the same as those for for-profit entities. Accordingly, this chapter focuses on those issues that are unique to NFPs.

Initial Recognition

8.05 Pursuant to FASB ASC 958-320-30-1 and FASB ASC 958-325-30-1, investments included within the scope of FASB ASC 958-320 and FASB ASC 958-325 are initially measured at their acquisition cost (including brokerage and other transaction fees) if they are purchased and are initially measured at fair value if they are received as a contribution or through an agency transaction. Pursuant to FASB ASC 815-10-30, all derivative instruments are measured initially at fair value. Investments that are accounted for under the equity method generally are measured initially at cost pursuant to FASB ASC 323-10-30, although FASB ASC 970-323-30 provides more specific guidance for real estate ventures, and FASB ASC 323-10-30-2 requires initial measurement at fair value for a retained investment in the common stock of an investee (including a joint venture) in a deconsolidation transaction.[†]

[†] The guidance in FASB ASC 323-10-30-2 is labeled as "Pending Content" due to the transition and open effective date information discussed in FASB ASC 810-10-65-3. It reflects changes made by

(continued)

8.06 Paragraphs 3.73–.94 of this guide discuss FASB ASC 820, *Fair Value Measurements and Disclosures*, which defines *fair value*, establishes a framework for measuring fair value, and requires disclosures about fair value measurements.[‡, ||] Chapter 5 of this guide discusses the classification of contributions.

Investment Income[2]

8.07 Per FASB ASC 958-320-45-2, dividend, interest, and other investment income should be reported in the period earned as increases in unrestricted net assets unless the use of the assets received is limited by donor-imposed restrictions. Donor restricted investment income should be reported as an increase in temporarily restricted net assets or permanently restricted net assets, depending on the type of restriction.[3]

8.08 For example, if there are no donor-imposed restrictions on the use of the income, it should be reported as an increase in unrestricted net assets. On the other hand, a donor may stipulate that a gift be invested in perpetuity with the income to be used to support a specified program. The initial gift creates permanently restricted net assets. Unless the NFP elects the alternative accounting policy described in paragraph 8.32, the investment income is temporarily restricted for support of the donor-specified program. If the restrictions on the income are met, the statement of activities should report a reclassification from temporarily restricted net assets to unrestricted net assets.

8.09 FASB ASC 958-225-45-14 specifies that a statement of activities should report the gross amounts of revenues and expenses. It also notes, however, that investment revenues may be reported net of related expenses, such as custodial fees and internal and external investment advisory costs, provided

---

(footnote continued)

ASU No. 2010-02, *Consolidation (Topic 810): Accounting and Reporting for Decreases in Ownership of a Subsidiary—a Scope Clarification*, issued in January 2010. Not-for-profit entities should apply the guidance in ASU No. 2010-02 for the first set of initial or annual financial statements for a reporting period beginning on or after December 15, 2009.

‡ Some of the guidance in FASB ASC 820, *Fair Value Measurements and Disclosures*, is labeled as "Pending Content" due to the transition and open effective date information discussed in FASB ASC 820-10-65. For example, ASU No. 2010-06, *Fair Value Measurements and Disclosures (Topic 820): Improving Disclosures about Fair Value Measurements*, is effective for interim and annual reporting periods beginning after December 15, 2009, except for the separate disclosures about purchases, sales, issuances, and settlements relating to level 3 measurements (see FASB ASC 820-10-50-2(c)(2)), which shall be effective for fiscal years beginning after December 15, 2010, and for interim periods within those fiscal years. Early adoption is permitted.

|| On June 29, 2010, FASB issued a proposed ASU, *Amendments for Common Fair Value Measurement and Disclosure Requirements in U.S. GAAP and IFRSs*, intended to develop common requirements for measuring fair value and for disclosing information about fair value measurements in U.S. generally accepted accounting principles and IFRSs. For many of the proposed requirements, FASB does not expect the amendments to result in changes in the application of FASB ASC 820. Other amendments would change a particular principle or requirement. The most notable of these changes are as follows: highest and best use and valuation premise, measuring the fair value of an instrument classified in shareholders' equity, measuring the fair value of instruments that are managed within a portfolio, and application of blockage factors and other premiums and discounts in a fair value measurement. The proposed standards also include additional disclosure requirements. Readers should be alert to the issuance of a final ASU.

2 Investment revenue is often referred to as income. It includes dividends, interest, rents, royalties, and similar payments on assets held as investments.

3 Paragraph 8.33 discusses an alternative accounting policy for circumstances in which temporary restrictions on investment income are met in the same reporting period as the income is recognized.

that the amount of the expenses is disclosed either in the statement of activities or in notes to financial statements.

Valuation Subsequent to Acquisition

Equity Securities With Readily Determinable Fair Value (Other Than Consolidated Subsidiaries and Equity Securities Reported Under the Equity Method) and All Debt Securities

8.10 FASB ASC 958-320-35-1 requires that investments in equity securities with readily determinable fair value and all investments in debt securities be measured at fair value in the statement of financial position.

Investments That Are Accounted for Under the Equity Method or a Fair Value Election

8.11 Investments in common stock and in-substance common stock of for-profit entities should be reported under the equity method if required by FASB ASC 323-10. (For additional information, see paragraph 3.49 of this guide.) Investments in certain for profit limited partnerships, unincorporated joint ventures, and limited liability companies should be reported under the equity method if required by FASB ASC 323-30 or FASB ASC 970-323. (For additional information, see paragraph 3.51 of this guide.) However, NFPs that choose to report investment portfolios at fair value in conformity with paragraph 8.15 or that make an election to report an investment at fair value pursuant to the "Fair Value Option" subsections of FASB ASC 825-10 may do so instead of applying the equity method of accounting to investments covered by this paragraph.

8.12 The FASB ASC glossary defines *in-substance common stock* as an investment in an entity that has risk and reward characteristics that are substantially similar to that entity's common stock. The characteristics of in-substance common stock are discussed at paragraphs 13–14 of FASB ASC 323-10-15. Paragraphs 1–18 of FASB ASC 323-10-55 provide examples applying the characteristics to various investments.

8.13 Per FASB ASC 958-810-15-4(d), an NFP with more than a minor interest in a for-profit real estate partnership, [for-profit real estate] limited liability company, or similar [for-profit real estate] entity should report a noncontrolling interest in such an entity using the equity method in accordance with the guidance in FASB ASC 970-323 unless that interest is reported at fair value in conformity with FASB ASC 958-810-15-4(e). NFPs that choose to report investment portfolios at fair value in conformity with the guidance in paragraph 8.15 or that make an election to report an investment at fair value pursuant to FASB ASC 825-10-25-1 (the fair value option) may do so instead of applying the equity method of accounting to investments covered by this paragraph.

Derivative Instruments

8.14 FASB ASC 815-10-25-1 and FASB ASC 815-10-35-1 require that investments in derivative instruments be reported as either assets or liabilities depending on the rights or obligations under the contracts and should be subsequently remeasured at fair value. Similarly, an embedded derivative shall be separated from the host contract and accounted for as a derivative instrument pursuant to FASB ASC 815-10 if and only if all of the criteria in FASB ASC 815-15-25-1 are met. Paragraphs 8.49–.56 of this guide further discuss derivative instruments.

Other Investments

8.15 Guidance concerning the carrying amounts of other investments subsequent to acquisition differs depending upon the type of NFP, as follows:

- Per paragraphs 1–2 of FASB ASC 958-325-35, institutions of higher education, including colleges, universities, and community or junior colleges, should subsequently report other investments at either of the following measures: (*a*) current market value or fair value or (*b*) carrying value (that is, those that were acquired by purchase are reported at cost and those that were contributed other investments are reported at their fair value at the date of the gift). However, the carrying value should be adjusted if there has been an impairment of value that is not considered to be temporary. The same measurement attribute should be used for all other investments excluding those for which the institution chose, at a specified election date, to measure at fair value pursuant to FASB ASC 815-15-25 or the "Fair Value Option" subsections of FASB ASC 825-10. (For more information about the election to report at fair value, see paragraphs 3.95–.97.) Investments in wasting assets are usually reported net of an allowance for depreciation or depletion.
- Per paragraphs 3–4 of FASB ASC 958-325-35, voluntary health and welfare entities should report other investments at either of the following measures: (*a*) carrying value (that is, cost if purchased and fair value at the date of the contribution if contributed) or (*b*) market value. The same measurement attribute should be used for all other investments excluding those for which the voluntary health and welfare entity chose, at a specified election date, to measure at fair value pursuant to FASB ASC 815-15-25 or the "Fair Value Option" subsections of FASB ASC 825-10. (For more information about the election to report at fair value, see paragraphs 3.95–.97.) If other investments are not equity securities and the market value of the portfolio of those investments is below the recorded amount, it may be necessary to reduce the carrying amount of the portfolio to market or to provide an allowance for decline in market value. If it can reasonably be expected that the voluntary health and welfare entity will suffer a loss on the disposition of an investment, an impairment loss should be recognized in the period in which the decline in value occurs.
- Per paragraphs 6–7 of FASB ASC 958-325-35, NFPs that are not colleges, universities, voluntary health and welfare entities, or health care entities should report other investments using one of the following measures: (*a*) fair value or (*b*) the lower of cost or fair value. The same measurement attribute should be used for all other investments excluding those for which the NFP chose, at a specified election date, to measure at fair value pursuant to FASB ASC 815-15-25 or the "Fair Value Option" subsections of

FASB ASC 825-10. (For more information about the election to report at fair value, see paragraphs 3.95–.97.) If other investments are not equity securities and are carried at the lower of cost or market value, declines in the value of those investments should be recognized if their aggregate market value is less than their carrying amount, recoveries of aggregate market value in subsequent periods should be recorded in those periods subject only to the limitation that the carrying amount should not exceed the original cost.

- Notwithstanding the preceding bullet points, if other investments are equity securities that are reported at cost (carrying value), all NFPs, regardless of type, should apply paragraphs 8–13 of FASB ASC 958-325-35 to determine if an impairment loss should be recognized. In conformity with FASB ASC 320-10-35-17, NFPs do not apply tests for other-than-temporary impairment to debt securities unless the NFP reports a performance indicator as defined in FASB ASC 954-205-45 (healthcare entities).

Fair Value Measurements

8.16 FASB ASC 820 defines fair value, establishes a framework for measuring fair value, and expands disclosures about fair value measurements.[‡,||] Paragraphs 3.73–.94 of this guide summarize FASB ASC 820 but are not intended as a substitute for reading FASB ASC 820 itself.

8.17 Some NFPs invest in hedge funds, private equity funds, real estate funds, venture capital funds, offshore fund vehicles, and funds of funds, collectively referred to as alternative investments. Many of these investees provide their investors with a net asset value per share (or its equivalent) that has been calculated in a manner consistent with FASB ASC 946, *Financial Services—Investment Companies*. If those investments do not have readily determinable fair values, FASB ASC 820-10-35-59 permits a reporting entity, as a practical expedient, to estimate the fair value of an investment within the scope of paragraphs 4–5 of FASB ASC 820-10-15 using the net asset value per share (or its equivalent, such as member units or an ownership interest in partners' capital to which a proportionate share of net assets is attributed) of the investment, if the net asset value per share of the investment (or its equivalent) is calculated in a manner consistent with the measurement principles of FASB ASC 946 as of the reporting entity's measurement date. FASB ASC 820-10-50-6A requires certain disclosures for these investments, regardless of whether net asset value is used as a practical expedient.

8.18 Technical Questions and Answers (TIS) sections 2220.18–.26 (AICPA, *Technical Practice Aids*) are intended to assist reporting entities in applying the provisions of FASB ASC 820 discussed in the preceding paragraph. TIS section 2220.27, "Determining Fair Value of Investments When the Practical Expedient Is Not Used or Is Not Available" (AICPA, *Technical Practice Aids*), assists reporting entities in determining the fair value of investments in circumstances in which the practical expedient (net asset value) is not used or is not available.

---

‡ See footnote ‡ in paragraph 8.06.

|| See footnote || in paragraph 8.06.

Unrealized and Realized Gains and Losses

8.19 Unrealized gains and losses arise from changes in the fair value of investments, exclusive of dividend and interest income recognized but not yet received and exclusive of any write-down of the carrying amount of investments for impairment. Unrealized gains and losses are recognized in some circumstances (for example, when the investments are carried at fair value), but not in others (for example, when the investments are carried at cost). Paragraph 8.15, however, provides guidance pertaining to circumstances in which unrealized losses on investments carried at cost should be recognized.

8.20 Realized gains and losses arise from selling or otherwise disposing of investments. If realized gains and losses arise from selling or otherwise disposing of investments for which unrealized gains and losses have been recognized in the statement of activities of prior reporting periods, the amount reported in the statement of activities as gains or losses upon the sale or other disposition of the investments should exclude the amount that has previously been recognized in the statement of activities. However, the components of that gain or loss may be reported as the realized amount (the difference between amortized cost and the sales proceeds) and the unrealized amount recognized in prior reporting periods. Table 8-1 illustrates this reporting.

Table 8-1

Facts

1. In 20X1, a not-for-profit entity with a December 31 year end purchases an equity security with a readily determinable fair value for $5,000.
2. At December 31, 20X1, the fair value of the security is $7,000.
3. During 20X2, the security is sold for $11,000.

Reporting Gains and Losses

20X1 Recognize a $2,000 gain and adjust the carrying value to $7,000. (The reported gain equals $7,000 fair value less $5,000 carrying value.)

20X2 Recognize a $4,000 gain and adjust the carrying value to zero. (The gain may be reported as the net of $11,000 selling price less the $7,000 carrying value at the time the security was sold. Alternatively, the gain may be displayed as the realized gain of $6,000 [$11,000 selling price less $5,000 cost] less the $2,000 unrealized gain previously recognized.)

8.21 To the extent that they are recognized, FASB ASC 958-320-45-1 requires that investment gains and losses should be reported in the statement of activities as increases or decreases in unrestricted net assets unless their use is temporarily or permanently restricted by explicit donor stipulations or by law.[4]

---

[4] Paragraph 8.33 discusses an alternative accounting policy for circumstances in which temporary restrictions on gains are met in the same reporting period as the gains are recognized.

Investment Pools

8.22 An NFP may pool part or all of its investments (including investments arising from contributions with different kinds of restrictions) for portfolio management purposes. The number and the nature of the pools may vary from NFP to NFP. When a pool is established, ownership interests are initially assigned (typically through unitization) to the various pool categories (sometimes referred to as *participants*) based on the market value of the cash and securities placed in the pool by each participant. Current market value is used to determine the number of units allocated to additional assets placed in the pool and to value withdrawals from the pool. Investment income and realized gains and losses (and any recognized unrealized gains and losses) are allocated equitably based on the number of units assigned to each participant.

Donor-Restricted Endowment Funds

8.23 The FASB ASC glossary defines a *donor-restricted endowment fund* as an endowment fund that is created by a donor stipulation requiring investment of the gift in perpetuity or for a specified term. Some donors may require that a portion of income, gains, or both be added to the gift and invested subject to similar restrictions. FASB ASC 958-205-45-14 states that

> when classifying an endowment fund, each source—original gift, gains and losses, and interest and dividends—must be evaluated separately. Each source is unrestricted unless its use is temporarily or permanently restricted by explicit donor stipulations or by law. Thus, an endowment fund that is created by a governing board from unrestricted net assets is classified as unrestricted because all three sources are free of donor restrictions. If an endowment fund is created by a donor, the donor may have placed different restrictions on each of the three sources. Generally, classification of the original gifts and the income earned by endowments is straightforward because usually donors explicitly state any time or purpose restrictions on those two sources. Determining how to classify gains on endowments may not be as easy because agreements with donors often are silent on how gains should be used and whether losses must be restored immediately from future gains, or not at all.

8.24 FASB ASC 958-205-45-28 and FASB ASC 958-205-45-33 provide guidance for determining the permanently restricted portion of a donor-restricted endowment fund. Those paragraphs state that

> an NFP that is subject to an enacted version of the Uniform Prudent Management of Institutional Funds Act (UPMIFA) shall classify a portion of a donor-restricted endowment fund of perpetual duration as permanently restricted net assets. The amount classified as permanently restricted shall be either (a) the amount of the fund that must be retained permanently in accordance with explicit donor stipulations (see paragraphs 958-605-45-3 through 45-4) or (b) the amount of the fund that, in the absence of explicit donor stipulations, the NFP's governing board determines must be retained (preserved) permanently consistent with the relevant law (see paragraph 958-205-45-21).
>
> In states that have enacted a version of the Uniform Management of Institutional Funds Act of 1972 (UMIFA) or states whose relevant

law is based on trust law, it is generally understood that at least the amount of the original gift(s) and any required accumulations is not expendable, although the value of the investments purchased may occasionally fall below that amount. Future appreciation of the investments generally restores the value to the required level. In states that have enacted its provisions, UMIFA describes "historic dollar value" as the amount that is not expendable.

8.25 Paragraphs 13–35 of FASB ASC 958-205-45 describe the presentation of endowment funds in the financial statements. That guidance is summarized in the following four paragraphs.

8.26 Unless gains and losses (net appreciation) are temporarily or permanently restricted by a donor's explicit stipulation or by a law that extends a donor's restriction to them, gains and losses (net appreciation) of a donor-restricted endowment fund are changes in unrestricted net assets. For example, if a donor stipulates that net gains be added to the principal of its gift until that endowed gift plus accumulated gains increases to a specified dollar level, the gains are permanently restricted. Similarly, if a donor states that a specific investment security must be held in perpetuity, the gains and losses on that security are subject to that same permanent restriction unless the donor specifies otherwise. However, if a donor allows the NFP to choose suitable investments, the gains are not permanently restricted unless the donor or the law requires that an amount be retained permanently.

8.27 In a state that has enacted a version of UMIFA, gains are unrestricted if the investment income is unrestricted or are temporarily restricted if the investment income is temporarily restricted by the donor unless the donor stipulates otherwise. In a state with UMIFA-based law, legal limitations may require the governing board to act to appropriate net appreciation for expenditure under a statutorily prescribed standard of ordinary business care and prudence. Per FASB ASC 958-205-45-20, reference to a standard of ordinary business care and prudence do not extend donor restrictions to the net appreciation on investments of a donor-restricted endowment fund. A requirement to exercise ordinary business care and prudence is not a limitation that is more specific than the broad limits of the environment in which charitable and other NFPs operate. Thus, a legal limitation that requires that a governing board exercise ordinary business care and prudence when appropriating net appreciation is not the equivalent of a law that extends a donor-imposed restriction and, therefore, by itself does not result in classification of net appreciation as donor-restricted, either permanently or temporarily. However, because UMIFA states that net appreciation may be appropriated "for the uses and purposes for which an endowment is established," the classification of income determines the classification of gains unless the donor stipulates otherwise.

8.28 In a state that has enacted a version of UPMIFA, legal limitations may state that, "unless stated otherwise in the gift instrument, the assets in an endowment fund are donor-restricted assets until appropriated for expenditure by the institution" (subsection 4(a) of UPMIFA). FASB ASC 958-205-45-30 states that for each donor-restricted endowment fund for which the restriction described in subsection 4(a) of UPMIFA applies, an NFP should classify the portion of the fund that is not classified as permanently restricted net assets as temporarily restricted net assets (time restricted) until appropriated for expenditure by the NFP. Pursuant to FASB ASC 958-205-45-31, in the absence of interpretation of the phrase *appropriated for expenditure* in subsection 4(a) of UPMIFA by legal or regulatory authorities (for example, court decisions or interpretations by state attorneys general), appropriation for expenditure is deemed to occur upon approval for expenditure, unless approval is for a future period, in which case appropriation is deemed to occur when that period is reached. Upon appropriation for expenditure, the time restriction expires to the extent of the amount appropriated and, in the absence of any purpose restrictions, results in a reclassification of that amount to unrestricted net assets. If the fund is also subject to a purpose restriction, the reclassification of the appropriated amount to unrestricted net assets would not occur until that purpose restriction also has been met, in accordance with the guidance beginning in FASB ASC 958-205-45-9. Pursuant to FASB ASC 958-205-45-11, temporarily restricted net assets with time restrictions are not available to support expenses until the time restrictions have expired.

8.29 In the absence of donor stipulations or law to the contrary, losses on the investments of a donor-restricted endowment fund shall reduce temporarily restricted net assets to the extent that donor-imposed temporary restrictions on net appreciation of the fund have not been met before a loss occurs. Any remaining loss shall reduce unrestricted net assets. Per FASB ASC 958-205-45-29, the amount of permanently restricted net assets is not reduced by losses on the investments of the fund or by an NFP's appropriations from the fund. If losses (or in UPMIFA states, appropriations) reduce the assets of a donor-restricted endowment fund below the level required by the donor stipulations or law, gains that restore the fair value of the assets of the endowment fund to the required level shall be classified as increases in unrestricted net assets.

8.30 After the fair value of the assets of the endowment fund equals the required level, gains that are restricted by the donor should be classified as increases in temporarily restricted net assets or permanently restricted net assets, depending on the donor's restrictions on the endowment fund.

8.31 FASB ASC 958-205-05-9 notes that because donor stipulations and laws vary, NFPs must assess the relevant facts and circumstances for their endowment gifts and their relevant laws to determine if net appreciation on endowments is available for spending or is permanently restricted.

8.32 In other words, classification of gains and losses (net appreciation) should be based on the underlying facts and circumstances. Donors or relevant law may require an NFP to retain permanently some portion of net appreciation on donor-restricted endowment funds. If limitations exist that preclude the use of net appreciation on permanently restricted net assets, either as a result of explicit or clear implicit donor stipulations or by the law of the relevant jurisdiction, the net gains are permanently restricted. In the absence of such a donor restriction or law, in a state with UMIFA-based law, gains on the investments of a donor-restricted endowment fund are unrestricted if the investment income is unrestricted or are temporarily restricted if the investment income is temporarily restricted by the donor because, in the absence of donor stipulations or law to the contrary, donor restrictions on the use of income of an endowment fund extend to the net appreciation on the endowment fund. In a state with UPMIFA-based legislation, gains on the investments of a donor-restricted endowment fund are temporarily restricted (time restricted) until appropriated for expenditure, and are also purpose restricted if the use of investment income is restricted as to purpose.

Financial Statement Presentation

8.33 FASB ASC 958-320-45-3 states that gains and investment income that are limited to specific uses by donor-imposed restrictions may be reported as increases in unrestricted net assets if the restrictions are met in the same reporting period as the gains and income are recognized, provided that the NFP has a similar policy for reporting contributions received,[5] reports consistently from period to period, and discloses its accounting policy in the notes to the financial statements.

8.34 Realized and unrealized losses on investments may be netted against realized and unrealized gains on a statement of activities.

8.35 FASB ASC 958-320-45-9 explains that some NFPs, in managing their endowment funds, use a spending-rate or total return policy. Those policies consider total investment return—investment income (interest, dividends, rents, and so forth) plus net realized and unrealized gains (or minus net losses). Typically, spending-rate or total return policies emphasize the use of prudence and a rational and systematic formula to determine the portion of cumulative investment return that can be used to support operations of the current period and the protection of endowment gifts from a loss of purchasing power as a consideration in determining the formula to be used. Example 1 (FASB ASC 958-320-55-4) illustrates a statement of activities and example disclosures of an NFP that uses a spending rate policy to include only a portion of its investment return in its operating measure.

8.36 Even if an NFP uses a spending-rate formula to determine how much of that return will be used for current operations, all investment income and recognized gains and losses should be reported on the statement of activities and classified as unrestricted unless restricted by the donor or applicable law. NFPs are permitted to provide information on the face of the statement of activities and the notes to the financial statements about the total return on investments by segregating the total return between operating and nonoperating components based on a spending-rate formula.

8.37 FASB ASC 958-320-45-6 explains that some NFPs, primarily health care entities, would like to compare their results to business entities in the same industry. An NFP with those comparability concerns may report in a manner similar to business entities by identifying securities as available-for-sale or held-to-maturity as described in paragraphs 1–6 of FASB ASC 320-10-25 and excluding the unrealized gains and losses on those securities from an operating measure within the statement of activities. Per FASB ASC 958-320-50-1, a reconciliation of investment return to amounts reported in the statement of activities is required to be presented if investment return is separated into operating and nonoperating amounts.

8.38 Example 1 (paragraphs 4–10 of FASB ASC 958-320-55) illustrates a statement of activities that reports a portion of investment return within a measure of operations. If investment return is separated into operating and nonoperating amounts, certain information, as discussed in paragraph 8.44 of

---

[5] Chapter 5, "Contributions Received and Agency Transactions," of this guide discusses the accounting policy for reporting contributions received if the organization meets donor-imposed restrictions on all or a portion of the amount contributed in the same reporting period as the contribution is received.

this guide, is required to be disclosed. Those disclosures are also illustrated in the example.

8.39 The majority of the disclosures for investments are located in the "Disclosure" subsections (sections 50) of FASB ASC 958-320, FASB ASC 958-325, and FASB ASC 825-10. The following paragraphs discuss the more common of those disclosures but are not intended as a substitute for reading the "Disclosure" subsections of FASB ASC. Certain of the disclosures are illustrated in FASB ASC 958-320-55.

8.40 Paragraphs 20–22 of FASB ASC 825-10-50 require that an NFP disclose all significant concentrations of credit risk arising from all financial instruments, including significant concentrations of credit risk arising from derivative instruments, whether from an individual counterparty or groups of counterparties. Further, as explained in FASB ASC 825-10-55-1, the terms of certain loan products may increase a reporting entity's exposure to credit risk and thereby may result in a concentration of credit risk.*

8.41 An individual concentration of risk could exist, for example, if an NFP invests a significant amount in the securities of a single corporation or government entity. A group concentration could exist, for example, if an NFP invests a significant amount in debt securities of a single industry or a single geographic region. Program loan investments that permit low payments in early years of the loan and higher payments later in the loan's life also may result in a concentration of credit risk.

8.42 Paragraphs 10–19 of FASB ASC 825-10-50 require various disclosures, including disclosures of fair value and carrying amounts for all financial instruments for which it is practicable to estimate that value, the method(s) and significant assumptions used to estimate the fair value of financial instruments, and the changes in the those methods and significant assumptions, if any, during the period.* FASB ASC 825-10-50-3 states that disclosures required by the "General" subsection of FASB ASC 825-10-50 are optional if an entity meets all of the following 3 criteria: (*a*) the entity is a nonpublic entity, (*b*) the entity's total assets are less than $100 million on the date of the financial statements, and (*c*) the entity has no instrument that, in whole or in part, is accounted for as a derivative instrument. For purposes of criterion (*a*), the FASB ASC glossary defines a *nonpublic entity* as

> any entity that does not meet any of the following conditions: (*a*) its debt or equity securities trade in a public market either on a stock exchange (domestic or foreign) or in the over-the-counter market, including securities quoted only locally or regionally, (*b*) it is a conduit bond obligor for conduit debt securities that are traded in a public market (a domestic or foreign stock exchange or an over-the-counter market, including local or regional markets), (*c*) it files with a regulatory agency in preparation for the sale of any class of debt or equity securities in a public market, or (*d*) it is controlled by an entity covered by the preceding criteria.

8.43 Investments that are reported under FASB ASC 958-320 and derivative financial instruments reported under FASB ASC 815 are already carried at fair value and would not require the disclosures of fair value and carrying

---

* See footnote * in chapter title.

amounts required by the preceding paragraph if they are separately reported in the body of the financial statements.

8.44 FASB 860-30-50-1A(a) requires that NFPs that enter into repurchase agreements or securities lending transactions disclose their policies for requiring collateral or other security. FASB ASC 860-30-50-1A(c) requires that if an NFP accepts collateral that it is permitted by contract or custom to sell or repledge, it should disclose (1) the fair value as of the date of each statement of financial position presented of that collateral, (2) the fair value as of the date of each statement of financial position presented of the portion of that collateral that it has sold or repledged, and (3) information about the sources and uses of that collateral.

8.45 For each period for which a statement of activities is presented, an NFP should disclose

a. pursuant to FASB ASC 958-320-50-1, the composition of investment return including, at a minimum, investment income, net realized gains or losses on investments reported at other than fair value, and net gains or losses on investments reported at fair value.

b. pursuant to FASB ASC 958-320-50-1, a reconciliation of investment return to amounts reported in the statement of activities if investment return is separated into operating and nonoperating amounts, together with a description of the policy used to determine the amount that is included in the measure of operations and a discussion of circumstances leading to a change, if any, in that policy. The reconciliation need not be provided if an NFP includes all investment return in its measure of operations or excludes it from that measure entirely.

c. the information required by FASB ASC 825-10-50-30, as modified by FASB ASC 815-10-15-7.*

d. the information required by FASB ASC 825-10-50-32 if the NFP made an election pursuant to FASB 825-10-25-4(d) or 9(e) during the period.*

8.46 Per FASB ASC 958-325-45-2, the statement of activities of an institution of higher education should set forth the total performance (that is, investment income and realized and unrealized gains and losses) of the other investment portfolio unless that information is disclosed in the notes.

8.47 For each period for which a statement of financial position is presented, an NFP should disclose

a. pursuant to FASB ASC 958-320-50-2, the aggregate carrying amount of investments by major types, for example, equity securities, U.S. Treasury securities, corporate debt securities, mortgage-backed securities, oil and gas properties, and real estate.

b. pursuant to FASB ASC 958-325-50-2(a), the basis for determining the carrying amount for investments within the scope of FASB ASC 958-325.

c. pursuant to FASB ASC 958-325-50-2(b), the method(s) and significant assumptions used to estimate the fair values of investments

---

* See footnote * in chapter title.

other than financial instruments if those other investments are reported at fair value.

d. pursuant to FASB ASC 958-205-50-2, the aggregate amount of the deficiencies for all donor-restricted endowment funds for which the fair value of the assets at the reporting date is less than the level required by donor stipulations or law.

e. the information required by FASB ASC 320-10-50-6(a) if the NFP holds cost-method investments in an unrealized loss position for which impairment losses have not been recognized.

f. the information required by FASB ASC 325-20-50-1 if the NFP has cost-method investments.

g. the information required by paragraphs 1–4 of FASB ASC 820-10-50 for investments measured at fair value, if applicable.

h. the information required by paragraphs 28–29 of FASB ASC 825-10-50, if the NFP has made an election as described in the "Fair Value Option" subsections of FASB ASC 825-10.*

i. pursuant to FASB ASC 958-205-50-1B(a), a description of the governing board's interpretation of the law(s) that underlies the NFP's net asset classification of donor-restricted endowment funds.

j. pursuant to FASB ASC 958-205-50-1B(b), a description of the NFP's policy(ies) for the appropriation of endowment assets for expenditure (its endowment spending policy(ies)).

k. pursuant to FASB ASC 958-205-50-1B(c), a description of the NFP's endowment investment policies. The description should include the NFP's return objectives and risk parameters; how those return objectives relate to the NFP's endowment spending policy(ies); and the strategies employed for achieving those return objectives.

l. pursuant to FASB ASC 958-205-50-1B(d), the composition of the NFP's endowment by net asset class at the end of the period, in total and by type of endowment fund, showing donor-restricted endowment funds separately from board-designated endowment funds.

m. pursuant to FASB ASC 958-205-50-1B(e), a reconciliation of the beginning and ending balance of the NFP's endowment, in total and by net asset class, including, at a minimum, all of the following line items (as applicable): investment return, separated into investment income (for example, interest, dividends, rents) and net appreciation or depreciation of investments; contributions; amounts appropriated for expenditure; reclassifications; and other changes.

8.48 For the most recent period for which a statement of financial position is presented, an NFP should disclose

a. pursuant to FASB ASC 958-320-50-3, the nature of and carrying amount for each individual investment or group of investments that represents a significant concentration of market risk, such as risks that result from the nature of the investments or from a lack of diversity of industry, currency, or geographic location.

---

* See footnote * in chapter title.

b. the information required by FASB ASC 320-10-50-6(b) if the NFP has cost-method investments in an unrealized loss position for which impairment losses have not been recognized.

c. the information required by FASB ASC 825-10-50-30, if the NFP has made an election as described in the "Fair Value Option" subsections of FASB ASC 825-10.*

Additionally, paragraphs 1–2 of FASB ASC 825-10-45 require that, if an NFP elects the fair value option, it display on the face of its statement of financial position (either by separate line items or parenthetically) the assets and liabilities reported at fair value separately from the carrying amounts of similar assets and liabilities measured using another measurement attribute.*

Accounting for Derivative Instruments and Hedging Activities*

8.49 Paragraphs 83–139 of FASB ASC 815-10-15 define a *derivative financial instrument*. FASB ASC 815-10-15-83 states that a *derivative instrument* is a financial instrument or other contract with all of the following characteristics:

a. Underlying, notional amount, payment provision. The contract has both of the following terms, which determine the amount of the settlement or settlements, and, in some cases, whether or not a settlement is required: (1) one or more underlyings and (2) one or more notional amounts or payment provisions or both.

b. Initial net investment. The contract requires no initial net investment or an initial investment that is smaller than would be required for other types of contracts that would be expected to have a similar response to changes in market factors.

c. Net settlement. The contract can be settled net by any of the following means: (1) its terms implicitly or explicitly require or permit net settlement, (2) it can readily be settled net by a means outside the contract, or (3) it provides for delivery of an asset that puts the recipient in a position not substantially different from net settlement.

8.50 The FASB ASC glossary defines an *underlying* as a variable that, along with either a notional amount or a payment provision, determines the settlement of a derivative instrument. Per paragraphs 88–89 of FASB ASC 815-10-15, an underlying usually is one or a combination of the following:

a. A security price or security price index

b. A commodity price or commodity price index

c. An interest rate or interest rate index

d. A credit rating or credit index

e. An exchange rate or exchange rate index

f. An insurance index or catastrophe loss index

g. A climatic or geological condition (such as temperature, earthquake severity, or rainfall), another physical variable, or a related index

---

* See footnote * in chapter title.

h. The occurrence or nonoccurrence of a specified event (such as a scheduled payment under a contract)

However, an underlying may be any variable whose changes are observable or otherwise objectively verifiable. An underlying may be a price or rate of an asset or liability but is not the asset or liability itself.

8.51 The FASB ASC glossary defines a *notional amount* as a number of currency units, shares, bushels, pounds, or other units specified in a derivative instrument. Sometimes other names are used. For example, the notional amount is called a *face amount* in some contracts. Per FASB ASC 815-10-15-92, the settlement of a derivative instrument with a notional amount is determined by interaction of that notional amount with the underlying. The interaction may be simple multiplication, or it may involve a formula with leverage factors or other constants. The FASB ASC glossary states that a *payment provision* specifies a fixed or determinable settlement to be made if the underlying behaves in a specified manner.

8.52 Options, futures, forwards, and swaps are common examples of derivative instruments. Investments in convertible debt securities are an example of an instrument with an embedded derivative. Unique to NFPs are embedded derivatives related to certain split interest agreements, as discussed in paragraphs 6.24–.28 of this guide. Accounting and reporting of investments in derivative instruments is subject to the requirements of FASB ASC 815. A brief summary of FASB ASC 815 is provided in paragraphs 8.48–.55 of this guide but is not intended as a substitute for the reading FASB ASC 815.

8.53 FASB ASC 815 establishes accounting and reporting standards for derivative instruments, including certain derivative instruments embedded in other contracts, (collectively referred to as derivatives) and for hedging activities. FASB ASC 815-10-05-4 explains that FASB ASC 815 requires that an entity recognize derivatives instruments, including certain derivative instruments embedded in other contracts, as assets or liabilities in the statement of financial position and measure them at fair value. If certain conditions are met, an entity may elect, under FASB ASC 815, to designate a derivative instrument in any one of the following ways: (*a*) a hedge of the exposure to changes in the fair value of a recognized asset or liability, or of an unrecognized firm commitment, that are attributable to a particular risk (referred to as a fair value hedge), (*b*) a hedge of the exposure to variability in the cash flows of a recognized asset or liability, or of a forecasted transaction, that is attributable to a particular risk (referred to as a *cash flow hedge*) or (*c*) a hedge of the foreign currency exposure of any one of the following: (1) an unrecognized firm commitment (a foreign currency fair value hedge), (2) an available-for-sale security (a foreign currency fair value hedge), (3) a forecasted transaction (a foreign currency cash flow hedge), or (4) a net investment in a foreign operation. FASB ASC 815-30-15-2 states that NFPs and other entities that do not report earnings are not permitted to use cash flow hedge accounting because they do not report earnings separately.

8.54 The accounting for changes in the fair value of a derivative (that is, gains and losses) depends on the intended use of the derivative and the resulting designation. The changes in fair value of derivative instruments or hedged items are classified as unrestricted unless their use is temporarily or permanently restricted by donors or by law.[6]

---

[6] Paragraph 8.32 discusses an alternative accounting policy for circumstances in which temporary restrictions on gains are met in the same period in which the gains are recognized.

8.55 FASB ASC 815 includes certain provisions regarding reporting of changes in the value of a derivative and a hedged item by NFPs and other entities that do not report earnings, as follows:

- FASB ASC 815-10-35-3 states that an entity that does not report earnings as a separate caption in a statement of financial performance (for example, an NFP or a defined benefit plan pension plan) shall recognize the gain or loss on a nonhedging derivative instrument as a change in net assets in the period of change.
- FASB ASC 815-25-35-19 states that an entity that does not report earnings as a separate caption in a statement of financial performance (for example, an NFP or a defined benefit pension plan) shall recognize the gain or loss on a hedging instrument as a change in net assets in the period of change unless the hedging instrument is designated as a hedge of the foreign currency exposure of a net investment in a foreign operation. In that circumstance, the provisions of FASB ASC 815-20-25-66 and paragraphs 1–2 of FASB ASC 815-35-35 shall be applied. Entities that do not report earnings shall recognize the changes in the carrying amount of the hedged item pursuant to paragraphs 1–4 of FASB ASC 815-25-35 in a fair value hedge as a change in net assets in the period of change.
- FASB ASC 815-30-15-3 states that consistent with the provisions of FASB ASC 958, *Not-for-Profit Entities*, the provisions of FASB ASC 815-30 do not prescribe how an NFP should determine the components of an operating measure, if one is presented.

8.56 The "Disclosure" subsections of FASB ASC 815 subtopics contain extensive disclosure requirements.

Auditing

8.57 Many audit objectives, controls, and auditing procedures for investments of NFPs are similar to those of other entities. For further information about auditing investments and implementing AU section 332, *Auditing Derivative Instruments, Hedging Activities, and Investments in Securities* (AICPA, *Professional Standards*), see the AICPA Audit Guide *Auditing Derivative Instruments, Hedging Activities, and Investments in Securities*. AU section 328, *Auditing Fair Value Measurements and Disclosures* (AICPA, *Professional Standards*), addresses audit considerations relating to the measurement and disclosure of assets, liabilities, and specific components of equity presented or disclosed at fair value in financial statements. In addition, the auditor may need to consider the specific audit objectives, selected controls, and auditing procedures that are unique to NFPs and that are presented at the end of this chapter.

8.58 Interpretation No. 1, "Auditing Investments in Securities Where a Readily Determinable Fair Value Does Not Exist," of AU section 332 (AICPA, *Professional Standards*, AU sec. 9332 par. .01–.04), provides additional guidance for auditing securities, such as hedge funds, for which a readily determinable fair value does not exist. NFPs may elect to report those securities at fair value as described in paragraph 8.15 of this guide. The interpretation states that in circumstances in which the auditor determines that the nature and extent of auditing procedures should include verifying the existence and testing the measurement of investments in securities, simply receiving a confirmation from a third party, either in aggregate or on a security-by-security basis, does not in and of itself constitute adequate audit evidence with respect to the valuation assertion in AU section 332. In addition, receiving confirmation from a third party for investments in aggregate does not constitute adequate audit evidence with respect to the existence assertion under AU section 332. Receiving confirmation from a third party on a security-by-security basis, however, typically would constitute adequate audit evidence with respect to the existence assertion under AU section 332. When auditing investments for which readily determinable fair value does not exist, auditors may find useful the practice aid *Alternative Investments—Audit Considerations*. That practice aid, which was developed and issued by the Alternative Investments Task Force, is available at www.aicpa.org/InterestAreas/AccountingAndAuditing/Resources/AudAttest/AudAttestGuidance/DownloadableDocuments/Alternative_Investments_Practice_Aid.pdf. In circumstances in which the auditor is unable to audit the existence or measurement of interests in investments in securities at the financial statement date, the auditor should consider whether that scope limitation requires the auditor to either qualify his or her opinion or to disclaim an opinion, as discussed in paragraphs .22–.26 of AU section 508, *Reports on Audited Financial Statements* (AICPA, *Professional Standards*). The practice aid states that the more complex or illiquid the underlying investments of an alternative investment are, the greater the inherent uncertainty in management's estimated fair value. As the inherent uncertainty in the estimate increases, as well as the significance of the alternative investments to the financial statements, auditors may consider inclusion of an emphasis of matter paragraph in the auditors' report. Such paragraphs are never required and are included solely at the auditor's discretion. The practice aid includes an example of an emphasis of matter paragraph.

Net Appreciation on Endowment Funds

8.59 As discussed in paragraphs 8.23–.32 of this guide, net appreciation on donor-restricted endowment funds should be reported as a change in unrestricted net assets unless the appreciation is temporarily or permanently restricted by explicit donor-imposed stipulations or by law.

8.60 As discussed in FASB ASC 958-205-05-8, laws concerning use of net appreciation of endowment funds that are donor-restricted may vary from jurisdiction to jurisdiction. For example, some jurisdictions follow trust law, and others follow an enacted version of either UMIFA or UPMIFA (including interpretations of those laws issued by state Attorneys General).

8.61 In July 2006, the National Conference of Commissioners on Uniform State Laws issued the UPMIFA as model legislation to be adopted, in whole or in part, by the individual states as a replacement for UMIFA. More than half of the states have adopted the provisions of UPMIFA (in whole or in part), and additional states have introduced legislation to change their laws. Readers should be alert to changes in their state law and the possible effects of those changes on classification of net assets. In August 2008, FASB issued guidance concerning the effect of the adoption of the model UPMIFA on the classification of net assets related to donor-restricted endowment funds, which is included in sections 45, 50, and 55 of FASB ASC 958-205. Paragraphs 8.23–.32 provide more information about that guidance.

8.62 Generally, in jurisdictions following trust law, net appreciation is not spendable and therefore should be added to permanently restricted net assets. Also, it has generally been interpreted that, absent donor restrictions, net appreciation is spendable under UMIFA and UPMIFA and therefore should not be added to permanently restricted net assets. Paragraphs 8.23–.32 provide further guidance about classification of net appreciation of endowment funds.

8.63 FASB ASC 958-205-55-1 states that how an enacted version of UPMIFA will be interpreted and enforced in a particular state will become clearer with the passage of time. Because the legislation is newly enacted, no case law currently exists for its interpretation. In the meantime, NFPs could look to other sources, such as the discussion that occurred in the legislative committees leading to the law adopted in a particular state, announcements from the state attorney general, a consensus of learned lawyers in the state, or similar information, to help them understand what the law requires. In the absence of new legislation, clarifying court decisions, additional guidance issued by the state attorney general, or similar developments, the governing board's interpretation of the relevant law should be consistent from year to year.

8.64 Auditors may find information available from State Societies of Certified Public Accountants, state Attorneys General, and industry publications useful in obtaining an understanding of these issues. As discussed in paragraph .07 of AU section 333, *Management Representations* (AICPA, *Professional Standards*), the representation letter ordinarily should be tailored to include additional appropriate representations, an example being where the representations from management about any interpretations made by the NFP's governing board concerning whether laws limit the amount of net appreciation of donor-restricted endowment funds that may be spent. However, for NFPs operating in jurisdictions in which there may be questions concerning interpretations of the applicable laws or in which there are conflicting interpretations by various legal counsel, auditors may find it helpful to request that the NFP obtain a specific opinion from legal counsel concerning interpretation of the legal requirements. AU section 336, *Using the Work of a Specialist* (AICPA, *Professional Standards*), provides guidance concerning circumstances in which the auditor relies on the representations or work of an attorney for other than litigation, claims, and assessments as addressed in AU section 337, *Inquiry of a Client's Lawyer Concerning Litigation, Claims, and Assessments* (AICPA, *Professional Standards*).

Audit Objectives and Procedures

8.65 The following table illustrates the use of assertions in developing audit objectives and designing substantive tests. The examples are not intended to be all-inclusive nor is it expected that all the procedures would necessarily be applied in an audit. The auditor should design and perform substantive procedures for all relevant assertions related to each material class of transactions, account balance, and disclosure to obtain sufficient appropriate audit evidence. The use of assertions in assessing risks and designing appropriate audit procedures to obtain audit evidence is described in paragraphs .14–.26 of AU section 326, *Audit Evidence* (AICPA, *Professional Standards*). Various audit procedures and the purposes for which they may be performed are described in paragraphs .27–.41 of AU section 326.

Auditing Considerations

Financial Statement Assertions	*Specific Audit Objectives*	*Examples of Selected Controls*	*Examples of Auditing Procedures*
Presentation and Disclosure			
Contributed Investments, Investment Income, Gains, and Losses			
Rights and obligations; Classification	Restrictions on contributed investments are reflected in the classification of net assets.	Contributions of investments and investment income, gains, and losses are reviewed for restrictions and management monitors compliance with restrictions.	Review donor correspondence to determine the existence of restrictions on, and classification of, investments and related income, gains, and losses.
	Restrictions on investment income, net realized gains, and net recognized unrealized gains that are imposed by donors or by law are reflected in the classification of revenue and gains.		Review minutes of governing board and governing board committee meetings for evidence of donor or statutory restrictions on, and classification of, investments and related income, gains, and losses. If specific investments are restricted, review investment transactions for the propriety of dispositions.
Reclassification of Restricted Net Assets			
Occurrence/ Existence; Classification	Restricted net assets are reclassified as unrestricted net assets in the statement of activities when restrictions are met on investment income or net appreciation restricted for support of donor-specified programs.		Determine that appropriate reclassifications are made in the statement of activities when restrictions are met on investment income or net appreciation restricted for donor-specified programs.

Chapter 9

Property, Plant, and Equipment

Introduction

9.01 Not-for-profit entities (NFPs) use various kinds of property and equipment to provide goods and services to beneficiaries, customers, and members. Property and equipment include all long-lived tangible assets held by NFPs, except collection items[1] and assets held for investment purposes.

9.02 Property and equipment commonly held by NFPs include the following:

- Land used as a building site not subject to depreciation
- Land improvements, buildings and building improvements, equipment, furniture and office equipment, library books, motor vehicles, and similar depreciable assets
- Leased property and equipment (capitalized in conformity with Financial Accounting Standards Board [FASB] *Accounting Standards Codification* [ASC] 840-30)*
- Improvements to leased property
- Construction in process
- Contributed use of facilities and equipment (recognized in conformity with the "Contributions Received" subsections of FASB ASC 958-605, as illustrated in paragraphs 23–25 of FASB ASC 958-605-55)

Recognition and Measurement Principles

9.03 NFPs acquire the use of property and equipment through purchases, trade-ins, self-construction, leases, and contributions. NFPs should apply the guidance in FASB ASC 360, *Property, Plant, and Equipment*, except when it conflicts with the specialized guidance for NFPs in FASB ASC 958-360.

9.04 Per FASB ASC 958-605-55-25, property and equipment used in exchange transactions (other than lease transactions), such as federal contracts, in which the resource provider retains legal title during the term of the arrangement should be reported as a contribution at fair value at the date received by the NFPs only if it is probable that the NFP will be permitted to keep the assets when the arrangement terminates. Per FASB ASC 958-360-50-4, the terms of such arrangements should be disclosed in notes to the financial statements.

---

[1] Because of their unique nature, collection items are reported differently from how other long-lived tangible assets are reported. Chapter 7, "Other Assets," of this Audit and Accounting Guide discusses accounting for collection items.

* On August 17, 2010, the Financial Accounting Standards Board (FASB) issued a proposed Accounting Standards Update (ASU), *Leases (Topic 840)*, which would make significant changes to the accounting requirements for both lessees and lessors. FASB initiated a joint project with the International Accounting Standards Board to develop a new approach to lease accounting that would ensure that assets and liabilities arising under leases are recognized in the statement of financial position. Readers should be alert to the issuance of a final ASU.

Contributed Property and Equipment

9.05 Pursuant to FASB ASC 958-605-25-2, 958-605-30-2, and 958-605-45-3, contributions of property and equipment (including unconditional promises to give property and equipment) should be recognized at fair value[2,†] at the date of contribution and, depending on donor restrictions and the NFP's accounting policy, should be included in permanently restricted, temporarily restricted, or unrestricted net assets. If the donors stipulate how or how long contributed property and equipment must be used by the NFP, the contribution should be reported as restricted support. If the donors do not specify such restrictions, the contribution should be reported as restricted support if the NFP has adopted an accounting policy of implying a time restriction on the use of such assets that expires over the assets' useful lives. In the absence of donor restrictions or an NFP's policy of implying time restrictions, contributions of long-lived assets should be reported as unrestricted support.

9.06 In practice, contributions of depreciable assets generally do not increase permanently restricted net assets. As noted in paragraph 120 of FASB Concepts Statement No. 6, *Elements of Financial Statements—a replacement of FASB Concepts Statement No. 3 (incorporating an amendment of FASB Concepts Statement No. 2)*, "receipt of a contribution increases permanently restricted net assets if the donor stipulates that the resources received must be maintained permanently and those resources are capable of providing future economic benefit indefinitely. Only assets that are not by their nature used up in carrying out the organization's activities are capable of providing economic benefits indefinitely."

9.07 Unconditional promises to give property and equipment should be recognized as receivables in conformity with paragraphs 8–10 of FASB ASC 958-605-25. Contributions of the use of property and equipment in which the donor retains legal title to the assets are discussed in paragraphs 5.100–.101.

9.08 Per FASB ASC 958-360-30-1, similar to items acquired in exchange transactions, the amount initially recognized for contributed property and equipment should include all the costs incurred by the entity to place those

---

[2] FASB *Accounting Standards Codification* (ASC) 820, *Fair Value Measurements and Disclosures*, defines *fair value* and establishes a framework for measuring fair value. Paragraphs 3.73–.94 discuss those standards. Some of the guidance in FASB ASC 820 is labeled as "Pending Content" due to the transition and open effective date information discussed in FASB ASC 820-10-65. For example, ASU No. 2010-06, *Fair Value Measurements and Disclosures (Topic 820): Improving Disclosures about Fair Value Measurements*, is effective for interim and annual reporting periods beginning after December 15, 2009, except for the separate disclosures about purchases, sales, issuances, and settlements relating to level 3 measurements (see FASB ASC 820-10-50-2(c)(2)), which shall be effective for fiscal years beginning after December 15, 2010, and for interim periods within those fiscal years. Early adoption is permitted. In addition, chapter 5, "Contributions Received and Agency Transactions," of this guide discusses measuring the fair value of contributed assets.

[†] On June 29, 2010, FASB issued a proposed ASU, *Amendments for Common Fair Value Measurement and Disclosure Requirements in U.S. GAAP and IFRSs*, intended to develop common requirements for measuring fair value and for disclosing information about fair value measurements in U.S. generally accepted accounting principles and International Financial Reporting Standards. For many of the proposed requirements, FASB does not expect the amendments to result in changes in the application of FASB ASC 820. Other amendments would change a particular principle or requirement. The most notable of these changes are: highest and best use and valuation premise, measuring the fair value of an instrument classified in shareholders' equity, measuring the fair value of instruments that are managed within a portfolio, and application of blockage factors and other premiums and discounts in a fair value measurement. The proposed standards also include additional disclosure requirements. Readers should be alert to the issuance of a final ASU.

assets in use. Examples of such costs include the freight and installation costs of contributed equipment and cataloging costs for contributed library books.

Depreciation and Amortization

9.09 Paragraph 149 of FASB Concept No. 6 describes depreciation as a "systematic and rational" process for allocating the cost of using up assets' service potential or economic benefit over the assets' useful economic lives. Depreciation should be recognized for contributed property and equipment as well as for plant and equipment acquired in exchange transactions.

9.10 Paragraphs 1–6 of FASB ASC 958-360-35 require all NFPs to recognize depreciation for all property and equipment except land used as a building site, certain works of art or historical treasures with extraordinarily long lives, and similar assets.

9.11 Per FASB ASC 958-360-35-7, the terms of certain grants and reimbursements from other entities may specify whether depreciation or the entire cost of the asset in the year of acquisition should be included as a cost of activities associated with those grants or reimbursements for contractual purposes (sometimes referred to as *allowable costs*). Those terms should not affect the recognition and measurement of depreciation for financial reporting purposes.

9.12 Paragraphs 1–2 of FASB ASC 958-360-45 provide guidance for reclassification of net assets upon the expiration of donor restrictions related to property, plant, and equipment. Depreciation expense should be reported in a statement of activities as a decrease in unrestricted net assets. If the property, plant, and equipment items being depreciated were contributed to the NFP with a donor-imposed restriction on the item's use, temporarily restricted net assets should, over time, be reclassified as unrestricted net assets in a statement of activities as those restrictions expire. The amount reclassified may or may not be equal to the amount of the related depreciation. The amount to be reclassified is based on the length of time indicated by the donor-imposed restrictions, and the amount of depreciation is based on the useful economic life of the asset. For example, a computer with an estimated useful economic life of 5 years may be contributed by a donor and restricted for a specific use by the NFP for 3 years. Reclassifications are also necessary if an NFP has adopted an accounting policy that implies a time restriction on contributions of property, plant, and equipment that expires over the useful life of the contributed assets. Pursuant to FASB ASC 958-225-45-3, reclassifications should be reported as separate items in a statement of activities.

9.13 FASB ASC 840-10-35-6 states that leasehold improvements that are placed in service significantly after and not contemplated at or near the beginning of the lease term should be amortized over the shorter of the following terms: (*a*) the useful life of the assets or (*b*) a term that includes required lease periods and renewals that are deemed to be reasonably assured (as used in the context of the definition of lease term) at the date the leasehold improvements are purchased.

Impairment or Disposal of Long-Lived Assets

9.14 The "Impairment or Disposal of Long-Lived Assets" subsections of FASB ASC 360-10 provide guidance whenever events or changes in circumstances indicate that the carrying amount of a long-lived asset (asset group)[3] may not be recoverable. This paragraph and the next two summarize that guidance but are not intended as a substitute for reading those subsections. FASB ASC 360-10-35-17 states that an impairment loss shall be recognized only if the carrying amount of the long-lived asset (or asset group) is not recoverable and exceeds its fair value. The carrying amount of a long-lived asset (asset group) is not recoverable if it exceeds the sum of the undiscounted cash flows expected to result from use and eventual disposition of the asset (asset group). FASB ASC 958-360-35-8 provides guidance for determining the appropriate cash flows of an NFP that relies in part on contributions to maintain its assets. That assessment shall be based on the carrying amount of the asset (asset group) at the date it is tested for recoverability, whether in use (see FASB ASC 360-10-35-33) or under development (see FASB ASC 360-10-35-34). An impairment loss should be measured as the amount by which the carrying amount of a long-lived asset (asset group) exceeds its fair value.

9.15 A long-lived asset is classified as held and used until it is disposed of or it meets the criteria to be classified as held for sale. An asset (disposal group) should be classified as held for sale in the period in which all of the criteria in FASB ASC 360-10-45-9 are met. If at any time afterwards the criteria are no longer met (except in certain limited circumstances beyond the entity's control, as discussed in FASB ASC 360-10-45-11), a long-lived asset (disposal group) classified as held for sale should be reclassified as held and used in accordance with FASB ASC 360-10-35-44. Further, if the criteria in FASB ASC 360-10-45-9 for classifying a long-lived asset (disposal group) as held for sale are met after the balance sheet date, but before the issuance of the financial statements, a long-lived asset (disposal group) should be classified as held and used in those financial statements when issued and certain disclosures are required.

9.16 A long-lived asset (disposal group) that is held for sale should be measured at the lower of its carrying amount or fair value less cost to sell. A long-lived asset should not be depreciated (amortized) while it is classified as held for sale. (Interest and other expenses attributable to the liabilities of a disposal group held for sale should continue to be accrued.) FASB ASC 205-20 provides guidance on when the results of operations of a component of an entity that either has been disposed of or is classified as held for sale would be reported as a discontinued operation in the financial statements of the entity. FASB ASC 205-20-55 is intended to help an entity determine whether the 2 conditions described in FASB ASC 205-20-45-1 are met and, if so, result in

---

[3] The FASB ASC glossary defines an *asset group* as the unit of accounting for a long-lived asset or assets to be held and used, which represents the lowest level for which identifiable cash flows are largely independent of the cash flows of other groups of assets and liabilities. The FASB ASC glossary states that a *disposal group* for a long-lived asset or assets to be disposed of by sale or otherwise represents assets to be disposed of together as a group in a single transaction and liabilities directly associated with those assets that will be transferred in the transaction. Per FASB ASC 360-10-15-4, examples of liabilities included in a disposal group are legal obligations that transfer with a long-lived asset, such as certain environmental obligations, and obligations that, for business reasons, a potential buyer would prefer to settle when assumed as part of a group, such as warranty obligations that relate to an acquired customer base. Per FASB ASC 360-10-35-24, in limited circumstances, a long-lived asset (for example, a corporate headquarters facility) may not have identifiable cash flows that are largely independent of the cash flows of other assets and liabilities and of other asset groups. In those circumstances, the asset group for that long-lived asset should include all assets and liabilities of the entity.

reporting the results of operations of a component of an entity in discontinued operations.‡

Asset Retirement Obligations

9.17 FASB ASC 410-20 establishes accounting standards for recognition and measurement of a liability for an asset retirement obligation and the associated asset retirement cost. It applies to legal obligations associated with the retirement of a tangible long-lived asset that result from the acquisition, construction, development, or normal operation of a long-lived asset, including any legal obligations that require disposal of a replaced part that is a component of a tangible long-lived asset, with exceptions for certain obligations. An entity is required to recognize a liability if the obligation to perform the asset retirement activity is unconditional, even though the timing or method of settlement may be uncertain. An entity should recognize the fair value of a liability for an asset retirement obligation in the period in which it is incurred if a reasonable estimate of fair value can be made. (An expected present value technique will usually be the only appropriate technique with which to estimate the fair value of a liability for an asset retirement obligation.) An entity should capitalize an asset retirement cost by increasing the carrying amount of the related long-lived asset by the same amount as the liability.

9.18 For example, an NFP would have an asset retirement obligation if it accepted a gift of a building with the stipulation that in 10 years the building would be destroyed and the land converted to a garden that would be open to the public.

Gains and Losses

9.19 Gains and losses recognized on property and equipment, including impairment losses, should be classified in a statement of activities as changes in unrestricted net assets unless explicit donor stipulations or law require their use to be restricted. In those situations, gains or losses should be classified as increases or decreases in temporarily restricted or permanently restricted net assets, as appropriate. Per FASB ASC 360-10-45-5, if a gain or loss is recognized on the sale of a long-lived asset (disposal group) that is not a component of an entity, it should be included in a subtotal, such as income from operations, if one is presented.

Financial Statement Presentation

9.20 FASB ASC 958-225-45-11 states that if a subtotal, such as income from operations, is presented, it shall include the amounts of an impairment loss recognized for a long-lived asset (asset group) to be held and used, pursuant to FASB ASC 360-10-45-4.

9.21 FASB ASC 958-360-50 and FASB ASC 360-10-50 list most of the disclosures required for property, plant, and equipment. The following paragraph

---

‡ On September 25, 2008, FASB issued an exposure draft of proposed FASB Staff Position (FSP) FAS 144-d, *Amending the Criteria for Reporting a Discontinued Operation*. The proposed FSP would define when a component of an entity should be reported in the "Discontinued Operations" section of the statement of activities and enhance the disclosure requirements for all components of an entity that have been disposed of or are classified as held for sale. In December 2009, FASB decided that the proposed guidance would be re-exposed. Readers should be alert to the issuance of a final ASU.

lists some of the more common of those disclosures, as well as other locations in FASB ASC that require disclosures about property, plant, and equipment.

9.22 A statement of financial position or related notes should include the balances of each major class of property and equipment. The basis of valuation—for example, cost for purchased items and fair value for contributed items—should also be disclosed. Separate disclosure should also be made of the following items:

- Nondepreciable assets
- Property and equipment not held for use in operations, for example, items held for sale or for investment purposes or construction in process
- FASB ASC 958-210-50-3 requires disclosure of the nature and amount of limitations on the use of cash and cash equivalents and assets whose use is limited, including assets restricted by donors to investment in property, plant, and equipment
- Improvements to leased facilities and equipment
- FASB ASC 840-30-50 requires disclosures about assets (and related obligations) recognized under capital leases[*]
- FASB ASC 835-20-50 requires disclosures about capitalized interest
- FASB ASC 205-20-50 requires disclosures about assets sold or held for sale
- Significant accounting policies concerning property and equipment, such as the following:
    - — The capitalization policy adopted
    - — Whether time restrictions are implied on the use of contributed long-lived assets (and contributions of assets restricted to purchase them) received without donor stipulations concerning how long the contributed assets must be used
    - — That donor-restricted contributions of long-lived assets are reported as unrestricted when restrictions are satisfied in the same reporting period in which the contributions are received, pursuant to FASB ASC 958-605-45-4, if that policy is adopted

9.23 Accumulated depreciation, either for each major class of property and equipment or in total, should be disclosed (*a*) as a deduction or parenthetically in a statement of financial position or (*b*) in the notes to the financial statements. The amount of depreciation expense for the period and the method or methods used to compute depreciation for the major classes of property and equipment should also be disclosed.

9.24 The notes to the financial statements should also include disclosures concerning the liquidity of the NFP's property and equipment, including information about limitations on their use. For example, information should be provided about

---

[*] See footnote * in paragraph 9.02.

- property and equipment pledged as collateral or otherwise subject to lien.
- property and equipment acquired with restricted assets where title may revert to another party, such as a resource provider.
- donor or legal limitations on the use of or proceeds from the disposal of property and equipment.
- impaired long-lived assets reported at fair value, as required by FASB ASC 820-10-50-5.

9.25 Example 3 in paragraph 5.134 illustrates how, in notes to the financial statements, an NFP might disclose alternative policies for implying time restrictions on the use of contributed long-lived assets (and contributions of assets restricted to purchase them) received without donor stipulations concerning how long the contributed assets must be used in notes to the financial statements. Paragraph 9.05 discusses those alternative accounting policies.

Auditing

9.26 As discussed in paragraphs 5.100–.101 of this guide, an NFP may have access to the use of property or equipment that is neither owned nor leased. For example, property or equipment may be provided by a related NFP (such as a religious order), by unrelated entity under affiliation programs, or by a governmental agency or unit. The auditor should inquire into, and the financial statements should disclose, the nature of any relationship between the NFP and the owners of the property or equipment. Contributions of property or its use received by the NFP are measured at fair value. AU section 328, *Auditing Fair Value Measurements and Disclosures* (AICPA, *Professional Standards*), addresses audit considerations relating to the measurement and disclosure of assets, liabilities, and specific components of equity presented or disclosed at fair value in financial statements.

9.27 Many audit objectives, controls, and auditing procedures for property and equipment of NFPs are similar to those of other entities. In addition, the auditor may need to consider the following specific audit objectives, selected controls, and auditing procedures that are unique to NFPs.

9.28 The following table illustrates the use of assertions in developing audit objectives and designing substantive tests. The examples are not intended to be all-inclusive nor is it expected that all the procedures would necessarily be applied in an audit. The auditor should design and perform substantive procedures for all relevant assertions related to each material class of transactions, account balance, and disclosure to obtain sufficient appropriate audit evidence. The use of assertions in assessing risks and designing appropriate audit procedures to obtain audit evidence is described in paragraphs .14–.26 of AU section 326, *Audit Evidence* (AICPA, *Professional Standards*). Various audit procedures and the purposes for which they may be performed are described in paragraphs .27–.41 of AU section 326.

Auditing Considerations

Financial Statement Assertions	*Specific Audit Objectives*	*Examples of Selected Controls*	*Examples of Auditing Procedures*
Transactions			
Contributed Property and Equipment			
Valuation and allocation	Contributed property and equipment is reported at fair value at the date of contribution.	Controls ensure that contributions of property and equipment are known and recorded and that documentation supports the determination of their fair value.	Review documentation supporting the determination of fair value.
Property and Equipment Additions			
Rights and obligations	Appropriate resource provider approvals, if required, have been obtained for property and equipment additions.	Management monitors compliance with resource provider regulations related to additions to property and equipment. Additions are authorized in the capital budget.	Determine compliance with resource provider requirements.
Presentation and Disclosures			
Rights and obligations; Classification	Restrictions on contributed property and equipment are reflected in the classification of net assets.	Contributions of property and equipment are reviewed for restrictions and management monitors compliance with restrictions.	Review donor correspondence to determine the presence or absence of restrictions. Review minutes of governing board and governing board committee meetings for evidence of donor restrictions. If specific property or equipment is restricted, review contributed property and equipment transactions for propriety of use and dispositions.

Auditing Considerations—continued

Financial Statement Assertions	*Specific Audit Objectives*	*Examples of Selected Controls*	*Examples of Auditing Procedures*
Presentation and Disclosures—continued			
Classification	Property and equipment is reported in the proper net asset class.		Review documentation underlying contributions of property and equipment for propriety of classification.
Property and Equipment Not Held for Use in Operations			
Classification	Property and equipment not used in operations but held as an investment or for sale is separately reported.	Property records segregate property and equipment not used for operating purposes.	Determine that property and equipment not held for operating purposes is reported separately.
Reclassification of Temporarily Restricted Net Assets			
Occurrence/ Existence; Classification	Temporarily restricted net assets are reclassified as unrestricted net assets in the statement of activities over the term of the donor-imposed restrictions or when placed in service if the donor did not specify a term and one is not implied.		Determine that appropriate reclassifications are made on the statement of activities over the term of the donor-imposed restrictions or when placed in service if the donor did not specify a term and one is not implied.

Chapter 10

Debt and Other Liabilities

Introduction

10.01 Many obligations of not-for-profit entities (NFPs) are similar to those of for-profit entities. This chapter considers debt and other liabilities that are not discussed elsewhere in this Audit and Accounting Guide and that present accounting and auditing issues unique to NFPs.

10.02 As discussed in paragraphs 3.95–.97 of this guide, the "Fair Value Option" subsections of Financial Accounting Standards Board (FASB) *Accounting Standards Codification* (ASC) 825-10 permit an NFP to irrevocably elect fair value as the initial and subsequent measure for certain financial liabilities, with changes in fair value recognized in the statement of activities as those changes occur. The following liabilities that might exist for NFPs are outside the scope of the "Fair Value Option" subsections and thus cannot be reported at fair value: employers' and plans' obligations for pension benefits, other postretirement benefits (including health care and life insurance benefits), postemployment benefits, deferred compensation arrangements, financial liabilities recognized under lease contracts, current and deferred tax assets and liabilities, and liabilities that require the NFP to provide services, rather than cash or another financial asset, to the obligee.*

10.03 FASB ASC 820-10-35-18A states that an issuer should not include the effect of an inseparable third-party credit enhancement in the fair value measurement of a liability if that liability is measured or disclosed at fair value on a recurring basis. For example, in determining the fair value of debt with a third-party guarantee, the issuer would consider its own credit standing and not that of the third-party guarantor.

Tax-Exempt Financing and Long-Term Debt

10.04 An NFP may finance part of its activities from the proceeds of tax-exempt bonds or other obligations issued through state and local financing authorities. FASB ASC 958-470-25-1 states that because the NFP is responsible for the repayment of those obligations, that financing should be recognized as a liability in its statement of financial position. The FASB ASC glossary defines *conduit debt obligation* as

> Certain limited-obligation revenue bonds, certificates of participation, or similar debt instruments issued by a state or local governmental

---

* On May 26, 2010, the Financial Accounting Standards Board (FASB) issued a proposed Accounting Standard Update (ASU), *Accounting for Financial Instruments and Revisions to the Accounting for Derivative Instruments and Hedging Activities*, intended to improve accounting for financial instruments. Among other changes, the proposed ASU reconsiders the recognition and measurement of financial instruments, addresses issues related to impairment of financial instruments, simplifies hedge accounting, and increases convergence in accounting for financial instruments with International Financial Reporting Standards (IFRSs). It would incorporate both amortized cost and fair value information about financial instruments held for collection or payment of cash flows. On January 31, 2011, FASB and the International Accounting Standards Board jointly issued a supplementary document, *Accounting for Financial Instruments and Revisions to the Accounting for Derivative Instruments and Hedging Activities: Impairment*, to address a number of questions that arose from the comments received on the proposed ASU. Readers should be alert to the issuance of a final ASU.

entity for the express purpose of providing financing for a specific third party (the conduit bond obligor) that is not a part of the state or local government's financial reporting entity. Although conduit debt securities bear the name of the governmental entity that issues them, the governmental entity often has no obligation for such debt beyond the resources provided by a lease or loan agreement with the third party on whose behalf the securities are issued. Further, the conduit bond obligor is responsible for any future financial reporting requirements.

10.05 FASB ASC 470, *Debt*, provides accounting and reporting guidance for borrowers. Its subtopics include modifications and extinguishments and troubled debt restructurings by debtors, as well as others. FASB ASC 470-50-40 provides guidance for exchanges of debt instruments between, or modifications of a debt instrument by, a debtor and a creditor in a nontroubled debt situation and how to account for changes in line-of-credit or revolving-debt arrangements (for example, changing interest rates, draw-down amounts, covenants, and maturity). FASB ASC 470-50-50 requires disclosures for in-substance defeasance of debt that occurred prior to the effective date of FASB Statement No. 125, *Accounting for Transfers and Servicing of Financial Assets and Extinguishments of Liabilities* (generally defeasances prior to December 31, 1996).

10.06 FASB ASC 860-30-50-1A requires disclosures if an entity pledges any of its assets as collateral. NFPs should disclose qualitative information about the relationship(s) between collateral assets and associated liabilities. For example, if assets are restricted solely to satisfy a specific obligation, the nature of restrictions placed on the assets should be disclosed.[†]

Current and Deferred Tax Liabilities

10.07 Although NFPs are generally tax-exempt under various Internal Revenue Code sections,[1] some may be subject to taxes on various portions of their income, such as federal excise taxes on investment income or federal and state income taxes on unrelated business income. FASB ASC 740, *Income Taxes*, provides guidance on recognizing (*a*) the amount of taxes payable (or refundable) for the current year and (*b*) deferred-tax liabilities (and assets) for the estimated future tax consequences of temporary differences and carryforwards.

10.08 NFPs adopt many tax positions relative to tax laws, including those adopted in determining whether tax is due, a refund is owed, or a tax return needs to be filed. A tax position could result in or affect the measurement of a current or deferred tax asset or liability in the statement of financial position.

[†] Certain requirements are labeled as "Pending Content" due to the transition and open effective date information discussed in paragraphs 2–3 of FASB *Accounting Standards Codification* (ASC) 860-10-65. Prior to the effective date of the changes made by ASU No. 2009-16, *Transfers and Servicing (Topic 860): Accounting for Transfers of Financial Assets*, certain of the disclosures in FASB ASC 860-30-50-1A were required only of public entities. (Public entities are entities that do not meet the definition of a nonpublic entity. Paragraph 8.42 of this guide provides the FASB ASC glossary definition of a *nonpublic entity*). The changes made by ASU No. 2009-16 to extend the requirements to all entities are effective as of the beginning of the reporting entity's first annual reporting period that begins after November 15, 2009, including interim periods within that year.

[1] Some not-for-profit entities (NFPs) may meet the definition of an NFP as discussed in paragraphs 1.01–.02 of this guide but may nevertheless not be tax-exempt under the Internal Revenue Code (IRC). For example, an NFP that may otherwise qualify for tax-exempt status under the IRC may lose its tax exemption because it has violated the private inurement rules applicable to tax-exempt entities. Chapter 15, "Tax Considerations," of this guide discusses various requirements for maintaining tax-exempt status under the IRC.

Chapter 15, "Tax Considerations," of this guide discusses tax issues concerning NFPs, including recognition and measurement guidance for a tax position taken or expected to be taken in a tax return.

Deferred Revenue

10.09 Resources received in exchange transactions from customers, patients, and other service beneficiaries for specific projects, programs, or activities that have not yet taken place should be recognized as liabilities to the extent that the earnings process has not been completed. For example, resources received from the advance sale of season theater tickets should be recognized as deferred revenue, representing the obligation to hold the performances. That revenue is earned as the theater performances are held.

Refunds Due to and Advances From Third Parties

10.10 Some NFPs receive (*a*) advances from third parties, such as government agencies and foundations, based on the estimated cost of providing services to constituents and (*b*) resources from third parties to be used to make loans to the NFP's constituents. Advances from third parties for services not yet performed, as well as refunds due to third parties for amounts previously received under such agreements, should be included as liabilities on a statement of financial position.

Promises to Give

10.11 The FASB ASC glossary defines a *promise to give* as "a written or oral agreement to contribute cash or other assets to another entity. A promise carries rights and obligations—the recipient of a promise to give has a right to expect that the promised assets will be transferred in the future, and the maker has a social and moral obligation, and generally a legal obligation, to make the promised transfer. A promise to give may be either conditional or unconditional." Per FASB ASC 958-605-25-11, conditional promises to give should not be recognized until the conditions are substantially met.[2] FASB ASC 720-25-25 requires contributions made to be recognized as expenses in the period made and as decreases of assets or increases of liabilities depending on the form of the benefits given. In accordance with FASB ASC 958-720-25-2, unconditional promises to give should be recognized at the time the donor has an obligation to transfer the promised assets in the future, which generally occurs when the donor approves a specific grant or when the recipient of the promise is notified. If a donor explicitly reserves the right to rescind an intention to contribute, or if a solicitation explicitly allows a donor to rescind the intention, a promise to give should not be recognized by the donor. If payments of the unconditional promise to give are to be made to a recipient over several fiscal periods and the recipient is subject only to routine performance requirements, a liability and an expense for the entire amount payable should be recognized. FASB ASC 958-720-30-1 requires that the liability and expense be measured initially at fair value.

---

[2] Chapter 5, "Contributions Received and Agency Transactions," of this guide provides additional guidance for recognizing conditional promises to give.

10.12 Per FASB ASC 958-720-25-3, if an NFP makes contributions or awards grants to other NFPs upon specific requests of others, the NFP may be acting as an agent, trustee, or intermediary in a transfer between the donor and the beneficiary specified by the donor (agency transaction). The terms *agent*, *trustee*, and *intermediary* are defined by the FASB ASC glossary. Paragraph 10.17 of this guide describes liabilities for amounts held for others in agency transactions. Paragraphs 5.07–.35 of this guide provide further guidance about agency transactions.

10.13 Per FASB ASC 958-405-35-1, if the present value of the amounts to be paid is used to measure fair value[3,‡] of an unconditional promise to give, the discount rate should be determined at the time the unconditional promise to give is initially recognized and should not be revised, unless the promise to give is subsequently remeasured at fair value pursuant to the "Fair Value Option" subsections of FASB ASC 825-10. The interest method, described in FASB ASC 835-30-35-2, should be used to amortize discounts. Per FASB ASC 958-405-45-1, the amortization of any discount related to unconditional promises to give should be reported as a component of contribution expense, in the same functional classification in which the promise to give was reported.

10.14 If contributions payable are measured using present value techniques and the NFP has not elected to measure the payable at fair value as described in paragraph 10.02 of this guide, methods of amortization other than the interest method may be used if the results are not materially different. The discount should be amortized between the date the promise to give is initially recognized and the date the cash or other contributed assets are paid.

10.15 In addition to disclosures required by FASB ASC 450-20-50,[||] FASB ASC 958-405-50 requires that the notes to financial statements include a schedule of unconditional promises to give that shows the total amount separated into amounts payable in each of the next 5 years, the aggregate amount due in more than 5 years, and for unconditional promises to give that are reported using present value techniques, the unamortized discount.

---

[3] Paragraphs 3.73–.94 of this guide discuss FASB ASC 820, *Fair Value Measurements and Disclosures*, which defines *fair value* and establishes a framework for measuring fair value. Paragraphs 4–20 of FASB ASC 820-10-55 provide standards for using present value techniques when the measurement objective is fair value. Some of the guidance in FASB ASC 820 is labeled as "Pending Content" due to the transition and open effective date information discussed in FASB ASC 820-10-65. For example, ASU No. 2010-06, *Fair Value Measurements and Disclosures (Topic 820): Improving Disclosures about Fair Value Measurements*, is effective for interim and annual reporting periods beginning after December 15, 2009, except for the separate disclosures about purchases, sales, issuances, and settlements relating to level 3 measurements (see FASB ASC 820-10-50-2(c)(2)), which shall be effective for fiscal years beginning after December 15, 2010, and for interim periods within those fiscal years. Early adoption is permitted.

[‡] On June 29, 2010, FASB issued a proposed ASU, *Amendments for Common Fair Value Measurement and Disclosure Requirements in U.S. GAAP and IFRSs*, intended to develop common requirements for measuring fair value and for disclosing information about fair value measurements in U.S. generally accepted accounting principles and IFRSs. For many of the proposed requirements, FASB does not expect the amendments to result in changes in the application of FASB ASC 820. Other amendments would change a particular principle or requirement. The most notable of these changes are as follows: highest and best use and valuation premise, measuring the fair value of an instrument classified in shareholders' equity, measuring the fair value of instruments that are managed within a portfolio, and application of blockage factors and other premiums and discounts in a fair value measurement. The proposed standards also include additional disclosure requirements. Readers should be alert to the issuance of a final ASU.

[||] On July 20, 2010, FASB issued a proposed ASU, *Disclosure of Certain Loss Contingencies*. The proposed ASU would retain the current qualitative disclosures in FASB ASC 450-20 for loss contingencies and enhance them by requiring additional disclosures, particularly for litigation contingencies. Readers should be alert to the issuance of a final ASU.

Annuity Obligations

10.16 Some contributions received by NFPs, such as interests in charitable gift annuity contracts and charitable remainder and lead trusts, impose obligations on the NFP to make future payments to others. Guidance for reporting such contributions, often referred to as *split-interest agreements*, is included in chapter 6, "Split-Interest Agreements," of this guide. Annuity obligations arising from split-interest gifts should be recognized as liabilities. Paragraphs 6.19–.29 of this guide discuss periodic revaluations of the obligations under split-interest agreements, including whether the discount rate assumptions should be revised at each measurement date to reflect current market conditions. Periodic revaluations of these obligations result in changes in the value of split-interest agreements, which should be included as changes in the appropriate net asset classes in a statement of activities.

Amounts Held for Others Under Agency Transactions

10.17 Some NFPs receive assets in agency transactions. Paragraphs 23–24 of FASB ASC 958-605-25 discuss recognition of resources received by intermediaries and agents in agency transactions. If cash and other financial assets are held under agency transactions, the NFP should report a liability to the specified beneficiary concurrently with its recognition of those assets received from the donor. If the assets received from the donor are donated materials, supplies, or other nonfinancial assets, the intermediary or recipient entity may choose either to (*a*) report the receipt of the asset as a liability to the beneficiary concurrent with recognition of the assets received or (*b*) not to report the transaction at all. The choice is an accounting policy that should be applied consistently from period to period. FASB ASC 958-605-50-4 states that an intermediary or other recipient entity should disclose its accounting policy for recognizing nonfinancial assets that it accepts from a donor on behalf of a specified beneficiary. Paragraphs 5.07–.20 of this guide discuss agency transactions in more detail.

Revenue Sharing and Other Agreements

10.18 FASB ASC 958-810-25-7 notes that some NFPs enter into agreements with other entities, such as sharing revenue, resulting in liabilities to those other entities. In such circumstances, those liabilities should be reported. If NFPs agree to share revenue from fundraising campaigns, the appropriate accounting depends on the relationship between the NFPs. FASB ASC 958-20 discusses agreements for which an NFP agrees to raise or hold contributions for a financially interrelated entity (see paragraph 5.26 of this guide). FASB ASC 958-605-25-24 discusses agreements in which an NFP agrees to raise or hold contributions for another NFP as its agent (see paragraph 10.17 of this guide).

Exit or Disposal Activities

10.19 FASB ASC 420, *Exit or Disposal Cost Obligations*, provides financial accounting and reporting standards for costs associated with exit or disposal activities, including restructurings. Per FASB ASC 420-10-15-4, an exit activity includes, but is not limited to, a restructuring, such as the sale or termination of a line of business, the closure of business activities in a particular location, the relocation of business activities from one location to another, changes in management structure, or a fundamental reorganization that affects the nature and focus of operations. FASB ASC 420 discusses recognition of liabilities for the costs of exit activities, including one-time termination benefits provided to current employees that are involuntarily terminated, costs to terminate a contract that is not a capital lease, costs to consolidate facilities or relocate employees, costs associated with a disposal activity covered by FASB ASC 205-20, and costs associated with an exit activity, including exit activities associated with an entity newly acquired in a merger or acquisition. FASB ASC 410-20 and paragraphs 9.17–.18 of this guide discusses exit and disposal obligations associated with the retirement (sale, abandonment, recycling, disposal, or other other-than-temporary idling) of tangible long-lived assets and the associated asset retirement costs.

Guarantees

10.20 An NFP that issues certain guarantees, including guarantees of the debt of others, should recognize a liability for those guarantees, even in circumstances in which it is not probable that payments will be required under the guarantee.

10.21 FASB ASC 460, *Guarantees*, establishes the accounting and disclosure requirements to be met by a guarantor for certain guarantees issued and outstanding. FASB ASC 460-10-25-4 requires that at the inception of a guarantee, a guarantor shall recognize in its statement of financial position a liability for that guarantee. Per paragraphs 2–3 of FASB ASC 460-10-30, if a guarantee is issued as a contribution to an unrelated party, the liability recognized at the inception of the guarantee shall be measured at its fair value unless at the inception of the guarantee, the contingent liability amount required to be recognized at inception of the guarantee by FASB ASC 450-20-30 is greater. If a guarantee is issued in a standalone arm's-length transaction with an unrelated party, the liability recognized at the inception of the guarantee may be the premium received or receivable by the guarantor as a practical expedient. Per FASB ASC 460-10-35-1, the liability that the guarantor initially recognized would typically be reduced as the guarantor is released from risk under the guarantee. Disclosures about guarantees are required by FASB ASC 460-10-50.

Contingencies[||]

10.22 In conformity with FASB ASC 450-20, notes to the financial statements may have to include information about, or a liability may have to be accrued for, loss contingencies. FASB ASC 958-450-25-1 provides the following examples of circumstances that may result in such contingencies:

- Noncompliance with donor-imposed restrictions on contributed assets
- A problem with the NFP's tax-exempt status, or that a determination letter regarding that status has not been received

[||] See footnote || in paragraph 10.15.

Pension and Other Defined Benefit Postretirement Plan Obligations

10.23 An NFP that sponsors a single-employer defined benefit pension or postretirement plan should recognize the overfunded or underfunded status of that plan in its statement of financial position. The NFP should also recognize changes in that funded status in the year in which the changes occur as changes in unrestricted net assets. The underfunded status of a plan is a liability, and the overfunded status of a plan is an asset.

10.24 For a single-employer defined benefit pension plan, FASB ASC 715-30-25-1 states that if the projected benefit obligation exceeds the fair value of plan assets, the employer should recognize in its statement of financial position a liability that equals the unfunded projected benefit obligation. If the fair value of plan assets exceeds the projected benefit obligation, the employer shall recognize in its statement of financial position an asset that equals the overfunded projected benefit obligation. Per FASB ASC 715-30-35-62, the measurements of plan assets and benefit obligations required shall be as of the date of the employer's fiscal year-end statement of financial position, with limited exceptions.

10.25 For single-employer defined benefit postretirement plans other than pensions, FASB ASC 715-60-25-1 and FASB ASC 715-60-35-6 state that an employer that sponsors 1 or more plans should recognize in its statement of financial position the funded statuses of those plans, and should measure the funded status for each plan as the difference between the fair value of plan assets and the accumulated postretirement benefit obligation. Per FASB ASC 715-60-35-121, the measurements of plan assets and benefit obligations should be as of the date of the employer's fiscal year-end statement of financial position, with limited exceptions.

Auditing

10.26 Many audit objectives, controls, and auditing procedures for debt and other liabilities of NFPs are similar to those of other entities. In addition, the auditor may need to consider the following specific audit objectives, selected controls, and auditing procedures that are unique to NFPs.

10.27 The following table illustrates the use of assertions in developing audit objectives and designing substantive tests. The examples are not intended to be all-inclusive nor is it expected that all the procedures would necessarily be applied in an audit. The auditor should design and perform substantive procedures for all relevant assertions related to each material class of transactions, account balance, and disclosure to obtain sufficient appropriate audit evidence. The use of assertions in assessing risks and designing appropriate audit procedures to obtain audit evidence is described in paragraphs .14–.26 of AU section 326, *Audit Evidence* (AICPA, *Professional Standards*). Various audit procedures and the purposes for which they may be performed are described in paragraphs .27–.41 of AU section 326.

Auditing Considerations

Financial Statement Assertions	*Specific Audit Objectives*	*Examples of Selected Controls*	*Examples of Auditing Procedures*
Transactions			
Contributions Made			
Occurrence	Amounts recognized as contributions made are properly authorized and are reported in the period in which they become unconditional.	Controls ensure that only unconditional contributions made and promises to give are recognized in the financial statements.	Examine documentation supporting recognition of contributions made including notification of donee and whether the contribution is conditional or unconditional.
Completeness	All unconditional contributions made are recognized.	Controls ensure that all unconditional contributions made are recognized in the financial statements.	Review minutes of governing board and governing board committee meetings for information about contributions.
Valuation and allocation	Contributions made are measured at fair value at initial recognition.	Controls ensure the appropriate valuation of contributions made, including promises to give, at the time of initial recognition.	Review and test the method used for valuing contributions made, including promises to give.
Account Balances			
Tax-Exempt Financing			
Completeness	Amounts related to tax-exempt debt are recognized in the financial statements.	Reconcile outstanding balances and other relevant data with information received from the trustee.	Confirm outstanding balances and other relevant data with trustee.

Auditing Considerations—continued

Financial Statement Assertions	*Specific Audit Objectives*	*Examples of Selected Controls*	*Examples of Auditing Procedures*
Account Balances—continued			
			Review minutes of governing board and governing board committee meetings for information about tax-exempt financing.
Promises to Give			
Occurrence	Amounts recognized as contributions payable represent valid unconditional promises to give.	Controls ensure that only unconditional promises to give are recognized in the financial statements.	Examine documentation supporting recognition of contributions payable, including information such as the absence of conditions and the periods over which the promises to give become due.
Completeness	All unconditional promises to give are recognized.	Controls ensure that all unconditional promises to give are recognized in the financial statements.	Review minutes of governing board and governing board committee meetings for information about promises to give.
Cut-off	All unconditional promises to give are recognized in the proper period.	Controls ensure that contributions made near fiscal period end are recorded in the appropriate period.	Review cash disbursements subsequent to year-end to ascertain that contributions made were recorded in the proper period.
Valuation and allocation	Contributions made and related liabilities expected to be paid beyond one year are measured using the method elected by the NFP.	Controls ensure the appropriate valuation of promises to give at the end of the fiscal period.	Review and test the method used for valuing promises to give payable more than one year from the date of the financial statements.

(continued)

Auditing Considerations—continued

Financial Statement Assertions	*Specific Audit Objectives*	*Examples of Selected Controls*	*Examples of Auditing Procedures*
Presentation and Disclosure			
Tax-Exempt Financing			
Completeness	Disclosures related to tax-exempt debt are adequate.	Management monitors compliance with bond covenants and is aware of possible events of default.	Review financing agreements to ascertain that information about tax-exempt financing is properly reported and disclosed.

Chapter 11

Net Assets

Introduction

11.01 The Financial Accounting Standards Board (FASB) *Accounting Standards Codification* (ASC) glossary defines *net assets* as "the excess or deficiency of assets over liabilities of a not-for-profit entity (NFP), which is classified into three mutually exclusive classes according to the existence or absence of donor-imposed restrictions."[1] As a residual interest, net assets cannot be measured independently of an NFP's assets and liabilities. Changes in net assets result from transactions and other events and circumstances in which total assets and total liabilities change by different amounts. In many NFPs, such changes include nonreciprocal transfers of assets received from donors who do not expect to receive either repayment or proportionate economic benefit in return. Display of and disclosures about net assets and changes in them are intended to assist donors and other users in assessing an NFP's efforts to provide goods and services to its constituencies, its efficiency and effectiveness in providing such services, and its continuing ability to do so.

11.02 Changes in net assets result from revenues, expenses, gains, and losses; those changes are discussed in chapters 5–10 and 12–13 of this guide. This chapter describes principles for reporting total net assets in statements of financial position and changes in total net assets in statements of activities, as well as related disclosures.

Net Asset Classes

11.03 Paragraphs 9–11 of FASB ASC 958-210-45 provide guidance for the classification of net assets. The amounts for each of three classes of net assets—permanently restricted, temporarily restricted, and unrestricted—are based on the existence or absence of donor-imposed restrictions.

11.04 The FASB ASC glossary defines a *donor-imposed restriction* as

> a stipulation that specifies a use for a contributed asset that is more specific than the broad limits resulting from the following: (*a*) the nature of the NFP, (*b*) the environment in which it operates, and (*c*) the purposes specified in its articles of incorporation or bylaws or comparable documents for an unincorporated association. A donor-imposed restriction on an NFP's use of the asset contributed may be temporary or permanent. Some donor-imposed restrictions impose limits that are permanent, for example, stipulating that resources be invested in perpetuity (not used up). Others are temporary, for example, stipulating that resources may be used only after a specified date, for particular programs or services, or to acquire buildings and equipment.

11.05 In addition to the three classes of net assets—(*a*) permanently restricted, (*b*) temporarily restricted, and (*c*) unrestricted—further disaggregation of total net assets may also be reported. For example, unrestricted net

---

[1] Though not-for-profit entities (NFPs) may use other terms, such as *equity*, this Audit and Accounting Guide uses the term *net assets* to describe the residual interest.

assets may be subdivided into board-designated net assets and undesignated net assets. Donor-imposed restrictions limit an NFP's ability to use or dispose of specific contributed assets or the economic benefits embodied in those assets. Donor stipulations should not be considered restrictions unless they include limitations on the use of contributed assets that are more specific than the broad limits imposed by the NFP's purpose and nature.

11.06 FASB ASC 958-210-45-6 states that generally, donor-imposed restrictions apply to net assets, not to specific assets. Donors may also restrict specific assets regarding their use (for example, land contributed for a park) or over time (for example, contributed securities that must be held in perpetuity). Paragraphs 3.06 and 11.27 of this guide discuss reporting requirements for specific assets that have been received with donor-imposed restrictions.

Permanently Restricted Net Assets

11.07 The FASB ASC glossary defines *permanently restricted net assets* as the part of net assets of an NFP resulting from the following: (*a*) contributions and other inflows of assets whose use by the NFP is limited by donor-imposed stipulations that neither expire by passage of time nor can be fulfilled or otherwise removed by the actions of the NFP, (*b*) other asset enhancements and diminishments subject to the same kinds of stipulations, and (*c*) reclassifications from or to other classes of net assets as a consequence of donor-imposed stipulations.

11.08 Permanently restricted net assets must be maintained by the NFP in perpetuity. For example, contributions of cash or securities restricted by the donor with the stipulation that they be invested in perpetuity (donor-restricted endowment funds) and contributions of collection items (if they are capitalized)[2] required by the donor to be maintained permanently in the NFP's collections should be recognized as increases in permanently restricted net assets.

11.09 Permanently restricted net assets may also change as a result of increases and decreases in existing assets that are subject to permanent restrictions. For example, FASB ASC 958-205-45-18 states that if a donor stipulates that net gains be added to the principal of its gift until that endowed gift plus accumulated gains increases to a specified dollar level, the gains are permanently restricted. Similarly, if a donor states that a specific investment security must be held in perpetuity, the gains and losses on that security are subject to that same permanent restriction unless the donor specifies otherwise. Increases in the carrying amounts of assets that are invested in perpetuity because of donor-imposed restrictions should be recognized as increases in permanently restricted net assets to the extent that donor stipulations or applicable law requires those increases to be retained permanently. Paragraphs 8.23–.32 of this guide further discuss the permanently restricted net assets of donor-restricted endowment funds.

Temporarily Restricted Net Assets

11.10 The FASB ASC glossary defines *temporarily restricted net assets* as the part of the net assets of an NFP that result from the following: (*a*)

---

[2] Chapter 7, "Other Assets," of this guide discusses accounting policies concerning the capitalization of collection items.

contributions and other inflows of assets whose use by the NFP is limited by donor-imposed stipulations that either expire by passage of time or can be fulfilled and removed by actions of the NFP pursuant to those stipulations, (*b*) other asset enhancements and diminishments subject to the same kinds of stipulations, and (*c*) reclassifications from or to other classes of net assets as a consequence of donor-imposed stipulations, their expiration by passage of time, or their fulfillment and removal by actions of the NFP pursuant to those stipulations.

11.11 Temporarily restricted net assets are those net assets whose use by the NFP has been limited by donors (*a*) to later periods of time or after specified dates or (*b*) to specified purposes.[3] For example, contributions restricted by the donor to use by the NFP over the next five years or to support a specific future program should be recognized as increases in temporarily restricted net assets. Contributions of assets (such as equipment or buildings) that by their nature are used up over time and that the donor stipulates must be used by the NFP should also be recognized as increases in temporarily restricted net assets.[4] Paragraphs 8.25–.32 of this guide discuss the temporarily restricted net assets of donor-restricted endowment funds.

11.12 Temporarily restricted net assets may also change as a result of increases and decreases in existing assets or the economic benefits embodied in those assets that are subject to donor-imposed temporary restrictions. For example, if the donor has stipulated that income earned on temporarily restricted net assets must be added to principal until the principal is spent for a restricted purpose, the income should be reported as increases in temporarily restricted net assets.

Unrestricted Net Assets

11.13 The FASB ASC glossary defines *unrestricted net assets* as the part of net assets of an NFP that is neither permanently restricted nor temporarily restricted by donor-imposed stipulations.

11.14 Unrestricted net assets include those net assets whose use is not restricted by donors, even though their use may be limited in other respects, such as by contract or by board designation. Changes in net assets arising from exchange transactions (except income and gains on assets that are restricted by donors or by law) should be included in the unrestricted class. Paragraphs 8.27 and 8.29 of this guide discuss the unrestricted net assets of donor-restricted endowment funds.

11.15 NFPs such as social and country clubs may issue membership interests, such as capital shares. As discussed in FASB ASC 958-405-25-3, if those interests are wholly or partially refundable when the member dies, moves away, resigns his or her membership, or at a fixed date, FASB ASC 480-10 provides guidance.

---

[3] Financial Accounting Standards Board (FASB) *Accounting Standards Codification* (ASC) 958-605-45-4 states that donor-restricted contributions whose restrictions are met in the same reporting period may be reported as unrestricted support provided that an NFP has a similar policy for reporting investment gains and income (see FASB ASC 958-320-45-3), reports consistently from period to period and discloses its accounting policy. Paragraph 5.68 provides further guidance concerning that policy.

[4] Some NFPs may adopt an accounting policy of implying time restrictions on contributed long-lived assets in the absence of explicit donor-imposed restrictions. Paragraphs 5.74–.77 provide additional guidance on alternative policies.

11.16 The following paragraph summarizes FASB ASC 480-10 only for interests that are mandatorily redeemable at a fixed date whose amounts either are fixed or are determined by reference to an external index, but is not intended as a substitute for reading FASB ASC 480-10. This guide will be updated to discuss other mandatorily redeemable interests issued by NFPs when FASB ASC 480-10-65 indicates that guidance has become effective for those interests.

11.17 An interest that is mandatorily redeemable at a fixed date for a fixed or indexed amount—that embodies an unconditional obligation requiring the issuer to redeem it by transferring its assets at a fixed date (or dates)—should be classified as a liability and initially measured at fair value. An interest that embodies a conditional obligation to redeem the instrument by transferring assets upon an event not certain to occur becomes mandatorily redeemable if that event occurs, the condition is resolved, or the event becomes certain to occur.

11.18 An interest that embodies a conditional obligation to redeem it upon an event not certain to occur (such as *only* upon moving from the community) is initially classified as unrestricted net assets. If the uncertain event occurs, the condition is resolved, or the event becomes certain to occur, and payment of a fixed or indexed amount is to be made at a fixed date (such as three months from the event's occurrence), the interest is reclassified as a liability.

11.19 Per FASB ASC 480-10-55-10, upon reclassification, the issuing NFP would measure the obligation at fair value and reduce net assets by the amount of that initial measure, recognizing no gain or loss. Subsequently, pursuant to FASB ASC 480-10-35-3, those mandatorily redeemable interests are measured at the present value of the amount to be paid at settlement using the rate implicit at inception if both the amount to be paid and the settlement date are fixed. If the amount to be paid varies by reference to an interest rate index, currency index, or another external index, those instruments are subsequently measured at the amount of cash that would be paid under the conditions specified in the contract if settlement occurred at the reporting date. The change in the liability amount from the prior period is reported as interest cost (reported as described in paragraph 13.51).

Noncontrolling Interests*

11.20 FASB ASC 958-810-45-1 states that noncontrolling interests in the equity (net assets) of consolidated subsidiaries should be reported as a separate component of the appropriate class of net assets in the consolidated statement of financial position of an NFP. That amount shall be clearly identified and described (for example, as *noncontrolling ownership interest in subsidiaries*) to distinguish it from the components of net assets of the parent, which includes the parent's controlling financial interest in its subsidiaries. The effects of donor-imposed restrictions, if any, on a partially owned subsidiary's net assets should be reported in accordance with FASB ASC 958-205 and 958-320.

* This guidance from FASB ASC 958-810-45 and FASB ASC 958-810- 50 is labeled as "Pending Content" due to the transition and open effective date information discussed in FASB ASC 810-10-65-1. It reflects changes made by FASB Statement No. 160, *Noncontrolling Interests in Consolidated Financial Statements—an amendment of ARB No. 51* NFPs apply the guidance in FASB Statement No. 160 prospectively in the first set of initial or annual financial statements for a reporting period beginning on or after December 15, 2009. See footnote 7 to paragraph 3.33 of this guide for additional information.

Paragraphs 4–6 of FASB ASC 958-810-50 require certain disclosures about noncontrolling interests.

11.21 FASB ASC 958-810-25-6 discusses an interest by an NFP in another NFP that is less than a complete interest. For example, an NFP may appoint 80 percent of the board of the other NFP. For NFPs other than health care entities (that is, within the scope of FASB ASC 954, *Health Care Entities*), if the conditions for consolidation in paragraphs 2–4 of FASB ASC 958-810-25 are met, the basis of that consolidation would not reflect a noncontrolling interest for the portion of the board that the reporting entity does not control because there is no ownership interest other than the interest of the reporting entity.

Reclassifications

11.22 Per FASB ASC 958-225-45-13, reclassifications of net assets—that is, simultaneous increases in one net asset class and decreases in another—should be made if any of the following events occur: (*a*) the NFP fulfills the purposes for which the net assets were restricted, (*b*) donor-imposed restrictions expire with the passage of time or with the death of a split-interest agreement beneficiary (if the net assets are not otherwise restricted), (*c*) a donor withdraws, or court action removes, previously imposed restrictions, or (*d*) a donor imposes restrictions on otherwise unrestricted net assets.[5]

11.23 For example, the amount of a donor's contribution that must be used by the NFP for a specified program would be reclassified from temporarily restricted to unrestricted net assets in the period in which the NFP conducts the program.[6] Paragraph 9.12 of this guide discusses reclassifications concerning the use of contributed depreciable assets.

Disclosure

11.24 FASB ASC 958-210-45-1 requires that a statement of financial position should report all of the following amounts: total assets, total liabilities, permanently restricted net assets, temporarily restricted net assets, unrestricted net assets, and total net assets. FASB ASC 958-225-45-1 requires that a statement of activities should report the following amounts for the period: the change in net assets, the change in permanently restricted net assets, the change in temporarily restricted net assets, and the change in unrestricted net assets. Per FASB ASC 958-225-45-2, the change in net assets should articulate to the net asset or equity reported in the statement of financial position.

11.25 Reclassifications of amounts between net asset classes should be reported separately from other transactions in the statement of activities. Specific changes in each net asset class should be aggregated into reasonably homogeneous groups.

11.26 FASB ASC 958-210-45-9 requires that information about the nature and amounts of different types of permanent restrictions or temporary

---

[5] Paragraph 5.65 discusses donors imposing restrictions on otherwise unrestricted net assets.

[6] A purpose restriction is often fulfilled when the NFP incurs an expense or recognizes a liability to a vendor to acquire goods or services that satisfies the restriction. Paragraph 5.72 of this guide discusses appropriate accounting when expenses are incurred for a purpose for which both unrestricted and temporarily restricted net assets are available.

restrictions be provided either by reporting their amounts on the face of the statement or by including relevant details in notes to financial statements.

11.27 For example, information about the following should be shown on the face of the financial statements or in the notes:

- Different kinds of permanent restrictions, such as those related to collection items and other specific assets to be held in perpetuity and to assets that have been contributed by donors with stipulations that they be invested in perpetuity
- Different kinds of temporary restrictions, such as those concerning the support of specific operating activities, use in specific future periods, or the acquisition of long-term assets

11.28 FASB ASC 958-210-45-11 permits information about self-imposed limits, including voluntary resolutions by the governing board to designate a portion of unrestricted net assets (such as board-designated endowments), to be provided in the notes to or on the face of financial statements.

11.29 Separate disclosures of significant limitations other than those imposed by donors are permitted to be made on the face of the financial statements or in the notes to the financial statements. For example, paragraphs 6.35–.36 discuss disclosure of annuity reserves that are required by the laws of the state where the NFP is located or by the state where the donor resides and voluntary reserves set aside as a cushion against unexpected actuarial losses.

Changing Net Asset Classifications Reported in a Prior Year

11.30 Technical Questions and Answers section 6140.23, "Changing Net Asset Classifications Reported in a Prior Year" (AICPA, *Technical Practice Aids*), discusses circumstances in which NFPs correct net asset classifications previously reported in prior years' financial statements. Individual net asset classes, rather than net assets in the aggregate (total net assets), are relevant in determining whether an NFP's correction of net asset classifications previously reported in prior years' financial statements is an error in previously issued financial statements.

Auditing

11.31 Because net assets cannot be measured independently of an NFP's assets and liabilities, the auditor's consideration of net asset balances generally focuses on the assertions about rights and obligations and presentation and disclosure. In addition, the auditor may need to consider the following specific audit objectives, selected controls, and auditing procedures that are unique to NFPs.

11.32 The following table illustrates the use of assertions in developing audit objectives and designing substantive tests. The examples are not intended to be all-inclusive nor is it expected that all the procedures would necessarily be applied in an audit. The auditor should design and perform substantive procedures for all relevant assertions related to each material class of transactions, account balance, and disclosure to obtain sufficient appropriate audit evidence. The use of assertions in assessing risks and designing appropriate audit procedures to obtain audit evidence is described in paragraphs .14–.26 of

AU section 326, *Audit Evidence* (AICPA, *Professional Standards*). Various audit procedures and the purposes for which they may be performed are described in paragraphs .27–.41 of AU section 326.

Auditing Considerations

Financial Statement Assertions	*Specific Audit Objectives*	*Examples of Selected Controls*	*Examples of Auditing Procedures*
Presentation and Disclosure			
Rights and obligations; Classification	Net assets are used and accounted for in accordance with donor restrictions.	Management monitors compliance with donor restrictions.	Review minutes of governing board and governing board committee meetings for evidence of donor restrictions.
	Temporarily restricted net assets are reclassified as unrestricted net assets in the statement of activities when donor-imposed restrictions have been fulfilled.	Controls ensure that reclassification of temporarily restricted net assets occurs when donor-imposed restrictions have been fulfilled.	Determine compliance with donor restrictions; test expenditures to determine that restricted net assets are used for their restricted purposes.
			Determine that appropriate reclassifications are reported in the statement of activities when donor-imposed restrictions have been fulfilled.

Chapter 12

Revenues and Receivables From Exchange Transactions

Introduction

12.01 This chapter discusses recognition, measurement, and display issues for revenues and related receivables arising from exchange transactions.* Because of the specialized nature of investment activities, they are discussed separately in chapter 8, "Investments," of this Audit and Accounting Guide. Chapter 5, "Contributions Received and Agency Transactions," of this guide includes guidance on distinguishing exchange transactions from contributions and agency transactions.

12.02 The Financial Accounting Standards Board (FASB) *Accounting Standards Codification* (ASC) glossary defines an *exchange transaction* as a reciprocal transfer between two entities that results in one of the entities acquiring assets or services or satisfying liabilities by surrendering other assets or services or incurring other obligations. The FASB ASC glossary's definition of *contribution* states that contributions differ from exchange transactions, which are reciprocal transfers in which each party receives and sacrifices something of approximately equal value.

Revenues

12.03 Paragraph 78 of FASB Statement of Financial Accounting Concepts No. 6, *Elements of Financial Statements—a replacement of FASB Concepts Statement No. 3 (incorporating an amendment of FASB Concepts Statement No. 2)*, defines *revenues* as "inflows or other enhancements of assets of an entity or settlements of its liabilities (or a combination of both) from delivering or producing goods, rendering services, or other activities that constitute the entity's ongoing major or central operations." Exchange transactions that give rise to revenues for not-for-profit entities (NFPs) typically involve their efforts to provide goods or services to members, clients, students, customers, and other beneficiaries for a fee.

12.04 FASB ASC 605-10-25-1 states that an entity's revenue-earning activities involve delivering or producing goods, rendering services, or other activities that constitute its ongoing major or central operations, and revenues are considered to have been earned when the entity has substantially accomplished what it must do to be entitled to the benefits represented by the revenues. Gains commonly result from transactions and other events that involve no earning

---

* On June 24, 2010, the Financial Accounting Standards Board (FASB) issued a proposed Accounting Standards Update (ASU), *Revenue from Contracts with Customers*, to improve and align with International Financial Reporting Standards (IFRSs) the financial reporting of revenue from contracts with customers and related costs. The core principle of the draft standard is that an entity should recognize revenue from contracts with customers when it transfers goods or services to the customer in the amount of consideration the entity receives, or expects to receive, from the customer. The proposed standards would replace most of the guidance in FASB *Accounting Standards Codification* (ASC) 605, *Revenue Recognition*. Readers should be alert for the issuance of the final ASU.

process, and for recognizing gains, being earned is generally less significant than being realized or realizable.

12.05 In some situations, judgment is required to determine whether an increase in net assets should be reported as a revenue or as a gain. That determination should be based on the relationship of the transaction to the NFP's activities. Transactions and other events that would properly be considered part of one NFP's ongoing major or central activities (and hence give rise to revenues) may be considered peripheral for other NFP's (and hence give rise to gains). For example, sales of computer equipment by a college store should be reported as revenues if such sales are considered part of the college's ongoing major or central activities. Sales of old computer equipment used in a museum's administrative offices would, however, be reported as gains if such sales are peripheral and if the equipment were sold above book value. Chapter 13, "Expenses, Gains, and Losses," of this guide discusses reporting gains from exchange transactions.

Recognition, Measurement, and Display

12.06 The recognition, measurement, and display of revenues and related receivables arising from exchange transactions are similar for both NFPs and for-profit entities. Revenues from exchange transactions should be recognized based on accrual accounting principles and should be measured by the increase in cash, receivables, or other assets or by the decrease in liabilities resulting from the transaction.[1] Revenues from exchange transactions should be reported as increases in unrestricted net assets in a statement of activities. As discussed in chapter 3, "Basic Financial Statements and General Financial Reporting Matters," of this guide, further classifications (for example, between operating and nonoperating) may be incorporated within a statement of activities beyond the required net asset classes.

12.07 Revenues from exchange transactions should generally be reported gross of any related expenses. Expenses that are directly related to specific gross revenues may, however, be displayed sequentially with those revenues. For example, gross revenues from special events less the direct costs related to those events, followed by a subtotal, may be reported in a statement of activities. Chapter 13 of this guide discusses reporting of special events.

12.08 Per FASB ASC 958-605-45-2, if the NFP regularly provides discounts (such as financial aid for students that is not reported as an expense, reduced fees for services, or free services) to certain recipients of its goods or services, revenues should be reported net of those discounts. Net revenue may be reported as a single line item in a statement of activities, or the gross revenue is permitted to be reported less the related discount, provided that the discount is displayed immediately beneath the revenue. Paragraphs 7–8 of FASB ASC 958-720-25 (paragraph 13.09 of this guide) provide guidance concerning whether reductions in amounts charged for goods or services should be reported as discounts or expenses.

---

[1] Consistent with generally accepted accounting principles, interest on loans made to students and to other individuals or organizations should be recognized as revenue when earned.

12.09 Unless measured at fair value in conformity with the "Fair Value Option" subsections of FASB ASC 825-10,[2] contributions receivable should be reported at the measures described in FASB ASC 958-310-35. Receivables arising from exchange transactions should be reported at net realizable value if the amounts are due within one year. Long-term receivables should be reported in conformity with FASB ASC 310-10-35. Pursuant to FASB ASC 310-10-45-4, a valuation allowance for uncollectible receivables should be deducted from the receivables to which the allowance relates and should be disclosed.[†]

---

[2] Paragraphs 3.95–.97 of this guide discuss the option for entities to report certain assets and liabilities at fair value in conformity with FASB ASC 815-15 or the "Fair Value Option" subsections of FASB ASC 825-10.

[†] On May 26, 2010, FASB issued a proposed ASU, *Accounting for Financial Instruments and Revisions to the Accounting for Derivative Instruments and Hedging Activities*, intended to improve accounting for financial instruments. Among other changes, the proposed ASU reconsiders the recognition and measurement of financial instruments, addresses issues related to impairment of financial instruments, simplifies hedge accounting, and, increases convergence in accounting for financial instruments with IFRSs. It would incorporate both amortized cost and fair value information about financial instruments held for collection or payment of cash flows. On January 31, 2011, FASB and the International Accounting Standards Board jointly issued a supplementary document, *Accounting for Financial Instruments and Revisions to the Accounting for Derivative Instruments and Hedging Activities: Impairment*, to address a number of questions that arose from the comments received on the proposed ASU. Readers should be alert for the issuance of a final ASU.

Chapter 13

Expenses, Gains, and Losses

Introduction

13.01 Generally, expenses, gains, and losses of not-for-profit entities (NFPs) are similar to those of for-profit entities and are recognized, measured, and displayed similarly. This chapter discusses certain expense, gain, and loss recognition, measurement, and display issues that are unique to NFPs and that are not covered elsewhere in this Audit and Accounting Guide.

Expenses

13.02 Paragraph 80 of Financial Accounting Standards Board (FASB) Concept No. 6, *Elements of Financial Statements—a replacement of FASB Concepts Statement No. 3 (incorporating an amendment of FASB Concepts Statement No. 2)*, defines *expenses* as "outflows or other using up of assets or incurrences of liabilities (or a combination of both) from delivering or producing goods, rendering services, or carrying out other activities that constitute the entity's ongoing major or central operations." Expenses are distinguished from losses, which are decreases in an NFP's net assets from peripheral or incidental transactions and from all other transactions and other events and circumstances affecting the NFP except those that result from expenses.

13.03 Per FASB *Accounting Standards Codification* (ASC) 958-225-45-7, a statement of activities should report expenses as decreases in unrestricted net assets. As discussed in paragraphs 3.12–.13 of this guide, further classifications (such as between operating and nonoperating) may be incorporated within a statement of activities beyond the required net asset classes.

13.04 FASB ASC 958-720-45-2 specifies that to help donors, creditors, and others in assessing an NFP's service efforts, including the costs of services and how it uses resources, a statement of activities or notes to financial statements should provide information about expenses reported by their functional classification, such as major classes of program services and supporting activities. FASB ASC 958-205-45-6 requires voluntary health and welfare entities[1] to report information about expenses by their functional classes, such as major classes of program services and supporting activities, as well as information about expenses by their natural classifications (such as salaries, rent, electricity, interest expense, depreciation, awards and grants to others, and professional fees), in a matrix format in a separate financial statement called a *statement of functional expenses*.[2] FASB ASC 958-720-45-16 states that other

---

[1] Voluntary health and welfare entities are defined in the Financial Accounting Standards Board (FASB) *Accounting Standards Codification* (ASC) glossary and in the glossary of this guide.

[2] Not-for-profit entities (NFPs) may have various kinds of functions. The discussion in this guide focuses on program, management and general, and fundraising for illustrative purposes, because the Accounting Standards Executive Committee (currently, the Financial Reporting Executive Committee) and the Not-for-Profit Organizations Committee (committees) believe the use of those functional classifications will likely become predominant practice. However, the committees neither encourage nor discourage the use of those or other functional classifications. Accordingly, the classifications used in the matrix may include program, management and general, and fundraising or other classifications, such as cost of sales or investing.

NFPs are encouraged, but not required, to provide information about expenses by their natural classification.

13.05 Reporting information about the functional classification of expenses may require the allocation of costs that benefit 2 or more functions. All references in this guide to the allocation of costs of informational materials and activities that include a fundraising appeal among functions are subject to the provisions of the "Accounting for Costs of Activities that Include Fundraising" subsections of FASB ASC 958-720, which are discussed in paragraphs 13.53–.92 of this guide.

13.06 There is no requirement to report losses by functional category.[3]

Expense Recognition Issues

13.07 Expenses are recognized when an NFP's economic benefits are used up in delivering or producing goods, rendering services, or other activities or when previously recognized assets are expected to provide reduced or no future benefits. Some expenses, such as cost of goods sold, are recognized simultaneously with revenues that result directly and jointly from the same transactions or other events as the expenses. Some expenses, such as salaries, are recognized when cash is spent or liabilities are incurred for goods and services that are used up either simultaneously with acquisition or soon after. Some expenses, such as depreciation, are allocated by systematic and rational procedures to the periods during which the related assets are expected to provide services. An expense or loss is also recognized if it becomes evident that the previously recognized future economic benefits of an asset have been reduced or eliminated, or that a liability has been incurred or increased, without associated economic benefits.

Fundraising Costs

13.08 Per FASB ASC 958-720-25-4, costs of fundraising, including the cost of special fundraising events, should be expensed as incurred. Costs are incurred when the item or service has been received. Fundraising costs incurred in one period, such as those made to obtain bequests, compile a mailing list of prospective contributors, or solicit contributions in a direct-response activity, may result in contributions that will be received in future periods. These costs also should be expensed as incurred. The FASB ASC glossary definition of *fundraising* is included in paragraph 13.43 of this guide.

Financial Aid and Other Reductions in Amounts Charged for Goods and Services

13.09 Some NFPs provide reductions in amounts charged for goods or services, such as financial aid provided by colleges and universities. Per FASB ASC 958-720-25-7, reductions in amounts charged for goods or services provided by an NFP should be reported as expenses if such reductions are given in exchange for goods or services provided to the NFP, such as part of a compensation package. Per FASB ASC 958-720-45-23, amounts reported as expenses for such reductions should be reported in the same functional classification in which the cost of the goods or services provided to the NFP are reported.

---

[3] Paragraphs 13.02 and 13.18–.22 of this guide discuss the differences between expenses and losses.

Per FASB ASC 958-720-25-8, if reductions in amounts charged for goods or services provided by an NFP are given other than in exchange for services provided to the NFP, those amounts should be reported as follows:

- As expenses to the extent that the NFP incurs incremental expense in providing such goods or services
- As discounts[4] if the NFP incurs no incremental expense in providing such goods or services

Advertising Costs

13.10 FASB ASC 720-35 provides recognition, measurement, and disclosure guidance for the advertising activities of all entities, including NFPs. (FASB ASC 720-35-15-3 specifically notes, however, that fundraising by NFPs is not within the scope of the subtopic.) FASB ASC 720-35-50 requires certain disclosures about advertising activities, including disclosure of total amount charged to advertising expense for each statement of activities presented.

13.11 FASB ASC 720-35-05-4 defines *advertising* as "the promotion of an industry, an entity, a brand, a product name, or specific products or services so as to create or stimulate a positive entity image or to create or stimulate a desire to buy the entity's products or services." Per FASB ASC 958-720-25-6, advertising by an NFP includes activities to create or stimulate a desire to use the NFP's products or services that are provided without charge.

13.12 Per FASB ASC 720-35-25-1 and FASB ASC 340-20-25-4, the costs of advertising should be expensed either as incurred or the first time the advertising takes place, subject to the following exception. The costs of direct-response advertising should be capitalized if both of the following conditions are met: (*a*) the primary purpose of the advertising is to elicit sales to customers who could be shown to have responded specifically to the advertising and (*b*) the direct-response advertising is expected to result in probable future benefits. Per FASB ASC 340-20-25-8, the probable future benefits of direct-response advertising activities are probable future revenues arising from that advertising in excess of future costs to be incurred in realizing those revenues. Per FASB ASC 958-720-25-6, if no future revenues are anticipated because the products or services advertised are being provided by the NFP without charge, there is no basis for capitalizing the costs of direct-response advertising after the first time the advertising takes place.

Start-Up Costs

13.13 FASB ASC 720-15 provides guidance on the financial reporting of start-up costs and organization costs. It requires costs of start-up activities, including organization costs to be expensed as incurred.

13.14 The FASB ASC glossary broadly defines *start-up activities* as those one-time activities related to any of the following: (*a*) opening a new facility, (*b*) introducing a new product or service, (*c*) conducting business in a new territory, (*d*) conducting business with an entirely new class of customer or beneficiary, (*e*) initiating a new process in an existing facility, or (*f*) commencing some new

---

[4] Chapter 12, "Revenues and Receivables From Exchange Transactions," of this guide provides guidance concerning display of discounts.

operations. Start-up activities include activities related to organizing a new entity (commonly referred to as organization costs).

13.15 FASB ASC 720-15-15 describes certain costs that may be incurred in conjunction with start-up activities that are outside the scope of FASB ASC 720-15. FASB ASC 720-15-55 provides examples to help entities determine what costs are and are not within its scope. Example 3 (paragraphs 8–10) of FASB ASC 720-15-55 describes an NFP that provides meals to the homeless is opening a shelter to house the homeless. The example shows the costs that might be incurred in conjunction with start-up activities and clarifies which costs are and are not within the scope of the subtopic.

Internal Use Computer Software Costs

13.16 FASB ASC 350-40 provides guidance on accounting for the costs of computer software developed or obtained for internal use. It identifies the characteristics of internal-use software and provides examples to assist in determining when computer software is for internal use.[5]

Contributions Made

13.17 The recognition rules for contributions made are discussed in chapter 10, "Debt and Other Liabilities," of this guide. Some transfers may appear to be contributions made but are actually reciprocal in nature. Paragraphs 5.30–.35 provide further guidance about a transfer made by an NFP for its own benefit or for the benefit of its affiliate.

Gains and Losses

13.18 *Revenues* are inflows of assets that result from an NFP's ongoing major or central operations and activities. *Gains* are increases in net assets resulting from an NFP's peripheral or incidental transactions and other events and circumstances affecting the NFP other than those that result from revenues. *Expenses* are outflows of assets or incurrences of liabilities that result from an NFP's ongoing major or central operations and activities. *Losses* are decreases in net assets from an NFP's peripheral or incidental transactions and other events and circumstances affecting the NFP other than those that result from expenses.

13.19 Gains and losses result both from an NFP's peripheral or incidental activities and from events and circumstances that stem from the environment and that are largely beyond the control of a particular organization and its management. Some gains and losses result from holding assets or liabilities while their values change, such as from changes in the fair value of securities or changes in foreign exchange rates. Other gains and losses result from natural catastrophes, such as fires, floods, and earthquakes. Still others result from transactions (such as an NFP's sale of buildings and equipment that are no longer needed for its ongoing operations, or from its winning or losing a lawsuit) that are only peripheral or incidental to the NFP.

13.20 Transactions resulting in revenues for one NFP may result in gains for another, which, in turn, determines how the related costs should be classified and displayed.

---

[5] Related literature includes FASB ASC 720-45, which provides guidance on costs associated with business process reengineering and IT transformation projects.

13.21 Per FASB ASC 958-225-45-14, a statement of activities should report the gross amounts of revenues and expenses (except for investment revenues and related expenses, which are permitted to be reported net of related expenses, as discussed in paragraph 8.09 and paragraphs 13.33–.34 of this guide). FASB ASC 958-225-45-15 states that a statement of activities may report gains and losses as net amounts if they result from peripheral or incidental transactions or from other events and circumstances that may be largely beyond the control of the NFP and its management.

13.22 Per FASB ASC 958-225-45-16, the frequency of the events and the significance of the gross revenues and expenses distinguish major or central events from peripheral or incidental events. Events are ongoing major and central activities if (*a*) they are normally part of an NFP's strategy and it normally carries on such activities or if (*b*) the event's gross revenues or expenses are significant in relation to the NFP's annual budget. Events are peripheral or incidental if they are not an integral part of an NFP's usual activities or if their gross revenues or expenses are not significant in relation to the NFP's annual budget. Accordingly, similar events may be reported differently by different NFPs based on the NFP's overall activities.

13.23 Per FASB ASC 958-225-45-8, gains and losses should be recognized as increases or decreases in unrestricted net assets unless their use is temporarily or permanently restricted by explicit donor stipulations or by law.

13.24 Losses need not be reported by their functional classification or in the matrix that presents information about expenses according to both their functional and natural classifications.

Reporting Costs Related to Sales of Goods and Services

13.25 Per FASB ASC 958-720-45-20, the way that costs related to sales of goods and services are displayed depends on whether the sales constitute a major or central activity of the NFP or a peripheral or incidental activity. For example, a not-for-profit museum that has a store that is a major or central activity should report and display separately the revenues from the store's sales and the related cost of sales. Cost of sales is permitted to be reported immediately after revenues from sale of merchandise, and may be followed by a descriptive subtotal, or cost of sales may be reported with other expenses. If the store sells merchandise that is related to the museum's program, the store would be a program service and the cost of the store's sales would be reported as a program expense. In other circumstances, cost of sales could be reported as a separate supporting service. For example, if operating a cafeteria is a major or central activity but is not related to the NFP's programs, the cafeteria's cost of sales would be reported as supporting services.

13.26 FASB ASC 958-720-45-22 states that, in contrast, a not-for-profit church that occasionally produces and sells a cookbook (considered to be a peripheral or incidental activity) has gains (or losses) from those sales, and the receipts and related costs are permitted to be offset and only the net gains (or losses) are reported.

13.27 Losses from the peripheral or incidental activities described in the previous paragraph are not classified as an expense, so they should not be reported by their functional classification.

Reporting the Cost of Special Events and Other Fundraising Activities

13.28 Some NFPs conduct fundraising or joint activities, including special social and educational events (such as symposia, dinners, dances, and theater parties) in which the attendee receives a direct benefit (for example, a meal or theater ticket).

13.29 FASB ASC 958-225-45-17 states that an NFP may report net amounts in its statement of activities for its special events if they result from peripheral or incidental transactions. However, so-called "special events" often are ongoing and major activities; if so, an NFP shall report the gross revenues and expenses of those activities. Costs netted against receipts from peripheral or incidental special events shall be limited to direct costs.

13.30 NFPs may report the gross revenues of special events and other fundraising activities with the cost of direct benefits to donors (for example, meals and facilities rental) displayed either (1) as a line item deducted from the special event revenues or (2) in the same section of the statement of activities as are other programs or supporting services and allocated, if necessary, among those various functions. Alternatively, the NFP could consider revenue from special events and other fundraising activities as part exchange (for the fair value the participant received) and part contribution (for the excess of the payment over that fair value) and report the two parts separately.

13.31 Paragraphs 11–15 of FASB ASC 958-225-55 (example 4) illustrate the guidance in FASB ASC 958-225-45-17. NFP B has a special event that is an ongoing and major activity with a ticket price of $100. The activity does not meet the audience criterion in paragraphs 13.74–.80, and, therefore, all costs of the activity, other than the direct donor benefits, should be reported as fundraising. The event includes a dinner that costs NFP B $25 and that has a fair value of $30. (Chapter 5, "Contributions Received and Agency Transactions," of this guide discusses the appropriate reporting if the meal or other items of value are donated to the NFP for resale.) In addition, NFP B incurs other direct costs of the event of $15 in connection with promoting and conducting the event, including incremental direct costs incurred in transactions with independent third parties and the payroll and payroll-related costs for the activities of employees who are directly associated with, and devote time to, the event. The other direct costs are unrelated to the direct benefits to donors and, accordingly, should not be included as costs of benefits to donors. The other direct costs include (*a*) $5 that otherwise might be considered management and general costs if they had been incurred in a different activity, and (*b*) fundraising costs of $10. In addition, NFP B has the following transactions, which are unrelated to the special event: unrestricted contributions of $200, program expenses of $60, management and general expenses of $20, and fundraising expenses of $20.

13.32 Paragraphs 13–15 of FASB ASC 958-225-55 illustrate three ways in which the NFP could display the results of the special event as part of its statement of activities, as follows:

Case A

Changes in unrestricted net assets:		
Contributions		$200
Special event revenue	100	
Less: Costs of direct benefits to donors	(25)	
Net revenues from special events		75
Contributions and net revenues from special events		275
Other expenses:		
Program		60
Management and general		20
Fundraising		35
Total other expenses		115
Increase in unrestricted net assets		$160

Case B

Changes in unrestricted net assets:	
Revenues:	
Contributions	$200
Special event revenue	100
Total revenues	300
Expenses:	
Program	60
Costs of direct benefits to donors	25
Management and general	20
Fundraising	35
Total other expenses	140
Increase in unrestricted net assets	$160

Case C

Changes in unrestricted net assets:		
Contributions		$270
Dinner sales	30	
Less: Costs of direct benefits to donors	(25)	
Gross profit on special events		5
Contributions and net revenues from special events		275
Other expenses:		
Program		60
Management and general		20
Fundraising		35
Total other expenses		115
Increase in unrestricted net assets		$160

Investment Revenues, Expenses, Gains, and Losses

13.33 Per FASB ASC 958-225-45-14, investment revenues may be reported net of related expenses, such as custodial fees and internal and external investment advisory costs, provided that the amount of the expenses is disclosed either on the face of the statement of activities or in notes to the financial statements. Per FASB ASC 958-205-45-6, expenses that are netted against investment revenues should be reported by their functional classification on the statement of functional expenses.

13.34 Realized and unrealized losses on investments may be netted against realized and unrealized gains on a statement of activities. Chapter 8, "Investments," of this guide includes a more detailed discussion of investment gains and losses.

Functional Reporting of Expenses

13.35 FASB ASC 958-720-45-2 requires the presentation, in either a statement of activities or the notes to the financial statements, of information about expenses reported by their functional classification, such as major classes of program services and supporting activities. *Program services* are defined in the FASB ASC glossary as "the activities that result in goods and services being distributed to beneficiaries, customers, or members that fulfill the purposes or mission for which the NFP exists. Those services are the major purpose for and the major output of the NFP and often relate to several major programs." *Supporting services* are defined in the FASB ASC glossary as "all activities of a not-for-profit entity (NFP) other than program services. Generally, they include management and general activities, fundraising activities, and membership-development activities." FASB ASC 958-720-45 provides examples of the kinds of activities that fall into each of those categories.

13.36 Program services may include cost of sales and costs of other revenue-generating activities that are program related. Supporting services may include, as one or more separate categories, cost of sales and costs of other revenue-generating activities that are not program related. Further elaboration of the kinds of activities that fall into each of the functional categories is provided in the following sections.

Functional Classifications

Program Services

13.37 The number of functional reporting classifications for program services varies according to the nature of the services rendered. For some NFPs, a single functional reporting classification may be adequate to portray what may, in effect, be a single, integrated program service that the NFP provides. In most cases, however, several separate and identifiable services are provided, and in such cases the expenses for program services should be reported by the kind of service function or group of functions.

13.38 FASB ASC 958-720-45-3 provides the following additional examples. A large university may have programs for student instruction, research, and patient care, among others. A federated fundraising entity's programs may include making contributions to NFPs supported by the federated fundraising organization. A health and welfare entity may have programs for health or family services, research, disaster relief, and public education, among others.

13.39 For guidance on what constitutes *major* classes of programs and supporting activities, NFPs may consider, among other sources, FASB ASC 280, *Segment Reporting*.[6]

13.40 Per FASB ASC 958-205-50-1, the financial statements should provide a description of the nature of the NFP's activities, including a description of each of its major classes of programs. If not provided in the notes to financial statements, the description can be presented on the statement of activities (for example, using column headings). Per FASB ASC 958-720-45-5, the components of total program expenses should be evident from the details provided on the face of the statement of activities, unless the notes to financial statements provide the information in FASB ASC 958-720-50-1(b); that is, the notes disclose total program expenses and provide information about why total program expenses disclosed in the notes do not articulate with the statement of activities. FASB ASC 958-720-50-1 provides the following example of a presentation in which the components of total program expenses are not evident from the details provided on the face of the statement of activities; cost of sales is not identified as either program or supporting services.

Supporting Services

13.41 NFPs may have various kinds of supporting activities, such as management and general, fundraising, and membership development. Some industries have functional categories of supporting activities that are prevalent in that industry. For example, colleges and universities typically have institutional support and institutional development activities. A single functional reporting classification is ordinarily adequate to portray each kind of supporting service. NFPs may, however, present more detailed disaggregated information for each kind of supporting service. For example, fundraising expenses and the corresponding support that is obtained may be reported separately for each kind of fundraising activity undertaken, either on the face of a statement of activities or in the notes to the financial statements.

13.42 Per the FASB ASC glossary, *management and general activities* are activities that are not identifiable with a single program, fundraising activity, or membership-development activity but that are indispensable to the conduct of those activities and to an entity's existence. Paragraphs 7–8 of FASB ASC 958-720-45 provide additional description of management and general activities. They include oversight; business management; general record keeping; budgeting; financing; soliciting funds other than contributions, including exchange transactions (whether program-related or not), such as government contracts, and related administrative activities; disseminating information to inform the public of the NFP's stewardship of contributed funds; announcements concerning appointments; the annual report; related administrative activities; and all management and administration except for direct conduct of program services or fundraising activities. The costs of oversight and management usually include the salaries and expenses of the governing board, the CEO of the NFP,

---

[6] FASB ASC 280, *Segment Reporting*, applies only to public business entities; however, the guidelines may be helpful to NFPs in determining the number of functional classifications that would be appropriate in their particular circumstances.

and the supporting staff. If such staff spend a portion of their time directly supervising program services or categories of other supporting services, however, their salaries and expenses should be allocated among those functions.

13.43 Per the FASB ASC glossary, *fundraising activities* are activities undertaken to induce potential donors to contribute money, securities, services, materials, facilities, other assets, or time. Paragraphs 9–10 of FASB ASC 958-720-45 provide additional description of fundraising activities. They include publicizing and conducting fundraising campaigns; maintaining donor mailing lists; conducting special fundraising events; preparing and distributing fundraising manuals, instructions, and other materials; and conducting other activities involved with soliciting contributions from individuals, foundations, government agencies, and others. Fundraising activities include soliciting contributions of services from individuals, regardless of whether those services meet the recognition criteria for contributions in the "Contributions Received" subsection of FASB ASC 958-605-25. (Paragraph 13.95 discusses how fundraising activities of federated fundraising organizations should be reported.) Per FASB ASC 958-720-50-1, the financial statements should disclose total fundraising expenses.

13.44 Per the FASB ASC glossary, *membership-development activities* include soliciting for prospective members and membership dues, membership relations, and similar activities. FASB ASC 958-720-45-12 states that if there are no significant benefits or duties connected with membership, the substance of membership-development activities may, in fact, be fundraising. Paragraphs 11–14 of FASB ASC 958-720-45 provide additional description of membership-development activities. When the substance of membership development is, in fact, fundraising, the related costs should be reported as fundraising costs. (See paragraphs 9–12 of FASB ASC 958-605-55 for indicators useful in determining the contribution and exchange portions of membership dues.)[7] Membership development activities may be conducted in conjunction with other activities. In circumstances in which membership development is conducted in conjunction with other activities but does not include soliciting contributions (for example, the NFP's membership dues are entirely exchange transactions and the activity is in part soliciting new members and in part program activities for existing members), the activity is not a joint activity, and the costs should be allocated to membership development and one or more other functions. For example, membership may entitle the members to group life and other insurance at reduced costs because of the NFP's negotiated rates and to a subscription to the NFP's magazine or newsletter. Under these circumstances, an appropriate part of the costs of soliciting members should be allocated to the membership-development function and a part to program services. In circumstances in which membership development is in part soliciting revenues from exchange transactions and in part soliciting contributions, the activity is a joint activity, as discussed in the "Accounting for Costs of Activities that Include Fundraising" subsections of FASB ASC 958-720. Those subsections are discussed in paragraphs 13.54–.93 of this guide but are not intended as a substitute for reading them.

Classification of Expenses Related to More Than One Function

13.45 Some expenses are directly related to, and can be assigned to, a single major program or service or a single supporting activity. Other expenses

---

[7] Chapter 5, "Contributions Received and Agency Transactions," and table 5-2 of this guide provide the guidance in paragraphs 9–12 of FASB ASC 958-605-55.

relate to more than one program or supporting activity, or to a combination of programs and supporting services. These expenses should be allocated among the appropriate functions. Examples include a direct mail solicitation that combines fundraising with program activities (subject to the provisions of paragraphs 13.53–.92), salaries of persons who perform more than one kind of service, and the rental of a building used for various programs and supporting activities.

Direct Identification Versus Allocation Methods[8]

13.46 Direct identification of specific expense (also referred to as *assigning* expenses) is the preferable method of charging expenses to various functions. If an expense can be specifically identified with a program or supporting service, it should be assigned to that function. For example, travel costs incurred in connection with a program activity should be assigned to that program.

13.47 If direct identification (that is, assignment) is impossible or impracticable, an allocation is appropriate. The techniques used to allocate are common to all entities, for-profit and NFP alike. A reasonable allocation of expenses among an NFP's functions may be made on a variety of bases. Objective methods of allocating expenses are preferable to subjective methods. The allocation may be based on related financial or nonfinancial data. The paragraphs that follow provide guidance (in addition to that presented throughout this chapter) on allocating or presenting certain costs that may be incurred by NFPs.[9]

13.48 Per FASB ASC 958-720-45-25, occupying and maintaining a building is not a separate supporting service.

13.49 The expenses associated with occupying and maintaining a building, such as depreciation, utilities, maintenance, and insurance, may be allocated among the NFP's functions based on the square footage of space occupied by each program and supporting service. If floor plans are not available and the measurement of the occupied space is impractical, an estimate of the relative portion of the building occupied by each function may be made.

13.50 Per FASB ASC 958-720-45-24, interest costs, including interest on a building's mortgage, should be allocated to specific programs or supporting services to the extent possible. Interest costs that cannot be allocated should be reported as part of the management and general function. (FASB ASC 835-20-50-1 requires disclosure of total interest costs incurred and the amount thereof that has been capitalized, if any.)

13.51 An NFP should evaluate its expense allocation methods periodically. The evaluation may include, for example, a review of the time records or activity reports of key personnel, the use of space, and the consumption of supplies and postage. The expense allocation methods should be reviewed by management and revised when necessary to reflect significant changes in the nature or level of the organization's current activities.

---

[8] This section provides general information about assigning and allocating costs among functional classifications. For costs incurred in joint activities, the guidance in this section is subject to the provisions of paragraphs 13.53–.92.

[9] The guidance found in U.S. Office of Management and Budget Circular A-122 may also be helpful in allocating costs.

Expenses of Materials and Activities That Combine Fundraising Activities With Activities That Have Elements of Another Function (Joint Activities)

13.52 FASB ASC 958-720-05-5 states that some NFPs solicit support through a variety of fundraising activities, including the following: direct mail, telephone solicitation, door-to-door canvassing, telethons, special events, and others. Sometimes fundraising activities are conducted with activities related to other functions, such as program activities or supporting services, such as management and general activities. Sometimes fundraising activities include components that would otherwise be associated with program or supporting services, but in fact support fundraising. The "Accounting for Costs of Activities that Include Fundraising" subsections of FASB ASC 958-720 establish financial accounting standards for accounting for costs of those joint activities and require financial statement disclosures about the nature of the activities for which joint costs have been allocated and the amounts of joint costs. The following paragraphs summarize those subsections but are not intended as a substitute for reading them.

13.53 The functional classifications of fundraising, program, and management and general are discussed throughout the "Accounting for Costs of Activities that Include Fundraising" subsections of FASB ASC 958-720 for purposes of illustrating how the guidance in these paragraphs would be applied by entities that use those functional classifications. Some entities have a functional structure that does not include fundraising, program, or management and general, or that includes other functional classifications, such as membership development. Use of those functional classifications is not intended to require reporting the functional classifications of fundraising, program, and management and general.

13.54 For example, some NFPs may conduct membership development activities. Per paragraphs 20–21 of FASB ASC 958-720-55, if there are no significant benefits or duties connected with membership, the substance of the membership development activities may, in fact, be fundraising. In such circumstances, the costs of those activities should be charged to fundraising. To the extent that member benefits are received, membership is an exchange transaction. In circumstances in which membership development is in part soliciting revenues from exchange transactions and in part soliciting contributions and the purpose, audience, and content of the activity are appropriate for achieving membership development, joint costs should be allocated between fundraising and the exchange transaction. Accounting for the costs of a joint activity is discussed in paragraphs 13.56–.92 of this guide.

Accounting for Joint Activities

13.55 Per FASB ASC 958-720-45-29, if the criteria of purpose, audience, and content are met, the costs of a joint activity should be classified as follows: (*a*) the costs that are identifiable with a particular function should be charged to that function and (*b*) joint costs should be allocated between fundraising and the appropriate program or management and general function. If any of the criteria are not met, all costs of the joint activity should be reported as fundraising costs, including costs that might be considered program or management and general costs if they had been incurred in a different activity, subject to the exception in the following sentence. Costs of goods or services provided in exchange transactions that are part of joint activities, such as costs of direct donor benefits of a special event (for example, a meal), should not be reported as fundraising.

13.56 FASB ASC 958-720-55-34 provides guidance for classifying costs of a joint activity that are identifiable with a particular functional classification. That paragraph provides the following example. The purpose for which costs other than joint costs are incurred may be fundraising, program, or management and general, depending on the context in which they are used in the activity undertaken. For example, if some pamphlets are used in program activities that include no fundraising, the cost of the pamphlets used in those separate program activities that include no fundraising should be charged to program. If some pamphlets are used in a joint activity and the criteria in FASB ASC 958-720-45-29 (paragraph 13.55) are met, the costs of materials that accomplish program goals and that are unrelated to fundraising, such as the costs of a program-related pamphlet included in a joint activity, should be charged to program, and joint costs, such as postage, should be allocated between fundraising and program. However, if the pamphlet is used in fundraising packets and the criteria are not met, the costs of the pamphlets used in the fundraising packets, as well as the joint costs, should be charged to fundraising.

13.57 In circumstances in which entities that have a functional structure that includes other functional classifications conduct joint activities, all costs of those joint activities should be charged to fundraising (or the category in which fundraising is reported), unless the purpose, audience, and content of those joint activities are appropriate for achieving those other functions.

Purpose

13.58 The purpose criterion is met if the purpose of the joint activity includes accomplishing program or management and general functions. Paragraphs 33–47 of FASB ASC 958-720-45 (reproduced in part in paragraphs 13.59–.72) provide guidance that should be considered in determining whether the purpose criterion is met. Paragraphs 35–39 of FASB ASC 958-720-45 (paragraph 13.59–.63) provide guidance pertaining to program functions only. FASB ASC 958-720-45-38 (paragraph 13.64) provides guidance pertaining to both program and management and general functions.

13.59 *Program functions*. To accomplish program functions, the activity should call for specific action by the audience that will help accomplish the NFP's mission. Actions that help accomplish the NFP's mission are actions that do either of the following: (*a*) benefit the recipient (such as by improving the recipient's physical, mental, emotional, or spiritual health and well-being) or (*b*) benefit society (such as by addressing societal problems). If the activity calls for specific action by the audience that will help accomplish the NFP's mission, the guidance in FASB ASC 958-720-45-38 (paragraphs 13.64–.72) should also be considered in determining whether the purpose criterion is met.

13.60 FASB ASC 958-720-55-4 provides the following examples of activities that call for specific action by the audience that will help accomplish the NFP's mission:

- An NFP's mission includes improving individuals' physical health. For that NFP, motivating the audience to take specific action that will improve their physical health is a call for specific action by the audience that will help accomplish the NFP's mission. An example of an activity that motivates the audience to take specific action that will improve their physical health is sending the audience a brochure that urges them to stop smoking and suggests specific methods, instructions, references, and resources that may be used to stop smoking.

- An NFP's mission includes educating individuals in areas other than the causes, conditions, needs, or concerns that the NFP's programs are designed to address (referred to as *causes*). For that NFP, educating the audience in areas other than causes or motivating the audience to otherwise engage in specific activities that will educate them in areas other than causes is a call for specific action by the audience that will help accomplish the NFP's mission. Examples of NFPs whose mission includes educating individuals in areas other than causes are universities and possibly other NFPs. An example of an activity motivating individuals to engage in education in areas other than causes is a university inviting individuals to attend a lecture or class in which the individuals will learn about the solar system. (Paragraphs 13.62–.63 provide further discussion of NFPs with educational missions.)
- Some educational activities that might otherwise be considered as educating the audience about causes may implicitly call for specific action by the audience that will help accomplish the NFP's mission. For example, activities that educate the audience about environmental problems caused by not recycling implicitly call for that audience to increase recycling. If the need for and benefits of the specific action are clearly evident from the educational message, the message is considered to include an implicit call for specific action by the audience that will help accomplish the NFP's mission.

13.61 FASB ASC 958-720-55-5 provides the following examples of activities that fail to call for a specific action by the audience that will help accomplish the NFP's mission:

- Educating the audience about causes or motivating the audience to otherwise engage in specific activities that will educate them about causes is not a call for specific action by the audience that will help accomplish the NFP's mission. Such activities are considered in support of fundraising.
- Asking the audience to make contributions is not a call for specific action by the audience that will help accomplish the NFP's mission.

13.62 Paragraphs 22–24 of FASB ASC 958-720-55 provide additional guidance for NFPs with educational missions, which is reproduced in this paragraph and the next. Most transactions in which a student attends a lecture or class are exchange transactions and are not joint activities. Such transactions are joint activities only if the activity includes fundraising. Some organizations have missions that include educating the public (students) in areas other than causes. FASB ASC 958-720-55-4 provides that, for those entities, educating the audience in areas other than causes or motivating the audience to engage in specific activities, such as attending a lecture or class, that will educate them in areas other than causes is considered a call for specific action by the recipients that will help accomplish the NFP's mission. Educating the audience about causes or motivating the audience to engage in specific activities that will educate them about causes without educating them in other subjects is not considered a call for specific action by the audience that will help accomplish the NFP's mission.

13.63 An example of a lecture or class that will educate students in an area other than causes is a lecture on the nesting habits of the bald eagle, given by the Save the Bald Eagle Society, an NFP whose mission is to save the bald eagle from extinction and educate the public about the bald eagle. An example of a lecture or class that will address particular causes is a lecture by the Bald Eagle Society on the potential extinction of bald eagles and the need to raise contributions to prevent their extinction. For purposes of applying this guidance, motivating the audience to attend a lecture on the nesting habits of the bald eagle is a call for specific action that will help accomplish the NFP's mission. If the lecture merely addresses the potential extinction of bald eagles and the need to raise contributions to prevent their extinction without addressing the nesting habits of the bald eagle, motivating the audience to attend the lecture is not considered a call for specific action by the recipient that will help accomplish the NFP's mission.

13.64 *Program and management and general functions*. Per FASB ASC 958-720-45-38, the following factors should be considered, in the order in which they are listed, to determine whether the purpose criterion is met:

a. The compensation or fees test (paragraphs 13.65–.68 of this guide)

b. The separate and similar activities test (paragraphs 13.69–.70 of this guide)

c. The other evidence test (paragraphs 13.71–.72 of this guide)

13.65 *The compensations or fees test*. Paragraphs 40–44 of FASB ASC 958-720-45 provide guidance for the compensation or fees test. The purpose criterion is not met if a majority of compensation or fees for any party's performance of any component of the discrete joint activity varies based on contributions raised for that discrete joint activity.

13.66 Some compensation contracts provide that compensation for performing the activity is based on a factor other than contributions raised, but not to exceed a specified portion of contributions raised. For example, a contract may provide that compensation for performing the activity is $10 per contact hour, but not to exceed 60 percent of contributions raised. In such circumstances, compensation is not considered based on amounts raised unless the stated maximum percentage is met. In circumstances in which it is not yet known whether the stated maximum percentage is met, compensation is not considered based on amounts raised unless it is probable that the stated maximum percentage will be met.

13.67 The compensation or fees test is a negative test in that it either (*a*) results in failing the purpose criterion or (*b*) is not determinative of whether the purpose criterion is met.

13.68 In considering the guidance in FASB ASC 958-720-45-38 (paragraph 13.64), the compensation or fees test is the preeminent guidance. Therefore, if the activity fails the compensation or fees test, the activity fails the purpose criterion and the separate and similar activities test should not be considered. If the purpose criterion is not failed based on the compensation or fees test, this factor (the compensation or fees test) is not determinative of whether the purpose criterion is met, and the factor in paragraphs 45–46 of FASB ASC 958-720-45-45 (paragraphs 13.69–.70) (separate and similar activities test) should be considered.

13.69 *The separate and similar activities test.* The purpose criterion is met if a similar program or management and general activity is conducted separately and on a similar or greater scale. That is, the purpose criterion is met if either of the following two conditions is met:

a. The first condition is met if both of the following are true:

  i. The program component of the joint activity calls for specific action by the recipient that will help accomplish the NFP's mission (see paragraphs 35–37 of FASB ASC 958-720-45, which are reproduced in part in paragraphs 13.59–.63).

  ii. A similar program component is conducted without the fundraising component using the same medium and on a scale that is similar to or greater than the scale on which it is conducted with the fundraising. Determining the scale on which an activity is conducted may be subjective. Factors to consider in determining the scale on which an activity is conducted may include dollars spent, the size of the audience reached, and the degree to which the characteristics of the audience are similar to the characteristics of the audience of the activity being evaluated.

b. The second condition is met if

  i. a management and general activity that is similar to the management and general component of the joint activity being accounted for is conducted without the fundraising component using the same medium and on a scale that is similar to or greater than the scale on which it is conducted with the fundraising.

13.70 If the purpose criterion is met based on the separate and similar activities test, the other evidence test (paragraphs 13.71–.72) should not be considered. If the separate and similar activities test is not determinative, the other evidence test should be considered.

13.71 *The other evidence test.* The compensation or fees test and the separate and similar activities test may not always be determinative because the attributes they consider may not be present. If the factors in paragraphs 40–44 of FASB ASC 958-720-45 (the compensation or fees test in paragraphs 13.65–.68) or paragraphs 44–45 of FASB ASC 958-720-45 (the separate and similar activities test in paragraphs 13.69–.70) do not determine whether the purpose criterion is met, other evidence may determine whether the criterion is met. All available evidence, both positive and negative, should be considered to determine whether, based on the weight of that evidence, the purpose criterion is met.

13.72 The following are examples of indicators that provide evidence for determining whether the purpose criterion is met:

a. FASB ASC 958-720-55-7 provides the following examples of indicators that provide evidence that the purpose criterion may be met:

i. *Measuring program results and accomplishments of the activity*. The facts may indicate that the purpose criterion is met if the NFP measures program results and accomplishments of the activity (other than measuring the extent to which the public was educated about causes).

ii. *Medium*. The facts may indicate that the purpose criterion is met if the program component of the joint activity calls for specific action by the recipient that will help accomplish the NFP's mission and if the NFP conducts the program component without a significant fundraising component in a different medium. Also, the facts may indicate that the purpose criterion is met if the NFP conducts the management and general component of the joint activity without a significant fundraising component in a different medium.

b. FASB ASC 958-720-55-8 provides the following examples of indicators that provide evidence that the purpose criterion may not be met:

i. *Evaluation*. The facts may indicate that the purpose criterion is not met if the evaluation of any party's performance of any component of the discrete joint activity varies based on contributions raised for that discrete joint activity.

ii. *Compensation*. The facts may indicate that the purpose criterion is not met if some, but less than a majority, of compensation or fees for any party's performance of any component of the discrete joint activity varies based on contributions raised for that discrete joint activity.

c. FASB ASC 958-720-55-9 provides the following examples of indicators that provide evidence that the purpose criterion may be either met or not met:

i. *Evaluation of measured results of the activity*. The NFP may have a process to evaluate measured program results and accomplishments of the activity (other than measuring the extent to which the public was educated about causes). If the NFP has such a process, in evaluating the effectiveness of the joint activity, the NFP may place significantly greater weight on the activity's effectiveness in accomplishing program goals or may place significantly greater weight on the activity's effectiveness in raising contributions. The former may indicate that the purpose criterion is met. The latter may indicate that the purpose criterion is not met.

ii. *Qualifications*. The qualifications and duties of those performing the joint activity should be considered. If a third party, such as a consultant or contractor, performs part or all of the joint activity, such as producing brochures or making telephone calls, the third party's experience and the range of services provided to the NFP should be considered in determining whether the third party is performing fundraising, program (other than educating the public about causes), or management and general activities on behalf of the NFP. If the NFP's employees perform part or all of the joint activity, the full range of their job duties should be considered in determining whether those employees are performing fundraising, program (other than educating the public about causes), or management and general activities on behalf of the NFP. For example, employees who are not members of the fundraising department and employees who are members of the fundraising department but who perform nonfundraising activities are more likely to perform activities that include program or management and general functions than are employees who otherwise devote significant time to fundraising.

iii. *Tangible evidence of intent*. Tangible evidence indicating the intended purpose of the joint activity should be considered. Examples of such tangible evidence include the following: (1) the NFP's written mission statement, as stated in its fundraising activities, bylaws, or annual report; (2) minutes of board of directors', committees', or other meetings; (3) restrictions imposed by donors (who are not related parties) on gifts intended to fund the joint activity; (4) long-range plans or operating policies; (5) written instructions to other entities, such as script writers, consultants, or list brokers, concerning the purpose of the joint activity, audience to be targeted, or method of conducting the joint activity; and (6) internal management memoranda.

Audience

13.73 A rebuttable presumption exists that the audience criterion is not met if the audience includes prior donors or is otherwise selected based on its ability or likelihood to contribute to the NFP. That presumption can be overcome if the audience is also selected for one or more of the reasons in FASB ASC 958-720-45-49 (paragraph 13.74*a–c*). In determining whether that presumption is overcome, NFPs should consider the extent to which the audience is selected based on its ability or likelihood to contribute to the NFP and contrast that with the extent to which it is selected for one or more of the reasons in FASB ASC 958-720-45-49 (paragraph 13.74*a–c*). For example, if the audience's ability or likelihood to contribute is a significant factor in its selection and it has a need for the action related to the program component of the joint activity, but having that need is an insignificant factor in its selection, the presumption would not be overcome.

13.74 FASB ASC 958-720-45-49 states that in circumstances in which the audience includes no prior donors and is not otherwise selected based on its ability or likelihood to contribute to the NFP, the audience criterion is met if the audience is selected for any of the following reasons:

a. The audience's need to use or reasonable potential for use of the specific action called for by the program component of the joint activity *b.* The audience's ability to take specific action to assist the NFP in meeting the goals of the program component of the joint activity

c. The NFP is required to direct the management and general component of the joint activity to the particular audience or the audience has reasonable potential for use of the management and general component

13.75 Paragraphs 11–15 of FASB ASC 958-720-55 provide additional guidance for the audience criterion, which is reproduced in this paragraph and the following 4 paragraphs. Some NFPs conduct joint activities that are special events, such as symposia, dinners, dances, and theater parties, in which the attendee receives a direct benefit (for example, a meal or theater ticket) and for which the admission price includes a contribution. For example, it may cost $500 to attend a dinner with a fair value of $50. In that case, the audience is required to make a $450 contribution in order to attend.

13.76 In circumstances in which the audience is required to make a contribution to participate in a joint activity, such as attending a special event, the audience's ability or likelihood to contribute is a significant factor in its selection. Therefore, in circumstances in which the audience is required to make a contribution to participate in a joint activity, the extent to which the audience is selected for the program or management and general reasons in FASB ASC 958-720-45-49 (paragraph 13.74) must be overwhelmingly significant in order to rebut the presumption that the audience criterion is not met.

13.77 The source of the names and the characteristics of the audience should be considered in determining the reason for selecting the audience. Some NFPs use lists compiled by others to reach new audiences. The source of such lists may indicate the purpose or purposes for which they were selected. For example, lists acquired from entities with similar or related programs are more likely to meet the audience criterion than are lists acquired from entities with dissimilar or unrelated programs. Also, the characteristics of those on the lists may indicate the purpose or purposes for which they were selected. For example, a list based on a consumer profile of those who buy environmentally friendly products may be useful to an NFP whose mission addresses environmental concerns and could therefore indicate that the audience was selected for its ability to take action to assist the NFP in meeting program goals. However, a list based on net worth would indicate that the audience was selected based on its ability or likelihood to contribute, unless there was a correlation between net worth and the program or management and general components of the activity.

13.78 Some audiences may be selected because they have an interest in or affinity to the program. For example, homeowners may have an interest in the homeless because they are sympathetic to the plight of the homeless. Nevertheless, including homeowners in the audience of a program activity to provide services to the homeless would not meet the audience criterion because they do not have a need or reasonable potential for use of services to the homeless.

13.79 An example of a joint activity in which the audience is selected because the NFP is required to direct the management and general component of the joint activity to the particular audience is an activity in which the NFP sends a written acknowledgment or other information to comply with requirements of the IRS to prior donors and includes a request for contributions. An example of a joint activity in which the audience is selected because the audience has reasonable potential for use of the management and general component is an activity in which the NFP sends its annual report to prior donors and includes a request for contributions.

Content

13.80 FASB ASC 958-720-45-50 states that the content criterion is met if the joint activity supports program or management and general functions, as follows:

- *a.* *Program*. The joint activity calls for specific action by the recipient that will help accomplish the NFP's mission (see paragraphs 35–37 of FASB ASC 958-720-45, which are reproduced in part in paragraphs 13.59–.64). If the need for and benefits of the action are not clearly evident, information describing the action and explaining the need for and benefits of the action is provided.
- *b.* *Management and general*. The joint activity fulfills one or more of the NFP's management and general responsibilities through a component of the joint activity.

13.81 Per FASB ASC 958-720-45-35, actions that help accomplish the NFP's mission are actions that either benefit the recipient or benefit society. FASB ASC 958-720-55-17 provides the following examples of actions that benefit the recipient (such as by improving the recipient's physical, mental, emotional, or spiritual health and well-being) or society (such as by addressing societal problems):

- *a.* Actions that benefit the recipient include the following:
  - i. *Stop smoking*. Specific methods, instructions, references, and resources should be suggested.
  - ii. *Do not use alcohol or drugs*. Specific methods, instructions, references, and resources should be suggested.
- *b.* Actions that benefit society include the following:
  - i. *Write or call*. The party to communicate with and the subject matter to be communicated should be specified.
  - ii. *Complete and return the enclosed questionnaire*. The results of the questionnaire should help the NFP achieve its mission. For example, if the NFP discards the questionnaire, it does not help the NFP achieve its mission.
  - iii. *Boycott*. The particular product or company to be boycotted should be specified.

13.82 Information identifying and describing the NFP, its causes, or how the contributions provided will be used is considered in support of fund-raising.

13.83 Per FASB ASC 958-720-45-53, activities that are undertaken in order to solicit contributions are fund-raising activities. For example, activities conducted to comply with requirements of regulatory bodies concerning soliciting contributions, such as the requirement by some states or other regulatory bodies that certain disclosures be included when soliciting contributions, are fundraising activities. For purposes of applying this guidance, communications that include such required disclosures are considered fundraising activities and are not considered management and general activities.

13.84 FASB ASC 958-720-55-18 provides the following examples of required disclosures that are considered fundraising activities:

- Information filed with the attorney general concerning this charitable solicitation may be obtained from the attorney general of [*the state*] by calling 123-4567. Registration with the attorney general does not imply endorsement.
- A copy of the registration and financial information may be obtained from the Division of Consumer Services by calling toll-free, within [*the state*], 1 (800) 123-4567. Registration does not imply endorsement, approval, or recommendation by [*the state*].
- Information about the cost of postage and copying, and other information required to be filed under [*the state*] law, can be obtained by calling 123-4567.
- The entity's latest annual report can be obtained by calling 123-4567.

Allocation Methods

13.85 The cost allocation methodology used should be rational and systematic, it should result in an allocation of joint costs that is reasonable, and it should be applied consistently given similar facts and circumstances. Paragraphs 25–31 of FASB ASC 958-720-55 (reproduced in appendix B [paragraph 13.100] of this chapter) provides explanations and examples of some acceptable allocation methods. The allocation of joint costs should be based on the degree to which costs were incurred for the functions to which the costs are allocated (that is, program, management and general, or fundraising). For purposes of determining whether the allocation methodology for a particular joint activity should be consistent with methodologies used for other particular joint activities, facts and circumstances that may be considered include factors related to the content and relative costs of the components of the activity. The audience should not be considered in determining whether the facts and circumstances are similar for purposes of determining whether the allocation methodology for a particular joint activity should be consistent with methodologies used for other particular joint activities. A change in cost allocation methodology should be evaluated in accordance with FASB ASC 250, *Accounting Changes and Error Corrections*, to determine if it is a change in accounting principle.

13.86 Paragraphs 32–33 of FASB ASC 958-720-55 provide the following information about which joint costs should be measured and allocated. Some costs, such as utilities, rent, and insurance (commonly referred to as *indirect costs*), may be joint costs. For example, the telephone bill for a department that, among other things, prepares materials that include both fundraising and program components may commonly be referred to as an indirect cost. Such telephone bills may also be joint costs. However, for some NFPs, it is impracticable to measure and allocate the portion of the costs that are joint costs. Considerations about which joint costs should be measured and allocated, such as considerations about materiality and the costs and benefits of developing and providing the information, are the same as considerations about cost allocations in other circumstances.

Incidental Activities

13.87 Some fundraising activities conducted in conjunction with program or management and general activities are incidental to such program or management and general activities. In circumstances in which a fundraising, program, or management and general activity is conducted in conjunction with another activity and is incidental to that other activity, and the criteria in FASB ASC 958-720-45-29 (paragraph 13.56) for allocation are met, joint costs are permitted but not required to be allocated and may therefore be charged to the functional classification related to the activity that is not the incidental activity. However, in circumstances in which the program or management and general activities are incidental to the fundraising activities, it is unlikely that the criteria in that paragraph to permit allocation of joint costs would be met.

13.88 Paragraphs 160–165 of FASB ASC 958-720-55 provide the following three examples of incidental activities. NFP Q conducts a fundraising activity by including a generic message, "Contributions to NFP Q may be sent to [*address*]" on a small area of a message that would otherwise be considered a program or management and general activity based on its purpose, audience, and content. That fundraising activity likely would be considered incidental to the program or management and general activity being conducted. NFP R conducts a program activity by including a generic program message such as "Continue to pray for [*a particular cause*]" on a small area of a message that would otherwise be considered fundraising based on its purpose, audience, and content. That program activity would likely be considered incidental to the fundraising activity being conducted. NFP S conducts a management and general activity by including the brief management and general message "We recently changed our phone number. Our new number is 123-4567" on a small area of a message that would otherwise be considered a program or fundraising activity based on its purpose, audience, and content. That management and general activity would likely be considered incidental to the program or fundraising activity being conducted.

Disclosures

13.89 FASB ASC 958-720-50-2 requires that an NFP that allocates joint costs should disclose all of the following in the notes to its financial statements:

a. The types of activities for which joint costs have been incurred

b. A statement that such costs have been allocated

c. The total amount allocated during the period and the portion allocated to each functional expense category

13.90 An NFP is also encouraged, but not required, to disclose the amount of joint costs for each kind of joint activity, if practical.

Additional Guidance

13.91 FASB ASC 958-720-55-2 (reproduced in appendix A [paragraph 13.98] of this chapter) includes a flowchart useful in accounting for joint activities. Paragraphs 35–159 of FASB ASC 958-720-55 (reproduced in appendix B [paragraph 13.99] of this chapter) illustrate the application of the purpose, audience, and content criteria to determine whether a program or management and general activity has been conducted along with the fundraising activity. Paragraph 25–31 of FASB ASC 958-720-55 (reproduced in appendix C [paragraph 13.100] of this chapter) illustrate allocation methods. Paragraphs 166–170 of FASB ASC 958-720-55 (reproduced in appendix D [paragraph 13.101] of this chapter) illustrate disclosures required when joint activities are conducted.

Support to Related Local and National NFPs

13.92 Some NFPs make payments or provide other support to local or national entities. The specific purposes and benefits of those payments may be determinable (for example, permission to raise funds in a specified geographical area, or the provision of joint purchasing arrangements and technical and fundraising assistance, functions that the NFP would otherwise have to carry out itself), or the purposes and benefits may be indeterminable. Payments in the form of grants and dues may also be made to related local and national entities.

13.93 Per FASB ASC 958-720-45-26, payments to related local and national NFPs should be reported by their functional classification to the extent that it is practicable and reasonable to do so and the necessary information is available, even if it is impossible to allocate the entire amount of such payments to functions. Payments to those entities that cannot be allocated to functions should be treated as a separate supporting service, reported on a statement of activities as a separate line item, and labeled "unallocated payments to local (or national) organizations."

Expenses of Federated Fundraising Entities

13.94 Per FASB ASB 958-720-45-27, federated fundraising entities solicit and receive designated and undesignated contributions and make grants and awards to other NFPs. The fundraising activities of federated fundraising entities, including activities related to fundraising on behalf of others, should be reported as fundraising expenses.

Income Taxes

13.95 Per FASB ASC 958-720-50-1, if an NFP incurs income tax expense, the financial statements of the NFP should disclose the amount of income tax expense and describe the nature of the activities that generated the taxes.

Auditing

13.96 Many audit objectives, controls, and auditing procedures for expenses, gains, and losses of NFPs are similar to those of other entities. In addition, the auditor may need to consider the following specific audit objectives, selected controls, and auditing procedures that are unique to NFPs.

13.97 The following table illustrates the use of assertions in developing audit objectives and designing substantive tests. The examples are not intended to be all-inclusive nor is it expected that all the procedures would necessarily be applied in an audit. The auditor should design and perform substantive procedures for all relevant assertions related to each material class of transactions, account balance, and disclosure to obtain sufficient appropriate audit evidence. The use of assertions in assessing risks and designing appropriate audit procedures to obtain audit evidence is described in paragraphs .14–.26 of AU section 326, *Audit Evidence* (AICPA, *Professional Standards*). Various audit procedures and the purposes for which they may be performed are described in paragraphs .27–.41 of AU section 326.

Auditing Considerations

Financial Statement Assertions	*Specific Audit Objectives*	*Examples of Selected Controls*	*Examples of Auditing Procedures*
Presentation and Disclosure			
Classification	Expenses are properly classified and displayed.	Controls ensure that expenses are properly classified and displayed.	Compare current period expenses in total and by functional classification with expectations based on prior-period expenses or budget, or both, and obtain explanations for variances from expectations. Determine that expenses have been properly assigned and allocated to functional and, if applicable, natural classifications.

13.98

Appendix A—Accounting for Joint Activities[1]

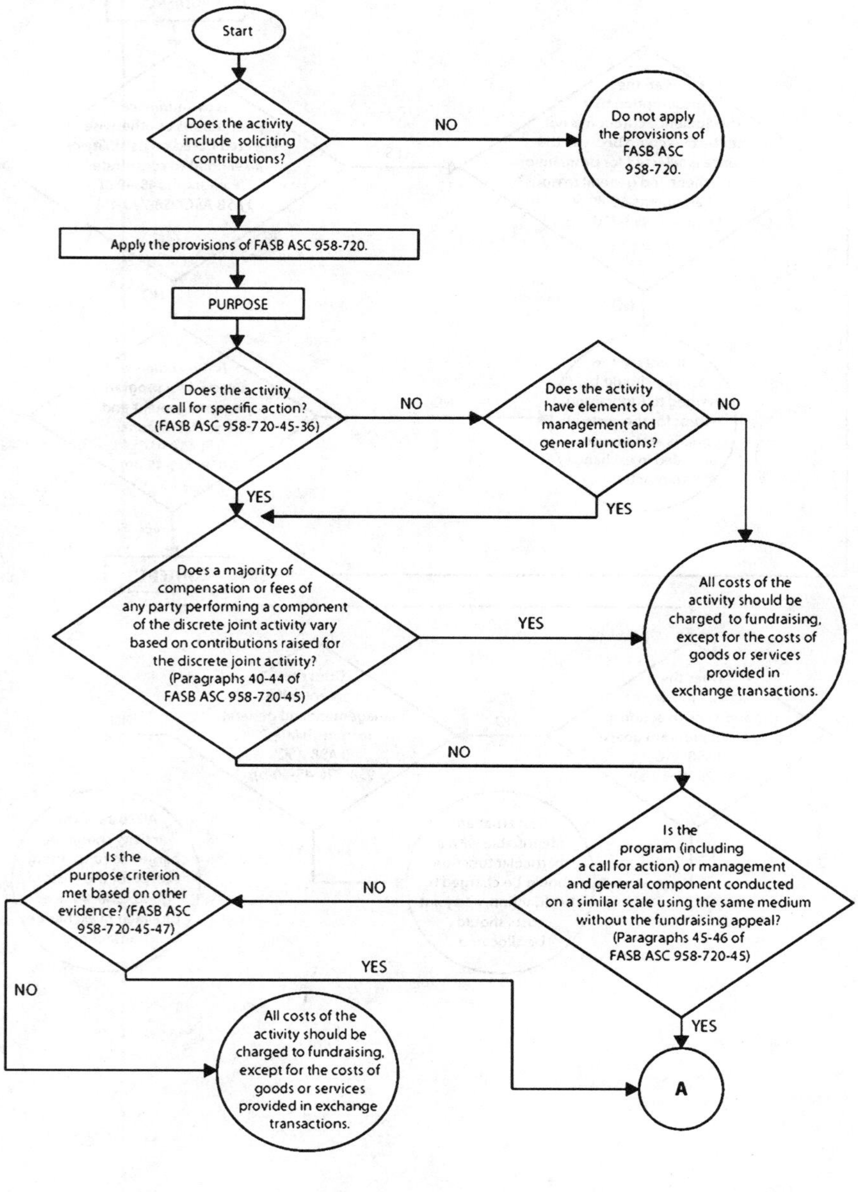

(continued)

[1] Note: This flowchart summarizes certain guidance in paragraphs 13.52–.91 and is not intended as a substitute for that guidance.

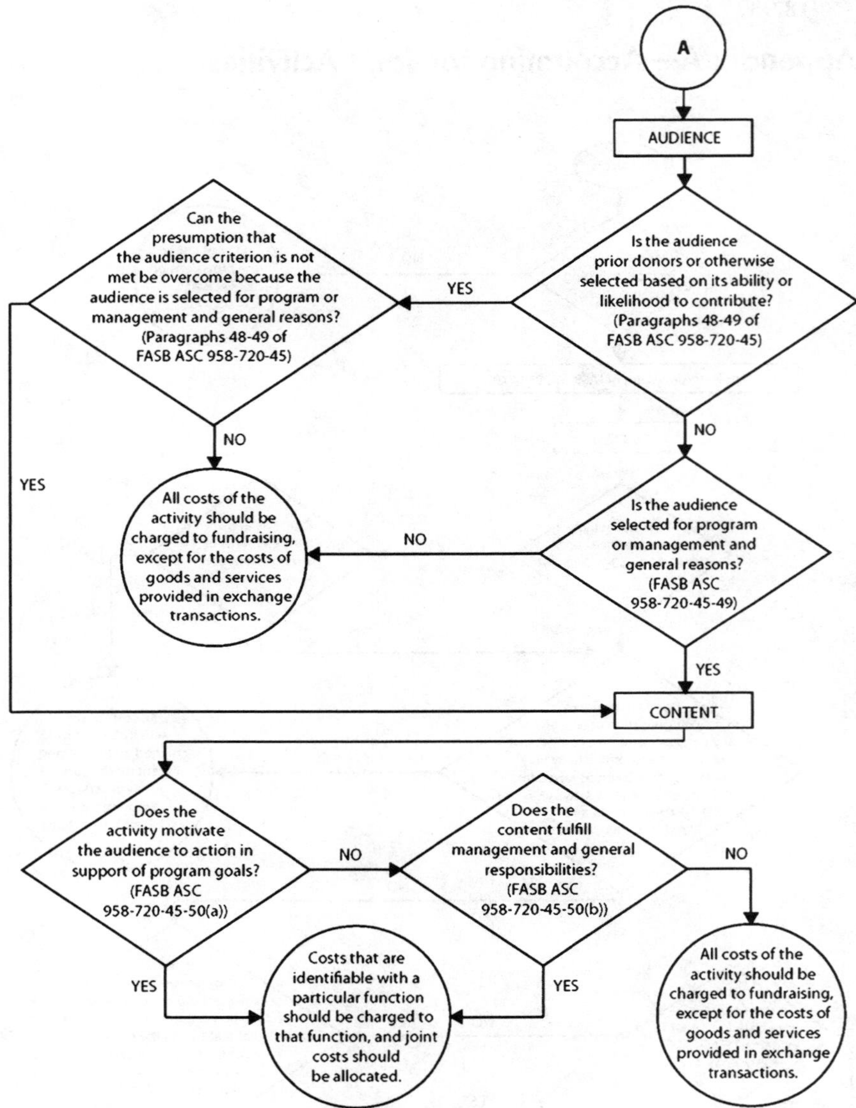
A
AUDIENCE
Is the audience prior donors or otherwise selected based on its ability or likelihood to contribute? (Paragraphs 48-49 of FASB ASC 958-720-45)
YES
Can the presumption that the audience criterion is not met be overcome because the audience is selected for program or management and general reasons? (Paragraphs 48-49 of FASB ASC 958-720-45)
NO
YES
All costs of the activity should be charged to fundraising, except for the costs of goods and services provided in exchange transactions.
NO
Is the audience selected for program or management and general reasons? (FASB ASC 958-720-45-49)
NO
YES
CONTENT
Does the activity motivate the audience to action in support of program goals? (FASB ASC 958-720-45-50(a))
NO
Does the content fulfill management and general responsibilities? (FASB ASC 958-720-45-50(b))
NO
YES
Costs that are identifiable with a particular function should be charged to that function, and joint costs should be allocated.
YES
All costs of the activity should be charged to fundraising, except for the costs of goods and services provided in exchange transactions.

13.99

Appendix B—Examples of Applying the Criteria of Purpose, Audience, and Content to Determine Whether a Program or Management and General Activity Has Been Conducted

Paragraphs 35–159 of Financial Accounting Standards Board (FASB) *Accounting Standards Codification* (ASC) 958-720-55 illustrate the application of the purpose, audience, and content criteria to determine whether a program or management and general activity has been conducted along with a fundraising activity. Those examples are reproduced in the following paragraphs.

Example 1: Mailing of Informational Materials

Facts

1. Not-for-profit entity (NFP) A's mission is to prevent drug abuse. NFP A's annual report states that one of its objectives in fulfilling that mission is to assist parents in preventing their children from abusing drugs.

2. NFP A mails informational materials to the parents of all junior high school students explaining the prevalence and dangers of drug abuse. The materials encourage parents to counsel children about the dangers of drug abuse and inform them about how to detect drug abuse. The mailing includes a request for contributions. NFP A conducts other activities informing the public about the dangers of drug abuse and encouraging parents to counsel their children about drug abuse that do not include requests for contributions and that are conducted in different media. NFP A's executive director is involved in the development of the informational materials as well as the request for contributions. The executive director's annual compensation includes a significant bonus if total annual contributions exceed a predetermined amount.

Conclusion

3. The purpose, audience, and content criteria are met, and the joint costs should be allocated.

4. The activity calls for specific action by the recipient (encouraging parents to counsel children about the dangers of drug abuse and informing them about how to detect drug abuse) that will help accomplish the NFP's mission. Therefore, the guidance in FASB ASC 958-720-45-38 (paragraph 13.64) should be considered. Neither of the factors in paragraphs 40–44 of FASB ASC 958-720-45 (the compensation or fees test in paragraphs 13.65–.68) or paragraphs 45–46 of FASB ASC 958-720-45 (the separate and similar activities test in paragraphs 13.69–.70) is determinative of whether the purpose criterion is met. (Although NFP A's executive director's annual compensation varies based on annual contributions, the executive director's compensation does not vary based on contributions raised for this discrete joint activity.) Therefore, other evidence, such as the indicators in paragraphs 6–9 of FASB ASC 958-720-55 (paragraph 13.72), should be considered. The purpose criterion is met based on the other evidence because (*a*) the program component of this activity calls for specific action by the recipient (encouraging parents to counsel children about the dangers of drug abuse) that will help accomplish the NFP's mission, and it otherwise conducts the program activity in this example without a request for contributions, and (*b*) performing such programs helps accomplish NFP A's mission. Note that had NFP A conducted the activity using the same medium on a scale that is similar to or greater than the scale on which it is conducted with the request for contributions, the purpose criterion would have been met under paragraphs 45–46 of FASB ASC 958-720-45 (paragraphs 13.64–.65).

5. The audience criterion is met because the audience (parents of junior high school students) is selected based on its need to use or reasonable potential for use of the action called for by the program component.

6. The content criterion is met because the activity calls for specific action by the recipient (encouraging parents to counsel children about the dangers of drug abuse and informing them about how to detect drug abuse) that will help accomplish the NFP's mission (assisting parents in preventing their children from abusing drugs), and it explains the need for and benefits of the action (the prevalence and dangers of drug abuse).

Example 2: Mailing to Prior Donors

Facts

7. Not-for-Profit Entity (NFP) B's mission is to reduce the incidence of illness from ABC disease, which afflicts a broad segment of the population. One of NFP B's objectives in fulfilling that mission is to inform the public about the effects and early warning signs of the disease and specific action that should be taken to prevent the disease.

8. NFP B maintains a list of its prior donors and sends them donor renewal mailings. The mailings include messages about the effects and early warning signs of the disease and specific action that should be taken to prevent it. That information is also sent to a similar-sized audience but without the request for contributions. Also, NFP B believes that recent donors are more likely to contribute than nondonors or donors who have not contributed recently. Prior donors are deleted from the mailing list if they have not contributed to NFP B recently, and new donors are added to the list. There is no evidence of a correlation between recent contributions and participation in the program component of the activity. Also, the prior donors' need to use or reasonable potential for use of the messages about the effects and early warning signs of the disease and specific action that should be taken to prevent it is an insignificant factor in their selection.

Conclusion

9. The purpose and content criteria are met. The audience criterion is not met. All costs, including those that might otherwise be considered program or management and general costs if they had been incurred in a different activity, should be charged to fundraising.

10. The activity calls for specific action by the recipient (action that should be taken to prevent ABC disease) that will help accomplish the entity's mission. Therefore, the guidance in FASB ASC 958-720-45-38 (paragraph 13.64) should be considered. The purpose criterion is met because (*a*) the program component of the activity calls for specific action by the recipient that will help accomplish the NFP's mission (to reduce the incidence of illness from the disease), and (*b*) the program is also conducted using the same medium on a scale that is similar to or greater than the scale on which it is conducted with the request for contributions (a similar mailing is done without the request for contributions, to a similar-sized audience).

11. The audience criterion is not met. The rebuttable presumption that the audience criterion is not met because the audience includes prior donors is not overcome in this example. Although the audience has a need to use or reasonable potential for use of the program component, that was an insignificant factor in its selection.

12. The content criterion is met because the activity calls for specific action by the recipient (actions to prevent ABC disease) that will help accomplish the entity's mission (to reduce the incidence of ABC disease), and it explains the need for and benefits of the action (to prevent ABC disease).

Example 3: Telephone Solicitation of Prior Donors

Facts

13. Not-for-profit entity (NFP) C's mission is to reduce the incidence of illness from ABC disease, which afflicts a broad segment of the population. One of NFP C's objectives in fulfilling that mission is to increase governmental funding for research about ABC disease.

14. NFP C maintains a list of its prior donors and its employees call them on the telephone reminding them of the effects of ABC disease, asking for contributions, and encouraging them to contact their elected officials to urge increased governmental funding for research about ABC disease. The callers are educated about ABC, do not otherwise perform fundraising functions, and are not compensated or evaluated based on contributions raised. NFP C's research indicates that recent donors are likely to contact their elected officials about such funding while nonrecent donors are not. Prior donors are deleted from the calling list if they have not contributed to NFP C recently, and new donors are added to the list.

Conclusion

15. The purpose, audience, and content criteria are met, and the joint costs should be allocated.

16. The activity calls for specific action by the recipient (contacting elected officials concerning funding for research about ABC disease) that will help accomplish the NFP's mission. Therefore, the guidance in FASB ASC 958-720-45-38 (paragraph 13.64) should be considered. Neither of the factors in paragraphs 40–44 of FASB ASC 958-720-45 (the compensation or fees test in paragraphs 13.65–.68) or paragraphs 45–46 of FASB ASC 958-720-45 (the separate and similar activities test in paragraphs 13.69–.70) is determinative of whether the purpose criterion is met. Therefore, other evidence, such as the indicators in paragraphs 6–9 of FASB ASC 958-720-55 (paragraph 13.72), should be considered. The purpose criterion is met based on the other evidence, because (*a*) the qualifications and duties of the personnel performing the activity indicate that it is a program activity (the callers are educated about ABC and do not otherwise perform fundraising functions), (*b*) the method of compensation for performing the activity does not indicate that it is a fundraising activity (the employees are not compensated or evaluated based on contributions raised), and (*c*) performing such programs helps accomplish NFP C's mission.

17. The audience criterion is met because the audience (recent donors) is selected based on its ability to assist NFP C in meeting the goals of the program component of the activity (recent donors are likely to contact their elected officials about such funding while nonrecent donors are not).

18. The content criterion is met because the activity calls for specific action by the recipient (contacting elected officials concerning funding for research about ABC disease) that will help accomplish the NFP's mission (to reduce the incidence of ABC disease), and it explains the need for and benefits of the action (to prevent ABC disease).

Example 4: Mailing Targeted Based on Program-Related Criteria

Facts: Case A

19. Not-for-profit entity (NFP) D's mission is to improve the quality of life for senior citizens. One of NFP D's objectives included in that mission is to increase the physical activity of senior citizens. One of NFP D's programs to attain that objective is to send representatives to speak to groups about the importance of exercise and to conduct exercise classes.

20. NFP D mails a brochure on the importance of exercise that encourages exercise in later years to residents over the age of 65 in 3 zip code areas. The last 2 pages of the 4-page brochure include a perforated contribution remittance form on which NFP D explains its program and makes an appeal for contributions. The content of the first 2 pages of the brochure is primarily educational; it explains how seniors can undertake a self-supervised exercise program and encourages them to undertake such a program. In addition, NFP D includes a second brochure on various exercise techniques that can be used by those undertaking an exercise program.

21. The brochures are distributed to educate people in this age group about the importance of exercising, to help them exercise properly, and to raise contributions for NFP D. These objectives are documented in a letter to the public relations firm that developed the brochures. The audience is selected based on age, without regard to ability to contribute. NFP D believes that most of the recipients would benefit from the information about exercise.

Conclusion: Case A

22. The purpose, audience, and content criteria are met, and the joint costs should be allocated. (Note that the costs of the second brochure should be charged to program because all the costs of the brochure are identifiable with the program function.)

23. The activity calls for specific action by the recipient (exercising) that will help accomplish the NFP's mission. Therefore, the guidance in FASB ASC 958-720-45-38 (paragraph 13.64) should be considered. Neither of the factors in paragraphs 40–44 of FASB ASC 958-720-45 (the compensation or fees test in paragraphs 13.65–.68) or paragraphs 45–46 of FASB ASC 958-720-45 (the separate and similar activities test in paragraphs 13.69–.70) is determinative of whether the purpose criterion is met. Therefore, other evidence, such as the indicators in paragraphs 6–9 of FASB ASC 958-720-55 (paragraph 13.72), should be considered. The purpose criterion is met based on the other evidence, because (*a*) performing such programs helps accomplish NFP D's mission, and (*b*) the objectives of the program are documented in a letter to the public relations firm that developed the brochure.

24. The audience criterion is met because the audience (residents over 65 in certain zip codes) is selected based on its need to use or reasonable potential for use of the action called for by the program component.

25. The content criterion is met because the activity calls for specific action by the recipient (exercising) that will help accomplish the NFP's mission (increasing the physical activity of senior citizens), and the need for and benefits of the action are clearly evident (explains the importance of exercising).

Facts: Case B

26. In this case, NFP D employs a fundraising consultant to develop the first brochure and pays that consultant 30 percent of contributions raised.

Conclusion: Case B

27. The content and audience criteria are met. The purpose criterion is not met, however, because a majority of compensation or fees for the fundraising consultant varies based on contributions raised for this discrete joint activity (the fundraising consultant is paid 30 percent of contributions raised). All costs should be charged to fundraising, including the costs of the second brochure and any other costs that otherwise might be considered program or management and general costs if they had been incurred in a different activity.

Example 5: Door-to-Door Canvass

Facts

28. Not-for-profit entity (NFP) E's mission is to protect the environment. One of NFP E's objectives included in that mission is to take action that will increase the portion of waste recycled by the public.

29. NFP E conducts a door-to-door canvass of a community that recycles a low portion of its waste. The purpose of the activity is to help increase recycling by educating the community about environmental problems created by not recycling, and to raise contributions. Based on the information communicated by the canvassers, the need for and benefits of the action are clearly evident. The ability or likelihood of the residents to contribute is not a basis for communities selected, and all neighborhoods in the geographic area are covered if their recycling falls below a predetermined rate. The canvassers are selected from individuals who are well-informed about NFP E's environmental concerns and programs and who previously participated as volunteers in program activities such as answering environmental questions directed to NFP E and developing program activities designed to influence legislators to take actions addressing those concerns. The canvassers have not previously participated in fundraising activities.

Conclusion

30. The purpose, audience, and content criteria are met, and the joint costs should be allocated.

31. The activity calls for specific action by the recipient (implicitly—to help increase recycling) that will help accomplish the entity's mission. Therefore, the guidance in FASB ASC 958-720-45-38 (paragraph 13.64) should be considered. Neither of the factors in paragraphs 40–44 of FASB ASC 958-720-45 (the compensation or fees test in paragraphs 13.65–.68) or paragraphs 45–46 of FASB

ASC 958-720-45 (the separate and similar activities test in paragraphs 13.69–.70) is determinative of whether the purpose criterion is met. Therefore, other evidence, such as the indicators in paragraphs 6–9 of FASB ASC 958-720-55 (paragraph 13.72), should be considered. The purpose criterion is met based on the other evidence, because (*a*) the qualifications and duties of the personnel performing the activity indicate that it is a program activity (the canvassers are selected from individuals who are well-informed about NFP E's environmental concerns and programs and who previously participated as volunteers in program activities such as answering environmental questions directed to NFP E and developing program activities designed to influence legislators to take actions addressing those concerns), and (*b*) performing such programs helps accomplish NFP E's mission (to protect the environment).

32. The audience criterion is met because the audience (neighborhoods whose recycling falls below a predetermined rate) is selected based on its need to use or reasonable potential for use of the action called for by the program component.

33. The content criterion is met because the activity calls for specific action by the recipient (implicitly—to help increase recycling) that will help accomplish NFP E's mission (to protect the environment), and the need for and benefits of the action are clearly evident (increased recycling will help alleviate environmental problems).

Example 6: Door-to-Door Solicitation Campaign

Facts

34. Not-for-profit entity (NFP) F's mission is to provide summer camps for economically disadvantaged youths. Educating the families of ineligible youths about the camps is not one of the program objectives included in that mission.

35. NFP F conducts a door-to-door solicitation campaign for its camp programs. In the campaign, volunteers with canisters visit homes in middle-class neighborhoods to collect contributions. NFP F believes that people in those neighborhoods would not need the camp's programs but may contribute. The volunteers explain the camp's programs, including why the disadvantaged children benefit from the program, and distribute leaflets to the residents regardless of whether they contribute to the camp. The leaflets describe the camp, its activities, who can attend, and the benefits to attendees. Requests for contributions are not included in the leaflets.

Conclusion

36. The purpose, audience, and content criteria are not met. All costs should be charged to fundraising.

37. The activity does not include a call for specific action because it only educates the audience about causes (describing the camp, its activities, who can attend, and the benefits to attendees). Therefore, the purpose criterion is not met.

38. The audience criterion is not met, because the audience is selected based on its ability or likelihood to contribute, rather than based on its need to use or reasonable potential for use of the action called for by the program component or its ability to take action to assist the NFP in meeting the goals of the program component of the activity. (NFP F believes that people in those neighborhoods would not need the camp's programs but may contribute.)

39. The content criterion is not met because the activity does not call for specific action by the recipient. (The content educates the audience about causes that the program is designed to address without calling for specific action.)

Example 7: Annual National Telethon

Facts

40. Not-for-profit entity (NFP) G's mission is to educate the public about lifesaving techniques in order to increase the number of lives saved. One of NFP G's objectives in fulfilling that mission, as stated in the minutes of the board's meetings, is to produce and show television broadcasts including information about lifesaving techniques.

41. NFP G conducts an annual national telethon to raise contributions and to reach the American public with lifesaving educational messages, such as summary instructions concerning dealing with certain life-threatening situations. Based on the information communicated by the messages, the need for and benefits of the action are clearly evident. The broadcast includes segments describing NFP G's services. NFP G broadcasts the telethon to the entire country, not merely to areas selected on the basis of giving potential or prior fundraising results. Also, NFP G uses national television broadcasts devoted entirely to lifesaving educational messages to conduct program activities without fundraising.

Conclusion

42. The purpose, audience, and content criteria are met, and the joint costs should be allocated.

43. The activity calls for specific action by the recipient (implicitly—to save lives) that will help accomplish the NFP's mission. Therefore, the guidance in FASB ASC 958-720-45-38 (paragraph 13.64) should be considered. The purpose criterion is met because (*a*) the program component of the activity calls for specific action by the recipient that will help accomplish NFP G's mission (to save lives by educating the public), and (*b*) a similar program activity is conducted without the fundraising using the same medium and on a scale that is similar to or greater than the scale on which it is conducted with the appeal (NFP G uses national television broadcasts devoted entirely to lifesaving educational messages to conduct program activities without fundraising).

44. The audience criterion is met because the audience (a broad segment of the population) is selected based on its need to use or reasonable potential for use of the action called for by the program activity.

45. The content criterion is met because the activity calls for specific action by the recipient (implicitly—to save lives) that will help accomplish the NFP's mission (to save lives by educating the public), and the need for and benefits of the action are clearly evident (saving lives is desirable).

Example 8: Television Broadcast Educating the Public

Facts

46. Not-for-profit entity (NFP) H's mission is to provide food, clothing, and medical care to children in developing countries.

47. NFP H conducts television broadcasts in the United States that describe its programs, show the needy children, and end with appeals for contributions.

NFP H's operating policies and internal management memoranda state that these programs are designed to educate the public about the needs of children in developing countries and to raise contributions. The employees producing the programs are trained in audiovisual production and are familiar with NFP H's programs. Also, the executive producer is paid $25,000 for this activity, with a $5,000 bonus if the activity raises over $1,000,000.

Conclusion

48. The purpose, audience, and content criteria are not met. All costs should be charged to fundraising.

49. The activity does not include a call for specific action because it only educates the audience about causes (describing its programs and showing the needy children). Therefore, the purpose criterion is not met. Also, note that if the factor in paragraphs 40–44 of FASB ASC 958-720-45 (the compensation or fees test, which is paragraphs 13.65–.68) were considered, it would not be determinative of whether the purpose criterion is met. Although the executive producer will be paid $5,000 if the activity raises over $1,000,000, that amount would not be a majority of the executive producer's total compensation for this activity, because $5,000 would not be a majority of the executive producer's total compensation of $30,000 for this activity. Also, note that if other evidence, such as the indicators in paragraphs 6–9 of FASB ASC 958-720-55 (paragraph 13.72), were considered, the purpose criterion would not be met based on the other evidence. Although the qualifications and duties of the personnel performing the activity indicate that the employees producing the program are familiar with NFP H's programs, the facts that some, but less than a majority, of the executive producer's compensation varies based on contributions raised, and that the operating policies and internal management memoranda state that these programs are designed to educate the public about the needs of children in developing countries with no call for specific action by recipients and to raise contributions, indicate that the purpose is fundraising.)

50. The audience criterion is not met because the audience is selected based on its ability or likelihood to contribute, rather than based on its need to use or reasonable potential for use of the action called for by the program component or its ability to take action to assist the NFP in meeting the goals of the program component of the activity. (The audience is a broad segment of the population of a country that is not in need of or has no reasonable potential for use of the program activity.)

51. The content criterion is not met because the activity does not call for specific action by the recipient that will help accomplish the NFP's mission. (The content educates the audience about the causes without calling for specific action.)

Example 9: Distribution of the Annual Report

Facts

52. Not-for-profit entity (NFP) I is a university that distributes its annual report, which includes reports on mission accomplishments, to those who have made significant contributions over the previous year, its board of trustees, and its employees. The annual report is primarily prepared by management and general personnel, such as the accounting department and executive staff. The activity is coordinated by the public relations department. Internal management memoranda indicate that the purpose of the annual report is to report on how management discharged its stewardship responsibilities, including the university's overall performance, goals, financial position, cash flows, and results of operations. Included in the package containing the annual report are requests for contributions and donor reply cards.

Conclusion

53. The purpose, audience, and content criteria are met, and the joint costs should be allocated.

54. The activity has elements of management and general functions. Therefore, no call for specific action is required. Neither of the factors in paragraphs 40–44 of FASB ASC 958-720-45 (the compensation or fees test in paragraphs 13.65–.68) or paragraphs 45–46 of FASB ASC 958-720-45 (the separate and similar activities test in paragraphs 13.69–.70) is determinative of whether the purpose criterion is met. Therefore, other evidence, such as the indicators in paragraphs 6–9 of FASB ASC 958-720-55 (paragraph 13.72), should be considered. The purpose criterion is met based on the other evidence, because (*a*) the employees performing the activity are not members of the fundraising department and perform other nonfundraising activities and (*b*) internal management memoranda indicate that the purpose of the annual report is to fulfill one of the university's management and general responsibilities.

55. The audience criterion is met because the audience is selected based on its reasonable potential for use of the management and general component. Although the activity is directed primarily at those who have previously made significant contributions, the audience was selected based on its presumed interest in NFP I's annual report (prior donors who have made significant contributions are likely to have an interest in matters discussed in the annual report).

56. The content criterion is met because the activity (distributing annual reports) fulfills one of the entity's management and general responsibilities (reporting concerning management's fulfillment of its stewardship function).

Example 10: Compliance With Internal Revenue Service Regulations

Facts

57. In accordance with internal management memoranda documenting its policies requiring it to comply with IRS regulations, not-for-profit entity (NFP) J mails prior donors the contribution substantiation documentation required by the IRS. The documentation is included on a perforated piece of paper. The information above the perforation line pertains to the documentation required by the IRS. The information below the perforation line includes a request for contributions and may be used as a donor reply card.

Conclusion

58. The purpose, audience, and content criteria are met, and the joint costs should be allocated. (Note that the costs of the information below the perforation line are identifiable with fundraising and therefore should be charged to fundraising.)

59. The activity has elements of management and general functions. Therefore, no call for specific action is required. Neither of the factors in paragraphs

40–44 of FASB ASC 958-720-45 (the compensation or fees test in paragraphs 13.65–.68) or paragraphs 45–46 of FASB ASC 958-720-45 (the separate and similar activities test in paragraphs 13.69–.70) is determinative of whether the purpose criterion is met. Therefore, other evidence, such as the indicators in paragraphs 6–9 of FASB ASC 958-720-55 (paragraph 13.72), should be considered. The purpose criterion is met based on the other evidence, because internal management memoranda indicate that the purpose of the activity is to fulfill one of NFP J's management and general responsibilities.

60. The audience criterion is met because the NFP is required to direct the management and general component of the activity to the particular audience. Although the activity is directed at those who have previously contributed, the audience was selected based on its need for the documentation.

61. The content criterion is met because the activity (sending documentation required by the IRS) fulfills one of the entity's management and general responsibilities (complying with IRS regulations).

Example 11: Mailing to Individuals Targeted Using a Rented List

Facts

62. Not-for-profit entity (NFP) K is an animal rights organization. It mails a package of material to individuals included in lists rented from various environmental and other NFPs that support causes that NFP K believes are congruent with its own. In addition to donor response cards and return envelopes, the package includes (*a*) materials urging recipients to contact their legislators and urge the legislators to support legislation to protect those rights, and (*b*) postcards addressed to legislators urging support for legislation restricting the use of animal testing for cosmetic products. The mail campaign is part of an overall strategy that includes magazine advertisements and the distribution of similar materials at various community events, some of which are undertaken without fundraising appeals. The advertising and community events reach audiences similar in size and demographics to the audience reached by the mailing.

Conclusion

63. The purpose, audience, and content criteria are met, and the joint costs should be allocated.

64. The activity calls for specific action by the recipient (mailing postcards to legislators urging support for legislation restricting the use of animal testing for cosmetic products) that will help accomplish the entity's mission. Therefore, the guidance in FASB ASC 958-720-45-38 (paragraph 13.64) should be considered. Neither of the factors in paragraphs 40–44 of FASB ASC 958-720-45 (the compensation or fees test in paragraphs 13.65–.68) or paragraphs 45–46 of FASB ASC 958-720-45 (the separate and similar activities test in paragraphs 13.69–.70) is determinative of whether the purpose criterion is met. Therefore, other evidence, such as the indicators in paragraphs 6–9 of FASB ASC 958-720-55 (paragraph 13.72), should be considered. The purpose criterion is met based on the other evidence, because (*a*) the program component of this activity calls for specific action by the recipient that will help accomplish the NFP's mission, and it otherwise conducts the program activity in this example without a request for contributions, and (*b*) performing such programs helps accomplish NFP K's mission.

65. The audience criterion is met because the audience (individuals included in lists rented from various environmental and other NFPs that support causes that NFP K believes are congruent with its own) is selected based on its ability to take action to assist the NFP in meeting the goals of the program component of the activity.

66. The content criterion is met because the activity calls for specific action by the recipient (mailing postcards to legislators urging support for legislation restricting the use of animal testing for cosmetic products) that will help accomplish the NFP's mission (to protect animal rights), and the need for and benefits of the action are clearly evident (to protect animal rights).

Example 12: Advertising of Ticket Subscription With a Request for Contributions

Facts

67. Not-for-profit entity (NFP) L is a performing arts entity whose mission is to make the arts available to residents in its area. NFP L charges a fee for attending performances and sends advertisements, including subscription forms, for the performances to residents in its area. These advertisements include a return envelope with a request for contributions. NFP L evaluates the effectiveness of the advertising based on the number of subscriptions sold as well as contributions received. In performing that evaluation, NFP L places more weight on the number of subscriptions sold than on the contributions received. Also, NFP L advertises the performances on local television and radio without a request for contributions but on a smaller scale than the mail advertising.

Conclusion

68. The purpose, audience, and content criteria are met, and the joint costs should be allocated.

69. The activity calls for specific action by the recipient (attending the performances) that will help accomplish the NFP's mission. Therefore, the guidance in FASB ASC 958-720-45-38 (paragraph 13.64) should be considered. Neither of the factors in paragraphs 40–44 of FASB ASC 958-720-45 (the compensation or fees test in paragraphs 13.65–.68) or paragraphs 45–46 of FASB ASC 958-720-45 (the separate and similar activities test in paragraphs 13.69–.70) is determinative of whether the purpose criterion is met. Therefore, other evidence, such as the indicators in paragraphs 6–9 of FASB ASC 958-720-55 (paragraph 13.72), should be considered. The purpose criterion is met based on the other evidence because (*a*) the NFP measures program results and accomplishments of the joint activity and in evaluating the effectiveness of the activity, the NFP places significantly greater weight on the activity's effectiveness in accomplishing program goals than on the activity's effectiveness in raising contributions (NFP L evaluates the effectiveness of the advertising based on the number of subscriptions sold as well as contributions received and places more weight on the number of subscriptions sold than on the contributions received), (*b*) it otherwise conducts the program activity without a request for contributions, and (*c*) performing such programs helps accomplish NFP L's mission (to make the arts available to residents in its area).

70. The audience criterion is met because the audience (a broad segment of the population in NFP L's area) is selected based on its need to use or reasonable potential for use of the action called for by the program component.

71. The content criterion is met because the activity calls for specific action by the recipient (attending the performances) that will help accomplish the NFP's mission (making the arts available to area residents), and the need for and benefits of the action are clearly evident (attending the performance is a positive cultural experience). (Note that the purchase of subscriptions is an exchange transaction and, therefore, is not a contribution.)

Example 13: University Lecture Series With Fair Value Admission

Facts

72. Not-for-profit entity (NFP) M is a university whose mission is to educate the public (students) in various academic pursuits. NFP M's political science department holds a special lecture series in which prominent world leaders speak about current events. The speakers command relatively high fees and, in order to cover costs and make a modest profit, the university sets a relatively expensive fee to attend. However, the tickets are priced at the fair value of the lecture and no portion of the ticket purchase price is a contribution. NFP M advertises the lectures by sending invitations to prior attendees and to prior donors who have contributed significant amounts, and by placing advertisements in local newspapers read by the general public. At some of the lectures, including the lecture being considered in this example, deans and other faculty members of NFP M solicit significant contributions from attendees. Other lectures in the series are conducted on a scale similar to the scale of the lecture in this example without requesting contributions. NFP M's records indicate that historically 75 percent of the attendees have attended prior lectures. Of the 75 percent who have attended prior lectures, 15 percent have made prior contributions to NFP M. Of the 15 percent who have made prior contributions to NFP M, 5 percent have made contributions in response to solicitations made at the events. (Therefore, one-half of 1 percent of attendees make contributions in response to solicitations made at the events. However, those contributions are significant.) Overall, the audience's ability or likelihood to contribute is an insignificant factor in its selection. NFP M evaluates the effectiveness of the activity based on the number of tickets sold, as well as contributions received. In performing that evaluation, NFP M places more weight on the number of tickets sold than on the contributions received.

Conclusion

73. The purpose, audience, and content criteria are met, and the joint costs should be allocated. The purchase of the tickets is an exchange transaction and, therefore, is not a contribution. As discussed in FASB ASC 958-720-45-29 (paragraph 13.55), costs of goods or services provided in exchange transactions that are part of joint activities, such as costs of direct donor benefits of a special event, should not be reported as fundraising. FASB ASC 958-225-45-17 (paragraph 13.29) provides guidance concerning reporting special events.

74. The activity calls for specific action by the recipient (attending the lecture) that will help accomplish the NFP's mission. Therefore, the guidance in FASB ASC 958-720-45-38 (paragraph 13.64) should be considered. The purpose criterion is met because (*a*) the program component of the activity calls for specific action by the recipient that will help accomplish the NFP's mission (educating the public [students] in various academic pursuits), and (*b*) the program is also conducted using the same medium on a scale that is similar to or greater than the scale on which it is conducted with the request for contributions (other lectures in the series are conducted on a scale similar to the scale of the lecture in this example without requesting contributions).

75. The audience criterion is met. The rebuttable presumption that the audience criterion is not met because the audience includes prior donors is overcome in this example because the audience (those who have shown prior interest in the lecture series, prior donors, a broad segment of the population in NFP M's area, and those attending the lecture) is also selected for its reasonable potential for use of the program component (attending the lecture). Although the audience may make significant contributions, that was an insignificant factor in its selection.

76. The content criterion is met because the activity calls for specific action by the recipient (attending the lecture) that will help accomplish the NFP's mission (educating the public [students] in various academic pursuits), and the need for and benefits of the action are clearly evident (attending the lecture is a positive educational experience).

Example 14: University Lecture Series With Contribution Inherent in the Admission

Facts

77. Not-for-profit entity (NFP) N is a university whose mission is to educate the public (students) in various academic pursuits. NFP N's political science department holds a special lecture series in which prominent world leaders speak about current events. Admission is priced at $250, which is above the $50 fair value of the lecture and, therefore, $200 of the admission price is a contribution. Therefore, the audience's likelihood to contribute to the NFP is a significant factor in its selection. NFP N advertises the lectures by sending invitations to prior attendees and to prior donors who have contributed significant amounts, and by placing advertisements in local newspapers read by the general public. NFP N presents similar lectures that are priced at the fair value of those lectures.

Conclusion

78. The purpose and criterion are met. The audience criterion is not met. All costs, including those that might otherwise be considered program or management and general costs if they had been incurred in a different activity, except for the costs of the direct donor benefit (the lecture), should be charged to fundraising. Note that the purchase of the tickets is an exchange transaction and, therefore, is not a contribution. As discussed in FASB ASC 958-720-45-29 (paragraph 13.55), costs of goods or services provided in exchange transactions that are part of joint activities, such as costs of direct donor benefits of a special event, should not be reported as fundraising.) FASB ASC 958-225-45-17 (paragraph 13.29) provides guidance concerning reporting special events.

79. The activity calls for specific action by the recipient (attending the lecture) that will help accomplish the NFP's mission. Therefore, the guidance in FASB ASC 958-720-45-38 (paragraph 13.64) should be considered. The purpose criterion is met because (*a*) the program component of the activity calls for specific action by the recipient that will help accomplish the NFP's mission (educating the public [students] in various academic pursuits), and (*b*) the program is also conducted using the same medium on a scale that is similar to or greater than the scale on which it is conducted with the request for contributions (other lectures in the series are conducted on a scale similar to the scale of the lecture in this example without including a contribution in the admission price.)

80. The audience criterion is not met. The rebuttable presumption that the audience criterion is not met because the audience is selected based on its likelihood to contribute to the NFP is not overcome in this example. The fact that the $250 admission price includes a $200 contribution leads to the conclusion that the audience's ability or likelihood to contribute is an overwhelmingly significant factor in its selection, whereas there is no evidence that the extent to which the audience is selected for its need to use or reasonable potential for use of the action called for by the program component (attending the lecture) is overwhelmingly significant.

81. The content criterion is met because the activity calls for specific action by the recipient (attending the lecture) that will help accomplish the NFP's mission (educating the public [students] in various academic pursuits), and the need for and benefits of the action are clearly evident (attending the lecture is a positive educational experience).

Example 15: Free Health Screenings

Facts

82. Not-for-profit Entity (NFP) O's mission is to reduce the incidence of illness from ABC disease, which primarily afflicts people over 65 years of age. One of NFP O's objectives in fulfilling that mission is to have all persons over 65 screened for ABC disease.

83. NFP O rents space at events attended primarily by people over 65 years of age and conducts free screening for ABC disease. NFP O's employees, who are educated about ABC disease and screening procedures and do not otherwise perform fundraising functions, educate interested parties about the effects of ABC disease and the ease and benefits of screening for it. NFP O also solicits contributions at the events. The effectiveness of the activity is evaluated primarily based on how many screening tests are performed, and only minimally based on contributions raised. The employees are not compensated or evaluated based on contributions raised.

Conclusion

84. The purpose, audience, and content criteria are met, and the joint costs should be allocated.

85. The activity calls for specific action by the recipient (being screened for ABC disease) that will help accomplish the NFP's mission. Therefore, the guidance in FASB ASC 958-720-45-38 (paragraph 13.64 should be considered. Neither of the factors in paragraphs 40–44 of FASB ASC 958-720-45 (the compensation or fees test in paragraphs 13.65–.68) or paragraphs 45–46 of FASB ASC 958-720-45 (the separate and similar activities test in paragraphs 13.69–.70) is determinative of whether the purpose criterion is met. Therefore, other evidence, such as the indicators in paragraphs 6–9 of FASB ASC 958-720-55 (paragraph 13.72), should be considered. The purpose criterion is met based on the other evidence, because (*a*) a process exists to evaluate measured program results and accomplishments and in evaluating the effectiveness of the joint activity, the NFP places significantly greater weight on the activity's effectiveness in accomplishing program goals than on the activity's effectiveness in raising contributions (NFP O evaluates the effectiveness of the activity based on the number of screening tests conducted as well as contributions received and places more weight on the number of tests conducted than on the contributions received); (*b*) the qualifications and duties of the personnel performing the activity indicate that it is a program activity (the employees are educated about ABC disease and the testing procedures and do not otherwise perform fundraising functions); (*c*) the method of compensation for performing the activity does not indicate that it is a fundraising activity (the employees are not compensated or evaluated based on contributions raised); and (*d*) performing such programs helps accomplish NFP O's mission (to prevent ABC disease).

86. The audience criterion is met because the audience (people over 65 years of age) is selected based on its need to use or reasonable potential for use of the action called for by the program component.

87. The content criterion is met because the activity calls for specific action by the recipient (being screened for ABC disease) that will help accomplish the NFP's mission (to reduce the incidence of ABC disease), and it explains the need for and benefits of the action (to prevent ABC disease).

Example 16: Public Television Membership Drive

Facts

88. Not-for-profit entity (NFP) P's mission is to provide cultural and educational television programming to residents in its area. NFP P owns a public television station and holds a membership drive in which it solicits new members. The drive is conducted by station employees and consists of solicitations that are shown during long breaks between the station's regularly scheduled programs. NFP P's internal management memoranda state that these drives are designed to raise contributions. NFP P evaluates the effectiveness of the activity based on the amount of contributions received. NFP P shows the programs on a similar scale, without the request for contributions. The audience is members of the general public who watch the programs shown during the drive. Station member benefits are given to those who contribute and consist of tokens of appreciation with a nominal value.

Conclusion

89. The purpose, audience, and content criteria are met, and the joint costs should be allocated. (Note that there would be few, if any, joint costs. Costs associated with the fundraising activities, such as costs of airtime, would be separately identifiable from costs of the program activities, such as licensing costs for a particular television program. Also, note that because no significant benefits or duties are associated with membership, member dues are contributions. Therefore, the substance of the membership-development activities is, in fact, fundraising.)

90. The activity calls for specific action by the recipient (watching the television program) that will help accomplish the NFP's mission. Therefore, the guidance in FASB ASC 958-720-45-38 (paragraph 13.64) should be considered. The purpose criterion is met because (*a*) the program component of the activity calls for specific action by the recipient that will help accomplish the NFP's mission, and (*b*) the program is also conducted using the same medium on a scale that is similar to or greater than the scale on which it is conducted with the request for contributions (NFP P shows the television programs on a similar scale, without the request for contributions).

91. The audience criterion is met. The rebuttable presumption that the audience criterion is not met because the audience is selected based on its likelihood to contribute is overcome in this example because the audience (members of the general public who watch the television programs shown during the drive) is also selected for its reasonable potential for use of the program component (watching the television programs). Although the audience may make contributions, that was an insignificant factor in its selection.

92. The content criterion is met because the activity calls for specific action by the recipient (watching the television programs) that will help accomplish the NFP's mission (providing cultural and educational television programming to residents in its area), and the need for and benefits of the action are clearly evident (watching the programs is a positive cultural and educational experience).

13.100

Appendix C—Allocation Methods

1. Paragraphs 26–31 of Financial Accounting Standards Board (FASB) *Accounting Standards Codification* (ASC) 958-720-55 provide the following information about commonly used cost allocation methods.

Physical Units Method

2. Joint costs are allocated to materials and activities in proportion to the number of units of output that can be attributed to each of the materials and activities. Examples of units of output are lines, square inches, and physical content measures. This method assumes that the benefits received by the fundraising, program, or management and general component of the materials or activity from the joint costs incurred are directly proportional to the lines, square inches, or other physical output measures attributed to each component of the activity. This method may result in an unreasonable allocation of joint costs if the units of output, for example, line counts, do not reflect the degree to which costs are incurred for the joint activity. Use of the physical units method may also result in an unreasonable allocation if the physical units cannot be clearly ascribed to fundraising, program, or management and general. For example, direct mail and telephone solicitations sometimes include content that is not identifiable with fundraising, program, or management and general; or the physical units of such content are inseparable.

Illustration

3. For example, assume a direct mail campaign is used to conduct programs of the not-for-profit entity (NFP) and to solicit contributions to support the organization and its programs. Further, assume that the appeal meets the criteria for allocation of joint costs to more than one function.

4. The letter and reply card include a total of 100 lines; 45 lines pertain to program because they include a call for action by the recipient that will help accomplish the NFP's mission, and 55 lines pertain to the fundraising appeal. Accordingly, 45 percent of the costs are allocated to program and 55 percent to fundraising.

Relative Direct Cost Method

5. Joint costs are allocated to each of the components on the basis of their respective direct costs. Direct costs are those costs that are incurred in connection with the multipurpose materials or activity and that are specifically identifiable with a function (program, fundraising, or management and general). This method may result in an unreasonable allocation of joint costs if the joint costs of the materials and activity are not incurred in approximately the same proportion and for the same reasons as the direct costs of the materials and activity. For example, if a relatively costly booklet informing the reader about the NFP's mission (including a call for action by the recipient that will help accomplish the NFP's mission) is included with a relatively inexpensive fundraising letter, the allocation of joint costs based on the cost of these pieces may be unreasonable, particularly if the booklet and letter weigh approximately the same and therefore contribute equally to the postage costs.

Illustration

6. For example, the costs of a direct mail campaign that can be specifically identified with program services are the costs of separate program materials and a postcard which calls for specific action by the recipient that will help accomplish the NFP's mission. They total $20,000. The direct costs of the fundraising component of the direct mail campaign consist of the costs to develop and produce the fundraising letter. They total $80,000. Joint costs associated with the direct mail campaign total $40,000 and would be allocated as follows under the relative direct cost method.

Program	$20,000/$100,000 × $40,000 = $8,000
Fundraising	$80,000/$100,000 × $40,000 = $32,000

Stand-Alone Joint-Cost-Allocation Method

7. Joint costs are allocated to each component of the activity based on a ratio that uses estimates of costs of items included in joint costs that would have been incurred had the components been conducted independently. The numerator of the ratio is the cost (of items included in joint costs) of conducting a single component independently; the denominator is the cost (of items included in joint costs) of conducting all components independently. This method assumes that efforts for each component in the stand-alone situation are proportionate to the efforts actually undertaken in the joint cost situation. This method may result in an unreasonable allocation because it ignores the effect of each function, which is performed jointly with other functions, on other such functions. For example, the programmatic impact of a direct mail campaign or a telemarketing phone message may be significantly lessened when performed in conjunction with a fundraising appeal.

Illustration

8. For example, assume that the joint costs associated with a direct mail campaign including both program and fundraising components are the costs of stationery, postage, and envelopes at a total of $100,000. The costs of stationery, postage, and envelopes to produce and distribute each component separately would have been $90,000 for the program component and $70,000 for the fundraising component. Under the stand-alone joint cost allocation method, the $100,000 in joint costs would be allocated as follows.

Program	$90,000/$160,000 × $100,000 = $56,250
Fundraising	$70,000/$160,000 × $100,000 = $43,750

13.101

Appendix D—Examples of Disclosures

1. Example 20 (paragraphs 167–170) of Financial Accounting Standards Board (FASB) *Accounting Standards Codification* (ASC) 958-720-55 illustrate the disclosures discussed in FASB ASC 958-720-50-2 (paragraphs 13.89–.90). Case A shows the required and encouraged information in narrative format. Case B reports that information in tabular format, as well as information concerning joint costs incurred for each kind of activity by functional classification, which is neither required nor encouraged, but which is not prohibited.

Case A: Narrative Format

Note X. Allocation of Joint Costs

In 20XX, Not-for-profit entity T conducted activities that included requests for contributions, as well as program and management and general components. Those activities included direct mail campaigns, special events, and a telethon. The costs of conducting those activities included a total of $310,000 of joint costs, which are not specifically attributable to particular components of the activities (joint costs). [Joint costs for each kind of activity were $50,000, $150,000, and $110,000 respectively.] These joint costs were allocated as follows.

Fundraising	$180,000
Program A	80,000
Program B	40,000
Management and general	10,000
Total	$310,000

Note that the bracketed sentence is a disclosure that is encouraged but not required.

Case B: Tabular Format

Note X. Allocation of Joint Costs

In 20XX, Not-for-profit entity T conducted activities that included appeals for contributions and incurred joint costs of $310,000. These activities included direct mail campaigns, special events, and a telethon. Joint costs were allocated as follows.

	Direct Mail	*Special Events*	*Telethon*	*Total*
Fundraising	$40,000	$50,000	$90,000	$180,000
Program A	10,000	65,000	5,000	80,000
Program B		25,000	15,000	40,000
Management and general		10,000		10,000
Total	$50,000	$150,000	$110,000	$310,000

Note that shading is used to highlight information that is not required, encouraged, or prohibited. However, NFPs may prefer to disclose it. Disclosing the total joint costs for each kind of activity ($50,000, $150,000, and $110,000) is encouraged but not required.

Chapter 14

Reports of Independent Auditors

Reports on Financial Statements

14.01 The guidance in AU section 508, *Reports on Audited Financial Statements* (AICPA, *Professional Standards*), applies to auditors' reports on the financial statements of not-for-profit entities (NFPs).[1] The facts and circumstances of each particular audit will govern the appropriate form of report. This chapter discusses the application of AU section 508 to report on the financial statements of NFPs in specific circumstances.

14.02 As noted in footnote 1 to chapter 2, "General Auditing Considerations," of this guide, NFPs are not issuers subject to oversight by the Public Company Accounting Oversight Board (PCAOB), and auditors are not required to follow auditing standards issued by the PCAOB in an audit of an NFP. Optional language may be added to the auditor's report on the financial statements to clarify that an audit conducted in accordance with generally accepted auditing standards (GAAS) does not require the same level of testing and reporting on internal control over financial reporting as an audit of an issuer when Section 404(b) of the Sarbanes Oxley Act of 2002 is applicable. See Interpretation No. 17, "Clarification in the Audit Report of the Extent of Testing of Internal Control Over Financial Reporting in Accordance With Generally Accepted Auditing Standards," of AU section 508 (AICPA, *Professional Standards*, AU sec. 9508 par. .85–.88), and footnote 10 of this chapter. Further, an auditor may be engaged to also follow PCAOB auditing standards in the audit of an NFP. See Interpretation No. 18, "Reference to PCAOB Standards in an Audit Report on a Nonissuer," of AU section 508 (AICPA, *Professional Standards*, AU sec. 9508 par. .89–.92).[2]

---

[1] Paragraph .30 of AU section 508, *Reports on Audited Financial Statements* (AICPA, *Professional Standards*), eliminates the requirement that the auditor add an uncertainties paragraph to the auditor's report if certain criteria are met. Paragraph .08 of AU section 508 requires that auditors identify in the auditor's report the country of origin of the auditing standards and accounting principles used. Paragraph .01 of AU section 530, *Dating of the Independent Auditor's Report* (AICPA, *Professional Standards*), requires that the auditor's report should not be dated earlier than the date on which the auditor has obtained sufficient appropriate audit evidence to support the opinion. Among other things, sufficient appropriate audit evidence includes evidence that the audit documentation has been reviewed and that the entity's financial statements, including disclosures, have been prepared and that management has asserted that they have taken responsibility for them. Technical Questions and Answers (TIS) section 9100.06, "The Effect of Obtaining the Management Representation Letter on Dating the Auditor's Report" (AICPA, *Technical Practice Aids*) (nonauthoritative), states that management will need to have reviewed the final representation letter and, at a minimum, have orally confirmed that they will sign the representation letter, without exception, on or before the date of the representations. The auditor will need to have the signed management representation letter in hand prior to releasing the auditor's report.

[2] Refer to paragraphs 85–98 of Public Company Accounting Oversight Board (PCAOB) Auditing Standard No. 5, *An Audit of Internal Control Over Financial Reporting That Is Integrated With an Audit of Financial Statements* (AICPA, *PCAOB Standards and Related Rules*, Auditing Standards), for the audit reports that should be used if the auditor is engaged to audit both a not-for-profit entity's (NFP's) (that is, a nonissuer's) financial statements and management's assessment of the effectiveness of internal control over financial reporting in accordance with PCAOB Auditing Standards.

14.03 If an auditor is engaged to report on the financial statements of a U.S. entity for use outside of the United States in conformity with accounting principles generally accepted in another country or in accordance with the International Standards on Auditing, the auditor should be aware of and consider the following additional interpretative publications:

- Interpretation No. 14, "Reporting on Audits Conducted in Accordance With Auditing Standards Generally Accepted in the United States of America and in Accordance With International Standards on Auditing," of AU section 508 (AICPA, *Professional Standards*, AU sec. 9508 par. .56–.59)
- Interpretation No. 19, "Financial Statements Prepared in Conformity With International Financial Reporting Standards as Issued by the International Accounting Standards Board," of AU section 508 (AICPA, *Professional Standards*, AU sec. 9508 par. .93–.97)
- AU section 534, *Reporting on Financial Statements Prepared for Use in Other Countries* (AICPA, *Professional Standards*), and related interpretations[*]

14.04 The auditor's standard report described in AU section 508 refers to *results of operations*, which is usually understood to refer to an enterprise's net income for a period together with other changes in net worth. As described in chapter 3, "Basic Financial Statements and General Financial Reporting Matters," of this Audit and Accounting Guide, an NFP's statement of activities reports the changes in net assets[3] for the period but does not purport to present the results of operations, as would an income statement of a for-profit entity.[4] Accordingly, the opinion paragraph of the auditor's report should refer to changes in net assets because that is more descriptive of the information in the statement of activities than results of operations.

Reports on Comparative Financial Statements[†]

14.05 As noted in chapter 3 of this guide, NFPs sometimes present comparative information for a prior year or years only in total rather than by net asset

---

[*] On November 9, 2010, the Auditing Standards Board (ASB), issued a proposed Statement on Auditing Standards (SAS), *Financial Statements Prepared in Accordance with a Financial Reporting Framework Generally Accepted in Another Country*, which would supersede AU section 534, *Reporting on Financial Statements Prepared for Use in Other Countries* (AICPA, *Professional Standards*). The proposed SAS would require an emphasis-of-matter paragraph that would highlight the financial reporting framework in any report also intended for use in the United States. It would also eliminate the concept of limited use of the report. Upon the finalization of all remaining SASs to be issued as part of the Clarity Project (that is, "clarified" SASs), one SAS will be issued containing all finalized but unissued clarified SASs in codified format. See the preface of this guide for further information on ASB's Clarity Project. This SAS is effective for audits of financial statements for periods ending on or after December 15, 2012.

[3] As discussed in paragraph 3.08, descriptive terms such as *change in equity* may be used.

[4] As discussed in chapter 3, "Basic Financial Statements and General Financial Reporting Matters," of this guide, an NFP may present an intermediate measure of operations within the statement of activities. As noted in chapter 3, however, if an intermediate measure of operations is reported, it must be in a financial statement that, at a minimum, reports the change in unrestricted net assets for the period. Such a statement would, therefore, ordinarily present more than merely the results of operations.

[†] On February 19, 2010, the ASB issued a proposed SAS, *Consistency of Financial Statements*, which would supersede AU section 420, *Consistency of Application of Generally Accepted Accounting Principles* (AICPA, *Professional Standards*). The proposed SAS would address the auditor's evaluation

(continued)

class. Paragraph .65 of AU section 508 provides requirements and guidance for reporting on comparative financial statements and states the following:

> The fourth standard of reporting requires that the auditor either express an opinion regarding the financial statements *taken as a whole* or an assertion to the effect that an opinion cannot be expressed in the auditor's report. Reference in the fourth reporting standard to the financial statements *taken as a whole* applies not only to the financial statements of the current period but also to those of one or more prior periods that are presented on a comparative basis with those of the current period. Therefore, a continuing auditor should update the report on the individual financial statements of the one or more prior periods presented on a comparative basis with those of the current period.

Footnote 24 to paragraph .65 of AU section 508 states the following:

> A continuing auditor need not report on the prior-period financial statements if only summarized comparative information of the prior period(s) is presented. For example, entities such as state and local governmental units may present prior-year financial information in their government-wide financial statements only for the total reporting entity rather than disaggregated by governmental activities, business-type activities, total primary government, and discretely presented component units. Also, not-for-profit organizations frequently present certain information for the prior period(s) in total rather than by net asset class. In some circumstances, the client may request the auditor to express an opinion on the prior period(s) as well as the current period. In those circumstances, the auditor should consider whether the information included for the prior period(s) contains sufficient detail to constitute a fair presentation in conformity with generally accepted accounting principles. In most cases, this will necessitate including additional columns or separate detail by reporting unit or net asset class, or the auditor would need to modify his or her report.

14.06 Though the financial reporting model for NFPs does not require fund reporting, Financial Accounting Standards Board (FASB) *Accounting Standards Codification* (ASC) 958, *Not-for-Profit Entities*, requires, however, that certain basic information, such as reporting total net assets and changes in net assets by net asset class, be provided. If the prior year(s) financial statements include the minimum information required by those standards for a complete set of financial statements (statement of financial position, statement of activities, statements of cash flows, and accompanying notes), the financial statements are not summarized information. Accordingly, a continuing auditor should report on them. Alternatively, if the prior year(s) financial statements are summarized and therefore do not include the minimum information required for a complete set of financial statements, a continuing auditor's report should not mention the

---

(footnote continued)

of the consistency of the financial statements between periods, including changes to previously issued financial statements and the effect of that evaluation on the auditor's report on the financial statements. Upon the finalization of all remaining SASs to be issued as part of the Clarity Project (that is, "clarified" SASs), one SAS will be issued containing all finalized but unissued clarified SASs in codified format. See the preface of this guide for further information on the ASB's Clarity Project. This SAS is effective for audits of financial statements for periods ending on or after December 15, 2012.

summarized information in the description of the financial statements audited or in the opinion paragraph. However, a continuing auditor should make clear the degree of responsibility that he or she is assuming in relation to the prior year(s) summarized information.[5] The introductory paragraph of the auditor's report should state (*a*) that the summarized information has been derived from a complete set of financial statements, (*b*) the date of the auditor's report on the complete financial statements,[6] and (*c*) the type of opinion expressed.[7,8] An example of an introductory paragraph with such a statement is as follows:

> We have audited the accompanying statement of financial position of XYZ Not-for-Profit Organization as of September 30, 20CY, and the related statements of activities and cash flows for the year then ended. These financial statements are the responsibility of XYZ Not-for-Profit Organization's management. Our responsibility is to express an opinion on these financial statements based on our audit. The prior year summarized comparative information has been derived from the Organization's 20PY financial statements and, in our report dated December 15, 20PY, we expressed an unqualified opinion on those financial statements.

14.07 As noted in paragraph 3.30, if the comparative financial information is summarized and does not include the minimum information required by FASB ASC 958—for example, if the statement of activities does not present revenues, expenses, gains, and losses by net asset class—certain disclosures about the nature of the information presented are required. If the disclosures required by paragraph 3.30 are omitted or are incomplete, the auditor should add a paragraph to his or her report calling the omitted or incomplete disclosure to the readers' attention. Such a paragraph might include the same wording that appears in the illustrative note presented as an example in paragraph 3.31 of this guide. To reduce the likelihood that a reader might misinterpret such a paragraph to be a qualified opinion on the current period financial statements, the paragraph should follow the opinion paragraph and should not be referred to in either the scope or opinion paragraphs of the auditor's report.

---

[5] AU section 508 discusses, in part, engagements in which the auditor is asked to report on an individual financial statement, such as a balance sheet, and not other individual financial statements, such as the statements of changes in net assets and cash flows (paragraph .33 of AU section 508), reports on comparative financial statements (paragraph .67 of AU section 508), and financial statements taken as a whole (paragraphs .05 and .65 of AU section 508). The guidance in AU section 508 ordinarily would not apply to circumstances in which the prior year(s) financial statements are summarized and, therefore, one or more of the individual financial statements do not include the minimum information necessary for a full generally accepted accounting principles (GAAP) presentation.

[6] Reference to the date of the original report removes any implication that records, transactions, or events after that date have been examined. The auditor does not have a responsibility to investigate or inquire further into events that may have occurred during the period between the date of the report on the complete financial statements and the date of the report on the summarized information.

[7] If the auditor's opinion on the complete financial statements was other than unqualified, the report should describe the nature of, and the reasons for, the qualification. The auditor should also consider the effect that any modification of the report on the complete financial statements might have on the report on the summarized information. For example, if the auditor's report on the complete financial statements referred to another auditor or included an explanatory paragraph because of a material uncertainty, a going concern matter, or an inconsistency in the application of accounting principles, the report on the summarized information should state that fact. However, no reference to the inconsistency is necessary if a change in accounting referred to in the auditor's report on the complete financial statements does not affect the comparability of the information being presented.

[8] If the prior year(s) summarized information has been derived from financial statements that were audited by another independent auditor, the report should state that fact, and the auditor should not express an opinion on that information.

Unqualified Opinions

14.08 The auditor's standard report contains an opinion that the financial statements are presented fairly, in all material respects, in conformity with generally accepted accounting principles (GAAP). That conclusion may be expressed only when the auditor has formed such an opinion on the basis of an audit performed in accordance with GAAS. An example of the auditor's standard report on financial statements covering a single year is as follows:

Independent Auditor's Report

We have audited the accompanying statement of financial position of XYZ Not-for-Profit Organization as of September 30, 20XX, and the related statements of activities and cash flows for the year then ended.[9] These financial statements are the responsibility of XYZ Not-for-Profit Organization's management. Our responsibility is to express an opinion on these financial statements based on our audit.

We conducted our audit in accordance with auditing standards generally accepted in the United States of America. Those standards require that we plan and perform the audit to obtain reasonable assurance about whether the financial statements are free of material misstatement. [*Optional: An audit includes consideration of internal control over financial reporting as a basis for designing audit procedures that are appropriate in the circumstances, but not for the purpose of expressing an opinion on the effectiveness of the Organization's internal control over financial reporting. Accordingly, we express no such opinion.*][10] An audit includes examining, on a test basis, evidence supporting the amounts and disclosures in the financial statements. An audit also includes assessing the accounting principles used and significant estimates made by management, as well as evaluating the overall financial statement presentation. We believe that our audit provides a reasonable basis for our opinion.

In our opinion, the financial statements referred to above present fairly, in all material respects, the financial position of XYZ Not-for-Profit Organization as of September 30, 20XX, and the changes in its

---

[9] Each of the statements presented, which may include a statement of functional expenses, should be identified in the introductory paragraph.

[10] This optional wording may be added to reports on the financial statement audits of NFPs in accordance with Interpretation No. 17, "Clarification in the Audit Report of the Extent of Testing of Internal Control Over Financial Reporting in Accordance With Generally Accepted Auditing Standards," of AU section 508 (AICPA, *Professional Standards*, AU sec. 9508 par. .85–.88), which provides reporting guidance for audits of nonissuers. (This wording may be added even in a report on the financial statements in an audit conducted in accordance with *Government Auditing Standards* or U.S. Office of Management and Budget Circular A-133, *Audits of States, Local Governments, and Non-Profit Organizations*, in which the auditor reports on internal control over financial reporting but does not express an opinion on that internal control. See the AICPA Audit Guide Government Auditing Standards *and Circular A-133 Audits*.) Interpretation No. 17 addresses how auditors may expand this report to explain that their consideration of internal control was sufficient to provide the auditor sufficient understanding to plan the audit and determine the nature, timing and extent of tests to be performed, but was not sufficient to express an opinion on the effectiveness of the internal control. If this optional wording is added, the remainder of the paragraph should read as follows:

> An audit also includes examining, on a test basis, evidence supporting the amounts and disclosures in the financial statements, assessing the accounting principles used and significant estimates made by management, as well as evaluating the overall financial statement presentation. We believe that our audit provides a reasonable basis for our opinion.

net assets and its cash flows for the year then ended in conformity with accounting principles generally accepted in the United States of America.

[*Signature*]

[*Date*][11]

Modified Reports and Departures From Unqualified Opinions

14.09 AU section 508 indicates the circumstances in which an explanatory paragraph is required to be added following the standard opinion paragraph.[12] The statement also provides examples of auditors' reports in these circumstances. In addition, AU section 508 indicates circumstances in which departures from GAAP and limitations on the scope of the audit would require a qualified opinion, an adverse opinion, and a disclaimer of opinion, and provides examples of auditors' reports in those circumstances. Examples of possible departures from GAAP that an auditor of an NFP's financial statements might encounter include the NFP's failure to (*a*) recognize or appropriately measure promises to give, contributed services, or depreciation on plant and equipment in conformity with GAAP, and (*b*) provide information about expenses reported by their functional classification. The auditor's inability to obtain sufficient competent evidential matter to audit (*a*) contributed services that the NFP has recorded or (*b*) receivables and revenues from fund-raising activities is an example of possible restrictions on the scope of the audit that an auditor of an NFP's financial statements might encounter.

Going Concern[‡]

14.10 AU section 341, *The Auditor's Consideration of an Entity's Ability to Continue as a Going Concern* (AICPA, *Professional Standards*), provides guidance to the auditor in evaluating whether there is substantial doubt about the entity's ability to continue as a going concern for a reasonable period of time, not to exceed one year beyond the date of the financial statements being audited. AU section 341 also provides guidance on reporting in that situation, including an example of an explanatory paragraph (following the opinion paragraph) in the

---

[11] AU section 530 requires that the auditor's report be dated no earlier than the date on which the auditor has obtained sufficient appropriate audit evidence to support the opinion on the financial statements. See www.aicpa.org/InterestAreas/AccountingAndAuditing/Resources/AudAttest/AudAttestGuidance/DownloadableDocuments/PracticeAlerts/pa_2007_1.pdf for a practice alert regarding application of this standard.

[12] Interpretation No. 12, "The Effect on the Auditor's Report of an Entity's Adoption of a New Accounting Standard That Does Not Require the Entity to Disclose the Effect of the Change in the Year of Adoption," of AU section 420 (AICPA, *Professional Standards*, AU sec. 9420 par. .69–.72), discusses whether to add an explanatory paragraph if an accounting standard does not require the NFP to disclose the effect of the change in accounting principle in the year of adoption. See also footnote †.

[‡] On October 10, 2008, the Financial Accounting Standards Board issued an exposure draft of a proposed statement, *Going Concern*, which would carry forward into the accounting standards the going concern guidance from AU section 341, *The Auditor's Consideration of an Entity's Ability to Continue as a Going Concern* (AICPA, *Professional Standards*), subject to several modifications to align the guidance with International Financial Reporting Standards. In June 2009, the project was broadened to address three additional areas: enhancing the disclosures of short-term and long-term risks, specifically risks for which there is more-than-remote likelihood of occurrence; defining substantial doubt in terms of an entity's ability to continue as a going concern; and defining when it is appropriate for an entity to apply the liquidation basis of accounting. Readers should be alert to the issuance of the final Accounting Standards Update.

auditor's report describing an uncertainty about the entity's ability to continue as a going concern. Paragraph 2.48 of this guide contains examples of conditions or events that are particularly applicable to NFPs and that might indicate that there could be substantial doubt about the NFP's continued existence.

Reporting on Supplementary Information

14.11 FASB ASC 958-720-45-4 states that information about an NFP's major programs (or segments) can be enhanced by reporting the interrelationships of program expenses and program revenues. Related nonmonetary information about program inputs, outputs, and results also is helpful. Generally, reporting that kind of information is feasible only in supplementary information or management explanations or by other methods of financial reporting.

14.12 Although nonmonetary information about an NFP's activities and programs may be informative and helpful to users of the financial statements, this information is not necessary for fair presentation of financial position, changes in net assets, or cash flows on which the auditor is reporting. In addition, this information may not be auditable if it is obtained from records outside the accounting system that are not subject to controls, rather than being obtained (or derived by analysis or computation) from records subject to controls. AU section 550A, *Other Information in Documents Containing Audited Financial Statements* (AICPA, *Professional Standards*), provides guidance to the auditor with regard to other information that may be included in audited financial statements. Paragraph .07 of AU section 550A refers to paragraph .13 of AU section 551A, *Reporting on Information Accompanying the Basic Financial Statements in Auditor-Submitted Documents* (AICPA, *Professional Standards*), which states that when the auditor disclaims an opinion on all or part of the accompanying information in a document that he submits to his client or to others, such information should either be marked as unaudited or should include a reference to the auditor's disclaimer of opinion. The wording of the disclaimer will vary according to the circumstances. Two examples follow:[||]

Disclaimer on All of the Information

> Our audit was conducted for the purpose of forming an opinion on the basic financial statements taken as a whole. The (identify the accompanying information) is presented for purposes of additional analysis and is not a required part of the basic financial statements. Such information has not been subjected to the auditing procedures applied

---

[||] In February 2010, the ASB issued three SASs: SAS No. 118, *Other Information in Documents Containing Audited Financial Statements* (AICPA, *Professional Standards*, AU sec. 550), SAS No. 119, *Supplementary Information in Relation to the Financial Statements as a Whole* (AICPA, *Professional Standards*, AU sec. 551), and SAS No. 120, *Required Supplementary Information* (AICPA, *Professional Standards*, AU sec. 558). SAS No. 118 addresses the auditor's responsibility in relation to other information in documents containing audited financial statements and the auditor's report thereon. SAS No. 119 addresses the auditor's responsibility when engaged to report on whether supplementary information is fairly stated, in all material respects, in relation to the financial statements as a whole. SAS No. 120 addresses the auditor's responsibility with respect to information that a designated accounting standard setter requires to accompany an entity's basic financial statements (referred to as required supplementary information). Together, the three SASs supersede AU section 550A, *Other Information in Documents Containing Audited Financial Statements*, AU section 551A, *Reporting on Information Accompanying the Basic Financial Statements in Auditor-Submitted Documents*, and AU section 558A, *Required Supplementary Information* (AICPA, *Professional Standards*). The SASs are effective for audits of financial statements for periods beginning on or after December 15, 2010. Early application is permitted.

in the audit of the basic financial statements, and, accordingly, we express no opinion on it.

Disclaimer on Part of the Information

Our audit was conducted for the purpose of forming an opinion on the basic financial statements taken as a whole. The information on pages XX–YY is presented for purposes of additional analysis and is not a required part of the basic financial statements. Such information, except for that portion marked "unaudited," on which we express no opinion, has been subjected to the auditing procedures applied in the audit of the basic financial statements, and, in our opinion, the information is fairly stated in all material respects in relation to the basic financial statements taken as a whole.

Bases of Accounting Other Than GAAP[13]

14.13 Some NFPs may find that financial statements prepared on the cash basis or the modified cash basis of accounting are adequate for their governing boards and other users. AU section 623, *Special Reports* (AICPA, *Professional Standards*), describes the auditor's reporting requirements when the financial statements are prepared on a comprehensive basis of accounting other than GAAP (other comprehensive basis of accounting [OCBOA]), including the cash receipts and disbursements basis of accounting and modifications of the cash basis having substantial support.[14]

14.14 AU section 623 also permits an auditor to issue a special report on financial statements that have been prepared in conformity with the requirements or financial reporting provisions of a governmental regulatory agency but that do not conform with GAAP or constitute OCBOA. In that instance, the auditor's report should include a separate paragraph at the end of the report stating that the report is intended solely for the information and use of those within the entity and the regulatory agency with which the report is being filed, and is not intended to be and should not be used by anyone other than these specified parties. Such a restrictive paragraph is appropriate, even though by law or regulation the auditor's report may be made a matter of public record. The auditor may use this form of report, however, only if the financial statements and report are intended solely for filing with the regulatory agency to whose jurisdiction the NFP is subject. Paragraph .04 of AU section 544, *Lack of Conformity With Generally Accepted Accounting Principles* (AICPA, *Professional Standards*), states that in circumstances in which the financial statements and reports will be used by parties or distributed by the entity to parties other than the regulatory agencies to whose jurisdiction the entity is subject, the auditor should use the standard form of report modified as appropriate because

---

[13] Interpretation No. 14, "Evaluating the Adequacy of Disclosure and Presentation in Financial Statements Prepared in Conformity With an Other Comprehensive Basis of Accounting (OCBOA)," of AU section 623, *Special Reports* (AICPA, *Professional Standards*, AU sec. 9623 par. .90–.95), provides guidance on evaluating the adequacy of disclosure and presentation in financial statements presented using OCBOA. TIS section 1500, *Financial Statements Prepared Under an Other Comprehensive Basis of Accounting* (AICPA, *Technical Practice Aids*), provides nonauthoritative guidance.

[14] The accrual basis of accounting is required by GAAP for a fair presentation of financial position, changes in net assets, and cash flows. Financial statements presented on the cash receipts and disbursements basis of accounting or using modifications of the cash basis having substantial support may be considered to present financial position, changes in net assets, and cash flows in conformity with GAAP only if they do not differ materially from financial statements prepared on an accrual basis.

of the departures from GAAP and then in an additional paragraph express an opinion on whether the financial statements are presented in conformity with the regulatory basis of accounting.[15]

Reporting on Prescribed Forms

14.15 Some NFPs prepare financial reports using forms prescribed by an affiliated entity. The auditor should review these forms and any accompanying preprinted auditor's report for compliance with GAAP and GAAS. If the financial statements prepared using the prescribed form do not conform with GAAP, either the auditor can attach a separate set of financial statements and report on them, or he or she can issue a report on the prescribed form but include a restriction on its distribution, as discussed previously. If the auditor considers the preprinted auditor's report inappropriate, he or she should prepare a separate report. When a separate report is used, the auditor should consider inserting language such as "See attached independent auditor's report" in the space provided for the auditor's signature on the preprinted form.

14.16 IRS Form 990, Return of Organizations Exempt from Income Tax, may be used in some states as an annual report by NFPs for reporting to both state and federal governments. Many states require an auditor's opinion on the financial statements included in an IRS Form 990. Interpretation No. 10, "Reports on the Financial Statements Included in Internal Revenue Form 990, 'Return of Organizations Exempt from Income Tax,'" of AU section 623 (AICPA, *Professional Standards*, AU sec. 9623 par. .47–.54), provides guidance on reporting on financial statements included in Form 990. (Paragraph .54 of that interpretation may no longer be relevant.)

Reports Required by *Government Auditing Standards*, the Single Audit Act Amendments of 1996, and OMB Circular A-133[#]

14.17 *Government Auditing Standards*, the Single Audit Act Amendments of 1996, and U.S. Office of Management and Budget (OMB) Circular A-133 broaden the auditor's responsibility to include reporting on not only an NFP's financial statements but also its internal control and its compliance with laws and regulations. AICPA Audit Guide Government Auditing Standards *and Circular A-133 Audits*, describes and illustrates the required reports. The report on internal control over financial reporting and on compliance and other matters and the report on compliance with requirements applicable to each major program and on the internal control over compliance required by *Government Auditing Standards* are restricted-use reports under the provisions of AU section 532, *Restricting the Use of an Auditor's Report* (AICPA, *Professional Standards*). Thus, those reports are not intended to be used for other purposes, such

---

[15] Interpretation No. 15, "Auditor Reports on Regulatory Accounting or Presentation When the Regulated Entity Distributes the Financial Statements to Parties Other Than the Regulatory Agency Either Voluntarily or Upon Specific Request," of AU section 623 (AICPA, *Professional Standards*, AU sec. 9623 par. .96–.98), issued in January 2005, provides an example of that report.

[#] In August 2010, the U.S. Government Accountability Office issued an exposure draft of the ninth edition of *Government Auditing Standards*. The proposed changes contained in the exposure draft update generally accepted government auditing standards to reflect major developments in the accountability and audit profession and emphasize specific considerations applicable to the government environment. Readers should be alert for the issuance of final standards.

as inclusion in an offering document for municipal securities filings. In addition, when an NFP's financial statements are included in an offering document as an "obligated person," it is generally advisable to use an auditor's report on the financial statements that does not refer to the *Government Auditing Standards* audit or to those reports.[**]

[**] On December 10, 2010, the ASB issued a proposed SAS, *Alert as to the Intended Use of the Auditor's Written Communication*, which would supersede AU section 532, *Restricting the Use of an Auditor's Report* (AICPA, *Professional Standards*). The proposed SAS has been clarified to indicate that it applies to auditor's reports and other written communications issued in connection with an engagement conducted in accordance with generally accepted auditing standards. It also eliminates the use of the term restricted use and instead addresses the intended use of such communications. Upon the finalization of all remaining SASs to be issued as part of the Clarity Project (that is, "clarified" SASs), one SAS will be issued containing all finalized by unissued clarified SASs in codified format. See the preface of this guide for further information on ASB's Clarity Project. This SAS is effective for audits of financial statements for periods ending on or after December 15, 2012.

Chapter 15
Tax Considerations

Introduction

15.01 This chapter discusses certain tax considerations relevant to not-for-profit entities (NFPs). It does not contain a detailed discussion of the Internal Revenue Code (IRC) and of rulings that have been issued by the IRS that apply to NFPs, nor is it intended as a substitute for appropriate research in resolving tax issues.

15.02 The tax considerations discussed in this chapter often result in an NFP (or its for-profit or not-for-profit subsidiaries) making a determination about whether a transaction or event must be reported in a tax return. The term *tax position* refers to a position in a previously filed tax return or a position expected to be taken in a future tax return that is reflected in measuring current or deferred income tax assets and liabilities for interim or annual periods. The term *tax position* encompasses, but is not limited to, the following:

- A decision to classify a transaction, entity, or other position in a tax return as tax exempt or subject to a lower rate of tax
- A decision not to file a tax return, such as a decision that a Form 990T need not be filed
- The characterization of income, such as a characterization of income as passive, or a decision to exclude reporting taxable income in a tax return
- An allocation or a shift of income between jurisdictions (federal, state, local, or foreign)
- An entity's status, including its status as a tax-exempt not-for-profit entity

The validity of a tax position is a matter of tax law. It is not controversial to recognize the benefit of a tax position in financial statements when the degree of confidence is high that that tax position will be sustained upon examination by a taxing authority. However, in some cases, the law is subject to varied interpretation, and whether a tax position will ultimately be sustained may be uncertain. Financial Accounting Standards Board (FASB) *Accounting Standards Codification* (ASC) 740-10-25-6, which applies to income taxes, limits the recognition of uncertain tax positions to only the financial statement effects of a tax position when it is more likely than not, based on the technical merits, that the position will be sustained upon examination.

15.03 Management generally should identify federal, state, and local laws and regulations that may have a direct and material effect on the determination of financial statement amounts. The auditor should make inquiries of management concerning the client's compliance with laws and regulations. An NFP's failure to maintain its tax-exempt status could have serious tax consequences and affect both its financial statements and related disclosures, and it could possibly require modification of the auditor's report. Failure to comply with tax laws and regulations could be an illegal act that may, as discussed in chapter 2, "General Auditing Considerations," of this Audit and Accounting Guide, have either a direct and material effect on the determination of financial statement amounts (for example, the result of an incorrect accrual for taxes on unrelated business income) or a material indirect effect on the financial statements that would require appropriate disclosures (for example, the result of a potential loss of tax-exempt status).

Basis of Exemption

15.04 The IRS determines whether an NFP qualifies for exemption from federal income tax. The following are some of the more common types of tax-exempt NFPs:

- Corporations, united funds, other funds, and foundations organized and operated (*a*) exclusively for religious, charitable, scientific, testing-for-public-safety, literary, or educational purposes; (*b*) to foster national or international amateur sports competition; or (*c*) for the prevention of cruelty to children or animals
- Civic leagues, NFPs operated exclusively for the promotion of social welfare, and certain local associations of employees
- Labor, agricultural, and horticultural organizations
- Business leagues, chambers of commerce, real estate boards, boards of trade, and professional football leagues that are not organized for profit
- Clubs organized for pleasure, recreation, and other not-for-profit purposes

15.05 Exemptions from state and local sales, real estate, and other taxes vary from state to state. NFPs are generally subject to the laws of the state of incorporation as well as the laws of states in which they conduct significant activities. Each state's laws govern exemption from its taxes and should be consulted for the applicable definitions and requirements.

15.06 Tax exemption is a privilege and not a right. At the federal level, the IRS has the authority to revoke exemptions for any one of several reasons. Furthermore, individual states have regulatory bodies that oversee NFPs and that can revoke their state tax-exempt status without regard to their federal tax-exempt status and even prevent them from operating. There are many potential threats to an NFP's federal tax-exempt status, of which the following are particularly important:

- Material changes in the NFP's character, purpose, or method of operation
- Private inurement
- Private benefit
- Commerciality
- Lobbying
- Political campaign activities
- Unrelated business income
- Failure of the NFP to meet the commensurate test
- Violation of public policy by the NFP

15.07 The IRS requires that NFPs disclose on Form 990 any changes in the kinds of exempt activities the NFP conducts, any changes in its governing documents, and whether there has been a liquidation, dissolution, or substantial contraction. If there has been a material change in the NFP's character, purpose, or method of operation, it may be appropriate to seek IRS guidance in the form of a private letter ruling.

15.08 NFPs are generally prohibited from making distributions to those who control or support them financially. IRS rules regulate transactions between an NFP and insiders. IRC provisions concerning such transactions are stricter for private foundations than for other NFPs. Insiders are individuals with a personal or private interest in the NFP, such as governing board members, officers, certain employees, and substantial contributors. Transactions between insiders and NFPs are permitted, but the NFP has the burden of proving that the transactions do not result in private inurement. The NFP must be able to satisfy the IRS that the transaction was reasonable, was adequately documented, had independent approval, and did not violate any law or regulation. Employee compensation can create an inurement problem if it is judged to be "unreasonably high."

15.09 The concept of private benefit prohibits an NFP from providing excessive benefits for the private interests of any specific individual or group—both insiders and outsiders. Incidental levels of private benefits are permitted, but the NFP is required to demonstrate that such benefits are a necessary concomitant of a public related benefit. The NFP generally should have sound policies for transactions with both insiders and outsiders, and these policies ordinarily should document that the transactions were appropriate and were approved by disinterested parties.

15.10 An NFP cannot qualify for tax exemption, or can have its tax-exempt status revoked, if it is, in reality, a commercial enterprise. Engaging in commercial activity, however, does not *per se* disqualify the NFP from tax-exempt status unless the commercial activity becomes the NFP's primary purpose. A gray area exists between commercial and noncommercial activities. To avoid problems with commerciality, many NFPs have found it advantageous to create separate for-profit subsidiaries.

15.11 The IRC allows public charities (but not private foundations) to lobby to influence federal, state, and local legislation (including initiatives and referenda), but it places limits on how much lobbying they can do. Membership organizations that are granted tax-exempt status under IRC Section 501(c)(4)(5) or (6) and lobby are required to make complex disclosures to their members or pay a proxy tax.

15.12 Public charities are prohibited from engaging in partisan political campaign activities. Prohibited political activities include contributing to candidates or political organizations, including, for example, in-kind contributions of services, publicity, advertising, paid staff time, facilities, and office space. Also prohibited are evaluating candidates and their positions on specific issues and encouraging voter registration for a specific political group. Permitted political activities include nonpartisan get-out-the-vote campaigns.

15.13 NFPs can lose their tax-exempt status if the IRS determines that too large a percentage of their income is from business activities unrelated to their specific exempt purposes. There is, however, no specific percentage of unrelated business income that can be designated as too large a percentage and is, therefore, not permissible. The facts and circumstances of each unrelated business income situation should be considered. Unrelated business income and the unrelated business income tax are discussed in more detail in paragraphs 15.18–.21.

15.14 An NFP can lose its tax-exempt status if it fails the commensurate test, which provides that the scope of the NFP's programs must be commensurate with its financial resources. The test requires that an NFP have a charitable program that is both real and, taking the NFP's circumstances and financial resources into account, substantial. This means that fund-raising expenses and administrative expenses should not be an excessive percentage of total expenses. Although no specific payout percentage has been established and individual facts and circumstances must be considered, low levels of program spending invite IRS scrutiny.

15.15 An NFP can also lose its tax exemption because it violates public policy, for example, through racial discrimination.

Federal and State Filing Requirements

15.16 Most tax-exempt organizations, except churches, must file annual information returns (Form 990 or Form 990-EZ) with the IRS. Those with less than $25,000 in gross receipts submit Form 990-N, also known as the e-Postcard, unless they choose to file a complete Form 990 or Form 990-EZ. Most states also have their own registration and filing requirements, some of which include audited financial statements. As stated in paragraph .05 of AU section 317, *Illegal Acts by Clients* (AICPA, *Professional Standards*), the auditor should consider laws and regulations that have a direct and material effect on the determination of financial statement amounts. An example of this would include the consideration of applicable tax laws that could affect a nonprofit's filing status or tax accruals.

Public Charities and Private Foundations

15.17 The IRS considers all charitable organizations (that is, those that are tax-exempt under IRC Section 501(c)(3)) to be private foundations unless they qualify as public charities (sometimes referred to as *nonprivate foundations*) under one of several IRC tests. Private foundations are subject to more restrictions under the tax law than are public charities. These restrictions include statutory prohibitions against self-dealing, excess business holdings, jeopardy investments, failing to distribute income, and taxable expenditures. In addition, private foundations are subject to an excise tax on their net investment income and are required to make annual distributions of five percent of the average market value of their noncharitable-use assets for charitable, educational, scientific, and similar purposes. (Noncharitable-use assets are assets that are not used or held for use directly in carrying on the NFP's exempt purpose; they include assets held for investment and the production of investment income.) Private foundations are also required to publish annually a notice that their annual reports are available for inspection. Public charities are exempt from federal unemployment taxes. Both public charities and private foundations may be exempt from property and sales taxes in some states.

Unrelated Business Income

15.18 Unrelated business income is gross income from an unrelated trade or business less expenses directly connected with the unrelated trade or business, certain net operating losses, and qualified charitable contributions. An unrelated trade or business of an exempt organization is any trade or business which is regularly carried on, and whose conduct is not substantially related to the exercise or performance of its exempt purpose. The IRS is primarily interested in how the unrelated business income was earned, not in how it is used, even if it is used to further the NFP's tax-exempt purpose. Unrelated business income is subject to federal corporate taxes on income, including the alternative minimum tax. (The first $1,000 of net unrelated business income is excluded from taxation, and corporate net operating losses and various tax credits are allowed.)

15.19 The unrelated-business-income tax requirements apply to all NFPs except (*a*) corporations that have been organized under Acts of Congress and that are instrumentalities of the United States and (*b*) certain charitable trusts not subject to the tax on private foundations.

15.20 Income from certain specified activities that might otherwise be considered unrelated business income is excluded from taxation. For example, unrelated business income does not include dividends, interest, royalties, and gains on the sale of property (unless that property was used in an unrelated trade or business). Unrelated business income also does not include income from activities in which substantially all of the work is done by volunteers, income from the sale of donated merchandise, and rents from real property. However, rents from debt-financed property, rents based on a percentage of net income rather than gross income, and rents on personal property are considered to be unrelated business income.

15.21 FASB ASC 740-10-55-225 provides examples of tax positions to be considered if an NFP enters into transactions that may be subject to income tax on unrelated business income. FASB ASC 740-10-50-15 requires that entities disclose the amounts of income tax-related interest and penalties recognized in the statement of activities, the total amounts of interest and penalties recognized in the statement of financial position, information about positions for which it is reasonably possible that the total amounts of unrecognized tax benefits will significantly increase or decrease within 12 months of the reporting date, and a description of tax years that remain subject to examination by major tax jurisdictions.

Auditing

15.22 As previously discussed, noncompliance with federal and state tax laws and regulations may have direct and material effects on an NFP's financial statements. Noncompliance may also, possibly through the loss of the NFP's tax-exempt status, have indirect effects on the statements. Because many NFPs depend on their tax-exempt status for funding purposes and could lose their funding if that status was revoked, such indirect effects may also indicate that there is substantial doubt about the NFP's ability to continue as a going concern.*

---

* On October 10, 2008, the Financial Accounting Standards Board issued an exposure draft of a proposed statement, *Going Concern*, which would carry forward into the accounting standards the going concern guidance from AU section 341, *The Auditor's Consideration of an Entity's Ability to Continue as a Going Concern* (AICPA, *Professional Standards*), subject to several modifications to align the guidance with International Financial Reporting Standards. In June 2009, the project

(continued)

15.23 Many audit objectives, controls, and auditing procedures for the tax provisions and liabilities of NFPs are similar to those of other entities. In addition, the auditor may need to consider the specific audit objectives, selected controls, and auditing procedures listed in the table in paragraph 15.24 that are unique to NFPs.

15.24 The following table illustrates the use of assertions in developing audit objectives and designing substantive tests. The examples are not intended to be all-inclusive, nor is it expected that all the procedures would necessarily be applied in an audit. The auditor should design and perform substantive procedures for all relevant assertions related to each material class of transactions, account balance, and disclosure to obtain sufficient appropriate audit evidence. The use of assertions in assessing risks and designing appropriate audit procedures to obtain audit evidence is described in paragraphs .14–.26 of AU section 326, *Audit Evidence* (AICPA, *Professional Standards*). Various audit procedures and the purposes for which they may be performed are described in paragraphs .27–.41 of AU section 326.

(footnote continued)

was broadened to address three additional areas: enhancing the disclosures of short-term and long-term risks, specifically risks for which there is more-than-remote likelihood of occurrence; defining substantial doubt in terms of an entity's ability to continue as a going concern; and defining when it is appropriate for an entity to apply the liquidation basis of accounting. Readers should be alert to the issuance of the final Accounting Standards Update.

Auditing Considerations

Financial Statement Assertions	*Specific Audit Objectives*	*Examples of Selected Controls*	*Examples of Auditing Procedures*
Account Balances			
Completeness	All liabilities and contingencies for taxes due and uncertain tax positions for the current and prior years are accrued or disclosed.	Tax returns are prepared and reviewed by knowledgeable personnel.	Inquire if tax returns have been filed on a timely basis.
			Review tax returns or filings and related correspondence for all "open" years.
			Review revenue agent's reports, if any, for evidence of additional liabilities or contingencies.
			Review minutes of governing board and governing board committee meetings and the accounting records for evidence of significant unrelated business income.
			Review the reasonableness of the computation of any unrelated business income tax liability.

(continued)

Auditing Considerations—continued

Financial Statement Assertions	*Specific Audit Objectives*	*Examples of Selected Controls*	*Examples of Auditing Procedures*
Presentation and Disclosure			
Rights and Obligations; Classification and Understandability	The NFP has obtained qualifying tax exemptions from the appropriate government authorities.	Management monitors compliance with applicable tax regulations.	Ascertain whether the NFP has been granted tax-exempt status.
			Review minutes of governing board meetings for changes in the NFP's governing instruments that could affect its tax-exempt status.
			Consider the effect of new, expanded, or unusual activities on the NFP's tax-exempt status.
Completeness	The NFP's tax-exempt status, any tax contingencies, and unrecognized tax benefits for uncertain tax positions are disclosed in the notes to the financial statements.		Determine whether the NFP's tax-exempt status, any tax contingencies, and unrecognized tax benefits for uncertain tax positions are appropriately disclosed in the notes to the financial statements.

Chapter 16

Fund Accounting

Introduction

16.01 Many not-for-profit entities (NFPs) have used fund accounting both for internal recordkeeping and for external financial reporting purposes. Fund accounting segregates assets, liabilities, and fund balances into separate accounting entities associated with specific activities, donor-imposed restrictions, or objectives. However, the financial reporting model for NFPs is based on net assets, classified solely on the basis of donor-imposed restrictions, and requires NFPs' external financial reporting to focus on aggregate information about the entity as a whole, rather than on individual funds.[1] Though fund accounting is not required by generally accepted accounting principles, some NFPs will continue to use fund accounting for internal recordkeeping purposes. Also, Financial Accounting Standards Board (FASB) *Accounting Standards Codification* (ASC) 958-205-45-3 permits the continued disclosure, for external financial reporting purposes, of disaggregated data classified by fund groups, provided that the information required by generally accepted accounting principles is presented. This chapter provides an overview of fund accounting and discusses the reporting of information derived from an internal fund accounting system in conformity with the reporting requirements of the net asset model.[2,3]

Fund Accounting and External Financial Reporting

16.02 Fund accounting is a system of recording resources whose use may be limited by donors, granting agencies, governing boards, or other individuals or entities or by law. To keep records of these limitations for internal purposes, some NFPs maintain separate funds for specific purposes. Each fund consists of a self-balancing set of asset, liability, and fund balance accounts. Prior to 1996, most NFPs prepared fund-accounting-based external financial statements by combining funds with similar characteristics into fund groups.

16.03 For external financial reporting purposes, the total of all assets and liabilities included in all funds and changes in net assets should be measured and reported on an NFP's financial statements in conformity with FASB ASC 958, *Not-for-Profit Entities*. Fund balances should be classified on a statement of financial position as unrestricted, temporarily restricted, or permanently restricted net assets based on the existence and type of donor-imposed

---

[1] Both fund balances and net assets represent residual interests in assets less liabilities. Fund balances, however, are not the same as net asset balances.

[2] The discussion in this chapter assumes paragraphs 9–12 of Financial Accounting Standards Board *Accounting Standards Codification* 958-205-45, concerning the recognition of expirations of donor-imposed restrictions, were applied prospectively when those standards were initially issued.

[3] The timing of recognition of changes in net assets under fund accounting and the net asset model may differ. For example, restrictions may expire under the net asset model in different periods than when expenses are reported in a fund. Accordingly, not-for-profit entities that continue to use fund accounting for internal recordkeeping purposes should generally keep records of all transactions and events that have been recognized under one model but not the other and should adjust opening fund accounting balances to amounts representing opening net assets.

restrictions.[4] For external financial reporting purposes, a fund balance may have to be divided among more than one net asset class.

16.04 FASB ASC 958-210-45-2 states that the requirement to display total assets and liabilities results in certain practical limits on how interfund items are displayed in a financial statement. For example, because receivables and payables between fund groups are not entity assets or liabilities, a statement of financial position should clearly label and arrange those interfund items to eliminate their amounts when displaying total assets or liabilities.

16.05 The remainder of this chapter describes seven commonly used kinds of funds and discusses how their fund balances should be reported based on the requirements of FASB ASC 958.

Unrestricted Current (or Unrestricted Operating or General) Funds

16.06 Unrestricted current funds (also called *unrestricted operating* or *general* funds) are used to record NFPs' activities that are supported by resources over which governing boards have discretionary control. Amounts designated by governing boards for specific purposes may be included in unrestricted current funds, or those amounts may be accounted for in other funds, such as plant funds, endowment funds, and loan funds. The principal sources of unrestricted current funds are unrestricted contributions from donors; exchange transactions with members, clients, students, customers, and others; and unrestricted investment income. Resources are used to help meet the costs of providing the NFP's programs and supporting services.

16.07 Fund balances of unrestricted current funds should be classified on a statement of financial position as unrestricted net assets unless donors have stipulated restrictions on the use of contributed assets that expire by passage of time. In those situations, net assets should be classified as temporarily restricted. Unrestricted fund balances that have been designated by governing bodies for specific purposes (such as quasi-endowment, funds functioning as endowment, funds for long-term investment, self-insurance reserve funds, or future development funds) should be classified as unrestricted net assets. Board designations are permitted to be disclosed, as discussed in chapters 3, "Basic Financial Statements and General Financial Reporting Matters," and 11, "Net Assets," of this guide.

Restricted Current (or Restricted Operating or Specific-Purpose) Funds

16.08 Restricted current funds (also called *restricted operating* or *specific-purpose* funds) are used to record NFPs' activities that are supported by resources whose use is limited by external parties to specific operating purposes. The principal sources of restricted current funds are contributions from donors; contracts, grants, and appropriations; endowment income; and other sources where resource providers have stipulated the specific operating purposes for which the resources are to be used.

---

[4] Accounting for contributions received with donor-imposed restrictions is discussed in chapter 5, "Contributions Received and Agency Transactions," of this guide.

16.09 Fund balances of restricted current funds represent net assets held for specified operating activities that have not yet been used. The portion of the fund balances, if any, that represents amounts contributed with donor-imposed restrictions should be classified as temporarily restricted net assets. Fund balances representing amounts received with limitations other than donor-imposed restrictions, such as contractual limitations, should be classified as unrestricted net assets. Any portion of the fund balances that represents unearned revenue resulting from exchange transactions should be classified as a liability.

Plant (or Land, Building, and Equipment) Funds

16.10 Some NFPs record plant and equipment (and resources held to acquire them) in a plant (or land, building, and equipment) fund or funds. A *plant fund* may be a single group of accounts or may be subdivided into some or all of the following subfund account groups:

- Unexpended plant funds
- Funds for renewal and replacement
- Funds for retirement of indebtedness
- Investment (or net investment) in plant

16.11 Unexpended plant fund balances and renewals and replacement fund balances represent net assets that have not yet been used to acquire, renew, and replace plant and equipment. Retirement-of-indebtedness fund balances represent net assets held to service debt related to the acquisition or construction of plant and equipment. The portion of those fund balances that represents amounts received with donor-imposed restrictions should be classified in a statement of financial position as temporarily restricted or permanently restricted net assets, depending on the nature of the restrictions. Other fund balances, including those arising under agreements with trustees under bond indentures and those designated by the NFP's governing board for the purchase, construction, renewal, or replacement of property and equipment should be classified as unrestricted net assets.[5]

16.12 Investment-in-plant fund balances represent assets invested in property and equipment less any liabilities related to those assets. These fund balances should be classified as permanently restricted net assets to the extent that (1) donors have imposed restrictions on the assets' use that neither expire by passage of time nor can be fulfilled or removed by actions of the NFP—for example, land that must be held in perpetuity—or (2) the proceeds from the ultimate sale or disposal of contributed assets must be reinvested in perpetuity. Amounts representing property and equipment donated or acquired with donor-imposed restrictions that expire by passage of time or that can be fulfilled or removed by actions of the NFP should be classified as temporarily restricted net assets. Amounts representing gifts of property and equipment received without donor-imposed restrictions about how long the assets must be used should be

---

[5] Board designations and other limitations on the use of unrestricted net assets stipulated by entities other than donors can be described on the face of the financial statements or in the notes. Chapters 3, "Basic Financial Statements and General Financial Reporting Matters," and 11, "Net Assets," of this guide discuss such disclosures.

classified as either unrestricted or temporarily restricted net assets, depending on the accounting policy adopted by the NFP.[6] Amounts representing property and equipment acquired with unrestricted resources or with resources whose use is limited by parties other than donors should be classified as unrestricted net assets. Significant limitations on the use of property and equipment should be described in notes to the financial statements.[7]

Loan Funds

16.13 Some NFPs use loan funds to account for loans made to students, employees, and other constituents and resources available for those purposes. The assets initially made available for the loans may be provided by donors or various governmental and other granting agencies or designated by governing boards. These entities or individuals may also stipulate qualifications for individual borrowers. Some loan funds are self-perpetuating—that is, the principal and interest repayments on outstanding loans are used to make additional loans. Other loan funds are created on a temporary basis, and the original resource providers must be repaid. In some situations, repayments may be forgiven by resource providers if certain conditions are met.

16.14 Fund balances of loan funds represent net assets available for lending. The portion of the fund balances representing net assets restricted by donors in perpetuity for use in making loans (for example, a revolving fund) should be classified as permanently restricted. The portion of the fund balances representing net assets temporarily restricted by donors (for example, if, each year, a portion of the fund may be used for the unrestricted purposes of the NFP) should be classified as temporarily restricted. Amounts that have been designated by governing boards to be used as loan funds, such as amounts designated as matching funds for government loan programs (for example, government loans to students that require colleges and universities to match a portion of those loans) and other amounts used for loans that have not been restricted by donors, should be classified as unrestricted net assets. Any portion of loan fund balances that represents refundable advances, such as under a government loan program, should be reported as a liability.

Endowment Funds

16.15 Some NFPs record cash, securities, or other assets held to provide income for the maintenance of the NFP in an endowment fund or funds. Three kinds of endowment may be identified: permanent endowment, term endowment, and quasi endowment, or funds functioning as endowment. *Permanent endowment* refers to amounts that have been contributed with donor-specified restrictions that the principal be invested in perpetuity; income from those investments may also be restricted by donors. *Term endowment* is similar to permanent endowment, except that at some future time or upon the occurrence of a specified future event, the resources originally contributed become available for unrestricted or purpose-restricted use by the entity. *Quasi endowment*

---

[6] Chapter 9, "Property, Plant, and Equipment," of this guide discusses alternative accounting policies concerning the contribution of long-lived assets received without donor-imposed restrictions.

[7] Examples of significant limitations on the use of property and equipment that should be described in the notes to the financial statements are provided in chapter 9 of this guide.

refers to resources designated by an entity's governing board to be retained and invested for specified purposes for a long but unspecified period.

16.16 Fund balances of endowment funds represent net assets for which various limitations exist on the use of the resources invested and, in some cases, on the income generated by those resources. Amounts that represent net assets restricted by donors in perpetuity should be classified as permanently restricted. If donor-imposed restrictions exist that preclude the use of gains and losses (net appreciation) on permanent endowment, either as a result of explicit or implicit donor stipulation or by the NFP's interpretation of the relevant law, those gains and losses should also be classified as permanently restricted. In the absence of such restrictions, those gains and losses should be classified as temporarily restricted or unrestricted, depending on the existence or absence of temporary restrictions imposed by the donor. Chapter 8, "Investments," of this guide provides additional information about the classification of the net assets of endowment funds.

16.17 Fund balances that represent term endowments for which the principal must be maintained for a specific period or must be used at the end of the term for a specified purpose should be classified as temporarily restricted net assets. Amounts representing resources that will be permanently restricted at the end of a specified term should be classified as permanently restricted net assets.

16.18 Fund balances that represent quasi endowments or other amounts designated by the NFP's governing board should be classified as unrestricted net assets unless donor-imposed restrictions exist on their use. Board designations are permitted to be disclosed, as discussed in chapters 3 and 11 of this guide.

Annuity and Life-Income (Split-Interest) Funds

16.19 Annuity and life-income (or split-interest) funds may be used by NFPs to account for resources provided by donors under various kinds of agreements in which the NFP has a beneficial interest in the resources but is not the sole beneficiary. These agreements include charitable lead and remainder trusts, charitable gift annuities, and pooled (life) income funds. Split-interest agreements are discussed in chapter 6, "Split-Interest Agreements," of this guide.

16.20 Fund balances of annuity and life-income funds represent an NFP's beneficial interest in the resources contributed by donors under split-interest agreements. Any portion of the fund balances representing amounts that will become part of permanent endowment when the agreements terminate should be classified as permanently restricted net assets. Any portion of the fund balances representing amounts that will be available for restricted purposes, or available for unrestricted use, by the entity when agreements terminate should be classified as temporarily restricted net assets. Any portion of the fund balances representing amounts that are available for unrestricted purposes should be classified as unrestricted net assets.

Agency (Or Custodian) Funds

16.21 Agency (or custodian) funds are used by NFPs to account for resources held by the entity as an agent for resource providers before those resources are transferred to third-party recipients specified by the resource providers. The entity has little or no discretion over the use of those resources. Accounting for agency transactions and distinguishing agency transactions from contributions are discussed in chapter 5, "Contributions Received and Agency Transactions," of this guide. Because the assets and liabilities are always equal in agency funds, no net assets are reported.

Summary

16.22 The following exhibit summarizes the net asset classes into which various kinds of fund balances will typically be classified.

Typical Classification of Fund Balances

	Net Asset Class		
Fund Type	*Permanently Restricted*	*Temporarily Restricted*	*Unrestricted*
Unrestricted Current (or Unrestricted Operating or General)	Not applicable	Contributions with donor-imposed restrictions that expire with the passage of time (not usually present in unrestricted current funds)	Unrestricted fund balances, including those designated by governing bodies for specific purposes
Restricted Current (or Restricted Operating or Specific Purpose)	Not applicable	Contributions with donor-imposed restrictions that expire with the passage of time or that can be fulfilled or removed by actions of the NFP	Unrestricted fund balances, including those designated by governing bodies for specific purposes[1]
Plant (or Land, Building, and Equipment)	Contributions with donor-imposed restrictions that do not expire with the passage of time or cannot be fulfilled or removed by actions of the NFP[2]	Contributions with donor-imposed restrictions that expire with the passage of time or that can be fulfilled or removed by actions of the NFP[3]	Unrestricted fund balances, including those designated by governing bodies for specific purposes[4]
Loan	Contributions with donor-imposed restrictions that do not expire with the passage of time or can not be fulfilled or removed by actions of the NFP	Contributions with donor-imposed restrictions that expire with the passage of time or that can be fulfilled or removed by actions of the NFP	Unrestricted fund balances, including those designated by governing bodies for specific purposes

Fund Type	*Net Asset Class* Permanently Restricted	Temporarily Restricted	Unrestricted
Endowment	Permanent endowment[5]	Temporary (or term) endowment[6]	Quasi endowment[7]
Annuity and Life-Income (Split Interests)	Donor-restricted in perpetuity	Amounts available for unrestricted or time-or-purpose restricted use when agreement terminates	Unrestricted fund balances, including those designated by governing bodies for specific purposes
Agency (or Custodian)	Not applicable	Not applicable	Not applicable

[1] Any portion of the fund balances representing unearned revenue from exchange transactions should be classified as a liability.

[2] This would include contributed assets such as land and capitalized collection items that must be held in perpetuity and other contributed assets when donors have stipulated that the proceeds from their ultimate sale or disposal must be reinvested in perpetuity.

[3] Amounts representing assets contributed without donor-imposed restrictions about how long the land, building, or equipment must be used should be classified as unrestricted or temporarily restricted net assets, depending on the accounting policy adopted by the NFP.

[4] Amounts representing assets contributed without donor-imposed restrictions about how long the land, building, or equipment must be used should be classified as unrestricted or temporarily restricted net assets, depending on the accounting policy adopted by the NFP.

[5] Includes gains and losses on permanent endowment when donor restrictions or law permanently preclude their use.

[6] Includes gains on permanent endowment when donor restrictions or law specify their use.

[7] Includes gains on permanent endowment when donors or laws do not restrict or specify their use.

Appendix A

Financial Accounting Standards Board Accounting Standards Codification 958, Not-For-Profit Entities, Topic Hierarchy

The purpose of this appendix is to assist readers in their understanding of the structure of the Financial Accounting Standards Board (FASB) *Accounting Standards Codification*™ (ASC).

- Within this guide, FASB ASC references follow the style articulated in FASB's notice to constituents, which can be found on the FASB ASC home page at http://asc.fasb.org/home. The basic reference format is FASB ASC 958-10-05-1, in which ASC stands for *Accounting Standards Codification*™,
- 958 is the topic (*Not-for-Profit-Entities*),
- 10 is the subtopic ("Overall"),
- 05 is the section ("Overview and Background"), and
- 1 is the paragraph.

The following table provides the list of subtopics and sections included within FASB ASC 958, *Not-for-Profit Entities*, as of March 1, 2011.

Topic	Subtopic	Section	Title
958			**Not-for-Profit Entities**
	10		Overall
		00	Status
		05	Overview and Background
		15	Scope and Scope Exceptions
		20	Glossary
		45	Other Presentation Matters
		60	Relationships
	20		Financially Interrelated Entities
		00	Status
		05	Overview and Background
		15	Scope and Scope Exceptions
		20	Glossary
		25	Recognition
		35	Subsequent Measurement
		45	Other Presentation Matters
		50	Disclosure
		55	Implementation Guidance and Illustrations
		60	Relationships

	75	XBRL Elements
30	Split-Interest Agreements	
	00	Status
	05	Overview and Background
	15	Scope and Scope Exceptions
	20	Glossary
	25	Recognition
	30	Initial Measurement
	35	Subsequent Measurement
	40	Derecognition
	45	Other Presentation Matters
	50	Disclosure
	55	Implementation Guidance and Illustrations
205	Presentation of Financial Statements	
	00	Status
	05	Overview and Background
	10	Objectives
	15	Scope and Scope Exceptions
	20	Glossary
	45	Other Presentation Matters
	50	Disclosure
	55	Implementation Guidance and Illustrations
	60	Relationships
	65	Transition and Open Effective Date Information
	75	XBRL Elements
210	Balance Sheet	
	05	Overview and Background
	15	Scope and Scope Exceptions
	20	Glossary
	45	Other Presentation Matters
	50	Disclosure
	55	Implementation Guidance and Illustrations
	60	Relationships
225	Income Statement	
	00	Status
	05	Overview and Background
	15	Scope and Scope Exceptions

	20	Glossary
	45	Other Presentation Matters
	50	Disclosure
	55	Implementation Guidance and Illustrations
	75	XBRL Elements
230	Statement of Cash Flows	
	00	Status
	05	Overview and Background
	15	Scope and Scope Exceptions
	20	Glossary
	55	Implementation Guidance and Illustrations
	75	XBRL Elements
310	Receivables	
	00	Status
	05	Overview and Background
	15	Scope and Scope Exceptions
	20	Glossary
	25	Recognition
	30	Initial Measurement
	35	Subsequent Measurement
	45	Other Presentation Matters
	50	Disclosure
	55	Implementation Guidance and Illustrations
320	Investments—Debt and Equity Securities	
	00	Status
	05	Overview and Background
	15	Scope and Scope Exceptions
	20	Glossary
	25	Recognition
	30	Initial Measurement
	35	Subsequent Measurement
	45	Other Presentation Matters
	50	Disclosure
	55	Implementation Guidance and Illustrations
	60	Relationships
	75	XBRL Elements

325	Investments—Other	
	00	Status
	05	Overview and Background
	15	Scope and Scope Exceptions
	20	Glossary
	25	Recognition
	30	Initial Measurement
	35	Subsequent Measurement
	45	Other Presentation Matters
	50	Disclosure
	60	Relationships
	75	XBRL Elements
360	Property, Plant, and Equipment	
	00	Status
	05	Overview and Background
	15	Scope and Scope Exceptions
	20	Glossary
	25	Recognition
	30	Initial Measurement
	35	Subsequent Measurement
	40	Derecognition
	45	Other Presentation Matters
	50	Disclosure
	55	Implementation Guidance and Illustrations
405	Liabilities	
	05	Overview and Background
	15	Scope and Scope Exceptions
	20	Glossary
	25	Recognition
	30	Initial Measurement
	35	Subsequent Measurement
	45	Other Presentation Matters
	50	Disclosure
	60	Relationships
450	Contingencies	
	00	Status
	05	Overview and Background

	15	Scope and Scope Exceptions
	20	Glossary
	25	Recognition
	50	Disclosure
470	Debt	
	05	Overview and Background
	15	Scope and Scope Exceptions
	25	Recognition
605	Revenue Recognition	
	00	Status
	05	Overview and Background
	15	Scope and Scope Exceptions
	20	Glossary
	25	Recognition
	30	Initial Measurement
	35	Subsequent Measurement
	45	Other Presentation Matters
	50	Disclosure
	55	Implementation Guidance and Illustrations
	75	XBRL Elements
715	Compensation—Retirement Benefits	
	00	Status
	05	Overview and Background
	15	Scope and Scope Exceptions
	20	Glossary
	25	Recognition
	35	Subsequent Measurement
	45	Other Presentation Matters
	50	Disclosure
	55	Implementation Guidance and Illustrations
	65	Transition and Open Effective Date Information
	75	XBRL Elements
720	Other Expenses	
	00	Status
	05	Overview and Background
	15	Scope and Scope Exceptions
	20	Glossary

	25	Recognition
	30	Initial Measurement
	45	Other Presentation Matters
	50	Disclosure
	55	Implementation Guidance and Illustrations
	60	Relationships
805	Business Combinations	
	00	Status
	05	Overview and Background
	10	Objectives
	15	Scope and Scope Exceptions
	20	Glossary
	25	Recognition
	30	Initial Measurement
	35	Subsequent Measurement
	45	Other Presentation Matters
	50	Disclosure
	55	Implementation Guidance and Illustrations
	65	Transition and Open Effective Date Information
	75	XBRL Elements
810	Consolidation	
	00	Status
	05	Overview and Background
	15	Scope and Scope Exceptions
	20	Glossary
	25	Recognition
	45	Other Presentation Matters
	50	Disclosure
	55	Implementation Guidance and Illustrations
	60	Relationships
	65	Transition and Open Effective Date Information
	75	XBRL Elements
815	Derivatives and Hedging	
	05	Overview and Background
	15	Scope and Scope Exceptions
	25	Recognition
	55	Implementation Guidance and Illustrations

840	Leases	
	05	Overview and Background
	15	Scope and Scope Exceptions
	20	Glossary
	55	Implementation Guidance and Illustrations

Appendix B

Information Sources

Further information on matters addressed in this guide is available through various publications and services listed in the table that follows. Many non-government and some government publications and services involve a charge or membership requirement.

Fax services allow users to follow voice cues and request that selected documents be sent by fax machine. Some fax services require the user to call from the handset of the fax machine, others allow the user to call from any phone. Most fax services offer an index document, which lists titles and other information describing available documents.

Electronic bulletin board services allow users to read, copy, and exchange information electronically. Most are available using a modem and standard communications software. Some bulletin board services are also available using one or more Internet protocols.

Recorded announcements allow users to listen to announcements about a variety of recent or scheduled actions or meetings.

All telephone numbers listed are voice lines, unless otherwise designated as fax (f) lines.

Information Sources

Organization	*General Information*	*Website*
American Institute of Certified Public Accountants	*Order Department* 220 Leigh Farm Road Durham, NC 27707 (888) 777-7077 *Audit and Accounting Technical Information Hotline* (877) 242-7212 Information about AICPA CPE programs is available by calling (888) 777-7077	*AICPA Home Page* The AICPA home page is currently located at www.aicpa.org.
Financial Accounting Standards Board	*Order Department* P.O. Box 5116 Norwalk, CT 06856-5116 (800) 748-0659	The FASB home page is currently located at www.fasb.org. The FASB *Accounting Standards Codification*™ can be accessed at http://asc.fasb.org/home.
U.S. Department of Education	Office of Inspector General U.S. Department of Education, 400 Maryland Avenue SW Washington, D.C. 20202 (800) 872-5327	The U.S. Department of Education home page is currently located at www.ed.gov.
U.S. Office of Management and Budget	Office of Administration Publications Office 725 17th Street NW Washington, D.C. 20503 (202) 395-3080 (202) 395-3888 (f)	The OMB home page is currently located at www.whitehouse.gov/omb/. Information pertaining to grants management is available at www.whitehouse.gov/omb/GRANTS.

Organization	*General Information*	*Website*
National Association of College and University Business Officers	1110 Vermont Avenue NW Suite 800 Washington, D.C. 20005 (202) 861-2500 (800) 462-4916 (202) 861-2583 (f)	The NACUBO home page is currently located at www.nacubo.org.
National Health Council	1730 M Street NW Suite 500 Washington, D.C. 20036 (202) 785-3910 (202) 785-5923 (f)	The National Health Council home page is located at www.nationalhealthcouncil.org.
Other		*The Rutgers Bulletin Board* at http://accounting.rutgers.edu/ includes various accounting related databases.
U.S. Government Accountability Office	U.S. GAO 441 G Street NW Washington, D.C. 20548 (202) 512-3000 Publications (866) 801-7077	The GAO has a home page at www.gao.gov.

Appendix C

References to AICPA Technical Practice Aids

The following nonauthoritative questions and answers, commonly referred to as Technical Questions and Answers (TISs), have been prepared by AICPA staff and are included in the AICPA publication *Technical Practice Aids*. The TISs have not been approved, disapproved, or otherwise acted upon by the Accounting Standards Executive Committee or any other senior technical committee of the AICPA. They are not sources of established accounting principles, nor are they sources of authoritative generally accepted auditing standards. AICPA staff believes the TISs listed in the following table may be useful and relevant for users of this guide. Other TISs, as well as Consensus Positions of the Financial Accounting Standards Board's Emerging Issues Task Force, may also be useful and relevant to users of this guide depending on the facts and circumstances.

TPA Reference No.	*Title*
1400.32	"Parent-Only Financial Statements and Relationship to GAAP"
1400.33	"Combining Financial Statements Prepared in Accordance With the Income Tax Basis of Accounting"
1500	*Financial Statements Prepared Under an Other Comprehensive Basis of Accounting*
1800.05	"Applicability of Fair Value Disclosure Requirements and Measurement Principles in Financial Accounting Standards Board (FASB) *Accounting Standards Codification* (ASC) 820, *Fair Value Measurements and Disclosures*, to Certain Financial Instruments"
2130.38	"Certificates of Deposit and FASB ASC 820, *Fair Value Measurements and Disclosures*"
2130.39	"Balance Sheet Classification of Certificates of Deposit"
2130.40	"Certificates of Deposit and FASB ASC 320"
2220.18	"Applicability of a Practical Expedient"
2220.19	"Unit of Account"
2220.20	"Determining Whether NAV Is Calculated Consistent With FASB ASC 946, *Financial Services—Investment Companies*"
2220.21	"Determining Whether an Adjustment to NAV Is Necessary"
2220.22	"Adjusting NAV When It Is Not as of the Reporting Entity's Measurement Date"
2220.23	"Adjusting NAV When It Is Not Calculated Consistent With FASB ASC 946"

(continued)

TPA Reference No.	*Title*
2220.24	"Disclosures—Ability to Redeem Versus Actual Redemption Request"
2220.25	"Impact of 'Near Term' on Classification Within Fair Value Hierarchy"
2220.26	"Categorization of Investments for Disclosure Purposes"
2220.27	"Determining Fair Value of Investments When the Practical Expedient Is Not Used or Is Not Available"
5250.14	"Application of Financial Accounting Standards Board (FASB) Interpretation No. 48, *Accounting for Uncertainty in Income Taxes* (codified in FASB Accounting Standards Codification [ASC] 740-10) to Taxes Other Than Income Taxes"
5250.15	"Application of Certain FASB Interpretation No. 48 (codified in FASB ASC 740-10) Disclosure Requirements to Nonpublic Entities That Do Not Have Uncertain Tax Positions"
5400.05	"Accounting and Disclosures Guidance for Losses From Natural Disasters—Nongovernmental Entities"
5600.07	"Determining a Lease Term for Accounting Purposes"
5600.08	"Lease Term for Accounting Purposes Differs From Term Stated in Lease (Part 1)"
5600.09	"Lease Term for Accounting Purposes Differs From Term Stated in Lease (Part 2)"
5600.10	"Rent Expense and Rent Revenue in an Operating Lease—General"
5600.11	"Rent Expense and Rent Revenue in an Operating Lease—Scheduled Increase in Rental Space"
5600.12	"Rent Expense and Rent Revenue in an Operating Lease—Rent Holiday"
5600.13	"Rent Expense and Rent Revenue in an Operating Lease—Scheduled Rent Increases"
5600.14	"Amortization/Depreciation of Leasehold Improvements in an Operating Lease (Part 1)"
5600.15	"Leasehold Improvements and Lease Term in an Operating Lease (Part 2)"
5600.16	"Landlord Incentive Allowance in an Operating Lease"
5600.17	"Cash Flows Statement Presentation of Landlord Incentive Allowance in an Operating Lease"
6140.01	"Inventory Valuation for a Not-For-Profit Scientific Entity"

TPA Reference No.	*Title*
6140.02	"Income Recognition of Membership Dues by Not-For-Profit Entity"
6140.03	"Lapsing of Time Restrictions on Receivables That Are Uncollected at Their Due Date"
6140.04	"Lapsing of Restrictions on Receivables if Purpose Restrictions Pertaining to Long-Lived Assets Are Met Before the Receivables Are Due"
6140.06	"Functional Category of Cost of Sales of Contributed Inventory"
6140.07	"Functional Category of Costs of Special Events"
6140.08	"Functional Category of the Costs of Direct Donor Benefits"
6140.09	"Reporting Bad Debt Losses"
6140.10	"Consolidation of Political Action Committee"
6140.11	"Costs of Soliciting Contributed Services and Time That Do Not Meet the Recognition Criteria in FASB ASC 958"
6140.12	"Nondiscretionary Assistance Programs"
6140.13	"Note to Sections 6140.14–.18—Implementation of FASB ASC 958—Classification of a Beneficiary's Interest in the Net Assets of a Financially Interrelated Fund-Raising Foundation (in the Beneficiary's Financial Statements)"
6140.14	"Application of FASB ASC 958—Classification of a Beneficiary's Interest in the Net Assets of a Financially Interrelated Fund-Raising Foundation (The beneficiary can influence the operating and financial decisions of the foundation to such an extent that the beneficiary can determine the timing and amount of distributions from the foundation.)"
6140.15	"Application of FASB ASC 958—Classification of a Beneficiary's Interest in the Net Assets of a Financially Interrelated Fund-Raising Foundation (The beneficiary cannot influence the operating and financial decisions of the foundation to such an extent that the beneficiary can determine the timing and amount of distributions from the foundation.)"
6140.16	"Application of FASB ASC 958—Classification of a Beneficiary's Interest in the Net Assets of a Financially Interrelated Fund-Raising Foundation (More Than One Beneficiary—Some Contributions Are Designated)"

(continued)

TPA Reference No.	*Title*
6140.17	"Application of FASB ASC 958—Classification of a Beneficiary's Interest in the Net Assets of a Financially Interrelated Fund-Raising Foundation (The beneficiary makes an expenditure that meets a purpose restriction on net assets held for its benefit by the recipient entity—The beneficiary can influence the operating and financial decisions of the recipient to such an extent that the beneficiary can determine the timing and amount of distributions from the recipient.)"
6140.18	"Application of FASB ASC 958—Classification of a Beneficiary's Interest in the Net Assets of a Financially Interrelated Fund-Raising Foundation (The beneficiary makes an expenditure that is consistent with a purpose restriction on net assets held for its benefit by the recipient entity—The beneficiary cannot influence the operating and financial decisions of the recipient to such an extent that the beneficiary can determine the timing and amount of distributions from the recipient.)"
6140.19	"Application of FASB ASC 958—Classification of Distributions From a Financially Interrelated Fund-Raising Foundation (Recipient Entity) to a Health Care Beneficiary"
6140.20	"NPEs Reporting No Fund-Raising Expenses"
6140.21	"Should an NPE Report Amounts Charged to the NPE by a Professional Fund-Raiser Gross, as Fund-Raising Expenses, or Net, as a Reduction of Contributions?"
6140.22	"In Circumstances in Which the Reporting NPE Undertakes a Transaction in Which Another NPE (Fund-Raising NPE) Raises Contributions on Behalf of the Reporting NPE, and the Reporting NPE Compensates the Fund-Raising NPE for Raising Those Contributions (Compensation Including, But Not Limited to, an Administrative Fee), Should the Reporting NPE Report the Fund-Raising NPE's Compensation Gross, as Fund-Raising Expenses, or Net, as a Reduction of Contributions?"
6140.23	"Changing Net Asset Classifications Reported in Prior Year"
6140.24	"Contributions of Certain Nonfinancial Assets, Such as Fundraising Material, Informational Material, or Advertising, Including Media Time or Space for Public Service Announcements or Other Purposes"
6140.25	"Multiyear Unconditional Promises to Give—Measurement Objective and the Effect of Changes in Interest Rates"

TPA Reference No.	*Title*
6960.12	"Allocation of Overhead"
8700.03	"Auditor's Responsibilities for Subsequent Events Relative to a Conduit Debt Obligor"
9070.06	"Decline in Market Value of Assets Subsequent to the Balance Sheet Date"

Appendix D

Schedule of Changes Made to the Text From the Previous Edition

As of March 1, 2011

This schedule of changes identifies areas in the text and footnotes of this guide that have been changed from the previous edition. Entries in the table of this appendix reflect current numbering, lettering (including those in appendix names), and character designations that resulted from the renumbering or re-ordering that occurred in the updating of this guide.

Reference	Change
Preface	Updated.
Former footnote * in heading before paragraph 1.05	Deleted.
Footnote 3 in heading before paragraph 1.05	Revised for clarification.
Paragraph 1.14	Revised for clarification.
Paragraph 1.28	Paragraphs A-2, A-28, A-31 revised for clarification.
Footnote 2 in paragraph 2.06	Revised to reflect the issuance of an exposure draft of the ninth edition of *Government Auditing Standards*.
Footnote 3 in paragraph 2.06	Revised to reflect the issuance of United States Office of Management and Budget (OMB) Circular A-133 Compliance Supplement.
Paragraph 2.07	Revised to reflect the issuance of Statement on Auditing Standards (SAS) No. 117, *Compliance Audits* (AICPA, *Professional Standards*, AU sec. 801); former footnote † deleted.
Footnote † in paragraph 2.19	Revised.
Footnote ‡ in paragraph 2.28	Revised.
Footnote ‖ in heading before paragraph 2.29	Added.
Former footnote † in paragraph 2.29	Deleted.
Footnote 7 in paragraph 2.30	Revised to reflect the issuance of OMB Circular A-133 Compliance Supplement.
Former footnote † in paragraph 2.32	Deleted.

(continued)

Reference	*Change*
Footnote 9 in paragraph 2.33	Revised to reflect the issuance of clarified SAS *Audit Considerations Relating to an Entity Using a Service Organization*.
Footnote 11 in paragraph 2.69	Revised to reflect the passage of time.
Footnote 12 in paragraph 2.74	Added to reflect the issuance of proposed SAS *Subsequent Events and Subsequently Discovered Facts;* added to reflect the issuance of Technical Questions and Answers (TIS) section 8700.03, "Auditor's Responsibilities for Subsequent Events Relative to a Conduit Debt Obligor" (AICPA, *Technical Practice Aids*); added to reflect the issuance of TIS section 9070.06, "Decline in Market Value of Assets Subsequent to the Balance Sheet Date" (AICPA, *Technical Practice Aids*).
Footnote † in paragraph 2.74	Revised for the passage of time.
Former footnote †† in paragraph 2.74	Deleted.
Footnote 13 in paragraph 2.74	Revised to reflect the revision of Interpretation No. 1, "Communicating Deficiencies in Internal Control Over Compliance in an Office of Management and Budget Circular A-133 Audit," of AU section 325, *Communicating Internal Control Related Matters Identified in an Audit* (AICPA, *Professional Standards*, AU sec. 9325 par. .01–.03).
Paragraph 2.76	Former footnotes † and ‡‡ deleted.
Footnote † in heading before paragraph 2.77	Revised.
Paragraph 3.01	Revised for clarification.
Paragraphs 3.34–.35	Former footnote † deleted.
Paragraph 3.36	Former footnotes ‡ and ǁ deleted.
Former footnote ‡ in paragraph 3.37	Deleted.
Paragraph 3.45	Revised to reflect the issuance of Financial Accounting Standards Board Accounting Standards Update (ASU) No. 2010-08, *Technical Corrections to Various Topics*.
Former footnote ** in paragraph 3.51	Deleted.
Former footnote †† in heading before paragraph 3.55	Deleted.

Reference	*Change*
Former footnote ## in paragraph 3.72	Deleted.
Footnote ‡ in heading before paragraph 3.73	Added.
Footnote ‖ in paragraph 3.74	Revised.
Paragraph 3.75	Added to reflect the issuance of TIS section 1800.05, "Applicability of Fair Value Disclosure Requirements and Measurement Principles in Financial Accounting Standards Board (FASB) *Accounting Standards Codification* (ASC) 820, *Fair Value Measurements and Disclosures*, to Certain Financial Instruments" (AICPA, *Technical Practice Aids*).
Paragraph 3.92	Former footnotes ††† and ‡‡‡ deleted.
Footnote # in heading before paragraph 3.95	Added.
Footnote †† in paragraph 3.100	Revised.
Paragraphs 3.103–.106	Added to reflect the issuance of ASU No. 2010-09, *Subsequent Events (Topic 855): Amendments to Certain Recognition and Disclosure Requirements*.
Paragraph 4.06	Added to reflect the issuance of TIS sections 2130.38–.40 (AICPA, *Technical Practice Aids*).
Footnote * in paragraph 5.20	Added.
Footnote 5 in paragraph 5.20	Revised for the passage of time.
Former footnote * in paragraph 5.69	Deleted.
Paragraph 5.97	Added to reflect the issuance of TIS section 6140.24, "Contributions of Certain Nonfinancial Assets, Such as Fundraising Material, Informational Material, or Advertising, Including Media Time or Space for Public Service Announcements or Other Purposes" (AICPA, *Technical Practice Aids*).
Footnote † in paragraph 5.101	Added.
Paragraph 5.104	Former footnote † deleted; footnote * added.

(continued)

Reference	*Change*
Footnote ‖ in paragraph 5.131	Added.
Former footnote ‡ in paragraph 5.136	Deleted.
Paragraph 6.02	Revised for clarification.
Footnote * in paragraph 6.05	Added.
Footnote 2 in paragraph 6.09	Revised for passage of time.
Footnote * in paragraph 6.09	Added.
Paragraph 6.34	Revised for clarification.
Paragraph 7.03	Footnote * revised for passage of time; footnote † added.
Footnote † in paragraph 7.09	Added.
Paragraphs 7.21–.22	Added to reflect the issuance of ASU No. 2010-07, *Not-for-Profit Entities (Topic 958): Not-for-Profit Entities: Mergers and Acquisitions*.
Footnote * in chapter 8 title	Added.
Former footnote * in paragraph 8.01	Deleted.
Paragraph 8.06	Footnote ‡ updated to reflect the passage of time; footnote ‖ added.
Former footnote * in heading before paragraph 8.11	Deleted.
Paragraph 8.16	Footnote ‡ added; footnote ‖ added; former footnote * deleted.
Former footnote ‖ in paragraph 8.17	Deleted.
Former footnote # in paragraph 8.25	Deleted.
Paragraph 8.40	Former footnote ** deleted; footnote * added.
Footnote * in paragraphs 8.42 and 8.45	Added.
Paragraph 8.47	Footnote * added; former footnote †† deleted.
Footnote * in paragraph 8.48	Added.
Footnote * in heading before paragraph 8.49	Revised.
Former footnote ‖ in paragraph 8.56	Deleted.

Reference	*Change*
Former footnote # in paragraph 8.61	Deleted.
Paragraph 8.62	Revised for clarification; footnote 7 deleted.
Footnote * in paragraph 9.02	Added.
Paragraph 9.05	Revised for clarification.
Footnote 2 in paragraph 9.05	Revised for passage of time.
Footnote † in paragraph 9.05	Added.
Footnote * in paragraph 9.22	Added.
Footnote * in paragraph 10.02	Added.
Former footnote * in paragraph 10.03	Deleted.
Former footnote ‡ in paragraph 10.08	Deleted.
Paragraph 10.13	Footnote 3 revised for passage of time; footnote ‡ added.
Footnote ǁ in paragraph 10.15 and 10.22	Revised.
Footnote ǁǀ in the heading in paragraph 10.22	Revised.
Paragraphs 11.01–.09	Revised for clarification.
Heading before paragraph 11.30 and paragraph 11.30	Added to reflect the issuance of TIS section 6140.23, "Changing Net Asset Classifications Reported in a Prior Year" (AICPA, *Technical Practice Aids*).
Footnote * in paragraph 12.01	Added.
Footnote † in paragraph 12.09	Added.
Footnote * in paragraph 14.03	Added.
Footnote † in heading before paragraph 14.05	Added.
Footnote 11 in paragraph 14.08	Revised for clarification.
Footnote 12 in paragraph 14.09	Revised for clarification.
Footnote # in heading before paragraph 14.17	Added.

(continued)

Reference	*Change*
Footnote ** in paragraph 14.17	Added.
Paragraph 15.02	Revised to reflect the issuance of TIS section 5250.14, "Application of Financial Accounting Standards Board (FASB) Interpretation No. 48, *Accounting for Uncertainty in Income Taxes* (codified in FASB *Accounting Standards Codification* (ASC) 740-10) to Taxes Other Than Income Taxes" (AICPA, *Technical Practice Aids*).
Former footnote * in paragraph 15.02	Deleted.
Paragraph 15.16	Revised for clarification.
Paragraph 15.21	Revised to reflect the issuance of TIS section 5250.15, "Application of Certain FASB Interpretation No. 48 (codified in FASB ASC 740-10) Disclosure Requirements to Nonpublic Entities That Do Not Have Uncertain Tax Positions" (AICPA, *Technical Practice Aids*).
Appendix A	Updated.
Appendix C	Updated.
Glossary	Updated.
Index	Updated.

Glossary

The following terms can be found in Financial Accounting Standards Board (FASB) *Accounting Standards Codification* (ASC) glossary:

acquiree. The business or businesses that the acquirer obtains control of in a business combination. This term also includes a nonprofit activity or business that a not-for-profit acquirer obtains control of in an acquisition by a not-for-profit entity (NFP).

acquirer. The entity that obtains control of the acquiree. However, in a business combination in which a variable interest entity is acquired, the primary beneficiary of that entity always is the acquirer.

acquisition by a not-for-profit entity. A transaction or other event in which a not-for-profit acquirer obtains control of one or more nonprofit activities or businesses and initially recognizes their assets and liabilities in the acquirer's financial statements. When applicable guidance in FASB ASC 805, *Business Combinations*, is applied by an NFP, the term *business combination* has the same meaning as this term has for an NFP. Likewise, a reference to business combinations in guidance that links to FASC ASC 805 has the same meaning as a reference to acquisitions by NFPs.

acquisition date. The date on which the acquirer obtains control of the acquiree.

activities. Activities are efforts to accomplish specific objectives. Some activities include producing and distributing materials. For example, if an NFP undertakes a mass mailing that includes a letter and a pamphlet, producing and distributing the letter and pamphlet are part of the activity. Other activities may include no materials, such as an annual dinner or a radio commercial.

affiliate. A party that, directly or indirectly through one or more intermediaries, controls, is controlled by, or is under common control with an entity.

agent. An entity that acts for and on behalf of another. Although the term *agency* has a legal definition, the term is used broadly to encompass not only legal agency, but also the relationships described in FASB ASC 958, *Not-for-Profit Entities*. A recipient entity acts as an agent for and on behalf of a donor if it receives assets from the donor and agrees to use those assets on behalf of or transfer those assets, the return on investment of those assets, or both to a specified beneficiary. A recipient entity acts as an agent for and on behalf of a beneficiary if it agrees to solicit assets from potential donors specifically for the beneficiary's use and to distribute those assets to the beneficiary. A recipient entity also acts as an agent if a beneficiary can compel the recipient entity to make distributions on its behalf.

agency transaction. A type of exchange transaction in which the reporting organization acts as an agent, trustee, or intermediary for another party that may be a donor or donee. See **agent**, **trustee**, and **intermediary**.

annuity gift. See **charitable annuity gift**.

annuity trust. See **charitable remainder trust**.

business. An integrated set of activities and assets that is capable of being conducted and managed for the purpose of providing a return in the form of dividends, lower costs, or other economic benefits directly to investors or other owners, members, or participants. Additional guidance on what a business consists of is presented in paragraphs 4–9 of FASB ASC 805-10-55.

business combination. A transaction or other event in which an acquirer obtains control of one or more businesses. Transactions sometimes referred to as *true mergers* or *mergers of equals* also are business combinations. See also **acquisition by a not-for-profit entity**.

charitable gift annuity. A transfer of assets to an NFP in connection with a split-interest agreement that is in part a contribution and in part an exchange transaction. The NFP accepts the contribution and is obligated to make periodic stipulated payments to the donor or a third-party beneficiary for a specified period of time, usually either a specified number of years or until the death of the donor or third-party beneficiary.

charitable lead trust. A trust established in connection with a split-interest agreement, in which the NFP receives distributions during the agreement's term. Upon termination of the trust, the remainder of the trust assets is paid to the donor or to third-party beneficiaries designated by the donor.

charitable remainder trust. A trust established in connection with a split-interest agreement, in which the donor or a third-party beneficiary receives specified distributions during the agreement's term. Upon termination of the trust, an NFP receives the assets remaining in the trust.

collections. Works of art, historical treasures, or similar assets that meet all of the following criteria: (*a*) they are held for public exhibition, education, or research in furtherance of public service rather than financial gain, (*b*) they are protected, kept unencumbered, cared for, and preserved, and (*c*) they are subject to an organizational policy that requires the proceeds of items that are sold to be used to acquire other items for collections. Collections generally are held by museums; botanical gardens; libraries; aquariums; arboretums; historic sites; planetariums; zoos; art galleries; nature; science; and technology centers, and similar educational, research, and public service organizations that have those divisions; however, the definition is not limited to those entities nor does it apply to all items held by those entities.

compensation or fees. Reciprocal transfers of cash or other assets in exchange for services performed.

conditional promise to give. A promise to give that depends on the occurrence of a specified future and uncertain event to bind the promisor.

contribution. An unconditional transfer of cash or other assets to an entity or a settlement or cancellation of its liabilities in a voluntary nonreciprocal transfer by another entity acting other than as an owner. Those characteristics distinguish contributions from exchange transactions, which are reciprocal transfers in which each party receives and sacrifices approximately equal value, from investments by owners and distributions to owners, which are nonreciprocal transfers between an entity and its owners; and from other nonreciprocal transfers, such as impositions of taxes or legal judgments, fines, and thefts, which are not voluntary transfers. In a contribution transaction, the value, if any, returned to the resource provider is incidental to potential public benefits. In an exchange transaction, the potential public benefits are secondary to the potential proprietary benefits to the resource provider. The term *contribution revenue* is used to apply to transactions that are part of the entity's ongoing major or central activities (revenues), or are peripheral or incidental to the entity (gains). See also **inherent contribution**.

contingent consideration. Usually an obligation of the acquirer to transfer additional assets or equity interests to the former owners of an acquiree as part of the exchange for control of the acquiree if specified future events occur or conditions are met. However, contingent consideration also may give the acquirer the right to the return of previously transferred consideration if specified conditions are met.

control of a not-for-profit entity. The direct or indirect ability to determine the direction of management and policies through ownership, contract, or otherwise.

control of a for-profit business. The same as the meaning of controlling financial interest in FASB ASC 810-10-15-8.

costs of joint activities. Costs incurred for a joint activity. Costs of joint activities may include joint costs and costs other than joint costs. Costs other than joint costs are costs that are identifiable with a particular function, such as fund raising, program, management and general, and cost of sales. For example, some costs incurred for printing, paper, professional fees, and salaries to produce donor cards are not joint costs, although they may be incurred in connection with conducting joint activities.

designated net assets. Unrestricted net assets subject to self-imposed limits by action of the governing board. Designated net assets may be earmarked for future programs, investment, contingencies, purchase or construction of fixed assets, or other uses.

donor-imposed condition. A donor stipulation that specifies a future and uncertain event whose occurrence or failure to occur give the promisor a right of return of the assets it has transferred or releases the promisor from its obligation to transfer its assets.

donor-imposed restriction. A donor stipulation that specifies a use for the contributed asset that is more specific than broad limits resulting from the following: (*a*) the nature of the NFP, (*b*) the environment in which it operates, and (*c*) the purposes specified in its articles of incorporation or bylaws, or comparable documents for an unincorporated association. A donor-imposed restriction on an NFP's use of the asset contributed may be temporary or permanent. Some donor-imposed restrictions impose limits that are permanent, for example, stipulating that resources be invested in perpetuity (not used up). Others are temporary, for example, stipulating that resources may be used only after a specified date, for particular programs or services, or to acquire buildings and equipment.

economic interest. An NFP's interest in another entity that exists if any of the following criteria are met: (*a*) the other entity holds or utilizes significant resources that must be used for the unrestricted or restricted purposes of the NFP, either directly or indirectly by producing income or providing services, or (*b*) the NFP is responsible for the liabilities of the other entity.

endowment fund. An established fund of cash, securities, or other assets to provide income for the maintenance of an NFP. The use of the assets of the fund may be permanently restricted, temporarily restricted, or unrestricted. Endowment funds generally are established by donor-restricted gifts and bequests to provide (*a*) a permanent endowment, which is to provide a permanent source of income, or a (*b*) term endowment, which is to provide income for a specified period.

equity interests. Used broadly to mean ownership interests of investor-owned entities; owner, member, or participant interests of mutual entities; and owner or member interests in the net assets of not-for-profit entities.

functional classification. A method of grouping expenses according to the purpose for which the costs are incurred. The primary functional classifications are program services and supporting activities.

funds functioning as endowment. Unrestricted net assets designated by an entity's governing board, rather than restricted by a donor or other outside agency, to be invested to provide income for a long but unspecified period. A board-designated endowment, which results from an internal designation, is not donor-restricted and is classified as unrestricted net assets. The governing board has the right to decide at any time to expend the principal of such funds. (Sometimes referred to as quasi-endowment funds.) See also **designated net assets**.

fund raising activities. Activities undertaken to induce potential donors to contribute money, securities, services, materials, facilities, other assets, or time.

funds held in trust by others. Resources held and administered, at the direction of the resource provider, by an outside trustee for the benefit of an NFP, frequently in connection with a split-interest agreement or permanent endowment.

goodwill. An asset representing the future economic benefits arising from other assets acquired in a business combination or an acquisition by an NFP that are not individually identified and separately recognized. For ease of reference, this term also includes the immediate charge recognized by NFPs in accordance with FASB ASC 958-805-25-29.

identifiable. An asset is identifiable if it meets either of the following criteria: (*a*) it is separable, that is, capable of being separated or divided from the entity and sold, transferred, licensed, rented, or exchanged, either individually or together with a related contract, identifiable asset, or liability, regardless of whether the entity intends to do so, or (*b*) it arises from contractual or other legal rights, regardless of whether those rights are transferable or separable from the entity or from other rights and obligations.

inherent contribution. A contribution that results if an entity voluntarily transfers assets (or net assets) or performs services for another entity in exchange for either no assets or for assets of substantially lower value and unstated rights or privileges of a commensurate value are not involved.

intangible assets. Assets (not including financial assets) that lack physical substance. (The term *intangible assets* is used to refer to intangible assets other than goodwill.)

intermediary. Although in general usage the term *intermediary* encompasses a broad range of situations in which an entity acts between two or more other parties, in this usage, it refers to situations in which a recipient entity acts as a facilitator for the transfer of assets between a potential donor and a potential beneficiary (donee) but is neither an agent or trustee nor a donee and donor.

joint activity. An activity that is part of the fund-raising function and has elements of one or more other functions, such as programs, management and general, membership development, or any other functional category used by the entity.

joint costs. The costs are the costs of conducting joint activities that are not identifiable with a particular component of the activity. For example, the cost of postage for a letter that includes both fund-raising and program components is a joint cost. Joint costs may include the following costs: salaries, contract labor, consultants, professional fees, paper, printing, postage, event advertising, telephones, airtime, and facility rentals.

lead interest. The right to the benefits (cash flows or use) of assets during the term of a split-interest agreement, which generally starts upon the signing of the agreement and terminates at either of the following times: (*a*) after a specified number of years (period-certain) or (*b*) upon the occurrence of a certain event, commonly either the death of the donor or the death of the lead interest beneficiary (life-contingent).

legal entity. Any legal structure used to conduct activities or to hold assets. Some examples of such structures are corporations, partnerships, limited liability companies, grantor trusts, and other trusts.

life income agreement. A form of split-interest agreement in which an NFP is obligated to make payments to the donor or a third-party beneficiary for that beneficiary's life. See **charitable gift annuity** and **charitable remainder trust**.

management and general activities. Activities that are not identifiable with a single program, fund-raising activity, or membership-development activity but that are indispensable to the conduct of those activities and to an entity's existence.

medium. A means of mass communication, such as direct mail, direct response advertising, or television.

membership-development activities. Membership-development activities include soliciting for prospective members and membership dues, membership relations, and similar activities. However, if no significant benefits or duties are connected with membership, however, the substance of membership-development activities may, in fact, be fund-raising.

merger date. The date on which the merger becomes effective.

merger of not-for-profit entities. A transaction or other event in which the governing bodies of two or more NFPs cede control of those entities to create a new NFP.

natural expense classification. A method of grouping expenses according to the kinds of economic benefits received in incurring those expenses. Examples of natural expense classifications include salaries and wages, employee benefits, supplies, rent, and utilities.

net assets. The excess or deficiency of assets over liabilities of an NFP, which is classified into three mutually exclusive classes according to the existence or absence of donor-imposed restrictions. See **unrestricted net assets, temporarily restricted net assets, and permanently restricted net assets**.

noncontrolling interest. The portion of equity (net assets) in a subsidiary not attributable, directly or indirectly, to a parent. A noncontrolling interest is sometimes called a *minority interest*.

nonprofit activity. An integrated set of activities and assets that is capable of being conducted and managed for the purpose of providing benefits, other than goods or services at a profit or profit equivalent, as a fulfillment of an entity's purpose or mission (for example, goods or services to beneficiaries, customers, or members). As with an NFP, a nonprofit activity possesses characteristics that distinguish it from a business or a for-profit business entity.

nonreciprocal transfer. A transaction in which an entity incurs a liability or transfers an asset to another entity (or receives an asset or cancellation of a liability) without directly receiving (or giving) value in exchange.

not-for-profit entity. An entity that possesses the following characteristics, in varying degrees, that distinguish it from a business entity: (*a*) contributions of significant amounts of resources from resource providers who do not expect commensurate or proportionate pecuniary return, (*b*) operating purposes other than to provide goods or services at a profit, and (*c*) absence of ownership interests like those of business enterprises. Entities that clearly fall outside this definition include the following: (*a*) all investor-owned enterprises and (*b*) entities that provide dividends, lower costs, or other economic benefits directly and proportionately to their owners, members, or participants, such as mutual insurance companies, credit unions, farm and rural electric cooperatives, and employee benefit plans.

owners. Used broadly to include holders of ownership interests (equity interests) of investor-owned entities, mutual entities, or NFPs. Owners include shareholders, partners, proprietors, or members or participants of mutual entities. Owners also include owner and member interests in the net assets of NFPs.

permanent restriction. A donor-imposed restriction that stipulates that resources be maintained permanently but permits the NFP to use up or expend part or all of the income (or other economic benefits) derived from the donated assets.

permanently restricted net assets. The part of the net assets of an NFP resulting from the following: (*a*) contributions and other inflows of assets whose use by the NFP is limited by donor-imposed stipulations that neither expire by passage of time nor can be fulfilled or otherwise removed by actions of the NFP, (*b*) other asset enhancements and diminishments subject to the same kinds of stipulations, and (*c*) reclassifications from (or to) other classes of net assets as a consequence of donor-imposed stipulations.

pooled income fund. A trust in which donors are assigned a specific number of units based on the proportion of the fair value of their contributions to the total fair value of the pooled income fund on the date of the donor's entry to the pooled fund. Until a donor's death, the donor (or the donor's designated beneficiary or beneficiaries) is paid the actual income (as defined under the arrangement) earned on the donor's assigned units. Upon the donor's death, the value of these assigned units reverts to the NFP.

program services. The activities that result in goods and services being distributed to beneficiaries, customers, or members that fulfill the purposes or mission for which the NFP exists. Those services are the major purpose for and the major output of the organization and often relate to several major programs.

promise to give. A written or oral agreement to contribute cash or other assets to another entity. A promise carries rights and obligations—the recipient of a promise to give has a right to expect that the promised assets will be transferred in the future, and the maker has a social and moral obligation, and generally a legal obligation, to make the promised transfer. A promise to give may be either conditional or unconditional.

quasi-endowment funds. See **funds functioning as endowment**.

reclassification. Simultaneous increase of one class of net assets and decrease of another, usually as a result of the release or lapsing of restrictions.

remainder interest. The right to receive all or a portion of the assets of a split-interest agreement at the end of the agreement's term.

remainder trust. See **charitable remainder trust**.

restricted support. Donor-restricted revenues or gains from contributions that increase either temporarily restricted net assets or permanently restricted net assets. See also **unrestricted support**.

spending-rate. The portion of total return on investments used for fiscal needs of the current period, usually used as a budgetary method of reporting returns of investments. It is usually measured in terms of an amount or a specified percentage of a moving average market value. Typically, the selection of a spending rate emphasizes the use of prudence and a systematic formula to determine the portion of cumulative investment return that can be used to support fiscal needs of the current period and the protection of endowment gifts from a loss of purchasing power as a consideration in determining the formula to be used.

split-interest agreement. An agreement in which a donor enters into a trust or other arrangements under which an NFP receives benefits that are shared with other beneficiaries. A typical split-interest agreement has the following two components: (*a*) a lead interest and (*b*) a remainder interest.

stipulation. A statement by a donor that creates a condition or restriction on the use of transferred resources.

supporting activities. All activities of an NFP other than program services. Generally, they include the following: (*a*) management and general activities, (*b*) fund raising activities, and (*c*) membership development activities.

temporarily restricted net assets. The part of the net assets of an NFP resulting from the following (*a*) contributions and other inflows of assets whose use by the NFP is limited by donor-imposed stipulations that either expire by the passage of time or can be fulfilled and removed by actions of the NFP pursuant to those stipulations, (*b*) other asset enhancements and diminishments subject to the same kinds of stipulations, and (*c*) reclassifications from or to other classes of net assets as a consequence of donor-imposed stipulations, their expiration by passage of time, or their fulfillment and removal by actions of the NFP pursuant to those stipulations.

temporary restriction. A donor-imposed restriction that permits the donee organization to use up or expend the donated assets as specified and that is satisfied either by the passage of time or by actions of the donee.

term endowment. An endowment fund established to provide income for a specified period. See **endowment fund**.

total return. A measure of investment performance that focuses on the overall return on investments, including interest and dividend income as well as realized and unrealized gains and losses on investments. Frequently used in connection with a spending-rate formula to determine how much of that return will be used for fiscal needs of the current period.

trustee. An entity that has a duty to hold and manage assets for the benefit of a specified beneficiary in accordance with a charitable trust agreement. In some states, NFPs are organized under trust law rather than as corporations. Those NFPs are not trustees as defined because, under those statutes, they hold assets in trust for the community or some other broadly described group, rather than for a specific beneficiary.

unconditional promise to give. A promise to give that depends only on passage of time or demand by the promisee for performance.

unrestricted net assets. The part of net assets of an NFP that is neither permanently restricted nor temporarily restricted by donor-imposed stipulations. The only limits on the use of unrestricted net assets are the broad limits resulting from the following: (*a*) the nature of the NFP, (*b*) the environment in which the NFP operates, (*c*) the purposes specified in the NFP's articles of incorporation or bylaws, and (*d*) limits resulting from contractual agreements with suppliers, creditors, and others entered into by the NFP in the course of its business. Unrestricted net assets generally result from revenues from providing services, producing and delivering goods, receiving unrestricted contributions, and receiving dividends or interest from investing in income-producing assets, less expenses incurred in providing services, producing and delivering goods, raising contributions, and performing administrative functions.

unrestricted support. Revenues or gains from contributions that are not restricted by donors. See also **restricted support**.

variance power. The unilateral power to redirect the use of the transferred assets to another beneficiary. A donor explicitly grants variance power if the recipient entity's unilateral power to redirect the use of the assets is explicitly referred to in the instrument transferring the assets. Unilateral power means that the recipient entity can override the donor's instructions without approval from the donor, specified beneficiary, or any other interested party.

voluntary health and welfare entities. An NFP that is formed for the purpose of performing voluntary services for various segments of society and that is tax exempt (organized for the benefit of the public), supported by the public, and operated on a not-for-profit basis. Most voluntary health and welfare entities concentrate their efforts and expend their resources in an attempt to solve health and welfare problems of our society and, in many cases, those of specific individuals. As a group, voluntary health and welfare entities include those NFPs that derive their revenue primarily from voluntary contributions from the general public to be used for general or specific purposes connected with health, welfare, or community services. For purposes of this definition, the general public excludes governmental entities when determining whether an NFP is a voluntary health and welfare entity.

The following is a list of additional terms that have been used in this guide:

board designated. See **designated net assets** and **endowment fund.**

corpus. The principal amount of a gift or trust. Usually refers to the portion of a split-interest gift or an endowment fund that must be maintained over a specified period or in perpetuity.

equity. See **net assets**.

gift annuity. See **charitable annuity gift**.

help accomplish the not-for-profit entity's mission. Actions that help accomplish the NFP's mission are actions that either benefit the recipient (such as by improving the recipient's physical, mental, emotional, or spiritual health and well-being) or benefit society (by addressing societal problems).

life tenant. One who possesses a life-use right to property, frequently used in connection with a split-interest agreement.

net income unitrust. A trust established in connection with a split-interest agreement, in which the donor or a third-party beneficiary receives distributions during the agreement's term of the lesser of the net income earned by the trust or a fixed percentage of the fair value of the trust's assets, with or without recovery and distribution of the shortfall in a subsequent year. Upon termination of the trust, an NFP receives the assets remaining in the trust.

net investment (equity) in land, buildings, and equipment. The total carrying value (after accumulated depreciation) of all property, plant, and equipment, less directly related liabilities. This amount is exclusive of real properties that are held for investment purposes.

program activities. See **program services.**

remainderman. The recipient of the corpus (remaining principal) of a trust upon termination.

restricted net assets. Resources whose use is restricted by donors as contrasted with those over which the NFP has complete control and discretion. Restricted net assets may be permanently or temporarily restricted.

Index

A

ACCOUNT BALANCE
- Audit risk 2.12

ACCOUNTING POLICY FOR CONTRIBUTED PROPERTY AND EQUIPMENT
- Illustrative disclosures .... 5.134 Ex. 3

ACCOUNTING STANDARDS CODIFICATION (ASC). *See* Financial Accounting Standards Board (FASB)

ACQUISITIONS. *See* Mergers and acquisitions
- Valuation of investments subsequent to. *See* Valuation subsequent to acquisition

ADVANCES FROM THIRD PARTIES 10.10

ADVERTISING
- Costs, expense recognition issues 13.10–.12
- Ticket subscription, advertising with request for contributions .... 13.99 Ex. 12

AGENCY FUNDS
- Fund accounting 16.21

AGENCY TRANSACTIONS
- Amounts held for others under 10.17
- Contributions received, distinguishing 5.07–.20
- Defined 5.07
- Gifts, representations made during solicitation 5.13
- Liability to specified beneficiary 5.15
- Materials, supplies, or other nonfinancial assets, donation of 5.16
- Measurement of fair value 5.20
- Perpetual trusts held by third party, fair value 5.18
- Rights of beneficiary 5.19
- Statement of cash flows 3.25

AGENT. *See also* Trustee or fiscal agent
- Defined, promises to give 10.12

AICPA CODE OF PROFESSIONAL CONDUCT
- Adherence to 1.28 (A-2)

AICPA TECHNICAL PRACTICE AIDS 1.07
- References to .... Appendix C

ALLOCATION METHODS
- Expenses 13.100
  - more than one function, classification of expenses related to .... 13.46–.51, ... 13.85–.86
  - physical units method 13.100
  - relative direct cost method 13.100
  - stand-alone-joint-cost-allocation method 13.100

ALTERNATIVE INVESTMENTS
- Auditing 8.58
- Investments, valuation subsequent to acquisitions 8.17

AMORTIZATION
- Property, plant, and equipment 9.09–.13

ANALYTICAL PROCEDURES 2.41–.43

ANNUAL REPORT, DISTRIBUTION OF .... 13.99 Ex. 9

ANNUITY AND LIFE-INCOME FUNDS
- Fund accounting 16.19–.20

ANNUITY OBLIGATIONS
- Debt and other liabilities 10.16

ANNUITY RESERVES
- Split-interest agreements 6.35

APB OPINIONS. *See* Mergers and Acquisitions

APPROPRIATED FOR EXPENDITURE, DEFINED 8.28

APPROPRIATIONS
- Exchange transactions 5.48

ASC (ACCOUNTING STANDARDS CODIFICATION). *See* Financial Accounting Standards Board (FASB); *specific ASC*

ASSERTIONS
- Evidence, use of in obtaining 2.34–.38

ASSET GROUP
- Property, plant, and equipment 9.14

ASSETS
- Beneficial interests in assets held by others
  - illustrative disclosures .... 5.134 Ex. 5
- Classification of
  - statements of financial position 3.06
- Exchange transactions 5.37
  - transfers of assets 5.41
- Long-lived assets
  - donor-imposed restrictions, recognition principles for contributions 5.75–.77
  - use of, recognition principles for contributions 5.100–.101
- Maturity of
  - statements of financial position 3.07
- Net assets. *See* Net assets
- Noncash
  - unconditional promises to give 5.112
  - underlying noncash assets, changes in fair value of 5.122–.127
- Retirement obligations
  - property, plant, and equipment 9.17–.18
- Subsequent measurement
  - nature of assets expected to be received, changes in 5.119

ASSETS—continued
· · underlying noncash assets, changes in fair value of 5.122–.127

ASSISTANCE
· Questions regarding 1.28 (A-16)

AUDIENCE
· More than one function, classification of expenses related to 13.73–.79, 13.91
· · examples 13.99

AUDIT COMMITTEE
· Communication about possible fraud to 2.79 (A-33)

AUDIT EVIDENCE
· Contributions received 5.140
· Debt and other liabilities 10.27
· Expenses 13.97
· FASB Concepts Statement No. 6 . . . . 9.28
· Gains and losses 13.97
· General considerations 2.34
· Net assets 11.32
· Other assets 7.28
· Split-interest agreements 6.63
· Tax considerations 15.24

AUDIT PLANNING 2.02–.18
· Audit risk 2.11–.13
· · account balance 2.12
· · material misstatement 2.12–.13
· GAAS (generally accepted auditing standards) 2.03, 2.08
· Independence 2.08–.10
· Scope of services 2.06–.07
· Specialist, use of work of 2.05
· Tolerable misstatement 2.18

AUDIT RISK 2.11–.13
· Account balance 2.12
· Material misstatement 2.12–.13

AUDIT RISK AND MATERIALITY IN CONDUCTING AN AUDIT 2.11

AUDIT TEAM, DISCUSSION AMONG 2.44

AUDITING. *See also* Understanding audits, reviews and compilations
· Alternative investments 8.58
· Audit planning. *See also* audit planning *for detailed treatment* 2.02–.17
· Benefits of 1.28 (A-2–A-4)
· Collection items 7.24–.27
· Completing 2.74
· Contributions received 5.135–.141
· Debt and other liabilities 10.26–.27
· Derivative instruments 8.57
· Evidence. *See also* Audit Evidence
· · fraud, considerations of . . . . 2.79 . . . . (A-28–A-29)
· · use of assertions in obtaining 2.34–.38
· Expenses 13.96–.97
· External financial statement user, benefits of audit 1.28 (A-12)
· Fraud, consideration of . . . . 1.28 (A-35), ... 2.79 (App. A)

AUDITING—continued
· · audit committee, communication about possible fraud to 2.79 (A-33)
· · communication about possible fraud 2.79 (A-33)
· · contributions 2.79 (A-15)
· · controls, management override of 2.79 (A-18)
· · documentation of auditor's consideration of fraud 2.79 (A-34)
· · engagement personnel, discussion regarding risks of material misstatement due to fraud 2.79 (A-5–A-9)
· · evidence, evaluation 2.79 (A-28–A-29)
· · expenses 2.79 (A-15)
· · guidance 2.79 (A-35)
· · identified risks, assessing after taking account evaluation of entity's programs and controls 2.79 (A-21–A-26)
· · information needed to identify risks of material misstatement due to fraud 2.79 (A-10–A-35)
· · key estimates 2.79 (A-19–A-20)
· · management, communication about possible fraud to 2.79 (A-33)
· · professional skepticism, importance of 2.79 (A-4)
· · response to misstatements that may be result of fraud 2.79 (A-30–A-32)
· · results of risk assessment 2.79 (A-27)
· · revenue recognition, improper . . . . 2.79 . . . . (A-16–A-17)
· Further audit procedures
· · designing and performing 2.64–.65
· GAAS (generally accepted auditing standards)
· · assurance level 1.28 (A-29)
· · errors 2.24
· · explained 1.28 (A-2)
· · fraud 2.24
· · fraud detection, guidance 2.79 (A-35)
· · management representation 2.75
· General considerations. *See also lines throughout this topic* 2.01–.79, 7.22
· Going concern considerations 2.77–.78
· Hedging activities 8.57
· Internal financial statement user, benefits of audit 1.28 (A-24)
· Inventory 7.23
· Investments 8.57–.58
· · alternative investments 8.58
· · derivative instruments 8.57
· · endowment funds, net appreciation 8.59–.64
· · hedging activities 8.57
· · objectives 8.65
· · procedures 8.65
· Management representation 2.75–.76
· Material misstatement, assessing risks of
· · overall responses 2.66
· · risk assessment and design of further audit procedures 2.60–.63
· · significant risks, identification of 2.63

AUDITING—continued
· Materiality
· · planning 2.14–.17
· · qualitative aspects. *See also* Materiality *for detailed treatment* 2.19–.33
· Misconceptions 1.28 (A-17–A-20)
· Misstatements, evaluating 2.72–.73
· Net assets 11.31–.32
· Professional skepticism
· · attitude of examiner 1.28 (A-34)
· · importance of 2.79 (A-4)
· Property, plant, and equipment 9.26–.28
· Reasonable cost 1.28 (A-33)
· Related party transactions 2.21–.23
· Review, use of instead of audit .... 1.28 .... (A-25–A-26)
· Risk assessment and design of further audit procedures 2.60–.71
· · designing and performing 2.64–.65
· · further audit procedures, designing and performing 2.64–.65
· · material misstatement, assessing risks of 2.60–.63
· · overall responses 2.66
· · significant risks, identification of 2.63
· Split-interest agreements 6.60–.63
· Test basis 1.28 (A-32)
· Understanding the entity, its environment, and its internal control 2.39–.59

AUDITING ACCOUNTING ESTIMATES 2.50

AUDITING DERIVATIVE INSTRUMENTS, HEDGING ACTIVITIES, AND INVESTMENTS IN SECURITIES 8.57

AUDITING FAIR VALUE MEASUREMENTS AND DISCLOSURES .... 5.138, 6.61, ... 7.23, 9.26

AUDITORS
· Independent. *See* Independent auditors' reports

THE AUDITOR'S COMMUNICATION WITH THOSE CHARGED WITH GOVERNANCE 2.06

THE AUDITOR'S CONSIDERATION OF AN ENTITY'S ABILITY TO CONTINUE AS A GOING CONCERN ... 2.77, 3.100, 14.10

AWARDS
· Exchange transactions 5.47–.48

B

BENEFICIAL INTERESTS IN ASSETS HELD BY OTHERS
· Illustrative disclosures .... 5.134 Ex. 5

BENEFICIARIES
· Rights of, agency transactions 5.19

BOARD OF TRUSTEES
· And audits 1.28 (A-2), 1.28 (A-28)

BOARD-DESIGNATED ENDOWMENTS
· Statements of financial position 3.11

BOARD-DESIGNATED NET ASSETS 11.05

BROADCASTING. *See also* Television
· U.S. GAAP 1.12

BUILDINGS
· Land, building, and equipment funds 16.10–.12

BUSINESS COMBINATIONS
· U.S. GAAP 1.15

C

CARRYOVER METHOD
· Mergers and acquisitions, financial statements 3.61

CASH AND CASH EQUIVALENTS 4.01–.06
· Certificate of deposit 4.06
· Definition of cash equivalents 4.02
· Financial statement presentation 4.03–.05
· Statement of cash flows 3.28

CASH CONTRIBUTIONS
· Donor-imposed restrictions, recognition principles for contributions 5.75, 5.77
· Unconditional promises to give .... 5.110 Exh. 5-1, 5.111

CASH EQUIVALENTS
· Certificate of deposit 4.06
· Statement of cash flows 3.28

CASH FLOWS STATEMENT. *See* Statement of cash flows

CERTIFICATE OF DEPOSIT 4.06

CHANGES MADE TO THE TEXT FROM PREVIOUS EDITION, SCHEDULE OF .... Appendix D

CHARITABLE GIFT ANNUITIES
· Split-interest agreements 6.52–.55
· · journal entries 6.64

CHARITABLE LEAD TRUSTS
· Split-interest agreements 6.38–.42
· · journal entries 6.64

CHARITABLE REMAINDER TRUSTS
· Split-interest agreements 6.47–.51
· · journal entries 6.64

COLLABORATIVE ARRANGEMENTS
· Financial statements 3.72

COLLECTION ITEMS
· Auditing 7.24–.27
· Defined 7.07
· Discussed 7.07–.13
· Illustrative disclosures 7.17
· Recognition principles for contributions 5.102

COMBINED FINANCIAL STATEMENTS
· Related entities, reporting for 3.57

COMMENSURATE TEST, FAILURE OF ... 15.14

COMMERCIAL ENTERPRISE
· Tax considerations 15.10

COMMON STOCK
· In-substance common stock, reporting for related entities 3.49
· U.S. GAAP 1.10

COMPARATIVE FINANCIAL INFORMATION
· Statement of cash flows 3.30–.31

COMPARATIVE FINANCIAL STATEMENTS
· Independent auditors' reports 14.05–.07

COMPENSATION OR FEES TEST
· More than one function, classification of expenses related to 13.65–.67

COMPILATIONS. *See also* Understanding audits, reviews and compilations
· Explanation 1.28 (A-40–A-43)
· Statements on Standards for Accounting and Review Services (SSARS), in accordance with 1.28 (A-40)

COMPLIANCE ATTESTATION 2.32

COMPLIANCE AUDITING
· Materiality 2.29

COMPLIANCE AUDITING CONSIDERATIONS IN AUDITS OF GOVERNMENTAL ENTITIES AND RECIPIENTS OF GOVERNMENTAL FINANCIAL ASSISTANCE 2.07

COMPUTER SOFTWARE COSTS, INTERNAL USE
· Expense recognition issues 13.16

CONCEPTUAL FRAMEWORK FOR AICPA INDEPENDENCE STANDARDS 2.08

CONDITIONAL PROMISES 5.78, 5.81

THE CONFIRMATION PROCESS 5.139

CONSIDERATION OF FRAUD IN A FINANCIAL STATEMENT AUDIT .... 2.24, ... 2.79 (App. A)

CONSOLIDATED FINANCIAL STATEMENTS. *See also* Related entities, reporting for *for detailed treatment* 3.32–.57

CONTENT
· More than one function, classification of expenses related to 13.80–.84, 13.91
· · examples 13.99

CONTINGENCIES 10.22

CONTRIBUTED PROPERTY AND EQUIPMENT 9.05–.08

CONTRIBUTED SERVICES
· Recognition principles for contributions 5.90–.93
· · illustrative disclosures .... 5.134 Ex. 4

CONTRIBUTIONS. *See also* Contributions received
· Defined 5.02
· Expense recognition issues 13.17
· Fraud, consideration of in audits 2.79 (A-15)
· Shortfalls 2.53

CONTRIBUTIONS RECEIVED 5.01–.140
· Accounting policy for contributed property and equipment
· · illustrative disclosures .... 5.134 Ex. 3
· Agency transactions, distinguishing 5.07–.20
· · definition of agency transactions 5.07
· · gifts, representations made during solicitation 5.13
· · liability to specified beneficiary 5.15
· · materials, supplies, or other nonfinancial assets, donation of 5.16
· · measurement of fair value 5.20
· · perpetual trusts held by third party, fair value 5.18
· · rights of beneficiary 5.19
· Auditing 5.135–.141
· Beneficial interests in assets held by others .... 5.134 Ex. 5
· Distinguishing contributions from other transactions 5.05–.49
· · agency transactions 5.07–.20
· · exchange transactions 5.36–.49
· · financially interrelated entities 5.26–.29
· · similar transactions that are revocable, repayable or reciprocal 5.30–.35
· · variance power 5.21–.25
· Donor-imposed restrictions
· · illustrative disclosures .... 5.134 Ex. 1
· Exchange transactions, distinguishing 5.36–.49
· · appropriations 5.48
· · asset transfers 5.41
· · assets, purchases of 5.37
· · awards 5.47–.48
· · employees' salaries, payments of 5.37
· · grants 5.47–.48
· · indicators useful in distinguishing .... 5.45 Table 5-1
· · membership dues 5.45–.46
· · premiums, costs of 5.39
· · sponsorships 5.47
· Financial statement presentation 5.129–.133
· Financially interrelated entities, distinguishing 5.26–.29
· · definition of financially interrelated entities 5.27
· · economic interest defined 5.29
· · ongoing economic interest in the net assets of another, defined 5.27
· Illustrative disclosures 5.134
· Introduction 5.01–.05
· Measurement principles for contributions 1.03–.27
· · discounting 5.113–.116
· · future cash flows 5.09
· · future fair value 5.112
· · nature of assets expected to be received, changes in 5.120–.121
· · securities, gifts of 5.122–.123
· · subsequent measurement 5.117–.128

CONTRIBUTIONS RECEIVED—continued
· · underlying noncash assets, changes in fair value of 5.122–.127
· Promises to give
· · illustrative disclosures . . . . 5.134 Ex. 2
· Recognition principles for contributions 5.50–.103
· · collection items 5.102
· · contributed services . . . . 5.90–.93, ... 5.134 Ex. 4
· · donor imposing condition 5.58–.61
· · donor imposing restriction 5.62–.77
· · gifts in kind 5.94–.99
· · long-lived assets, use of 5.100–.101
· · promises to give 5.78–.89
· · split-interest agreements 5.103
· · utilities, contributed 5.100–.101
· Similar transactions that are revocable, repayable or reciprocal, distinguishing 5.30–.35
· · control, defined 5.31
· · equity transactions 5.33
· · reciprocal transactions, described 5.33
· Variance power, distinguishing 5.21–.25
· · definition of variance power 5.21
· · unaffiliated, defined 5.23

CONTROL
· Defined, similar transactions that are revocable 5.31
· Management override of controls
· · fraud, consideration of in audits 2.79 (A-18)
· Related entities, reporting for 3.38

CONVERTIBLE DEBT 1.11

COST OF CONTROL, QUESTIONS REGARDING 1.28 (A-16)

CREDIT RISK
· Investments, financial statement presentation 8.40–.41

CRITERIA OF PURPOSE, AUDIENCE, AND CONTENT, EXAMPLES OF APPLICATION OF
· Annual report, distribution of . . . . 13.99 Ex. 9
· Door-to-door canvass . . . . 13.99 Ex. 5
· Door-to-door solicitation campaign . . . . 13.99 Ex. 6
· Health screenings, free . . . . 13.99 Ex. 15
· Internal Revenue Service regulations, compliance . . . . 13.99 Ex. 10
· Mailing
· · informational materials . . . . 13.99 Ex. 1
· · prior donors . . . . 13.99 Ex. 2
· · program-related criteria, based on . . . . 13.99 Ex. 4
· · rented list, use of . . . . 13.99 Ex. 11
· Prior donors
· · mailing to . . . . 13.99 Ex. 2
· · telephone solicitation . . . . 13.99 Ex. 3
· Program-related criteria, mailing targeted based on . . . . 13.99 Ex. 4

CRITERIA OF PURPOSE, AUDIENCE, AND CONTENT, EXAMPLES OF APPLICATION OF—continued
· Rented list, mailing to individuals targeted using . . . . 13.99 Ex. 11
· Television
· · annual national telethon . . . . 13.99 Ex. 7
· · broadcast educating public . . . . 13.99 Ex. 8
· · public television membership drive . . . . 13.99 Ex. 16
· Ticket subscription, advertising with request for contributions . . . . 13.99 Ex. 12
· University lecture series
· · with contribution inherent in admission . . . . 13.99 Ex. 14
· · with fair value admission . . . . 13.99 Ex. 13

CURRENT AND DEFERRED TAX LIABILITIES 10.07–.08

CUSTODIAN FUNDS
· Fund accounting 16.21

D

DEBT AND OTHER LIABILITIES 10.01–.27
· Advances from third parties 10.10
· Agency transactions, amounts held for others under 10.17
· Annuity obligations 10.16
· Auditing 10.26–.27
· Contingencies 10.22
· Current and deferred tax liabilities 10.07–.08
· Deferred revenue 10.09
· Defined benefit postretirement plan obligations 10.23–.25
· Exit or disposal activities 10.19
· Guarantees 10.20–.21
· Introduction 10.01–.03
· Pension plan obligations 10.23–.25
· Promises to give 10.11–.15
· · agent, defined 10.12
· · defined 10.11
· · intermediary, defined 10.12
· · Ttrustee, defined 10.12
· Refunds to third parties 10.10
· Revenue sharing 10.18
· Split-interest agreements 10.16
· Tax-exempt financing and long-term debt 10.04–.06
· Third-party enhancement 10.03

DECISION TREES
· Financial statements . . . . 3.107 (App. A)

DEFERRED CHARGES
· Recognition and measurement 7.06

DEFERRED REVENUE 10.09

DEFERRED TAX LIABILITIES 10.07–.08

DEFINED BENEFIT POSTRETIREMENT PLAN OBLIGATIONS 10.23–.25

DEFINITION OF NOT-FOR-PROFIT ENTITY
· FASB 1.01

DEPRECIATION
· Property, plant, and equipment 9.09–.13

DERIVATIVE INSTRUMENTS
· Accounting for 8.49–.56
· · accounting and reporting standards 8.53–.54
· · changes, reporting 8.55
· · definition 8.49
· · disclosures 8.56
· · forwards 8.52
· · futures 8.52
· · notional amount, defined 8.51
· · options 8.52
· · swaps 8.52
· · underlying, defined 8.50
· Auditing 8.57
· Investments
· · financial statement presentation 8.43
· · valuation subsequent to acquisitions 8.14

DIRECT IDENTIFICATION VERSUS ALLOCATION METHODS
· More than one function, classification of expenses related to 13.46–.51

DIRECT MAIL SOLICITATION
· More than one function, classification of expenses related to 13.45

DISCLOSURES
· Derivative instruments 8.56
· Expenses
· · examples 13.101
· · more than one function, classification of expenses related to 13.89–.90
· · narrative format 13.101
· · tabular format 13.101
· Financial statements
· · donor-imposed restrictions, noncompliance 3.99–.101
· · fair value measures, use of 3.94
· · mergers and acquisitions, financial statements 3.71
· · risks and uncertainties 3.102
· Hedging activities, accounting for 8.56
· Net assets 11.24–.29
· · board-designated net assets 11.28
· · permanently restricted net assets 11.24, 11.26–.27
· · reclassifications 11.25
· · temporarily restricted net assets 11.25–.27
· · unrestricted net assets 11.24

DISCOUNTS
· Measurement principles for contributions 5.113–.116
· Rates
· · fair value measures, use of 3.86–.87

DISPLAY
· Exchange transactions, revenues and receivables from 12.06–.09

DISPOSAL ACTIVITIES
· Debt and other liabilities 10.19

DOCUMENTATION
· Fraud, consideration of 2.79 (A-34)
· Promises to give 5.86

DONOR STIPULATIONS 8.24, 8.26, 8.31

DONOR-IMPOSED CONDITIONS. *See also* Donor-imposed restrictions; Donor-restricted endowment funds
· Recognition principles for contributions 5.58–.61
· · definition 5.51

DONOR-IMPOSED RESTRICTIONS
· Defined 11.04
· Endowment funds. *See* Donor-restricted endowment funds
· Financial statements
· · noncompliance 3.99–.101
· · statement of activities 3.15
· · statements of financial position 3.06, 3.08
· Internal control 2.59
· Net assets 11.03–.06
· · permanently restricted 11.04–.05, 11.07–.09
· · temporarily restricted 11.04–.05, 11.10–.12
· Recognition principles for contributions 5.62–.77
· · cash contributions 5.75, 5.77
· · definition 5.53
· · employee's salary 5.73
· · expenses incurred 5.72
· · expiration of 5.71
· · illustrative disclosures . . . . 5.134 Ex. 1
· · long-lived assets 5.75–.77
· · use of classification 5.67
· Statement of cash flows 3.27
· Statements of financial position 3.06, 3.08

DONOR-RESTRICTED ENDOWMENT FUNDS 8.23–.32
· Appropriated for expenditure, defined 8.28
· Defined 8.23
· Determination of restricted portion 8.24
· Donor stipulations 8.24, 8.26, 8.31
· Gains and losses, classification of 8.32
· Permanently restricted net assets 8.26, 8.29
· Temporarily restricted net assets 8.30
· Unrestricted net assets 8.27

DOOR-TO-DOOR CANVASS . . . . 13.99 Ex. 5

DOOR-TO-DOOR SOLICITATION CAMPAIGN . . . . 13.99 Ex. 6

E

ECONOMIC INTEREST DEFINED
· Financially interrelated entities 5.29

ECONOMIC INTEREST, EXISTENCE OF
· Related entities, reporting for 3.38

EDUCATING INDIVIDUALS
· More than one function, classification of expenses related to 13.60–.63

EDUCATING PUBLIC
· Television broadcast . . . . 13.99 Ex. 8

EDUCATIONAL INSTITUTIONS. *See* Higher education institutions

EMPLOYEES' SALARIES
· Donor-imposed restrictions, recognition principles for contributions 5.73
· Payments of, exchange transactions 5.37

ENDOWMENT FUNDS. *See also* Donor-restricted endowment funds
· Fund accounting 16.15–.18
· Net appreciation, auditing 8.59–.64
· Permanent endowment, defined 16.15
· Quasi endowment, defined 16.15
· Term endowment, defined 16.15

ENDOWMENTS 4.04

ENGAGEMENT PERSONNEL
· Discussion regarding risks of material misstatement due to fraud 2.79 (A-5–A-9)

ENTERTAINMENT INDUSTRY
· U.S. GAAP 1.12

ENTITY AND ENVIRONMENT, UNDERSTANDING. *See* Understanding the entity, its environment, and its internal control

EQUIPMENT. *See also* Property, plant, and equipment
· Accounting policy, illustrative disclosures . . . . 5.134 Ex. 3
· Land, building, and equipment funds 16.10–.12

EQUITY. *See also* Net assets
· Change in, statement of activities 3.13
· Contributions received, distinguishing 5.33

EQUITY SECURITIES WITH READILY DETERMINABLE FAIR VALUE 8.10

EQUITY TRANSACTIONS 5.33

ERRORS
· Materiality 2.24

EVIDENCE
· Assertions, use of in obtaining 2.34–.38
· Audits. *See also* Audit Evidence
· · fraud, considerations of 2.79 (A-28–A-29)
· · use of assertions in obtaining 2.34–.38

EXCHANGE TRANSACTIONS
· Appropriations 5.48
· Assets
· · purchases of 5.37
· · transfers 5.41
· Awards 5.47–.48
· Contributions received, distinguishing 5.36–.49
· · indicators useful in distinguishing . . . . 5.45 Table 5-1

EXCHANGE TRANSACTIONS—continued
· Defined 5.36, 12.02
· Employees' salaries, payments of 5.37
· Grants 5.47–.48
· Membership dues 5.45–.46
· · contributions and exchange portions . . . . 5.45 Table 5-2
· Premiums, costs of 5.39
· Revenues and receivables from 12.01–.09
· · definition of exchange transaction 12.02
· · recognition, measurement, and display 12.06–.09
· · revenues, discussed 12.03–.05
· Sponsorships 5.47

EXEMPTION, BASIS OF 15.04–.15
· Commensurate test, failure of 15.14
· And commercial enterprise 15.10
· Common types of exemptions 15.04
· Form 990 . . . . 15.07
· In-kind contributions 15.12
· Private benefit concept 15.09
· Private charities 15.11
· Private foundations 15.11
· As privilege 15.06
· Prohibited distributions 15.08
· Prohibited transactions 15.12
· Public charities 15.12
· Public policy violation 15.15
· And state of incorporation, laws of 15.05
· Unrelated business income 15.13

EXIT OR DISPOSAL ACTIVITIES 10.19

EXPENSE RECOGNITION ISSUES 13.07–.17
· Advertising costs 13.10–.12
· Computer software costs, internal use 13.16
· Contributions made 13.17
· Financial aid 13.09
· Fundraising costs 13.08
· Goods and services, reductions in amounts charged for 13.09
· Internal use computer software costs . . . 13.16
· Start-up costs 13.13–.15

EXPENSES 13.01–.17
· Allocation methods 13.100
· · more than one function, classification of expenses related to . . . . 13.46–.51, ... 13.85–.86
· · physical units method 13.100
· · relative direct cost method 13.100
· · stand-alone-joint-cost-allocation method 13.100
· Auditing 13.96–.97
· Classification of
· · statement of activities 3.18, 3.20
· Disclosures
· · examples 13.101
· · narrative format 13.101
· · tabular format 13.101
· Donor-imposed restrictions, recognition principles for contributions 5.72

EXPENSES—continued
· Expense recognition issues 13.07–.17
· · advertising costs 13.10–.12
· · computer software costs, internal use 13.16
· · contributions made 13.17
· · financial aid 13.09
· · fundraising costs 13.08
· · goods and services, reductions in amounts charged for 13.09
· · internal use computer software costs 13.16
· · start-up costs 13.13–.15
· Federated fundraising entities ... 13.38; 13.94
· Fraud, consideration of in audits ... 2.79 (A-15)
· Functional classifications 13.37–.44
· · federated fundraising entities 13.38
· · fundraising activities, defined 13.43
· · management and general activities, defined 13.42
· · membership-development activities, defined 13.44
· · program services 13.37–.40
· · supporting services 13.41–.44
· Functional reporting of 13.35–.94
· · federated fundraising entities 13.38; 13.94
· · functional classifications 13.37–.44
· · more than one function, classification of expenses related to 13.45–.94
· Income taxes 13.95
· Introduction 13.01
· Investment revenues 13.33–.34
· Joint activities
· · accounting for 13.55–.57
· · purpose 13.58
· More than one function, classification of expenses related to 13.45–.94
· · allocation methods ... 13.46–.51, 13.85–.86
· · audience 13.73–.79, 13.91, 13.99
· · compensation or fees test 13.65–.67
· · content 13.80–.84, 13.91, 13.99
· · direct identification versus allocation methods 13.46–.51
· · direct mail solicitation 13.45
· · disclosures 13.89–.90
· · educating individuals 13.60–.63
· · fundraising activities combined with elements of another function 13.52–.54
· · incidental activities 13.87–.88
· · indirect costs 13.86
· · joint activities 13.52–.57
· · local NFPs, support to 13.92–.93
· · management and general functions 13.64
· · mortgages 13.50
· · national NFPs, support to 13.92–.93
· · other evidence test 13.71–.72
· · program functions 13.59, 13.64
· · purpose criterion 13.58–.72, 13.91
· · separate and similar activities test 13.68–.70
· Statement of functional expenses 3.21

EXTERNAL FINANCIAL REPORTING AND FUND ACCOUNTING 16.02–.05

EXTERNAL FINANCIAL STATEMENT USER, BENEFITS OF AUDIT 1.28 (A-12)

F

FAIR VALUE ADMISSION, UNIVERSITY LECTURE SERIES .... 13.99 Ex. 13

FAIR VALUE, DETERMINATION
· Gifts in kind 5.96

FAIR VALUE DISCLOSURE
· Investments, financial statement presentation 8.42

FAIR VALUE HIERARCHY 3.89–.93

FAIR VALUE MEASURES, USE OF 3.73–.97
· Agency transactions 5.20
· Cash flows 3.86–.87
· Contributions received. *See* Measurement principles for contributions
· Cost approach to valuation 3.81
· Definition of fair value 3.74–.81
· Disclosures 3.94
· Discount rates 3.86–.87
· Fair value hierarchy 3.89–.93
· Fair value options 3.95–.98
· Financial statements. *See also lines throughout this topic* 3.01–.30
· Income approach to valuation 3.82, 3.88
· Inventory 7.03–.05
· Investments, valuation subsequent to acquisitions 8.16–.18
· Liabilities 3.79–.80, 3.90
· And location 3.81
· Market participant assumptions 3.93
· Present value techniques 3.85–.88
· Prioritizing inputs 3.90
· Reliability of inputs 3.91
· Valuation techniques 3.82–.88
· Value-in-exchange 3.78
· Value-in-use 3.78

FAIR VALUE OPTIONS 3.95–.98

FASB. *See* Financial Accounting Standards Board (FASB)

FASB STAFF POSITIONS. *See* Financial Accounting Standards Board (FASB)

FASB STATEMENTS. *See* Financial Accounting Standards Board (FASB)

FEDERATED FUNDRAISING ENTITIES
· Expenses 13.38; 13.94

FINANCIAL ACCOUNTING STANDARDS BOARD (FASB)
· Accounting standards codification (ASC)
· · explained 1.05
· Definition of not-for-profit entity 1.01
· FASB Concepts Statement No. 1
· · net assets 11.01

FINANCIAL ACCOUNTING STANDARDS BOARD (FASB)—continued
· FASB Concepts Statement No. 2 ....9.06
· · expenses 13.03
· FASB Concepts Statement No. 3
· · exchange transactions................12.03
· · expenses 13.03
· · net assets 11.01
· FASB Concepts Statement No. 6
· · exchange transactions................12.03
· · expenses 13.03
· · net assets 11.01
· · property, plant, and equipment ... 9.06, 9.09
· FASB Concepts Statement No. 7........5.118
· FASB Statement No. 12
· · grandfathered U.S. GAAP guidance 1.20
· · tax-exempt financing and long-term debt 10.05
· FASB Statement No. 121
· · grandfathered U.S. GAAP guidance 1.16
· FASB Statement No. 141
· · grandfathered U.S. GAAP guidance..................1.15–.16, 1.20
· FASB Statement No. 141(Revised)
· · grandfathered U.S. GAAP guidance 1.20
· FASB Statement No. 144
· · grandfathered U.S. GAAP guidance 1.16, 1.20
· FASB Statement No. 164
· · goodwill...............................7.20
· · grandfathered U.S. GAAP guidance..................1.15–.16, 1.19
· FASB Statement No. 165
· · grandfathered U.S. GAAP guidance 1.15
· FASB Statement No. 168
· · grandfathered U.S. GAAP guidance 1.15

FINANCIAL AID
· Expense recognition issues.............13.09

FINANCIAL STATEMENT PRESENTATION. *See also* Financial statements
· Contributions received............5.129–.133
· Discussed...........................7.14–.16
· Investments 8.33–.48
· · credit risk..........................8.40–.41
· · derivative financial instruments 8.43
· · fair value disclosure....................8.42
· · health care entities 8.37
· · higher education institutions............8.46
· · operations, measure of 8.38
· · realized and unrealized losses 8.34
· · repurchase agreements................8.44
· · restricted endowment funds 8.47
· · spending rate formula..................8.36
· Property, plant, and equipment 9.20–.25
· Split-interest agreements 6.32–.26

FINANCIAL STATEMENTS. *See also* Financial statement presentation
· Cash and cash equivalents 4.03–.05
· Collaborative arrangements..............3.72
· Comparative. *See* Comparative financial statements

FINANCIAL STATEMENTS—continued
· Disclosures
· · donor-imposed restrictions, noncompliance.................3.99–.101
· · not considered elsewhere 3.98–.102
· · risks and uncertainties................3.102
· Donor-imposed restrictions
· · noncompliance 3.99–.101
· · statement of activities 3.15
· · statements of financial position ... 3.06, 3.08
· External financial statement user, benefits of audit 1.28 (A-12)
· Fair value measures, use of 3.73–.97
· · cash flows 3.86–.87
· · cost approach to valuation 3.82
· · definition of fair value..............3.75–.81
· · disclosures............................3.94
· · discount rates......................3.86–.87
· · fair value hierarchy 3.89–.93
· · fair value options 3.95–.98
· · income approach to valuation.....3.82, 3.88
· · liabilities 3.79–.80, 3.90
· · and location 3.81
· · market participant assumptions 3.93
· · present value techniques 3.85–.88
· · prioritizing inputs 3.90
· · reliability of inputs 3.91
· · valuation techniques................3.82–.88
· · value-in-exchange 3.78
· · value-in-use 3.78
· Independent auditors' reports 14.01–.04
· Internal financial statement user, benefits of audit 1.28 (A-24)
· Introduction 3.01–.04
· Mergers and acquisitions............3.58–.71
· · acquisition by not-for-profit entity ... 3.62–.70
· · carryover method......................3.61
· · definition of merger of not-for-profit entities 3.60
· · disclosures............................3.71
· · goodwill...............................3.70
· · intangible assets.......................3.61
· Related entities, reporting for........3.32–.57
· · another NFP, relationship with 3.34–.43
· · combined financial statements..........3.57
· · for-profit entity, relationships with.............................3.44–.54
· · guidance 3.33
· · special-purpose leasing entities, consolidation of 3.55–.56
· Statement of activities 3.12–.20
· · classes of net assets 3.18
· · classification of net assets 3.14
· · classification of revenues, expenses, gains and losses....................3.18, 3.20
· · donor-imposed restrictions 3.15
· · equity, change in 3.13
· · focus of..............................3.13
· · formats 3.17
· · measure of operations 3.19
· · net assets, change in 3.13
· · reclassifications, defined 3.15

FINANCIAL STATEMENTS—continued
· · subtotal, appropriately labeled . . . 3.16
· Statement of cash flows . . . 3.22–.31
· · agency transactions . . . 3.25
· · cash equivalents . . . 3.28
· · comparative financial information . . . 3.30–.31
· · donor-imposed restrictions . . . 3.27
· · GAAP, in conformity with . . . 3.30–.31
· · gross cash payments . . . 3.26
· · gross cash receipts . . . 3.26
· · maturities of less than three months . . . 3.29
· · operating activities, defined . . . 3.24
· · purpose of . . . 3.23
· · short-term highly liquid investments . . . 3.28
· Statement of functional expenses . . . 3.21
· Statements of financial position . . . 3.05–.11
· · assets and liabilities, classification of . . . 3.06
· · audited financial statements prepared in conformity with GAAP . . . 1.21
· · board-designated endowments . . . 3.11
· · donor-imposed restrictions . . . 3.06, 3.08
· · focus of . . . 3.06
· · and liquidity . . . 3.07
· · maturity of assets and liabilities . . . 3.07
· · net assets, classification of . . . 3.09
· · permanently restricted net assets, defined . . . 3.10
· · self-imposed limits . . . 3.11
· · unrestricted net assets, defined . . . 3.11
· · voluntary resolutions . . . 3.11

FINANCIALLY INTERRELATED ENTITIES
· Contributions received, distinguishing . . . 5.26–.29
· Defined . . . 5.27
· Economic interest defined . . . 5.29
· Ongoing economic interest in the net assets of another, defined . . . 5.27

FISCAL AGENT. *See* Trustee or fiscal agent

FLOWCHARTS AND DECISION TREES
· Relationships with other entities . . . 3.107 (App. A)

FOREIGN COUNTRIES
· Independent auditors' reports . . . 14.03

FORM 990 . . . 14.16, 15.07, 15.16

FORM 990-EZ . . . 15.16

FORM 990-N . . . 15.16

FORM 990T . . . 15.02

FOR-PROFIT ENTITY, RELATIONSHIPS WITH
· Financial statements . . . 3.44–.54
· Related entities, reporting for . . . 3.44–.54
· · common stock . . . 3.49
· · guidance . . . 3.44
· · in-substance common stock . . . 3.49
· · joint ventures . . . 3.49
· · limited liability companies . . . 3.46, 3.51
· · limited partnerships . . . 3.46–.47
· · majority voting interest . . . 3.45
· · minority rights . . . 3.45
· · real estate general partnerships . . . 3.52

FOR-PROFIT ENTITY, RELATIONSHIPS WITH—continued
· · real estate limited liability companies . . . 3.51
· · real estate partnerships . . . 3.51
· · significant influence, defined . . . 3.49
· · voting stock . . . 3.48, 3.50

FORWARDS . . . 8.52

FRAUD
· Audits, consideration of fraud . . . 1.28 (A-35), 2.79 (App. A)
· · audit committee, communication about possible fraud to . . . 2.79 (A-33)
· · communication about possible fraud . . . 2.79 (A-33)
· · contributions . . . 2.79 (A-15)
· · controls, management override of . . . 2.79 (A-18)
· · documentation of auditor's consideration of fraud . . . 2.79 (A-34)
· · engagement personnel, discussion regarding risks of material misstatement due to fraud . . . 2.79 (A-5–A-9)
· · evidence, evaluation . . . 2.79 (A-28–A-29)
· · expenses . . . 2.79 (A-15)
· · guidance . . . 2.79 (A-35)
· · identified risks, assessing after taking account evaluation of entity's programs and controls . . . 2.79 (A-21–A-26)
· · information needed to identify risks of material misstatement due to fraud . . . 2.79 (A-10–A-35)
· · key estimates . . . 2.79 (A-19–A-20)
· · management, communication about possible fraud to . . . 2.79 (A-33)
· · misappropriation of assets . . . 2.79 (A-2)
· · professional skepticism, importance of . . . 2.79 (A-4)
· · response to misstatements that may be result of fraud . . . 2.79 (A-30–A-32)
· · results of risk assessment . . . 2.79 (A-27)
· · revenue recognition, improper . . . 2.79 (A-16–A-17)
· Material misstatement due to
· · engagement personnel, discussion regarding risks of . . . 2.79 (A-5–A-9)
· · information needed to identify risks of material misstatement due to fraud . . . 2.79 (A-10–A-35)
· Materiality . . . 2.24

FRAUD DETECTION IN A GAAS AUDIT . . . 2.79 (A-35)

FUND ACCOUNTING . . . 16.01–.22
· Agency funds . . . 16.21
· Annuity and life-income funds . . . 16.19–.20
· Custodian funds . . . 16.21
· Defined . . . 1.22, 16.02
· Endowment funds . . . 16.15–.18
· And external financial reporting . . . 16.02–.05
· Fund balances, typical classification . . . 16.22
· General funds . . . 16.06–.07
· Land, building, and equipment funds 16.10–.12

FUND ACCOUNTING—continued
· Loan funds........................16.13–.14
· And net asset classes...............1.22–.27
· Plant funds.......................16.10–.12
· Self-balancing..........................1.23
· Specific-purpose funds............16.08–.09
· Split-interest funds................16.19–.20
· Unrestricted current (or unrestricted operating or general) funds................16.06–.07

FUND BALANCES, TYPICAL CLASSIFICATION.................16.22

FUNDRAISING ACTIVITIES
· Combined with elements of another function........................13.52–.54
· Defined..............................13.43
· Gains and losses................13.28–.32

FUNDRAISING COSTS
· Defined..............................13.08
· Expense recognition issues............13.08

FUNDS OF FUNDS 8.17

FUTURE CASH FLOWS
· Measurement principles for contributions..........................5.09

FUTURE FAIR VALUE
· Measurement principles for contributions........................5.112

FUTURES..............................8.52

G

GAAP. *See* U.S. GAAP

GAAS (GENERALLY ACCEPTED AUDITING STANDARDS)
· Assurance level..................1.28 (A-29)
· Audit planning.....................2.03, 2.08
· Explained 1.28 (A-2)
· Fraud detection, guidance 2.79 (A-35)
· Independent auditors' reports
· · unqualified opinions...................14.08
· Management representation 2.75

GAINS AND LOSSES 13.18–.34
· Classification of
· · statement of activities............3.18, 3.20
· Definition of gains.....................13.18
· Donor-restricted endowment funds 8.32
· Fundraising activities, reporting costs of.............................13.28–.32
· Income taxes.........................13.95
· Introduction...........................13.01
· Investment revenues..............13.33–.34
· Property, plant, and equipment...........9.19
· Realized, investments.........8.19–.21, 8.34
· As results of..........................13.19
· Revenues or gains, classification of contributions as..................13.18–.34
· Sales of goods and services, reporting costs related to.......................13.25–.27
· Special events, reporting costs of.............................13.28–.32
· Unrealized, investments.......8.19–.21, 8.34

GENERAL AUDITING CONSIDERATIONS. *See* Auditing

GENERAL FUNDS
· Fund accounting..................16.06–.07

GIFTS
· Representations made during solicitation, agency transactions 5.13

GIFTS IN KIND
· Fair value, determination.................5.96
· Recognition principles for contributions.....................5.94–.99

GOING CONCERNS
· Audits..............................2.77–.78
· Independent auditors' reports............14.10

GOODS AND SERVICES, SALES OF
· Gains and losses 13.25–.27

GOODWILL
· Discussed..........................7.18–.20
· Mergers and acquisitions, financial statements............................3.70

GOVERNMENT AUDITING STANDARDS
· Audit planning..........................2.06
· Compliance auditing....................2.29
· Independent auditors' reports..........14.17

GOVERNMENTAL AUDITS
· Materiality, planning 2.17

GRANTS
· Exchange transactions..............5.47–.48

GROSS CASH PAYMENTS
· Statement of cash flows.................3.26

GROSS CASH RECEIPTS
· Statement of cash flows.................3.26

GUARANTEES
· Debt and other liabilities 10.20–.21

H

HEALTH CARE ENTITIES
· Investments, financial statement presentation............................8.37

HEALTH CARE SERVICES.................1.04

HEALTH SCREENINGS, FREE.......................13.99 Ex. 15

HEDGING ACTIVITIES
· Accounting for......................8.49–.56
· · changes, reporting 8.55
· · disclosures............................8.56
· · notional amount, defined 8.51
· · underlying, defined....................8.50
· Auditing 8.57

HIGHER EDUCATION INSTITUTIONS
· Investments
· · financial statement presentation 8.46
· · valuation subsequent to acquisitions 8.15

HISTORICAL TREASURES. *See* Collection items

I

IASB. *See* International Accounting Standards Board (IASB)

IFRS. *See* International Financial Reporting Standards (IFRS)

ILLEGAL ACTS
· Materiality 2.25–28

INCIDENTAL ACTIVITIES
· Expenses, classification of expenses related to more than one function 13.87–.88

INCOME APPROACH TO VALUATION 3.82, 3.88

INCOME TAXES
· Expenses 13.95
· Gains and losses 13.95

INDEPENDENCE. *See also* Independent auditors' reports

INDEPENDENCE
· Audit planning 2.08–.10

INDEPENDENT AUDITORS' REPORTS 14.01–.17
· On comparative financial statements 14.05–.07
· · taken as a whole, described 14.05
· Departures from unqualified opinions 14.09
· On financial statements 14.01–.04
· · foreign countries 14.03
· · results of operations 14.04
· Going concerns 14.10
· *Government Auditing Standards*, reports required by 14.17
· OMB Circular A-133, reports required by 14.17
· Other comprehensive basis of accounting (OCBOA) 14.13–.14
· Proscribed forms, reporting on 14.15–.16
· Single Audit Act Amendments of 1996, reports required by 14.17
· Supplementary information 14.11–.12
· Unqualified opinions 14.08
· · departures from 14.09

INDIRECT COSTS
· Expenses, classification of expenses related to more than one function 13.86

INDUSTRY CHARACTERISTICS
· Environment, understanding 2.47–.53

INFORMATION SOURCES . . . . Appendix B

INFORMATIONAL MATERIALS, MAILING . . . . 13.99 Ex. 1

IN-KIND CONTRIBUTIONS
· And exemption 15.12

IN-SUBSTANCE COMMON STOCK
· Investments, valuation subsequent to acquisitions 8.12
· Related entities, reporting for 3.49

INTANGIBLE ASSETS
· Goodwill 7.18–.20
· Other than goodwill 7.21–.22
· Mergers and acquisitions, financial statements 3.61

INTERMEDIARY
· Defined, promises to give 10.12

INTERNAL CONTROL
· Donor restrictions 2.59
· Long-lived assets 2.59
· Reporting requirements 2.59
· Understanding of 2.54–.59

INTERNAL CONTROL—INTEGRATED FRAMEWORK 2.57

INTERNAL FINANCIAL STATEMENT USER, BENEFITS OF AUDIT 1.28 (A-24)

INTERNAL REVENUE SERVICE REGULATIONS, COMPLIANCE
· Criteria of purpose, audience, and content, examples of application of . . . . . 13.99 Ex. 10

INTERNAL USE COMPUTER SOFTWARE COSTS
· Expense recognition issues 13.16

INTERNATIONAL ACCOUNTING STANDARDS BOARD (IASB) 1.07

INTERNATIONAL FINANCIAL REPORTING STANDARDS (IFRS) 1.07

INTERPRETATIONS, PROFESSIONAL STANDARDS. *See* Professional Standards Interpretations

INTRODUCTION/EXPLANATION OF GUIDE
· Applicability to entities 1.02
· Fund accounting and net asset classes 1.22–.27
· GAAS (generally accepted auditing standards) 1.28 (A-2)
· Net asset classes 1.22–.27
· Nongovernmental NFPs
· · applicability to entities 1.02
· Scope of guide 1.01–.04
· Understanding audits, reviews and compilations . . . . 1.28 (App. A)
· U.S. GAAP 1.05–.14
· · accounting Standards Updates 1.09
· · and AICPA Code of Professional Conduct 1.05
· · audited financial statements prepared in conformity with GAAP 1.21
· · broadcasting 1.12
· · business combinations 1.15
· · common stock 1.10
· · convertible debt 1.11
· · entertainment industry 1.12
· · grandfathered guidance 1.15–.20
· · mergers and acquisitions 1.15–.20
· · pooling of interests 1.15
· · procedures 1.28 (A-2)
· · reviews in accordance with 1.28 (A-36)

INTRODUCTION/EXPLANATION OF GUIDE—continued
· · share-based payments 1.11
· · stock purchase warrants 1.11

INTANGIBLE ASSETS

INVENTORY 7.02–.05
· Auditing 7.23
· Fair value measures 7.03–.05

INVESTMENT INCOME 8.07–.09

INVESTMENT POOLS 8.22

INVESTMENT REVENUES
· Expenses 13.33–.34
· Gains and losses 13.33–.34

INVESTMENTS 8.01–.65
· Alternative investments 8.17
· Auditing 8.57–.58
· · alternative investments 8.58
· · derivative instruments 8.57
· · endowment funds, net appreciation 8.59–.64
· · hedging activities 8.57
· · objectives 8.65
· · procedures 8.65
· Certificate of deposit 4.06
· Derivative instruments 8.14
· · accounting and reporting standards 8.53–.54
· · accounting for 8.49–.56
· · changes, reporting 8.55
· · definition 8.49
· · disclosures 8.56
· · forwards 8.52
· · futures 8.52
· · notional amount, defined 8.51
· · options 8.52
· · swaps 8.52
· · underlying, defined 8.50
· Donor-restricted endowment funds . . . 8.23–.32
· · appropriated for expenditure, defined . . . 8.28
· · defined 8.23
· · determination of restricted portion 8.24
· · gains and losses, classification of 8.32
· Endowment funds, net appreciation 8.59–.64
· Equity method, investments accounted for under 8.11–.13
· Equity securities with readily determinable fair value 8.10
· Fair value election, investments accounted for under 8.11–.13
· Fair value measurements 8.16–.18
· Financial statement presentation 8.33–.48
· · credit risk 8.40–.41
· · derivative financial instruments 8.43
· · fair value disclosure 8.42
· · health care entities 8.37
· · higher education institutions 8.46
· · operations, measure of 8.38
· · realized and unrealized losses 8.34
· · repurchase agreements 8.44

INVESTMENTS—continued
· · restricted endowment funds 8.47
· · spending rate formula 8.36
· Funds of funds 8.17
· Hedging activities
· · accounting for 8.49–.56
· · changes, reporting 8.55
· · disclosures 8.56
· · notional amount, defined 8.51
· · underlying, defined 8.50
· Higher education institutions 8.15
· Initial recognition 8.05–.06
· In-substance common stock, defined 8.12
· Introduction 8.01–.04
· Investment income 8.07–.09
· Investment pools 8.22
· Offshore fund vehicles 8.17
· Private equity funds 8.17
· Split-interest gifts 8.02
· Total investment return 8.35
· Unrealized and realized gains and losses 8.19–.21, 8.34
· U.S. GAAP 8.04
· Valuation subsequent to acquisition 8.10–.18
· · alternative investments 8.17
· · derivative instruments 8.14
· · equity method, investments accounted for under 8.11–.13
· · equity securities with readily determinable fair value 8.10
· · fair value election, investments accounted for under 8.11–.13
· · fair value measurements 8.16–.18
· · funds of funds 8.17
· · higher education institutions 8.15
· · in-substance common stock, defined 8.12
· · offshore fund vehicles 8.17
· · private equity funds 8.17
· · venture capital funds 8.17
· · voluntary health and welfare agencies . . . 8.15
· Venture capital funds 8.17
· Voluntary health and welfare agencies 8.15

J

JOINT ACTIVITIES
· Accounting for 13.55–.57, 13.98
· Expenses, classification of expenses related to more than one function 13.52–.57
· Purpose 13.58

JOINT VENTURES
· Related entities, reporting for 3.49

L

LACK OF CONFORMITY WITH GENERALLY ACCEPTED ACCOUNTING PRINCIPLES 14.14

LAND, BUILDING, AND EQUIPMENT FUNDS
· Fund accounting 16.10–.12

LEAD INTERESTS, DEFINED............6.02

LEASES
· Below-market lease payments 5.101
· Capital lease disclosures 9.22

LECTURE SERIES. *See* University lecture series

LIABILITIES. *See also* Debt and other liabilities
· Classification of, statements of financial position 3.06
· Fair value measures, use of....3.79–.80, 3.90
· Maturity of, statements of financial position 3.07
· To specified beneficiary, agency transactions 5.15

LIMITED LIABILITY COMPANIES
· Real estate limited liability companies 3.51
· Related entities, reporting for 3.46, 3.51

LIMITED PARTNERSHIPS
· Related entities, reporting for........3.46–.47

LIQUIDITY
· Statements of financial position 3.07

LOAN FUNDS
· Fund accounting.................. 16.13–.14

LOCAL NFPs, SUPPORT TO
· Expenses, classification of expenses related to more than one function........... 13.92–.93

LOCATION
· Fair value measures, use of............. 3.81

LONG-LIVED ASSETS
· Donor-imposed restrictions, recognition principles for contributions......... 5.75–.77
· Impairment or disposal of 9.14–.16
· Internal control........................ 2.59
· Use of, recognition principles for contributions.................. 5.100–.101

LONG-TERM DEBT
· Tax-exempt financing and 10.04–.06

LOSS OF EXEMPTION
· Commensurate test, failure of 15.14
· Political campaign activities............. 15.12
· Public policy violations 15.15
· Unrelated business income 15.13

M

MAILING
· Criteria of purpose, audience, and content, examples of application of
· · informational materials.......... 13.99 Ex. 1
· · prior donors.................... 13.99 Ex. 2
· · program-related criteria, based on............................ 13.99 Ex. 4
· · rented list, use of............. 13.99 Ex. 11

MAJORITY VOTING INTEREST
· Related entities, reporting for 3.35–.36, 3.40

MANAGEMENT
· Communication about possible fraud to 2.79 (A-33)

MANAGEMENT AND GENERAL ACTIVITIES, DEFINED 13.42

MANAGEMENT AND GENERAL FUNCTIONS
· Expenses, classification of expenses related to more than one function 13.64

MANAGEMENT REPRESENTATIONS
· Audits............................. 2.75–.76
· Endowments.......................... 8.64
· Representation letters.................. 2.75

MARKET PARTICIPANT ASSUMPTIONS
· Fair value measures, use of............. 3.93

MATERIAL MISSTATEMENT
· Assessing risks of 2.60–.63
· Audit risk.......................... 2.12–.13
· Fraud, due to
· · engagement personnel, discussion regarding risks of..................... 2.79 (A-5–A-9)
· · information needed to identify risks of material misstatement due to fraud 2.79 (A-10–A-35)

MATERIALITY
· Compliance auditing..................... 2.29
· Errors 2.24
· Fraud.................................. 2.24
· Illegal acts......................... 2.25–.28
· Planning........................... 2.14–.17
· · governmental audits 2.17
· Qualitative aspects................. 2.19–.33
· · compliance auditing................... 2.29
· · errors............................... 2.24
· · fraud................................ 2.24
· · illegal acts 2.25–228
· · related party transactions.......... 2.21–.23
· · service organizations, processing of transactions by 2.33
· · single audits and related considerations 2.30–.32
· Related party transactions........... 2.21–.23
· Service organizations, processing of transactions by....................... 2.33
· Single audits and related considerations 2.30–.32

MATERIALS, SUPPLIES, OR OTHER NONFINANCIAL ASSETS, DONATION OF
· Agency transactions..................... 5.16

MEASURE OF OPERATIONS
· Statement of activities.................. 3.19

MEASUREMENT PRINCIPLES FOR CONTRIBUTIONS
· Discounting..................... 5.113–.116
· Future cash flows 5.09
· Future fair value....................... 5.112
· Subsequent measurement........ 5.117–.128
· · generally...................... 5.117–.119
· · nature of assets expected to be received, changes in 5.120–.121

MEASUREMENT PRINCIPLES FOR CONTRIBUTIONS—continued
· · securities, gifts of 5.122–.123
· · underlying noncash assets, changes in fair value of 5.122–.127

MEMBERSHIP DUES
· Exchange transactions 5.45–.46

MEMBERSHIP-DEVELOPMENT ACTIVITIES, DEFINED 13.44

MERGERS AND ACQUISITIONS
· APB Opinion No. 16
· · grandfathered U.S. GAAP guidance 1.15–.19
· APB Opinion No. 17
· · grandfathered U.S. GAAP guidance 1.19–.20
· Financial statements 3.58–.71
· · acquisition by not-for-profit entity ... 3.62–.70
· · carryover method 3.61
· · definition of merger of not-for-profit entities 3.60
· · disclosures 3.71
· · goodwill 3.70
· · intangible assets 3.61

MINORITY RIGHTS
· Related entities, reporting for 3.45

MISSTATEMENTS. *See also* Material misstatement
· Evaluating 2.72–.73

MORTGAGES
· Expenses, classification of expenses related to more than one function 13.50

N

NATIONAL NFPs, SUPPORT TO
· Expenses, classification of expenses related to more than one function 13.92–.93

NET APPRECIATION
· Endowment funds 8.59–.64
· · donor-restricted 8.32

NET ASSETS 11.01–.31
· Auditing 11.31–.32
· Board-designated net assets 11.05
· Classes 11.03–.06
· · and fund accounting 1.22–.27
· · statement of activities 3.18
· Classification of
· · statement of activities 3.14
· · statements of financial position 3.09
· Change in classification from prior year 11.30
· Disclosures 11.24–.29
· · board-designated net assets 11.28
· · permanently restricted net assets 11.24, 11.26–.27
· · reclassifications 11.25
· · temporarily restricted net assets 11.25–.27

NET ASSETS—continued
· · unrestricted net assets 11.24
· Donor-imposed restrictions 11.03–.06
· · defined 11.04
· · permanently restricted net assets ...... 8.24, ... 8.26, 8.29, 11.04–.05, 11.07–.09
· · temporarily restricted net assets 11.04–.05, 11.10–.12
· Introduction 11.01–.02
· Noncontrolling interests 11.20–.21
· Ongoing economic interest in the net assets of another, defined 5.27
· Permanently restricted net assets ...... 11.04, ... 11.05, 11.07–.09
· · defined 3.10, 11.07
· · disclosures 11.24, 11.26–.27
· · statements of financial position 3.10
· Reclassifications 11.22–.23
· Temporarily restricted net assets .... 8.26, ... 8.30, 11.04, 11.05, 11.10–.12
· · defined 11.10
· · disclosures 11.26–.27
· Unrestricted net assets .... 8.23, 8.27, ... 11.04–.05, 11.13–.19
· · defined 3.11, 11.13
· · disclosures 11.24
· · investment income 8.08

NET INCOME UNITRUSTS
· Split-interest agreements 6.18, 6.30

NONCONTROLLING INTERESTS IN THE EQUITY 11.20–.21

NONGOVERNMENTAL NOT-FOR-PROFIT ENTITIES (NFPs). *See specific topic*

NOT-FOR-PROFIT ENTITIES (NFPs). *See specific topic*

NOTIONAL AMOUNT, DEFINED 8.51

O

OCBOA. *See* Other comprehensive basis of accounting (OCBOA)

OFFSHORE FUND VEHICLES
· Investments, valuation subsequent to acquisitions 8.17

OMB CIRCULAR A-133
· Generally 2.06
· Independent auditors' reports 14.17
· Single audits and related considerations 2.30–.32

ONGOING ECONOMIC INTEREST IN THE NET ASSETS OF ANOTHER, DEFINED 5.27

OPERATING ACTIVITIES, DEFINED
· Statement of cash flows 3.24

OPERATIONS, MEASURE OF
· Investments, financial statement presentation 8.38

OPTIONS 8.52

OTHER COMPREHENSIVE BASIS OF ACCOUNTING (OCBOA)
· Independent auditors' reports 14.13–.14

OTHER EVIDENCE TEST
· Expenses, classification of expenses related to more than one function 13.71–.72

OTHER INFORMATION IN DOCUMENTS CONTAINING AUDIT FINANCIAL STATEMENTS 14.12

P

PARTNERSHIPS
· Limited partnerships 3.46–.47
· Real estate general partnerships 3.52
· Real estate partnerships 3.51

PCAOB. *See* Public Company Accounting Oversight Board (PCAOB)

PENSION PLAN OBLIGATIONS 10.23–.25

PERFORMING AUDIT PROCEDURES IN RESPONSE TO ASSESSED RISKS AND EVALUATING THE AUDIT EVIDENCE OBTAINED 2.63

PERMANENT ENDOWMENT, DEFINED 16.15

PERMANENTLY RESTRICTED NET ASSETS. *See* Net assets

PERPETUAL INTEREST HELD BY THIRD PARTY
· Split-interest agreements 6.43–.46
· · journal entries 6.64

PERPETUAL TRUSTS HELD BY THIRD PARTY
· Fair value 5.18

PHYSICAL UNITS METHOD OF ALLOCATION.....................13.100

PLANT FUNDS
· Fund accounting 16.10–.12

POLITICAL CAMPAIGN ACTIVITIES 15.12

POOLED (LIFE) INCOME FUNDS
· Split-interest agreements 6.56–.59
· · journal entries 6.64

POOLED INCOME FUNDS
· Defined 6.56
· Split-interest agreements 6.18, 6.30

POOLING OF INTERESTS................1.15

PREMIUMS, COSTS OF
· Exchange transactions 5.39

PREPAID EXPENSES
· Recognition and measurement 7.06

PRESENT VALUE TECHNIQUES
· Fair value measures, use of 3.85–.88

PRIOR DONORS
· Criteria of purpose, audience, and content, examples of application of
· · mailing to .... 13.99 Ex. 2
· · telephone solicitation...........13.99 Ex. 3

PRIORITIZING INPUTS
· Fair value measures, use of............. 3.90

PRIVATE BENEFIT CONCEPT 15.09

PRIVATE CHARITIES
· And exemption.........................15.11

PRIVATE EQUITY FUNDS
· Investments, valuation subsequent to acquisitions 8.17

PRIVATE FOUNDATIONS
· And exemption.........................15.11
· Tax considerations 15.17

PROFESSIONAL ETHICS EXECUTIVE COMMITTEE 2.10

PROFESSIONAL SKEPTICISM
· Attitude of examiner...............1.28 (A-34)
· Importance of......................2.79 (A-4)

PROFESSIONAL STANDARDS (AU sec.) INTERPRETATIONS
· Interpretation No. 1 of AU section 322 ... 8.58
· Interpretation No. 1 of AU section 328 ... 6.62
· Interpretation No. 10 of AU section 623..........................14.16
· Interpretation No. 14 of AU section 508..........................14.03
· Interpretation No. 17 of AU section 508..........................14.02
· Interpretation No. 18 of AU section 508..........................14.02
· Interpretation No. 19 of AU section 508..........................14.03

PROGRAM FUNCTIONS
· Expenses, classification of expenses related to more than one function 13.59, 13.64

PROGRAM SERVICES
· Expenses 13.37–.40

PROGRAM-RELATED CRITERIA, MAILING TARGETED BASED ON ...... 13.99 Ex. 4

PROHIBITED DISTRIBUTIONS
· And exemption.........................15.08

PROHIBITED TRANSACTIONS
· And exemption.........................15.12

PROMISES TO GIVE 5.78–.89
· Agent, defined 10.12
· Conditional promises 5.78, 5.81
· Debt and other liabilities 10.11–.15
· · agent, defined.......................10.12
· · defined 10.11
· · intermediary, defined 10.12
· · trustee, defined 10.12
· Defined.........................5.78, 10.11
· Documentation..........................5.86
· Intermediary, defined...................10.12
· Permanently restricted classification......5.83
· Promises to give .... 5.134 Ex. 2
· Recognition principles for contributions......................5.78–.89
· · promises to give................5.134 Ex. 2

PROMISES TO GIVE—continued
· Trustee, defined 10.12
· Unconditional promises .... 5.78, 5.80, ... 5.82–.84
· · cash .... 5.110 Exh. 5-1, 5.111
· · noncash assets 5.112
· · not measured subsequently at fair value .... 5.128 Illus.
· Wording 5.89

PROPERTY, PLANT, AND EQUIPMENT 9.01–.28
· Auditing 9.26–.28
· Financial statement presentation 9.20–.25
· Introduction 9.01–.02
· Leased property 9.02
· Recognition and measurement principles 9.03–.19
· · allowable costs 9.11
· · amortization 9.09–.13
· · asset group 9.14
· · asset retirement obligations 9.17–.18
· · contributed property and equipment 9.05–.08
· · depreciation 9.09–.13
· · gains and losses 9.19
· · long-lived assets, impairment or disposal of 9.14–.16

PROSCRIBED FORMS, REPORTING ON
· Independent auditors' reports 14.15–.16

PUBLIC COMPANY ACCOUNTING OVERSIGHT BOARD (PCAOB) 14.02

PUBLIC CHARITIES
· And exemption 15.12

PUBLIC CORPORATIONS 1.03

PUBLIC POLICY VIOLATION
· And exemption 15.15

PUBLIC TELEVISION MEMBERSHIP DRIVE .... 13.99 Ex. 16

Q

QUASI-ENDOWMENTS 4.04
· Defined 16.15

R

REAL ESTATE GENERAL PARTNERSHIPS
· Related entities, reporting for 3.52

REAL ESTATE LIMITED LIABILITY COMPANIES
· Related entities, reporting for 3.51

REAL ESTATE PARTNERSHIPS
· Related entities, reporting for 3.51

REALIZED GAINS AND LOSSES
· Investments 8.19–.21, 8.34

RECEIVABLES
· Exchange transactions. *See* Exchange transactions

RECIPROCAL TRANSACTIONS
· Contributions received, distinguishing 5.30–.35
· Reciprocal transactions, described 5.33

RECLASSIFICATIONS
· Net assets 11.22–.23

RECOGNITION AND MEASUREMENT. *See also* Recognition principles for contributions
· Exchange transactions
· · revenues and receivables from 12.06–.09
· Property, plant, and equipment 9.03–.19
· · allowable costs 9.11
· · amortization 9.09–.13
· · asset group 9.14
· · asset retirement obligations 9.17–.18
· · contributed property and equipment 9.05–.08
· · depreciation 9.09–.13
· · gains and losses 9.19
· · long-lived assets, impairment or disposal of 9.14–.16
· Split-interest agreements. *See* Split-interest agreements

RECOGNITION PRINCIPLES FOR CONTRIBUTIONS. *See also* Recognition and measurement 5.50–.102
· Collection items 5.102
· Contributed services 5.90–.93
· · illustrative disclosures .... 5.134 Ex. 4
· Donor-imposed conditions 5.58–.61
· · defined 5.51
· Donor-imposed restrictions 5.62–.77
· · cash contributions 5.75, 5.77
· · defined 5.53
· · employee's salary 5.73
· · expenses incurred 5.72
· · expiration of 5.71
· · illustrative disclosures .... 5.134 Ex. 1
· · long-lived assets 5.75–.77
· · use of classification 5.67
· Gifts in kind 5.94–.99
· Long-lived assets, use of 5.100–.101
· Promises to give 5.78–.89
· · conditional promises 5.78, 5.81
· · defined 5.78
· · documentation 5.86
· · illustrative disclosures .... 5.134 Ex. 2
· · permanently restricted classification 5.83
· · unconditional promises .... 5.78, 5.80, ... 5.82–.84
· · wording 5.89
· Revenues or gains, classification of contributions as 5.56
· Split-interest agreements 5.103
· Utilities, contributed 5.100–.101

REFUNDS TO THIRD PARTIES 10.10

RELATED ENTITIES, REPORTING FOR. *See also* Related party transactions 3.32–.57
· Another NFP, relationship with 3.34–.43

RELATED ENTITIES, REPORTING FOR—continued
· · control, existence of 3.38
· · economic interest, existence of 3.38
· · less than complete interest 3.41
· · majority voting interest 3.35–.36, 3.40
· · ownership, explained 3.34
· Combined financial statements 3.57
· For-profit entity, relationships with 3.44–.54
· · common stock 3.49
· · guidance 3.44
· · in-substance common stock 3.49
· · joint ventures 3.49
· · limited liability companies 3.46, 3.51
· · limited partnerships 3.46–.47
· · majority voting interest 3.45
· · minority rights 3.45
· · real estate general partnerships 3.52
· · real estate limited liability companies 3.51
· · real estate partnerships 3.51
· · significant influence, defined 3.49
· · voting stock 3.48, 3.50
· Guidance 3.33
· Significant influence, defined 3.49
· Special-purpose leasing entities, consolidation of 3.55–.56

RELATED PARTIES 2.21

RELATED PARTY TRANSACTIONS
· Materiality 2.21–.23

RELATIVE DIRECT COST METHOD OF ALLOCATION 13.100

RELIABILITY OF INPUTS
· Fair value measures, use of 3.91

REMAINDER INTERESTS
· Defined 6.02

RENTED LIST, MAILING TO INDIVIDUALS TARGETED USING
· Criteria of purpose, audience, and content, examples of application of . . . . . 13.99 Ex. 11

REPAYABLE TRANSACTIONS. *See* Similar transactions that are revocable, repayable or reciprocal, distinguishing

REPORTING ON FINANCIAL STATEMENTS PREPARED FOR USE IN OTHER COUNTRIES 14.03

REPORTING ON INFORMATION ACCOMPANYING THE BASIC FINANCIAL STATEMENTS IN AUDITOR-SUBMITTED DOCUMENTS 14.12

REPORTS AND REPORTING. *See specific topic*

REPRESENTATION LETTERS 2.75

REPURCHASE AGREEMENTS
· Investments, financial statement presentation 8.44

RESPONSIBILITIES AND FUNCTIONS OF THE INDEPENDENT AUDITOR 2.79 (A-1)

RESTRICTED CURRENT (OR RESTRICTED OPERATING OR SPECIFIC-PURPOSE FUNDS)
· Fund accounting 16.08–.09

RESTRICTED ENDOWMENT FUNDS
· Investments, financial statement presentation 8.47

REVENUE RECOGNITION, IMPROPER
· Fraud, consideration of in audits 2.79 (A-16–A-17)

REVENUE SHARING 10.18

REVENUES
· Classification of
· · gains or revenues, classification of contributions 5.56
· · statement of activities 3.18, 3.20
· Deferred 10.09
· Exchange transactions. *See* Exchange transactions
· Investment revenues
· · expenses 13.33–.34
· · gains and losses 13.33–.34

REVIEWS. *See also* Understanding audits, reviews and compilations
· Explanation 1.28 (A-36–A-39)
· Statements on Standards for Accounting and Review Services (SSARS), in accordance with 1.28 (A-36)
· Unusual items or trends, identification of 1.28 (A-39)

REVOCABLE AGREEMENTS
· Split-interest agreements 6.06

REVOCABLE TRANSACTIONS. *See* Similar transactions that are revocable, repayable or reciprocal, distinguishing

RISK. *See also* audit risk; Risk assessment; Risks and uncertainties
· Concentration of 8.40–.41
· Financial statements disclosures 3.102
· Material misstatement due to fraud
· · engagement personnel, discussion regarding risks of 2.79 (A-5–A-9)
· · information needed to identify risks of material misstatement due to fraud 2.79 (A-10–A-35)

RISK ASSESSMENT
· Further audit procedures, design of 2.60–.71
· · material misstatement 2.60–.63
· · overall responses 2.66
· · performing and designing 2.64–.65
· Procedures 2.40

RISKS AND UNCERTAINTIES
· Financial statement disclosures 3.102

S

SALARIES, PAYMENTS OF
· Donor-imposed restrictions, recognition principles for contributions 5.73
· Exchange transactions 5.37

SALES OF GOODS AND SERVICES
· Gains and losses 13.25–.27

SARBANES OXLEY ACT OF 2002.......14.02

SECURITIES, GIFTS OF
· Measurement principles for contributions 5.122–.123

SELF-IMPOSED LIMITS
· Statements of financial position 3.11

SEPARATE AND SIMILAR ACTIVITIES TEST
· Expenses, classification of expenses related to more than one function........... 13.68–.70

SERVICE ORGANIZATIONS 2.33

SERVICE ORGANIZATIONS, PROCESSING OF TRANSACTIONS BY.................2.33

SERVICES
· Contributed, recognition principles for contributions......................5.90–.93
· · illustrative disclosures...........5.134 Ex. 3
· Sales of, gains and losses 13.25–.27

SHARE-BASED PAYMENTS
· U.S. GAAP 1.11

SHORTFALLS
· Contributions 2.53

SHORT-TERM HIGHLY LIQUID INVESTMENTS
· Statement of cash flows 3.28

SINGLE AUDIT ACT AMENDMENTS OF 1996...........................2.06
· Independent auditors' reports.......... 14.17

SINGLE AUDITS AND RELATED CONSIDERATIONS
· Materiality 2.30–.32

SPECIAL EVENTS, REPORTING COSTS OF
· Gains and losses 13.28–.32

SPECIALIST, USE OF WORK OF
· Audit planning 2.05

SPECIAL-PURPOSE LEASING ENTITIES, CONSOLIDATION OF 3.55–.56

SPECIFIC-PURPOSE FUNDS
· Fund accounting.................. 16.08–.09

SPENDING RATE FORMULA
· Investments, financial statement presentation........................... 8.36

SPLIT-INTEREST AGREEMENTS 6.01–.64
· Annuity reserves 6.35
· Auditing 6.60–.63
· Charitable gift annuities 6.52–.55
· · journal entries 6.64
· Charitable lead trusts 6.38–.42
· · journal entries 6.64
· Charitable remainder trusts.......... 6.47–.51

SPLIT-INTEREST AGREEMENTS—continued
· · journal entries 6.64
· Debt and other liabilities................10.16
· Examples of........................ 6.37–.59
· · charitable gift annuities 6.52–.55
· · charitable lead trusts 6.38–.42
· · charitable remainder trusts 6.47–.51
· · perpetual interest held by third party 6.43–.46
· · pooled (life) income funds.......... 6.56–.59
· Financial statement presentation..... 6.32–.26
· Journal entries 6.64
· Lead interests, defined 6.02
· Net income unitrusts 6.18, 6.30
· Perpetual interest held by third party 6.43–.46
· · journal entries 6.64
· Pooled (life) income funds 6.56–.59
· · journal entries 6.64
· Pooled income funds 6.18, 6.30
· Recognition and measurement principles 6.04–.31
· · net income unitrusts 6.18, 6.30
· · pooled income funds 6.18, 6.30
· · revocable agreements, recognition of ... 6.06
· · termination of agreement, recognition upon 6.31
· · unconditional irrevocable agreements 6.08–.29
· · unrelated third party as trustee or fiscal agent..................... 6.14–.17, 6.21
· Recognition principles for contributions........................ 5.103
· Remainder interests, defined............ 6.02
· Revocable agreements, recognition of.... 6.06
· Termination of agreement, recognition upon.................................. 6.31
· Trustee or fiscal agent, NFP as...... 6.08–.13, 6.22–.29
· Types of........................... 6.02–.03
· Unconditional irrevocable agreements
· · trustee or fiscal agent, NFP as.................... 6.08–.13, 6.22–.29
· Unrelated third party as trustee or fiscal agent...................... 6.14–.17, 6.21
· Voluntary reserves 6.36

SPLIT-INTEREST FUNDS
· Fund accounting.................. 16.19–.20

SPLIT-INTEREST GIFTS
· Investments............................. 8.02

SPONSORSHIPS
· Exchange transactions 5.47

SSARS. *See* Statements on Standards for Accounting and Review Services (SSARS)

STAND-ALONE-JOINT-COST-ALLOCATION METHOD 13.100

START-UP COSTS
· Defined.................................13.14
· Expense recognition issues 13.13–.15

STATE OF INCORPORATION, LAWS OF
· And exemption 15.05

STATEMENT OF ACTIVITIES 3.12–.20
· Classes of net assets 3.18
· Classification of net assets 3.14
· Classification of revenues, expenses, gains and losses 3.18, 3.20
· Donor-imposed restrictions 3.15
· Equity, change in 3.13
· Focus of 3.13
· Formats 3.17
· Measure of operations 3.19
· Net assets, change in 3.13
· Reclassifications, defined 3.15
· Subtotal, appropriately labeled 3.16

STATEMENT OF CASH FLOWS....... 3.22–.31
· Agency transactions 3.25
· Cash equivalents 3.28
· Comparative financial information 3.30–.31
· Donor-imposed restrictions 3.27
· GAAP, in conformity with 3.30–.31
· Gross cash payments 3.26
· Gross cash receipts 3.26
· Maturities of less than three months 3.29
· Operating activities, defined 3.24
· Purpose of 3.23
· Short-term highly liquid investments 3.28

STATEMENT OF FUNCTIONAL EXPENSES 3.21

STATEMENTS OF FINANCIAL POSITION 3.05–.11
· Assets and liabilities, classification of 3.06
· Board-designated endowments 3.11
· Donor-imposed restrictions 3.06, 3.08
· Focus of 3.06
· And liquidity 3.07
· Maturity of assets and liabilities 3.07
· Net assets, classification of 3.09
· Permanently restricted net assets, defined 3.10
· Self-imposed limits 3.11
· Unrestricted net assets, defined 3.11
· Voluntary resolutions 3.11

STATEMENTS OF POSITION
· SOP 78-10 .... 3.43

STATEMENTS ON STANDARDS FOR ACCOUNTING AND REVIEW SERVICES (SSARS)
· Compilations in accordance with, generally 1.28 (A-40)
· Reviews in accordance with, generally 1.28 (A-36)

STOCK. *See* Common stock; Voting stock

STOCK PURCHASE WARRANTS
· U.S. GAAP 1.11

SUBSEQUENT MEASUREMENT. *See* Measurement principles for contributions

SUBSIDIARIES
· Noncontrolling ownership interest in 11.20

SUBSEQUENT EVENTS 2.74, 5.69

SUPPLEMENTARY INFORMATION
· Independent auditors' reports 14.11–.12

SUPPORTING SERVICES
· Expenses 13.41–.44

SWAPS 8.52

T

TAX CONSIDERATIONS. *See also* Income taxes 15.01–.24
· Auditing 15.22–.24
· Exemption, basis of 15.04–.15
· · commensurate test, failure of 15.14
· · and commercial enterprise 15.10
· · common types of exemptions 15.04
· · form 990 .... 15.07
· · in-kind contributions 15.12
· · private benefit concept 15.09
· · private charities 15.11
· · private foundations 15.11
· · as privilege 15.06
· · prohibited distributions 15.08
· · prohibited transactions 15.12
· · public charities 15.12
· · public policy violation 15.15
· · and state of incorporation, laws of 15.05
· · unrelated business income 15.13
· Federal filing requirements 15.16
· Filing requirements 15.16
· Management's role 15.03
· Private foundations 15.17
· Public charities 15.17
· State filing requirements 15.16
· Tax position, defined 15.02
· Unrelated business income 15.18–.21

TAX-EXEMPT FINANCING AND LONG-TERM DEBT 10.04–.06

TELEPHONE SOLICITATION
· Prior donors .... 13.99 Ex. 3

TELETHON
· Annual national .... 13.99 Ex. 7

TELEVISION
· Criteria of purpose, audience, and content, examples of application of
· · annual national telethon .... 13.99 Ex. 7
· · broadcast educating public ...... 13.99 Ex. 8
· · public television membership drive .... 13.99 Ex. 16

TEMPORARILY RESTRICTED NET ASSETS. *See* Net assets

TERM ENDOWMENT, DEFINED 16.15

TERMINATION OF AGREEMENTS
· Split-interest agreements 6.31

THIRD PARTIES
· Advances from 10.10
· Refunds due to 10.10

TICKET SUBSCRIPTION, ADVERTISING WITH REQUEST FOR CONTRIBUTIONS
· Criteria of purpose, audience, and content, examples of application of ..... 13.99 Ex. 12

TOLERABLE MISSTATEMENT
· Audit planning 2.18

TOTAL INVESTMENT RETURN 8.35

TRAINING
· Questions regarding 1.28 (A-16)

TRUSTEE. *See also* Trustee or fiscal agent
· Defined, promises to give 10.12

TRUSTEE OR FISCAL AGENT, SPLIT-INTEREST AGREEMENTS
· NFP as 6.08–.13, 6.22–.29
· Unrelated third party as 6.14–.17, 6.21

U

UMIFA. *See* Uniform Management of Institutional Funds Act of 1972 (UMIFA)

UNAFFILIATED, DEFINED
· Variance power 5.23

UNCERTAINTIES. *See* Risks and uncertainties

UNCONDITIONAL PROMISES ..... 5.78, 5.80, ... 5.82–.84
· Cash .... 5.110 Exh. 5-1
· Noncash assets 5.112
· Not measured subsequently at fair value .... 5.128 Illus.

UNDERLYING, DEFINED 8.50

UNDERSTANDING AUDITS, REVIEWS AND COMPILATIONS .... 1.28 (App. A)
· Audits 1.28 (A-1–A-35)
· Benefits of an audit 1.28 (A-2–A-4)
· Compilations 1.28 (A-40–A-43)
· Control weaknesses, questions regarding 1.28 (A-16)
· Cost of control, questions regarding 1.28 (A-16)
· Discussion of 1.28 (A-29–A-35)
· Frequently asked questions 1.28 (A-6–A-28)
· Review 1.28 (A-36–A-39)
· Training and assistance, questions regarding 1.28 (A-16)

UNDERSTANDING THE ENTITY AND ITS ENVIRONMENT AND ASSESSING THE RISKS OF MATERIAL MISSTATEMENTS 2.39, 2.79 (A-10), 5.136, 7.25

UNDERSTANDING THE ENTITY, ITS ENVIRONMENT, AND ITS INTERNAL CONTROL. *See also* Understanding the Entity and Its Environment and Assessing the Risks of Material Misstatements 2.39–.59
· Analytical procedures 2.41–.43

UNDERSTANDING THE ENTITY, ITS ENVIRONMENT, AND ITS INTERNAL CONTROL—continued
· Audit team, discussion among 2.44
· Environment and entity, understanding 2.45–.53
· Industry characteristics 2.47–.53
· Internal control 2.54–.59
· Risk assessment procedures 2.40

UNIFORM MANAGEMENT OF INSTITUTIONAL FUNDS ACT OF 1972 (UMIFA) 8.24, 8.27–.28

UNIFORM PRUDENT MANAGEMENT OF INSTITUTIONAL FUNDS ACT (UPMIFA) 8.61, 8.63

UNITED STATES OFFICE OF MANAGEMENT AND BUDGET
· OMB Circular A-133
· · generally 2.06
· · single audits and related considerations 2.30–.32

UNITIZATION 8.22

UNIVERSITY LECTURE SERIES
· With contribution inherent in admission .... 13.99 Ex. 14
· With fair value admission .... 13.99 Ex. 13

UNQUALIFIED OPINIONS
· Independent auditors' reports 14.08
· · departures from unqualified opinions ... 14.09

UNREALIZED GAINS AND LOSSES
· Investments 8.19–.21, 8.34

UNRELATED BUSINESS INCOME
· Tax considerations 15.18–.21
· · exemption 15.13

UNRELATED THIRD PARTY AS TRUSTEE OR FISCAL AGENT
· Split-interest agreements 6.14–.17, 6.21

UNRESTRICTED CURRENT (OR UNRESTRICTED OPERATING OR GENERAL) FUNDS
· Fund accounting 16.06–.07

UNRESTRICTED NET ASSETS. *See* Net assets

UNUSUAL ITEMS OR TRENDS, IDENTIFICATION OF
· Reviews 1.28 (A-39)

UPMIFA. *See* Uniform Prudent Management of Institutional Funds Act (UPMIFA)

U.S. GAAP 1.05–.14
· Accounting Standards Updates 1.09
· AICPA Code of Professional Conduct 1.05
· Audited financial statements prepared in conformity with 1.21
· Broadcasting 1.12
· Business combinations 1.15
· Common stock 1.10
· Convertible debt 1.11
· Entertainment industry 1.12

U.S. GAAP—continued
· Grandfathered guidance............1.15–.20
· Independent auditors' reports
· · unqualified opinions..................14.08
· Industry characteristics...........2.51, 2.53
· Investments............................8.04
· Mergers and acquisitions...........1.15–.20
· Pooling of interests.....................1.15
· Reviews in accordance with........1.28 (A-36)
· Share-based payments.................1.11
· Statement of cash flows............3.30–.31
· Stock purchase warrants...............1.11

UTILITIES, CONTRIBUTED
· Recognition principles for contributions..................5.100–.101

V

VALUATION SUBSEQUENT TO ACQUISITION
· Investments........................8.10–.18
· · alternative investments.................8.17
· · derivative instruments..................8.14
· · equity method, investments accounted for under..........................8.11–.13
· · equity securities with readily determinable fair value..............................8.10
· · fair value election, investments accounted for under..........................8.11–.13
· · fair value measurements..........8.16–.18
· · funds of funds..........................8.17
· · higher education institutions............8.15
· · in-substance common stock, defined....8.12
· · offshore fund vehicles..................8.17
· · private equity funds....................8.17
· · venture capital funds...................8.17
· · voluntary health and welfare agencies...8.15

VALUATION TECHNIQUES
· Fair value measures, use of.........3.82–.88

VALUE-IN-EXCHANGE
· Fair value measures, use of..............3.78

VALUE-IN-USE
· Fair value measures, use of..............3.78

VARIANCE POWER
· Contributions received, distinguishing.....................5.21–.25
· Defined..................................5.21
· Unaffiliated, defined.....................5.23

VENTURE CAPITAL FUNDS
· Investments, valuation subsequent to acquisitions..........................8.17

VOLUNTARY HEALTH AND WELFARE ENTITIES
· Investments, valuation subsequent to acquisitions..........................8.15
· Statement of functional expenses........3.21

VOLUNTARY RESOLUTIONS
· Statements of financial position..........3.11

VOTING INTEREST
· Majority voting interest, reporting for related entities.....................3.35–.36, 3.40

VOTING STOCK
· Related entities, reporting for......3.48, 3.50

W

WORKS OF ART. ***See* Collection items**

Y

YELLOW BOOK. ***See* Government Auditing Standards**